South
Africa & India
Shaping the Global
South

South Africa & India
Shaping the Global South

Edited by
Isabel Hofmeyr and
Michelle Williams

WITS UNIVERSITY PRESS

Published in South Africa by:
Wits University Press
1 Jan Smuts Avenue
Johannesburg
2001
www.witspress.co.za

First published 2011

ISBN 978-1-86814-538-6

Cover and text design by Prins
Typesetting by Pamset
Printed and bound by Ultra Litho (Pty) Ltd.

Table of Contents

Socio-political Comparisons

Acknowledgements

This volume arises out of a number of research initiatives associated with the Centre for Indian Studies in Africa (CISA) at the University of the Witwatersrand (www.cisa-wits.org). Started in 2006 as a network of researchers under the title 'South Africa–India Research Thrust', CISA hosted seminars, conferences, public events, cultural performances and literary festivals as well as producing a range of publications. This volume represents a selection of work undertaken at CISA over the last five years.

The articles are drawn from academic publications and are collected together here to provide more ready access to a wider readership. The introduction, chapters 2, 4, 7, 9, 10 and 11 appeared as a special issue of the Journal of Asian and African Studies 44 (1) 2009 and are reproduced with the permission of Sage. Chapter 3 arose from a colloquium on 'South Africa-India: Re-imagining the Disciplines' held at the University of the Witwatersrand in 2006. The papers from this event appeared in a special issue of the South African Historical Journal 57 2007 and chapter 3 is reproduced with the permission of Taylor and Francis. Chapters 5 and 6 are taken from a special issue of Historia 54 (1) 2009 which emerged from a colloquium 'The Bonfire of 1908: Passive Resistance Then and Now' held at the University of the Witwatersrand in 2008 with support from the Consulate General of India in Johannesburg. These two pieces are reproduced with the permission of the journal Historia. Chapter 1 first appeared in a collection of essays *Cosmopolitan Thought Zones: South Asia and the Global Circulation of Ideas* edited by Kris Manjapra and Sugata Bose (London: Palgrave Macmillan, 2010) and is reproduced with the permission of Palgrave MacMillan.

The publications described above as well as this volume were enabled by funding from the University of the Witwatersrand and the National Research Foundation.

We thank all our colleagues who assisted with the organization of these events and those who took part in them. Our thanks as well to the staff at Wits University Press for their smooth handling of this volume.

Abbreviations and acronyms

ANC	African National Congress
ASC	Anti-Segregation Council
BCCI	Board of Control for Cricket of India
BJP	Bharatiya Janata Party
BRIC	Brazil, India, China
BRICSA	Brazil, India, China and South Africa
CAA	Constitutional Amendment Act
COSATU	Congress of South African Trade Unions
CPI(M)	Communist Party of India (Marxist)
CPSA	Communist Party of South Africa
CST	Colonialism of a Special Type
EPW	Economic and Political Weekly
GEAR	Growth, Employment and Redistribution policy
GDP	Gross domestic product
GOI	Government of India
HIV/AIDS	Human immunnodeficiency virus/acquired immune deficiency syndrome
IBSA	India – Brazil – South Africa
INC	Indian National Congress
IPL	Indian Premier League
IPP	International Printing Press
JNNURM	Jawaharlal Nehru National Urban Renewal Mission
JP	Jaya Prakash Narayan
LSG	Liberal Study Group
NAD	Natal Archives Depot
NDR	National Democratic Revolution
NGO	non-governmental organisation
NIA	Natal Indian Association
NIC	Natal Indian Congress
NSFU	National Seamen's and Firemen's Union
PAC	Pan Africanist Congress
PRC	Passive Resistance Council
PRI	Panchayati Raj Institution
RDP	Reconstruction and Development Programme
RSS	Rashtriya Swayamsevak Sangh
SACP	South African Communist Party
SACTU	South African Congress of Trade Unions
SAIC	South African Indian Congress
SANCO	South African National Civic Organisation
SC	Scheduled Caste
ST	Scheduled Tribe
TAC	Treatment Action Campaign
ULB	Urban local body
TIC	Transvaal Indian Congress
TRC	Truth and Reconciliation Commission
VHP	Vishva Hindu Parishad

Introduction

South Africa–India: Historical Connections, Cultural Circulations and Socio-political Comparisons

Introduction | *Isabel Hofmeyr and Michelle Williams*

Pick up any South African newspaper or tune in to any broadcast programme and before long one is likely to come across an item on India. Whether an advertisement for a particular model of Tata or Mahindra motor car, or a report on the growing trade and investment links between the two countries, each day brings mounting evidence of the marked intensification of relations between South Africa and India.

This Indian presence in the South African media may seem unremarkable. As a rising world economic power, India probably currently features more in most international media than it used to. South Africa has one of the largest Indian diasporic populations and one may hence expect India-related stories. However, the Indian presence in the South African media is noteworthy in two respects: firstly, the reporting on India appears in the mainstream media rather than those aimed specifically at South African Indian communities and, secondly, the discussion of India in the South African media tends to explore the economic synergies that exist between the two countries rather than discussing India's rise in general.

This focus on these new economic possibilities in turn forms part of a series of state and public policies that specifically seek to bolster South Africa–India interactions. Prior to South Africa's political transition in 1994, there were no formal economic ties between the two countries. In 2008/2009 total trade amounted to over US$4 billion. Since 2001 it has grown at a phenomenal rate of 22 per cent per annum, and the two governments set a target of US$10 billion in trade by 2010. Investment has grown almost as rapidly, and today there are at least 50 major corporations from each country operating in the other, and as many as 20 or 25 others exploring the possibility of investing from one to the other. Both states are committed to increasing these figures by making use of their growing number of bilateral agreements and the trilateral possibilities opened up by the India–Brazil–South Africa initiative (commonly know as IBSA). Growth in commercial ties has seen the establishment of bilateral business associations and similar bodies, but has also stimulated the expansion of linkages in other social arenas beyond the market.

Other factors promote closer South Africa–India exchanges. There are long-standing historical links between the two countries inaugurated by 17th-century slavery at the Cape, where about one-quarter of the slaves were from South Asia, and then, from the 1860s, by the arrival of indentured labourers followed by merchants. The two countries share cross-cutting anti-colonial histories in which the figure of Gandhi has been central. The African National Congress and South African Communist Party drew on ideas and strategies from Indian nationalist struggles, while India was one of the first countries to provide support for the anti-apartheid movement. Both countries are middle-ranking powers in the Global South and both are vibrant democracies with strong traditions of public debate and press freedom. In addition to facing similar social issues such as HIV/AIDS, poverty and unemployment, both states are characterised by extreme linguistic, ethnic and religious diversity. Both are grappling with the issues presented by a rapidly rising middle class characterised by a mixture of high-minded political ideals encountering new modes of materialism and consumerism.

Given this context, it is not surprising that there has been a groundswell of academic interest in projects with a South Africa–India dimension. Across the disciplinary spectrum there has been a turn towards India, with increasing numbers of South African academics seeking out Indian partners with whom they can start to track the emerging interactions between the two countries, while analysing both the possible future implications of these new realities and their pasts.

The chapters drawn together in this volume arise out of an interdisciplinary project based at the University of the Witwatersrand in Johannesburg.[1] The project draws together about two dozen scholars working in software engineering, public health, economics, education, social sciences and the humanities. Research themes include trade and investment patterns between the two countries, comparative constitutional law, Indian Ocean cultural exchanges, English in secondary schools in Johannesburg and Delhi, HIV/AIDS in South Africa and India, and comparative topics (urbanisation in both countries; the Communist Parties of South Africa and Kerala). This research has expanded rapidly and in 2008 the university established a Centre of Indian Studies in Africa, where Professor Dilip Menon has been appointed to the Chair of Indian Studies.

The work arising out of this group consciously attempts to speak to the new relations that have emerged between South Africa and India. This volume presents an opportunity to profile this research. We begin by discussing older traditions of scholarship that have addressed relations between the two regions. We then turn to consider the new scholarship that is emerging and the directions that this work suggests. The first set of chapters in this volume focus on the historical connections between India and South Africa, where the flow of ideas, people and merchandise has interlaced the histories in interesting and often unexpected ways. The chapters in this section explore these issues through the circulation of the printing press, maritime flows, interlocking worlds of war, the processes of decolonisation and cultural forms of resistance. The second set of chapters draw our attention to socio-political comparisons that look at iconic struggle leaders, democratic deepening, popular participation, migration and political party ideologies. Through the two rubrics – historical connections and socio-political comparisons – the chapters explore the interwoven histories and complex experiences of India and South Africa.

South Africa/India: Uneasy historiographies

Despite centuries of interaction, Africa and India today remain largely sundered domains of analysis. Set in relations of opposition by colonial rule and then by a Cold War Area studies map, 'Africa' and 'India/South Asia' in the academy appear to have little to do with each other. When they are configured, this configuration is usually characterised by uneasy stereotypes of extremity. On one side stand narratives of shoulder-to-shoulder Bandung-style anti-colonial solidarity, especially apparent in accounts of Indian involvement in the anti-apartheid movement (e.g. see Gupta, 2003). On the other are quasi-colonial views to be found in India of Africa as 'the dark continent', a view that draws implicitly on older ideas of civilisationism that rank 'Indian' civilisation above that of 'Africa' (Hofmeyr, 2007:61). These contrasting views offer a stark binary set of explanations, with either too much solidarity on the one side or too little on the other.

Complicating this picture has been the difficulties of pursuing transnational study in an academy dominated by national and regional frameworks. The two regions that are now South Africa and India have been linked by transnational flows of labour (first slavery and then indenture), as well as intellectual and cultural exchange. The scholarship that has sought to understand these processes was undertaken in a context of nationally based historiographies and the dominance of Area Studies training. This work has necessarily encountered difficulties in asserting the primacy of transnational processes in the face of national and regional models of analysis. However, with the transnational turn in the social sciences occasioned by the processes of globalisation and the emergence of a post-Cold War order, questions of transnationalism have come into their own.

These frameworks have in turn opened up new possibilities for thinking about interactions between South Africa and India and have permitted revisions of earlier historiographies that addressed the interaction between these two regions.

Indentured historiographies: The one-way problem

The movement of Indian indentured labour and then 'free passenger' Indians – largely merchants to Natal in the 1860s – has generated a strong tradition of scholarship (Bhana & Brain, 1990). However, as Uma Dhupelia-Mesthrie (2007) has pointed out, this scholarship manifests various problems: it tends to homogenise the 'Indian community' without looking in detail at its faultlines, and it is primarily social and economic history, with little cultural exploration. A recent major work on indenture by Ashwin Desai and Goolam Vahed (2007) has taken up this challenge and provides a detailed insight into the social, cultural and religious contours of everyday indenture experience. It also addresses another problem with older indentured historiography, namely that it focusses mainly on 'Indian experience'. Desai and Vahed (2007:8) narrate this experience 'against the backdrop of White rule and its oppressive relationship with the Zulu'.

An additional problem with older historiography is that it manifests what we may call the 'one-way problem'. Put briefly, studies tend to examine movement from India to South Africa, without asking what implications this migration had back in India. As Dhupelia-Mesthrie (2007) points out, this problem is equally apparent in the fact that the indentured diaspora tends mainly to be studied in the diaspora itself, with comparatively few historians in India turning their attention to this question, a process exacerbated by the strongly nationalist stamp of Indian historiography.

Fortunately, this 'one-way problem' has started to shift through the pioneering work of Tejaswini Niranjana (1999) on Trinidad and John Kelly (1991) on Fiji. Both these scholars demonstrate how the indentured diaspora feeds back into debates in Indian nationalism and is used in a variety of ways. For some early 20th-century Indian nationalists, the indentured diaspora becomes the outer boundaries of the nation, and the maltreatment of workers – and particularly Hindu women – in the diaspora is portrayed as a transgression of the nation. This transgression is used to mobilise sympathy and support for nationalist struggles in India. As Niranjana (1999) argues, the diaspora could also become a conduit for imaginatively and actually expelling the unwanted parts of the nation. Pivoting on the upper-caste/middle-class Indian women as its imagined centre, Indian nationalist discourse depended on a disavowal of the lower-caste woman. As Niranjana demonstrates, the figure of the undesirable woman could be relegated to the outer reaches of the diaspora, enabling a 'pure' concept of the gendered nation to take shape.

This important work opens the way to reinsert the indentured diaspora into the story of Indian nationalism itself. Such a reconfiguration has occurred in relation to the post-1960s diaspora, which was more middle class and hence generally attracted more attention. Along with the transnational turn in the social sciences, the way is clear to factor the less glamorous indentured diaspora back into Indian historiography, demonstrating how the nation's peripheries were important in its imaginative formation. Or, as Metcalf (2007:3) notes: 'Abroad … Indians came face to face with their nationality.'

'Africa' in 'India'

Another body of work that is starting to reverse the one-way flow is that which asks about the meanings of Africa in India. In India itself, there is often a perception that apart from Gandhi, Gujarati traders and Siddis (the latter being Africans who from the 13th century moved from North and East Africa to India as servants, soldiers, slaves, sailors, policemen, traders, bureaucrats and concubines [Jayasuriya & Pankhurst, 2003]), India has little to do with Africa. Indeed, it is not uncommon to find quasi-colonial perceptions in India of Africa as 'the dark continent' (Hofmeyr, 2007:61).

However, as new work is starting to indicate, Africa itself played a formative role in the imagining of India, constituting a boundary for the imagination of the nation. This process is particularly clear in relation to Gandhi, whose pejorative comments on Africans have often been noted. One way to make sense of this discourse is to examine it as part of Gandhi's imagination of India that began to emerge in South Africa, where for the first time he confronted a cross section of Indian society. Gandhi's conception of India was initially imagined as a dominion within the British Empire. In this configuration, India shared a boundary with the empire. A primary marker for this boundary was the 'native' or 'Africa', which came to represent an imaginative boundary of 'India'. 'Africa' hence constitutes one of the limits of 'India', a boundary reinforced by ideas of civilisationism (Hofmeyr, 2007).

Gandhi's years in South Africa obviously provide a major focus within the historiographies of South Africa–India interactions. However, as Surendra Bhana and Goolam Vahed (2005) point out, this scholarship tends to be dominated by national paradigms of analysis. Scholars in and of India have tended to see Gandhi as 'an extension of traditions in India' (Bhana & Vahed, 2005:11). Scholars of South Africa such as Maureen Swan (1985) place him in a South African context, with little reference to the Indian background. Elsewhere, there is a strong awareness that Gandhi's work in South Africa was central to Indian nationalism (Brown, 1996; Markovits, 2003:78–85), yet this relationship awaits in-depth study. Quoting Markovits, Dhupelia-Mesthrie (2007:23) points out that the South African years represent the 'real black hole in Gandhi's life', an absence in part created by the fact that during the apartheid years, historians in India were unable to visit South Africa.

Other ways in which Africa featured in Indian nationalist thought are starting to emerge from P. K. Datta's (2007) seminal work on the depictions of the Anglo-Boer War in India (which is included in this volume). An avowedly international event, the Anglo-Boer War was taken up allegorically by different groups in India. As Datta (2007:39) indicates, the war crystallised 'an ambivalence towards colonial authority that deepened skepticism of the Raj' and served to weaken ideas of imperial loyalism. Datta explores the idea that imperial subjecthood provided a discourse to claim rights within the British Empire (from one place to another), but was fundamentally flawed owing to the structured inequalities of the empire. The contradictions of this idea were powerfully revealed in the Anglo-Boer War and its aftermath in both India and South Africa.

Indian Ocean studies

Under the influence of Braudelianism and world systems theory, Indian Ocean historiography accelerated from the 1980s, producing a rich vein of work on the historical unities, commonalities and discontinuities of this early modern maritime world. In an excellent account of this scholarship, Markus Vink (2007) sets out these themes: monsoon and trade winds, port cities, littorals (Pearson, 1998; 2003; 2006), ships and seafarers (Gupta, 2004), religion and trade (Risso, 1995), long-distance commerce (Chaudhuri, 1985; Gupta, 2004; Prakash, 2004) and the Portuguese presence (Subrahmanyam, 1997b; Pearson, 1998).

One strand in this skein has become important to current debates on transnationalism, i.e. the notion that the early modern Indian Ocean world offers an instance of transregional trade without the state.[2] Discussing how the Hadrami diaspora engaged with the Indian Ocean region, Engseng Ho (2006:xxi) notes:

> Their enterprises overseas were not backed by [a] ... mobile, armed state. The Portuguese, Dutch, and English in the Indian Ocean were strange new traders who brought their states with them. They created militarized trading-post empires in the Indian Ocean ... and were wont to do business at the point of a gun. Hadramis and other non-Europeans – such as Gujaratis, Bohras, Chettiars, Buginese, and Malays – did not. Rather than elbow their way in, they comported themselves to local arrangements wherever they went.

T. N. Harper (2002:158) puts the point succinctly: 'The globalization of European imperialism was an extension of the nation state. The globalism [of diasporas] was not.' This precedent of transoceanic trading systems uncoupled from a militarised state has proved productive in terms of rethinking the nation state today. Three prominent writers on the Indian Ocean – Amitav Ghosh (1992; 2008), Abdulrazak Gurnah (1994; 2005) and Engseng Ho (2004; 2006) – explore these old trading diasporas of the Indian Ocean world as a way of relativising the nation state. For Ghosh, the cosmopolitanism of the older diasporic networks offers a counterpoint to the narrowness of the modern nation state system. For Gurnah, the nation state is subsumed into the transnational networks above it and the loyalties of family and lineage below it. For Ho, the nation state is overshadowed by more epic entanglements as the universalistic ambitions of old diasporas and new empires encounter one another.

While the initial impetus in Indian Ocean historiography was towards early modern patterns of trade and diaspora, more recently there has been a growing emphasis on 19th- and 20th-century histories (Ewald, 2000; Vergès, 2003; Bose, 2005; Metcalf, 2007). One productive strand in this scholarship has been around the notion of Indian Ocean public spheres emerging from the 1880s to the First World War. As Mark Ravinder Frost's work (2002; 2004; 2010) has demonstrated, these public spheres were rooted in the port cities of the ocean and grew out of the intellectual and religious activities of the cross-cutting diasporas that gathered in these entrepôts.

Dedicated to projects of reform, these intelligentsias pursued a variety of universalisms (pan-Islam, pan-Buddhism, theosophy, imperial citizenship, Hindu reformism), which they formulated by sharing ideas via circulating periodicals and intellectuals (Arya Samaj missionaries, Sufis, pilgrims and scholars). Utilising the growing communication channels of empire, these networks operated most visibly in the extensive periodical press produced in these 'information ports' (Cole, 2002:344) and circulated actively between them. These journals quoted avidly from one another, enacting a quoting circle around the ocean (Hofmeyr, 2008).

These periodicals constitute an experimental site in which ideas of nationalism and diasporic discourses could be explored in relation to one another. An apt example is the extensive field of diasporic ideas of Indianness apparent in terms such as 'overseas Indian', 'colonial-born Indian', 'Indians abroad' and 'Greater India'. The complexity of each of these terms is apparent from a quick glance at the idea of 'Greater India'. As Susan Bayly (2004) demonstrates, this idea was first articulated in the 1920s by French-influenced Bengali scholars and focussed on the ancient cultural diffusion of Hinduism and Buddhism from India into East and South-East Asia. This idea of India as an early and benign coloniser appealed to a range of constituencies: Indian Indologists seeking to claim an active role for India; Hindu supremacists wanting evidence of ancient Vedic glories; anti-colonialists like Subhas Chandra Bose and his Indian National Army and Ghadarists like Taraknath Das, who saw their military activities as armed wings of Greater India; and, finally, those interested in the Indian indentured diaspora, or what was known as the 'new' Greater India, as opposed to the ancient. Greater India could provide an idea of nationhood that stretched diasporically across time and space and importantly could be both anti-colonial and colonising at the same time.

This idea of Indian Ocean public spheres is a useful one for considering the interactions between South Africa and India. Some of the chapters in the first section of this book develop this idea by exploring connections between southern Africa and India, and exchanges in the Indian Ocean more generally. Together, these chapters explore a range of lateral linkages within the Indian Ocean and enrich our picture of both Indian Ocean public spheres and the historiographies of interactions between southern Africa and India.

Isabel Hofmeyr's chapter in this volume focusses on cosmopolitanism in the Indian Ocean through the lens of Gandhi's printing press and textual migration. Hofmeyr explores the idea that the port cities of the Indian Ocean 'constituted a network of textual exchange and circulation that built on, sustained and invented forms of cosmopolitan universalism across the Indian Ocean'. She suggests that the circulation of print across the Indian Ocean interpolated with cosmopolitanism in unexplored and interesting ways. The chapter looks at the connection between textual migration and an emerging cosmopolitanism by exploring the social relationships that developed around Gandhi's printing press.

Keeping the Indian Ocean as their focal point, Pamila Gupta examines the itinerant movement of Goans in the Indian Ocean (and beyond) in the 20th century and Jonathan Hyslop explores the Indian Ocean lascars in the age of steam. Using a life history approach, Gupta examines three distinct periods of Goan migration in the Indian Ocean: the 1920s (a period of migration from Portuguese India to Mozambique); the 1950s and 1960s as the decolonisation of Goa started to bite; and then the post-1975 movement (mainly to Portugal) as Goans left Mozambique after its independence, with a small number remaining. These movements demonstrate not only Indian Ocean links but also faultlines. Goans generally found themselves precariously poised in the Portuguese empire: in Goa they found themselves as colonised Portuguese subjects, while in Mozambique they became a type of coloniser defined as superior to Africans, but below white Portuguese. As itinerants, Goan migrants unsettle supposedly clear boundaries of race within empire and render provisional ideas of high colonial rule and its stark categories of ruling. Decolonisation also begins to look different if viewed through a Goan lens: rather than being one discrete event, decolonisation comprises an ensemble of processes, one of which is further migration.

Gupta's chapter demonstrates the interwoven relationship of empire and diaspora, a theme taken up by Jonathan Hyslop. He examines Indian Ocean seafarers in the age of steam navigation, tracing the interactions of British sailors and African and Asian seamen (lascars) in an imperial communication system. Moving away from the existing focus of examining lascars in British ports, the chapter explores the lateral linkages between port cities in the Indian Ocean. As steam replaced sail, labour relations on ships became increasingly industrialised and racialised. Enfranchised British workers used their unions to win better wages and working conditions for themselves. Captains and shipowners in turn increasingly turned to African and Asian seamen, who were seen as more tractable. While the lateral linkages across the sea opened up new routes of communication, the increasing racialisation of the workforce added new faultlines to the Indian Ocean world.

Shifting to an investigation of Gandhi's *satyagraha*[3] legacies in the South African political arena, Goolam Vahed's chapter scrutinises the influences of Gandhism from the perspective of an individual life, that of Dr G. M. 'Monty' Naicker (1910–78), a political activist who drew heavily on Gandhian ideas. Naicker was involved in Natal Indian politics and played a leading role in the 1946–48 Passive Resistance Campaign challenging the increasing segregationist measures in Durban. As Vahed suggests, Naicker and others in the South African Indian Congress were in dialogue with Gandhi and Nehru, a dialogue that was crucial in propagating non-violent forms of resistance and feeding ideas between Indian and African nationalist thinking.

Emerging comparative perspectives

The experiences of India and South Africa have also been explored through scholarship comparing them. While still working largely within nationally based historiographies, scholars are beginning to look at social, political and economic processes experienced by India and South Africa in order to better understand each individual case. Indeed, comparative research is especially fruitful in trying to understand the complexities of India and South Africa, as both countries (and scholarship on the countries) have tended to see themselves as exceptional, reducing social and political phenomena to the uniqueness of their respective societies. Comparing them with each other helps to dispel notions of exceptionalism and makes us look to local, national, *and* global processes and forces shaping the countries. Thus, using the comparative method strengthens analyses by focussing attention on factors that may have been overlooked in a single-case analysis.

Looking at southern Africa alongside India yields fascinating similarities and differences in their histories. The early colonial histories bear resemblance involving layers of Portuguese, Dutch and British incursion. In the 20th century their histories diverged markedly when in 1947 India gained independence and became the largest democracy in the world. Less than a year later the apartheid regime officially took power in South Africa, putting the country on a very different trajectory. Yet their histories would converge again by century's end, and despite important differences in their struggles, the Indian National Congress and the African National Congress bear striking similarities. Moreover, in both South

Africa and India, Communist Parties have found their voices expressed in oppositional politics and institutional arenas, and both societies enjoy robust civic associations and vibrant labour movements.

Alongside these achievements, however, are also disturbing trends. According to the 2009 *Human Development Report* of the United Nation Development Programme (UN, 2009), South Africa registers the third-highest income inequality in the world. In addition to high levels of poverty, South Africa has some of the most violent crime rates in the world. India, too, manifests extreme levels of inequality and poverty, and has seen incessant communal (religious) violence since independence. While formal democracy has been consolidated in both countries, as Patrick Heller shows in this volume, the power of the elite continues to act on subaltern classes in devastating ways. The goal of deepening democracy has proven more elusive in both India and South Africa.

Development indicators are illustrative of the achievements and challenges faced by each country. While India's economy grew at 7.2 per cent per year against South Africa's 4.8 per cent between 1998 and 2008,[4] India has not opened its economy in terms of exports and imports to the same degree as South Africa. India's poverty rate of 34.3 per cent of the population living below US$1 a day is far higher than South Africa's poverty rate of 10.7 per cent.[5] Yet India's income share of the lowest 20 per cent of the population is 8.1 per cent, which compares favourably with South Africa's income share of the lowest 20 per cent of the population of 3.5 per cent. Comparing the countries across a series of indicators throws up contradictory processes. On a number of indicators, such as per capita gross national income, literacy, internet use and tertiary enrolment, South Africa ranks favourably against India. These achievements, however, have not translated into increased youth employment, nor have they produced the phenomenal growth rates found in India. At the same time, India's spectacular growth has not increased literacy rates or reduced poverty. Clearly, these are complex societies with contradictory processes shaping the countries' development trajectories; see Table 1.

Table 1: India and South Africa compared

Indicator	India	South Africa
Population	1.1 billion	48 million
Gross national income per capita (Atlas method) (2009)	US$1,040	US$5,820
Gross domestic product (GDP) growth, % per annum, 1998–2008	7.2	4.1
GDP growth, % per annum, 2008–10	7.3	1.2
Openness: exports + imports, % of GDP (2006)	32.5	53.2
Income share of lowest 20% (2006)	8.1	3.5
Poverty rate, % of population < US$1 per day (2006)	34.3	10.7
Infant mortality, per 1,000 live births (2009)	52	48
Youth unemployment rate, % (2006)	10.5	60.1
Literacy rate, % (2009)	66	88
Tertiary enrolment ratio, % (2006)	11.4	15.3
Internet users, per 1,000 people (2006)	55	109

Source: World Bank (2006a; 2006b; 2009a; 2009b)

Given these similarities between South Africa and India, one might expect a strong tradition of comparative work. This as yet does not fully exist, part of the reason being that under apartheid Indian scholars could not visit South Africa. The situation is fortunately beginning to change and a field of comparative work is starting to emerge. A problem with comparative work, however, is that it often focusses on large-scale policy-oriented studies. Put simply, these studies tend to compare very general phenomena in as many cases as possible in order to draw policy outcomes through the comparisons. They are often funded by well-resourced northern foundations that are more interested in the immediate policy implications for South Africa and India than in a deeper understandings of causes, processes and sequences of events. Fortunately, a growing body of emerging work on South Africa and India is providing an alternative body of comparative studies.

Beyond the obvious similarities that India and South Africa share, such as common histories of British imperialism, iconic liberation movements, successful democratic consolidation in two heterogeneous societies and two of the most remarkable leaders of the 20th century (Mahatma Gandhi and Nelson Mandela), scholars are also exploring the less obvious areas of comparison. The work of Crain Soudien (2007), for example, looks at inclusion and exclusion in Indian and South African schools. Soudien shows how similar processes of elite values (Anglo, middle class in South Africa and upper caste in India) reproduce exclusion despite advocating normative inclusion. Another example of comparative scholarship is Claire Bénit-Gbaffou's and Stéphanie Tawa Lama-Rewal's emerging research on urban governance, participation, and the voice of the poor in South African and Indian cities, which looks at the relative incapacity of the urban poor to influence policy, despite the fact that they constitute a numerical majority. The chapters in this volume contribute to this tradition of comparative work that seeks to understand unfamiliar ground in new and exciting ways.

Socio-political comparisons

Without losing the historical integrity of the specifics of each case, the chapters in this section search for common themes. Taking as their focal points different topics, they converge in showing the striking similarities and important differences between India and South Africa. The five chapters represent aspects of comparative work that can be explored in regional analyses. They range in topic from political parties and democracy to migrant histories, and in scope from the local to the national levels. All the chapters compare some facet of India and South Africa and in the process tell interesting and illuminating stories.

Picking up on the legacies of Gandhian ideas on South Africa, Crain Soudien's chapter asks how Gandhian ideas might be applied to current social theory on Africa. Soudien argues that current thinking on Africa is caught in one of two positions: either a reproduction of Western modernity or a wishful nativism that seeks to retrieve a pure Africanness apparently untouched by the ravages of colonialism and modernity. He asks how we can transcend the sterility of these two positions, which are characterised by envy or revenge. Highlighting two aspects of Gandhian thinking – a critique of 'masculinised conceits of civilisation' and their reliance on violence, and a non-teleological approach to the past that allows it to become a site of contingency and experimentation – Soudien argues that Gandhian thinking leads us beyond the 'logic of dominance'

Patrick Heller compares India and South Africa using the indices of democratic consolidation and democratic deepening as his central organising principles. He shows how both South Africa and India are relatively successful cases of democratic consolidation in terms of state capacity and the rule of law. However, Heller problematises these achievements by asking whether consolidating democratic institutions in India and South Africa has translated into democratic deepening in which citizens are able to meaningfully participate in political life. In this regard, South Africa and India have not fared very well. Citizens in both countries struggle to *practise* citizenship, because the effective points of interface with the state are limited and the nature of state-civil society relations has tended to favour state control. In addition to these vertical limitations between the state and civil society, Heller also points to horizontal limitations within civil society. By carefully examining South Africa and India, Heller shows how consolidating and deepening democracy require very different logics and very different configurations of the balance of power between the state and civil society.

Claire Bénit-Gbaffou and Stéphanie Tawa Lama-Rewal explore a similar idea from a different perspective. Looking at the different experiences of decentralisation and local democracy in India and South Africa, they show a striking difference in the two experiences. In India, the focus has been on rural areas, with cities remaining almost invisible (at least in the literature), whereas South Africa has emphasised the metropolitan areas. They argue that 'the idea that natural location of local democracy is in *rural* India has been extremely widespread, among politicians and scholars, at least until the 2000s'. This contrasts markedly with South Africa, where there has not been a rural bias, but rather a strong focus on the urban political field.

In her chapter, Michelle Williams compares the ideological visions of the communist parties in South Africa and the Indian state of Kerala. In response to the rise of neoliberal globalisation and the failures of 20th-century socialism, during the 1990s the communist parties in South Africa and Kerala embarked on a journey of ideological renewal that highlights radically democratic egalitarian alternatives. Williams shows how both parties theorised remarkably similar visions of 'socialist democracy' around four common themes: participatory democracy, a new developmental state, the coexistence of capitalism and socialism, and the extension of civil society and the state in the economy. Their ideological renewal grew out of an appreciation that socialist alternatives could not be conceived as a predetermined model of social organisation, but rather had to be understood as a process of extending democratic practices of collective decision making and the progressive empowerment of subalterns to participate in the development of society.

Phil Bonner's chapter explores differences between the historiographies on migrancy in the two countries. Central to South Africa's segregationist and then apartheid order has been a migrant labour system held in place by a raft of repressive measures: land dispossession, taxation, pass systems, compounds, segregation. In the South African historiography, migrancy is treated as synonymous with institutionalised compulsion and coercion. India has large-scale migrancy, but without this barrage of coercive interventions. Focussing on Bombay (now Mumbai) and Calcutta (now Kolkata), the chapter outlines how migrancy in the Indian case has been sustained by a series of factors across town and country that encouraged the maintenance of a rural base and discouraged the movement of families to towns, and kept oscillatory migrancy in place. Bonner also compares questions of generation, gender, race and social stability across the two historiographies. In South African migration, young men and women moved first, a 'generationally skewed' pattern that is as evident in the Indian case. In terms of gender, far more women moved in the South African context than in the Indian, raising the question of why and how the Indian working class became so overwhelmingly male. In South Africa, race became a critical issue as the power of white settler society came to define African urbanisation as pathological and as something that had to be reversed by a series of repressive state measures. In the South African case, migrancy produced 'chronic family instability' and high levels of juvenile delinquency, which were not evident to nearly the same degree in India. Comparing these historiographies shows up their aporias in productive ways.

In his chapter, Eric Worby concludes the book by exploring the common preoccupation of all the authors with what he calls 'civic virtue' and 'private ethics'. Using the example of cricket, he demonstrates how civic virtue and personal ethics dovetail in performance in the game. Worby shows how 'in the transnational ethical field constituted by cricket, it is fairly easy to see how personal morality is persistently mapped into arguments about public values, as well as the political institutions and practices that sustain them'. It is this very same intermingling of personal morality, public values, and political institutions and practices that makes possible the conversations in this volume.

Rethinking the South: Towards some conclusions

For some commentators, we are beginning to move towards a 'post-American world' (Zakaria, 2008) in which the unilateral dominance of the United States will wane. The rise of India and China most powerfully signals this shift and raises pressing questions about the shape of such a 'post-American' world – and the Global South within it.

Yet as we start to feel some of the changes precipitated by the rise of Asia, questions about the idea of the Global South move to the fore insistently. Can this category hold together as India and China strive for superpower status? What are the limits and possibilities of this concept as we move forward? Can the idea of the Global South with its roots in Third Worldist discourses speak to the ambiguities and complexities of a changing world order?

The term itself has become common currency, but its genealogies and lineages are less clear. The term 'South' initially emerged in the 1980s from the Brandt Commission on international development, which popularised a North/South or rich/poor vocabulary (Dirlik, n.d.). The collapse of the Eastern bloc and Soviet Union in 1989 precipitated a shift from a Cold War three-worlds model towards a division of developed and developing nations, the 'North' and the 'South'. In this context, the term 'Global South' came to stand in as a proxy for the term 'Third World'. In a post-Cold War order, older ideas of the Third World and non-alignment appeared to have become redundant, but these nations continued to share strategic objectives and interests. In recognition of this imperative, the Non-Aligned Movement called its tenth summit in September 1992 in Jakarta, Indonesia, to discuss how the developing nations might regroup in the changed geopolitical order. The summit affirmed the importance of a North–South axis, as opposed to the East–West Cold War axis. Clovis Maksoud, the eminent diplomat and long-standing permanent observer of the League of Arab States at the United Nations, comments: 'The Jakarta Declaration implicitly recognised the dawn of a new era, in which the terms "Third World" and "non-aligned" have been subsumed by the term "Global South"' (Maksoud 1993:34). The persistence of the Non-Aligned Movement and the growing importance of the G-77 group (which focusses on a unitary voice for the 'developing nations' in the United Nations) point to the continued need for collective action among these nations.

The idea of the Global South, then, will continue to be an important concept that will shape intergovernmental activity, non-governmental organisation priorities and trade agendas. What will its role be in setting academic and research priorities? Taken together, the chapters in this collection provide some answers to this question by probing the limits and possibilities of one set of axes in the Global South, namely the links between South Africa and India.

On the possibilities side of the equation, the chapters point to the productive and as yet unexplored histories and comparative possibilities within the Global South. The pieces point to new histories of linkage and circulation, whether these be Goan migrants, lascars or typographers moving in and around the Indian Ocean. The comparative possibilities point to new historiographical insights, as histories of labour, social movements and urban governance are placed side by side and as social theory from different parts of the Global South is brought into conversation.

Yet at the same time, these pieces also point to the growing contradictions within the category of 'the South' and its earlier incarnations. As Hofmeyr's chapter indicates, Gandhi's cosmopolitanism met its limits in ideas of civilisational hierarchies between India and Africa. While ideologies of Third Worldist solidarity and Afro-Asian cooperation have obscured such divisions, new histories of Bandung are starting to reveal the complexities and struggles within and between different players, ideologies and interests, and how these shaped the contours of these movements (Amrith, 2005; Burton, 2006; Burton, Espiritu & Wilkins, 2006; Chatterjee, 2006b; Abraham, 2008).

In some cases, the gaps of power between different parts of the Global South are considerable and can constitute what Antoinette Burton (2006:151) has termed 'semi-imperialisms'. These faultlines and semi-imperialisms will continue to play themselves out, especially as new alliances and competitions emerge in the 'post-American' Indian Ocean. In this changing arena, unexpected 'lateral' cultural forms will take shape. Hindi film continues to make its way to many parts of Africa and finds new audiences there (Larkin, 1997). Reverse flow is apparent in the South African film *Mr Bones*, which has been circulating in India. The film comes from Leon Schuster, the king of South African slapstick. Its plot concerns a white boy who falls from an aeroplane and grows up in a 'tribe' and becomes a 'witch doctor'. Translated into a range of Indian languages, the film has been a runaway success in cinemas and on TV.

In some senses, *Mr Bones*' travels are to be expected: slapstick stereotypes travel easily. Yet such examples also seem counter-intuitive: they unsettle the elevated moral agendas of South–South cooperation, in which slapstick does not really belong. Equally out of place would be the growing trend of South–South spying, a phenomenon that is now routine in the Indian Ocean: since 2007, for example, India has opened up listening posts in Madagascar and Mozambique to track shipping lanes and keep an eye on the Chinese. As a post-Cold War and possibly 'post-American' world coalesces, understanding South–South slapstick and South–South spying will become increasingly important.[6] The chapters in this collection seek to lay the groundwork for an environment in which we can start to make sense of new phenomena such as these that will speak to the complexities of a new and confusing world order.

Historical
Connections

chapter 1-5

<table>
1

Chapter
</table>

Gandhi's Printing Press: Indian Ocean Print Cultures and Cosmopolitanisms

Isabel Hofmeyr

Introduction

At low tide from the beach at Porbandar in Gujarat, one can just glimpse the tip of a shipwreck. Originally the SS Khedive, this vessel is the subject of a double legend. The first is that it carried Mohandas Gandhi on one of his voyages between Bombay and Durban; the second is that the ship sank with Gandhi's printing press on board.[7]

This is not the only report of a phantom printing press associated with Gandhi. More than a century earlier another account had emerged, this time on the other side of the Indian Ocean, in Durban. Towards the end of 1896 Gandhi was headed for this port on his way back from Bombay. Angry white mobs awaited his arrival, claiming he was organising an 'Asiatic Invasion'. Rumours circulated that Gandhi had a printing press and 30 compositors on board. According to the Natal media, the lynch mob intended first to attack Gandhi and then the printing press (*Natal Witness*, 11 January 1897).

In part, this phenomenon of the phantom printing press can be easily explained. In the Durban case, it had been well known for some years that Gandhi wished to acquire such a press in order to start a newspaper that could speak for the interests of Indian merchants in Natal (Pyarelal, 1986:63–65). The alarm that much of white Natal society felt at this idea expressed itself in the rumour of the imaginary press. White artisans were equally perturbed at the prospect of cheap compositors coming to undercut the market.

A few years later, in 1898, Gandhi did indeed play a part in purchasing a press that was to print his newspaper, *Indian Opinion*, which became pivotal in his *satyagraha* campaigns. When Gandhi returned to India in 1914, newspapers continued to be a key component of his non-cooperation movements. Gandhi, the newspaper and the printing press were closely associated, and hence the memory of his printing press persisting in legend is understandable. Indeed, Gandhi's press has become something of a minor icon in his life story. A chapter of his autobiography discusses his printing press in South Africa (Gandhi, M., 1957:302–4), while the presses he used feature in exhibitions and museums (*Satyagraha*, n.d.).

Yet, pertinent as these explanations are, they do not clarify one important aspect of these stories: both are accounts of a printing press at sea. In the Durban case, the idea of a press coming across the waters from Bombay sparks alarm and aggression. In the Porbandar case, the press remains a symbol of Gandhi, but one that has been lost in the Indian Ocean. Both stories ask us to think about the printing press in the context of the Indian Ocean.

This chapter takes up this invitation by placing Gandhi's printing press in the framework of an Indian Ocean public sphere as a way of exploring cosmopolitanism in the Indian Ocean region. As groundbreaking work by Mark Ravinder Frost (2002) and scholars such as T. N. Harper (2002), Sugata Bose (2005), Engseng Ho (2006) and Thomas Metcalfe (2007) indicates, the imperial port cities of the Indian Ocean sustained a distinctive public sphere that flourished from the 1880s until the First World War and supported various modes of cosmopolitanism.

The Indian Ocean was the site of several overlapping diasporas whose educated classes gathered in the ports around the ocean. As Frost (2002: 937) notes:

> Entrepôts like Bombay, Madras, Calcutta, Rangoon and Singapore witnessed the emergence of a non-European, Western-educated professional class that serviced the requirements of expanding international commercial interests and the simultaneous growth of the imperial state.

These centres supported intelligentsias drawn from various Indian Ocean diasporas who 'developed habits of intellectual sociability that become organized and systematic'. Sharing similar concerns for reform, these groups oversaw parallel campaigns for religious revival, social and educational improvement and constitutional change' (Frost, 2002:937). Positioned as 'nodal points in an imperial network of steamer routes, telegraph lines and railways', these cities functioned as relay stations for ideas, texts, commodities and people (Frost, 2002:939).

To Frost's map we could of course add other ports, namely Mombasa, Zanzibar, Beira, Lourenco Marques (the modern Maputo) and Durban. Together, these cities constituted a network of textual exchange and circulation that built on, sustained and invented forms of cosmopolitan universalism across the Indian Ocean. Some of these universalisms were religious in character and, as Frost (2002:939) points out, were apparent in pan-Buddhist, pan-Islamic (and, one might add, pan-Hindu) movements. There were also traditions of transnational social organisation, like anarchism or socialism, that were anti-colonial in character. Beliefs in a colour-blind, rights-bearing imperial citizenship provided yet another template of universalism. Such diasporic universalisms have long been obscured, falling outside studies of empire, on the one hand, and studies of the nation, on the other. With the transnational turn in the humanities and social sciences, such networks are moving to the fore and are helping to revise understandings of colonial encounter not as the interaction of the local and the global, but rather as an encounter of different universalisms.

These distinctive public spheres of the South offer several analytical possibilities. In relation to studies of print culture, this zone of circulation opens up new maps for thinking about textual migration. Frost (2002:940) notes that in 1920 the number of books, pamphlets and newspapers that passed through the Colombo post office to and from other parts of the British Empire was equal to, if not greater than, the number of equivalent items passing between Colombo and Britain. The South–South traffic of books and newspapers matched the equivalent traffic on a North–South axis. What were these books and pamphlets? Where did they come from and where were they headed? What kinds of reading and writing publics did they convene on their oceanic circuits and what kinds of communities of belief did they bring into being? Put differently, what modes of cosmopolitanism did this circulation of print enable?

This chapter is a very modest initial attempt to draw this bigger picture. Drawing on existing work on the Indian Ocean public sphere, the chapter seeks to build on Frost's model by asking what the analytical grammar of such an Indian Ocean cultural world might be. Put differently, how in methodological terms might one gain an analytical grasp on a field as diverse as the Indian Ocean? The chapter proposes that the printing presses be considered as a key element in that grammar. One way, then, to think about the Indian Ocean is as a series of interrelated printing presses spread around the port cities. The chapter looks at one such press by way of a methodological experiment. It asks what we might learn by examining the social relationships that developed around the press, the types of socialities it entailed, the ideas of printing and publishing that it generated, and the kinds of audiences it called into being. The personnel of the press were drawn from across the Indian Ocean and brought with them different ideas and ideals of printing and publishing.

Gandhi's printing press: A biography

The International Printing Press (IPP) came into the world in considerable style on the evening of 29 November 1898. An opening ceremony attended by a crowd of nearly a hundred inaugurated the press at 113 Grey Street, next door to the Natal Indian Congress Hall. Proceedings got under way with the Congress organist playing *God Save the Queen*. Next followed speeches. The proprietor, Madanjit Viyavaharik, told the predominantly Indian audience that '[t]he press is not mine alone – it is yours also'. Gandhi then read letters of good wishes and the press was declared open. What the Natal press described as 'a priest from Verulam [a settlement north of Durban]' apostrophised the press with some Gujarati verses extolling the virtues of the printing arts and indicated that 'they had to thank Queen Victoria for the freedom which enabled them to obtain the privileges and blessings accruing from printing' (Pyarelal, 1980:193–94).

The IPP itself comprised two hand-operated presses: the first an Albion Press (the most widely used press in the British Empire), the second a platen jobber, as well as 1,000 lbs of English type, which had been acquired second hand in Durban. Hindi, Gujarati, Tamil, Urdu and Marathi type was ordered from India (Pyarelal, 1980:193). The press undertook general job printing. It printed the monthly magazine of the theosophical society and a short-lived newspaper called the *Volunteer*, as well as booklets and pamphlets (Pyarelal, 1986:434; Natal Archives Depot [NAD], CSO 1735, 1903/6053). From June 1903 the newspaper *Indian Opinion* was printed at 113 Grey Street.

The press could do work in a range of languages: Gujarati, Tamil, Hindi, Urdu, Hebrew, Marathi, Sanscrit, Zulu and Dutch, according to an advertisement on the newspaper's cover on the 11 June 1903. Its personnel were multilingual and drawn from across the Indian Ocean and beyond. The foreman, a Mr Oliver from Mauritius, oversaw a staff of typesetters and machinemen. The English compositors included a French-speaking Mauritian; a man from St Helena; and, in the parlance of the day, a 'Cape coloured', Mr Mannering. The Gujarati typesetters were Kababhai and Virji Damodar, with Virji doing Hindi as well. Moothoo, a colonial-born Indian, undertook the Tamil composing, while Raju Govindswamy ('Mr Sam', as he was known) was in charge of machines and binding (Pyarelal, 1986:434). Also colonial-born, Govindswamy had started his career as a 'kitchenboy' in Umkomaas, then moved on to being a messenger on the railways, before becoming an assistant in a printer's firm at 30 shillings per month, where he was recruited by Madanjit (Meer, 1969:56–57). By Natal standards, wages were generous and ranged from £8 to £18 per month in an industry whose average wage was £12 (Downes, 1952:80).

The move to Phoenix

Like many small printing establishments in Durban, the IPP struggled to break even. The launch of *Indian Opinion* exacerbated this financial strain. Madanjit Viyavaharik was nominally the proprietor of the paper, but the enterprise was kept afloat by Gandhi's money and the editorial skills of M. H. Nazar, the newspaper's first editor. Worried about the press, Gandhi sent Alfred West, whom he had met through vegetarian circles in Johannesburg, to investigate. West reported deep financial chaos. Madanjit, who had been wanting to return to India for some time, ceded the press to Gandhi to settle the debts he had accrued and duly left. In early October 1904 Gandhi caught the overnight train down to Durban to sort out the affairs of the press, and on the journey famously read Ruskin's *Unto this Last*, which inspired him to take the radical departure of setting up his first ashram, Phoenix, 14 miles north of Durban. The press was laboriously moved by oxwagon to Phoenix and reassembled in a corrugated-iron shed built from donated material. Those who joined Phoenix were to earn £3 a month and be entitled to an acre of land. If the press made a profit (which it never did), it would be shared among the settlers, as they called themselves. Two press employees, one of whom was Sam Govindswamy, retained their original salaries (Pyarelal, 1986:435–37).

Directing operations mainly from Johannesburg, Gandhi soon instituted major changes in the press, seeking to fashion it into a utopian instrument that would stand beyond the market and the state. He first stopped all jobbing printing, seeing this as a distraction from the real work of producing the newspaper, and then in 1912 decided to dispense with advertisements, except those promoting socially useful objects (Bhattacharya, 1965:118).

The changing letterheads of the press reflect these shifts. An early letterhead from March 1904, when the IPP still operated from Durban, presents the press as a commercial operation ('artistic and general printers') undertaking jobbing printing of various kinds (wedding cards, visiting cards, ball programmes, etc.) in a range of languages (NAD, CSO 1758, 1904/2954). By 1907 the letterhead had lost some of its commercial flair (NAD, CSO 1848, 8564/1907). Thereafter, the press's sole function was to print *Indian Opinion* (NAD, II 1/180 I 1058/1911). Another barometer of these shifts comes from the memoir of Prabhudas Gandhi (1957:46) who spent part of his childhood at Phoenix. He describes these years of mounting asceticism as a period when there was 'no more fun and frolic'.

As several historians have demonstrated, the newspaper *Indian Opinion* became central to the success of Gandhi's campaigns. The paper kept people informed, spurred them on and provided the world with information as to what was going on (Mesthrie, 1987:99–126). Equally pivotal was the press itself, which became central to Phoenix and operated as an embodiment of its utopian ideals. At its height, and before *satyagraha* imprisonments took their toll, Phoenix was home to about 40 people and everyone – adults and children alike – was involved in at least some aspect of the printing process. Typesetting was mandatory for all, some proving more adept than others, with Gandhi describing himself as a dunce (Gandhi, M., 1957:304). All men assisted with operating the press, which sometimes ran on oil engines and at other times was operated by hand. Everyone folded the newspapers, put them in wrappers and pasted on addresses (Gandhi, P., 1957:45; Dhupelia-Mesthrie, 2004:74).

The press was also a leveller, with everyone undertaking physical labour whatever their caste or religious background: in the words of Prabhudas Gandhi (1957:55), 'Germans, English, Africans, Chinese, Parsis, Muslims, Jews and Hindus' laboured together on the press.

Among the settlers at Phoenix were several of Gandhi's relatives, as well as his immediate family. The core functions of the press were family run. Chaganlal, a nephew, ran the accounts and the Gujerati section; Maganlal, another nephew, oversaw composing and did other skilled jobs. However, this was not a family business in the normal sense. As Prabhudas Gandhi (1957:18) noted in his memoir: 'In Gandhi's ashram the place of blood ties was taken by common ideology and a common devotion to duty' Or as Lloyd and Susanne Rudolph (2006) have indicated, Gandhi's ashrams were modern institutions in which entry and exit were by choice rather than lineage.

The press also became central to Gandhi's educational philosophy. Part of Phoenix's work involved running an informal boarding school for children from both the settlement and beyond. Prabhudas Gandhi attended this school and has left a description of his routine. After an early start, students attended school from 9 to 11 a.m., after which they spent half an hour digging in the fields. When students complained and asked whether this digging couldn't happen early in the morning, Gandhi replied: 'You must get into the habit of working in the fields in the heat of the sun. Today you are studying here, but if the struggle starts and you have to go to jail, who will then let you rest in the shade?' At 11.30 a.m. the students bathed, had lunch and worked on their own while the adults were busy in the press. At 3 p.m. the children went to the press and received vocational training or assisted with press work. At 5 p.m. the children returned to work in the fields till sunset (Gandhi, P., 1957:114–15).

Gandhi saw Phoenix as a training ground for *satyagrahis* and for prison. There was hence a rigorous labour regime, of which the press formed a part. Working a hand-operated iron press is noisy and involves long hours. It is physically demanding and those who did it on a full-time basis often developed back and kidney problems from the constant strain of pulling the bar of the press (Rummonds, 2004:598). Typesetters too developed aching fingers and felons (painful, pus-producing infections at the ends of their fingers) (Rummonds, 2004:265). Since most settlers at Phoenix never worked full-time at the press, they probably avoided these ailments. They were nonetheless subject to the labour disciplines of the printshop, which increasingly became part of the project of training for *satyagraha*.

The press, then, was a fulcrum of social relationships in Phoenix, which was at times known as the IPP settlement. When the manager of the press, Alfred West, married in July 1908, the wedding was reported in *Indian Opinion* as though the bride were marrying into the company (4 July 1908).

The idea that everyone worked equally on the press was probably something of an illusion. A core of people were devoted to the running of the press, two of whom earned commercial salaries. Also, it is clear from some accounts that the press, like all concerns in Natal, relied on cheap African labour. Millie Polak (1931:53–54) reports:

> The printing-press, at this time, had no mechanical means at its disposal, for the oil-engine had broken down, and at first animal power was utilized, two donkeys being used to turn the handle of the machine. But Mr. Gandhi, ever a believer in man doing his own work, soon altered this, and four hefty Zulu girls were procured for a few hours on printing day. These took the work in turns, two at a time, while the other two rested; but every male able-bodied settler, Mr. Gandhi included, took his turn at the handle, and thus the copies of the paper were 'ground out'.

In his autobiography, Gandhi notes his preference for a hand-operated press, which he regarded as more uplifting. He writes: 'There came a time when we deliberately gave up the use of the engine and worked with hand-power only. Those were, to my mind, the days of the highest moral uplift for Phoenix' (Gandhi, M., 1957:303–4).

There is, of course, an irony when this claim is set against Millie Polak's description indicating that the hardest physical labour was done by four Zulu women. On the face of it, Phoenix stood beyond the wage economy, since in theory settlers did not receive salaries, only a £3 grant. However, as we have seen, two members of the press did receive commercially linked salaries and so the press at least was not entirely extricated from the relations of the market. One does not know what the Zulu women were paid, if anything. Their absence from Gandhi's account points to the extent to which his press was a South African one that relied, if only in small part, on cheap African labour.

Gandhi was to leave South Africa in 1914. The press continued at Phoenix under the guidance of his son, Manilal, who edited *Indian Opinion* until his death in 1956. The presses were preserved in a museum at Phoenix, but have not survived intact. During internecine fighting in the early 1980s in Natal, Phoenix was looted and burned. The story of Manilal and the press has been masterfully told by Uma Dhupelia-Mesthrie (2004) and need not detain us here. Instead, let us ask what we might learn from the biography of the press between 1898 and 1914.

The IPP and Indian Ocean cosmopolitanism

The IPP had two clear chapters in its early life, one in Grey Street in Durban and the other out at Phoenix; one apparently as a commercial operation, the other as anti-commercial – two commonsense categories that we take for granted. Yet to use such stark oppositions is to miss the uniqueness of the early IPP, as well as the ways in which Gandhi built on that legacy.

One way to grasp this uniqueness is to compare and contrast the IPP with similar printing establishments of the time in Durban. By the turn of the century the city was home to 14 presses, all of them white-owned, except for the IPP. The IPP was located in Grey Street; the *Indian Opinion* office was in Mercury Lane. Grey Street fell into what had emerged informally as the Indian area, while Mercury Lane was located in the 'white' foreshore of the city, although there was some porousness between these areas. This flexibility was, however, rapidly disappearing as the Natal colonial state started to implement ever-more rigorous forms of municipal segregation (Swanson, 1983).

With regard to the print shops in the 'white' area, these would generally have been staffed by white men, except for very menial positions, which would have been occupied by Indians and/or Africans. The white printers were united by strong bonds of solidarity. Most printers had done apprenticeships in Britain, parts of the empire or Natal, and belonged to the well-organised and vocal South African Typographical Union (Downes, 1952). These workplace networks promoted a marked sense of racial protectionism and white labourism. These networks spread into other areas. One key institution of colonial Natal society was the volunteer military regiment, which supplemented the small imperial standing army and promoted a widespread ethic of militarised masculinity, as Rob Morrell (2001) has demonstrated. At times, men who worked together signed up for these regiments, as did a group of typographers, who joined the Frontier Light Horse in 1879 in the lead-up to the Anglo-Zulu war (Downes, 1952:16). In the 'Asiatic Invasion' crisis of 1896, this cross between the volunteer regiment and the workplace became apparent: lynch mobs were organised into divisions according to their professions, such as railwaymen, carpenters and joiners, store assistants, plasterers and bricklayers, saddlers, and tailors – and, of course, printers (*Natal Witness*, 15 January 1897).

The establishment at 113 Grey Street was somewhat different. Firstly, the staff members were diverse, being drawn, as we have seen, from Mauritius, St Helena, Gujarat, South India, Durban and parts of southern Africa. One employee was a member of the South African Typographical Union and had had to seek permission to work for an Indian (Downes, 1952:99). The other workers were not unionised.

Another distinctive feature of the press was its use of different languages. For commercial printing, this would have involved typesetting in a range of different languages and scripts. As *Indian Opinion* got going, the work of translation became central to the print-shop activities. The newspaper first appeared in four languages – English, Gujarati, Hindi and Tamil – although the latter two were subsequently dropped. Even working with two languages, the process of translation formed part of the labour processes of the press. Some pieces were written in Gujarati, but others were translations from English. In theory, what should have happened was that the Gujarati compositor would translate articles from English and then set them in Gujarati. However, the reality was that compositors were not always fluent in English. The long-suffering Nazar had to summarise the gist of the article for them in Gujarati so that they could then typeset it. Type in Indian languages was always in short supply and the compositor at one point enjoined Nazar to avoid words with the Gujarati letter 'a', since stocks of this character were particularly low (Bhana & Hunt, 1989:112).

The IPP shop floor drew together different traditions of printing that workers brought with them from different regions of the Indian Ocean. It is difficult to know exactly what these traditions were, but in the case of India we can hazard some speculations thanks to the rich research on 19th- and early 20th-century printing history (Shaw, 1977a; 1977b; Ghosh, 2006; Pinto, 2007; Stark, 2004; 2007). This work demonstrates the diverse forms of printing and publishing that arose from regionally specific configurations of factors such as existing scribal and manuscript traditions; the presence of state-, mission- and European-owned printing; and, in the second half of the 19th century, a significant rise of indigenous printer-publishers. This latter category varied enormously. At the top end, as Ulrike Stark (2004:254) demonstrates, the Nawal Kishore Press in Lucknow was a substantial operation with 350 hand presses, a 'considerable number' of steam presses and 900 employees. At the bottom end, as Anindita Ghosh (2006) demonstrates, the small presses of Batalla huddled together in narrow lanes in the north of Calcutta producing a steady stream of popular almanacs, pamphlets and images. While any generalisation is difficult, Stark (2007:2) notes that Indian printer-publishers assumed complex roles of 'entrepreneur, publicist, literary patron, philanthropist, disseminator of knowledge and educator'. This formulation usefully reminds us that the line between commercial and non-commercial is not inevitable or automatic, and some Indian firms straddled this divide, functioning as commercial concerns deeply committed to projects of social reform. The IPP was not dissimilar. While a commercial operation, it was equally pledged to social reform through both *Indian Opinion* and its links to the Natal Indian Congress.

The move to Phoenix did not represent a complete break with these traditions. Gandhi certainly sloughed off the more obviously commercial operations of the press, possibly because of his experience at the hands of the lynch mob arranged, as we have seen, into artisanal units, including one comprising printers. This printers' platoon made visible the links of capitalism and militarism, and might have provided an early intimation of this theme, which was to become so important in Gandhi's thinking.

While he toned down the commercial aspects, he played up the idea of the press as a mode of social reform, using the IPP as a theatre to display a new utopian and cosmopolitan world where everyone, at least on the face of it, dirtied their hands by operating the press, a task in India generally reserved for the lower castes. As different nationalities, religions and races worked side by side, the press enacted a modernist idea of the family business tied together not by lineage, but by common ideas. The press was central to Gandhi's *satyagraha* campaigns. Not only did it produce *Indian Opinion*, but its labour routines formed part of the programme of disciplining and preparing *satyagrahis*. The press was also important in Gandhi's educational experiments.

In the context of Durban, the IPP at Phoenix was not the only press of its kind. Outside Durban there were three Christian presses, which were likewise more ideological than market driven. These were the mission presses of the American Board of Commissioners for Foreign Missions at Adams College, the Trappist-run presses at Mariannhill and John Dube's press at Ohlange Institute. Gandhi had visited the two latter presses, which are often cited as possible models for Phoenix (Swan, 1985:59; Mesthrie, 1987:110). Like the press at Phoenix, these other ones were located outside the city and tended to be anti-urban and anti-industrial.

While all of these presses sought to operate beyond the constraints of the market, Gandhi's press aimed to move beyond the state as well. While he was in South Africa, Gandhi appeared to pay little attention to copyright, a position he refined in India through his reiterated rejections of copyright law as a form of private property that prevented the free circulation of ideas (Bhattacharya, 1965:113). At least in Natal, mission presses generally observed copyright legislation studiously. For Gandhi, then, texts were meant to circulate as widely and as freely as possible, moving beyond the market and the state, and bringing into being a new type of reader in that utopian and necessarily cosmopolitan space.

But what were the nature and boundary of this utopian space and what was its ideal reader? The first point to note is that Gandhi's ideal reader was someone who took his/her task seriously to the point of seeing himself/herself as a distant collaborator in the press and the newspaper. At the height of Gandhi's *satyagraha* campaign in India, the newspapers *Young India* and *Harijan* sold in tens of thousands and started to make a profit. Some advisors urged Gandhi to lower the price of the papers. He refused, feeling that the cover price represented a form of commitment from the reader, who had a responsibility and a role to play in the production of the newspaper. In Gandhi's words, readers should be 'as much interested in the upkeep of the papers as the managers and the editors are' (quoted in Bhattacharya, 1965:107).

In this spirit, he frequently enjoined readers to be conscientious and dedicated. They should read and reread articles, act on them, and recruit new readers. He urged readers of *Indian Opinion* to keep a scrapbook into which they could paste important articles that could then be reread. When the Gujarati section of *Indian Opinion* ran a biography series, the newspaper wrote:

> We hope that readers of this journal will read [these] lives and follow them in practice ... We have suggested earlier that each one of our subscribers should maintain a file on *Indian Opinion*. We remind [readers again] on this occasion (quoted in Bhattacharya, 1965:20).

At other times he urged readers to copy out sections of newspapers and pass them on to friends or to read the paper to non-literate colleagues (Bhattacharya, 1965:140–41).

In his textual practice, Gandhi aimed to establish, in his own words, 'an intimate and clean bond between the editor and the readers' (quoted in Bhattacharya, 1965:75). Towards this end, he refined his famed spare prose style by, as he phrased it, writing with 'not one word more than necessary' (quoted in Bhattacharya, 1965:79). This mode of composition constituted a form of spiritual discipline, as Gandhi explained:

> The reader can have no idea of the restraint I have to exercise from week to week in the choice of topics on my vocabulary. It is a training for me. It enables me to peep into myself and make discoveries of my weakness. Often my vanity dictates a smart expression or my anger a harsh adjective. It is a terrible ordeal but a fine exercise to remove these weeds (quoted in Bhattacharya, 1965:80).

This almost puritanical plain style became the rhetorical means through which he could invent the idea of speaking directly to the reader. His concern for the reader also stretched to the physical appearance of texts. Gandhi liked neat handwriting and clean printing: 'good printing can create a valuable spiritual state in the reader' (quoted in Bhattacharya, 1965:103).

The importance of the reader was reiterated in *Hind Swaraj*, the book in which Gandhi enunciated his core political philosophy. The preface to the English translation appeared in *Indian Opinion* on 2 April 1910. This document explained that the book takes the form of a dialogue between an editor and readers that, in Gandhi's words in the preface, 'took place between several friends, mostly readers of *Indian Opinion* and myself'.

Since *Hind Swaraj* sets out Gandhi's key ideas, the reader of *Indian Opinion* is an extremely significant figure. Much of the book enunciates a proto-nationalist vision of 'India' that is brought into being by readers in South Africa. Such a reader must be able to move effortlessly between South Africa and India and must understand that 'India' is an idea that emerges in part in South Africa. Such a reader must be able to operate within the Indian

Ocean and understand the relationships emerging across it. Indeed, one way of reading *Indian Opinion* is as a site for experimenting with genres that bring such an Indian Ocean reader into being. Let us look at three quick examples of genres of circulation that take on this work: the cutting, the Indian Ocean travelogue and the booklet.

Like many newspapers of the time that could not afford foreign correspondents, *Indian Opinion* included excerpts from other newspapers. Often, these were from papers across the Indian Ocean in places like Beira, Zanzibar, Mombasa, Nairobi, Bombay, Madras and Rangoon. These papers in turn excerpted material from *Indian Opinion* and one another. Together, this form of textual practice constituted a quoting circle that enacted an Indian Ocean textual circuit.

Another use of the cutting in *Indian Opinion* pertained to reporting developments in South Africa via India. A report in the edition of 26 September 1910 reads: 'Mr G. A. Natesan writes in the Indian Review: A cable from South Africa brings the news that the British Indians in the Transvaal are taking a vow of passive resistance as a protest against the recent Asiatic Amendment Bill.' In part, this cutting validates local struggles by demonstrating international interest in the event. Yet such cuttings illustrate a mode of simultaneous reading as if the event were taking place in India and South Africa at the same time and as if the reader could inhabit both spaces.

Other instances of such South Africa–India reading strategies were common. Under the heading 'The National Congress and Indians in South Africa', the 12 December 1903 edition noted that an important meeting was to he held at 'Tata Mansions, Waudby Road'. The meeting was in fact to take place in Bombay, but it is taken for granted that every reader knew where Waudby Road was. Similarly, in terms of time, readers are expected to have the ability to imagine interlocking time schemes across the Indian Ocean. One report on 19 November 1903 reads: 'By the time this issue of "Indian Opinion" reaches India, preparations for the meeting of the national assembly will have very far advanced.'

Another way of creating circuits of significance was through Indian Ocean travel writing. The most visible version of this genre was the travelogue of moving between Bombay and Durban, and stopping at each of the intermediate ports. The form was generally reserved for political celebrities whose progress from port to port was reported in extensive details. In the case of G. K. Gokhale, the Indian National Congress notable who visited South Africa in 1912, the newspaper hyped up his visit by reporting his elaborate farewell in Bombay and then his reception in Mombasa, Zanzibar and Beira, as well as his progress through South Africa.[8] It is as if the person were invented through travel, becoming more 'real' and visible with each successive newspaper report.

In addition to producing a newspaper, the IPP produced a series of small booklets, many of them reruns of material in the paper. In all, about ten such titles were produced (Hofmeyr, 2008).

Some of these explored Indian Ocean themes. One pertinent example is a retelling of the Hindu epic Ramayana by J. L. P. Erasmus, a Boer commandant who had been captured by the British during the Anglo-Boer War. Along with 9,000 others, he was sent as a prisoner of war to India. He was held in various locations in northern India and was finally released in Amritsar. Before returning to South Africa, Erasmus befriended a lawyer and through him learned a lot about Indian religion and history. On his return home, he must have linked up with Gandhi or Henry Polak (probably through the legal world, since Erasmus was also a lawyer).[9] Erasmus's lectures on the Ramayana given to the Transvaal Philosophical Society were printed in the newspaper and then brought out in book form. The book remained an *Indian Opinion* stalwart and was still being advertised in the 1930s. The genesis of the book requires one to think about unusual cosmopolitan links and axes in the Indian Ocean.

Indian Opinion ran advertisements for its own books and for some that it imported from India and Britain. It advocated the idea that to buy a book was to enter a political and philanthropic contract, very often with an Indian Ocean component. In 1914 C. F. A. Andrews, a Christian priest and Gandhi's right-hand man, published his lectures on Tagore. *Indian Opinion* urged readers to buy the book and reminded them that proceeds would go to Santiniketan, the school of Rabindranath Tagore, the Indian poet (1 April 1914). The first biography of Gandhi by Joseph Doke appeared in 1909. Readers were encouraged to buy the book, since any profits would be devoted to the cause of passive resistance (22 May 1909). Buying a book hence constituted an act of ethical solidarity often across the Indian Ocean.

Gandhi's view of books was an unusual one. For him, books were not commodities, they should not be copyrighted, they were certainly transnational, and stood somewhere between a newspaper and a book. In other words, they defied what we today regard as key characteristics of a book – it is copyrighted; it is produced in a national space; it is distinct from a newspaper, magazine or pamphlet; and it is a commodity bought by the reader.

Today these booklets are very difficult to track down, having made their way into surprisingly few libraries. They conform closely to Meredith McGill's analysis of such under-the-radar texts. McGill (2003) examines the pre-Civil War era in the United States (the 1830s and 1840s) and directs her attention to this unindexed world of uncopyrighted newspapers and periodicals; book-magazines (books masquerading as magazines to elude postal charges); and what were then legitimate reprints at a time when international copyright law was not in place and many saw reprinting as a triumph of American democracy over British publishing monopolies:

> Texts that circulate without authors' names attached frequently remain unindexed and untraceable, as do authored texts that are published without their authors' knowledge or consent. Unauthorized reprinting escapes the enumerative strategies of bibliographers and collectors who remain tied to authorial intention and the principle of scarcity as grounds of value. The mass-cultural circulation of high-cultural texts confounds our critical taxonomies even as the transnational status of reprinted texts makes it difficult for us to assimilate them into national literary narratives (McGill, 2003:2–3).

Gandhi's printing policies certainly conformed to these principles, but extended them even further by seeking to move beyond the marketplace entirely. Gandhi pursued an avowedly utopian cosmopolitan idea of printing, publishing and reading that took shape in the Indian Ocean. For him, the production and consumption of books should not be separated, but should form part of a continuous ethical community in which printers, authors and readers become comrades.

These ideas have not survived the forces of the capitalist market that Gandhi so abhorred. Like the legend of his printing press on the SS Khedive, his textual experiments have disappeared into the archive of lost Indian Ocean utopias. They are nonetheless worth salvaging, not least for the new light they can throw on print culture and cosmopolitanism.

The IPP was avowedly cosmopolitan in its personnel, methods of working, textual products and their envisaged audiences. It supported a form of textual circulation and modes of reading that straddled the Indian Ocean and helped bring into being the universalisms and cosmopolitanisms uniting different groups across the sea. Commenting on the wide range of people who visited Phoenix, Prabhudas Gandhi (1957:58) notes: 'our jungle school had the atmosphere of an international university.' His observation reminds us of the remarkable cosmopolitanism of Phoenix, which the press had helped to create. The comment also underlines that like all cosmopolitan projects, this one had boundaries. Prabhudas imagines himself on the Gujarati frontier marked by what he saw as 'the jungle' and its African inhabitants. Like the Zulu women erased from Gandhi's account of the press, however, Africans were never to be numbered among the fraternity of Gandhi's cosmopolitanism.

2

Chapter

Steamship Empire:
Asian, African and British Sailors in the
Merchant Marine c. 1880–1945

Jonathan Hyslop

In late 1942 a young Bengali man called Syed Ali from Kalijuri in the Sylhet district decided to go to sea. In Calcutta, he found work in the engine room on the British merchant marine steamship *SS McLeith*, which was sailing for Cape Town (Choudhury, 1995:94). It was a dangerous time to sail the southern Indian Ocean. The Japanese navy had launched a significant submarine offensive against Allied shipping in the seas north-east of the Natal coast and German submarines were also occasionally striking off South Africa. The bodies of dead sailors were washing up on the Durban beachfront (Keane, 1995). But with war raging in nearby Burma, staying at home could not have been a very attractive option either. From the beginning of the voyage Syed Ali was bullied by the *serang* (boatswain or supervisor) of the stokehold, a man called Attik, from Ishkapur. In Cape Town, the ship docked for a short stay and the crew were given shore leave. To escape his persecutor, Syed Ali deliberately overstayed his leave and the ship sailed without him. The port police directed the young man to a seamen's boarding house and he was told by an official that he should remain there. There were several other Sylhetis in the boarding house, and one of them, a serang from Dinapur, turned out to be a friend of Syed Ali's uncle. This serang promised to find a berth for the lad when he next got a ship, and soon they sailed off together on the *SS McNeill* for Colombo in Ceylon (now Sri Lanka).

Syed Ali remained on this ship for a long period, plying the route back and forth between Colombo and Cape Town. Eventually paid off at Colombo, the now experienced seaman returned to Calcutta and spent a month visiting his family. He needed to get work again and back in Calcutta was offered a job on the *SS Murdoch*. But his papers had a 'black mark' because of his desertion of his ship on his first voyage, and this was an obstacle to getting employed. He went to see two local men who had connections with the seamen's union led by the powerful organiser Aftab Ali. These two worthies used their influence to solve the problem. The ship then went to Bombay and on to Cape Town. There, the news came that the war was over. The crew received a bonus and went out celebrating. But Syed

Ali was saving his money. The ship was now going to sail for Britain and he intended to stay there. In Manchester, Syed Ali, who spoke no English, equipped with only a few pounds in his pocket and some warm clothes given by a friend, disembarked and headed for London. This was the beginning of a new life for him, for he was to settle in Britain (Choudhury, 1995:94–95).

Although there has been a vast development of the literature on the Indian Ocean in recent decades, I think it would be fair to say that its most distinguished contributors (Chaudhuri, 1985; McPherson, 1993; Pearson, 1998; Subrahmanyam, 2005) have written primarily on the age of sail, whereas the epoch of steam has been less well served. The aim of this chapter is thus to identify some of the key issues concerning Indian Ocean seafarers of the age of steam navigation. In doing so, Syed Ali's story is a useful point of departure. His journeys stood at the end of a period of about 70 years in which the sea trade of the world had been dominated by the coal-burning steamships of the British merchant marine. Sailors of African and Asian origin had been present on British ships since the 18th century and had formed a very significant proportion of the merchant and fighting naval forces in the Napoleonic Wars. But their numbers fell very sharply thereafter until the mid-19th century. The introduction of the steamship saw a new reversal of the trend, with African and Asian sailors again becoming a central component of British marine power. This development was met with considerable resistance from British seamen, largely framed in racial terms, for they saw the new workers as a cheap labour force that would undermine their position. It also generated decades of intra-bureaucratic struggle within and between the various ministries of the British state and the viceroy's government of India over the management of this workforce.

In the work of those who have paid central attention to the Indian Ocean steamship sailor, there is a strange imbalance. This work seems to have been focussed disproportionately on the history of seafarers in British ports and on the regulation of the lives of these sailors by the British authorities (Dixon, 1980; Visram, 1986; Tabili, 1994; Frost, 1995). Of course, there is a good and valid political reason for this – the concern of historians to examine the history of immigration and official racism in Britain, which became such a central issue in the country's late 20th-century politics. But Syed Ali's life reminds us that this was not the whole story. Syed Ali's maritime experience was chiefly of the ports of the Indian Ocean – Cape Town, Colombo and Calcutta, in his case – and of the shipboard microworld. The life of the maritime cities of the Indian Ocean littoral and their lateral connections across that ocean are surely at least as important to explore as the metropolis–periphery relationship and the social world of Cardiff or South Shields, but they have had less attention. Moreover, Syed Ali's story is not one simply of subordination to the power of the British imperial authorities, but of circumventing them – he jumped ship in Cape Town, used family connections to find a new job, got his union contacts to fix his papers and settled in Britain without asking anyone's permission. Rather than effectively containing and policing the sailors, the colonial state leaked like an old rowing boat. For all the attempts to regulate people like Syed Ali, the port was at the limits of the power to control, rather than exemplifying irresistible governmentality. Thus, I want to propose that attention needs to shift to the world of sailors in Indian Ocean ports and on board ships, and to their active role in shaping their futures. In this, I follow the important leads given by the work of Broeze (1997) and his collaborators on coastal cities, Ewald (2000) on the crucial role of African maritime workers in the Indian Ocean, and Balachandran (2003) on the need to move away from a victimological reading of the sailor's experience.

Syed Ali also poses a challenge for South African historiography. As in other parts of the world, the many books by South African ship enthusiasts and company historians tell us almost nothing about sailors. But serious South African social historians have done no better. With minor exceptions, almost no work examines the lives of seafarers. Shamil Jeppie's (2007:8–14) recent call for the study of aspects of civil society in South Africa beyond the range of conventional political narratives is thus both extremely timely and relevant to our present concerns. The maritime world of South African ports and their global shipboard and port extensions should be a significant area for research. The one part of this social world that has been examined to some extent is that of dock workers, especially in relation to the development of black trade unionism since the 1920s (Hemson, 1977; Bradford, 1987; Beinart & Bundy, 1987). Usually, however, the specifically maritime character of this world is seldom addressed. It may be worth asking new questions about the cultural impact of the maritime life within inland South Africa. For example, Isaiah Shembe, the founder of the extraordinarily successful syncretic religious movement based in Natal, was a former dock worker.[10] Could his experience of the Indian Ocean world not have been a factor in the evolution of his thought? Similarly, in his great autobiography, *Tell Freedom*, Peter Abrahams (1970) writes of growing up in a Johannesburg slum before the Second World War with an 'Ethiopian' father who had had adventures in many lands; but as far as I am aware, none of the literary scholars who have written about Abrahams has investigated who this father was. Almost certainly, on the slight evidence that Abrahams gives us, he would have been a sailor from the Horn of Africa, which raises interesting questions about the connections of the ports to the South African interior.

What sort of analytical framework might help us come to terms with analysing this vanished world? A useful point of departure is provided by Tony Ballantyne's recent work on the Sikh diaspora. Ballantyne (2006:81) focusses on

> two interwoven, overlapping but occasionally independent sets of webs. The first is composed of the imperial structures largely produced to meet the needs of British merchants, missionaries, and administrators .... The second set of webs was largely constructed by Punjabis themselves, who fashioned them to meet their needs within a world that was being remade by colonialism and migration.

For Ballantyne (2006:69), the British Empire functioned as

> a system of exchange and mobility where key institutions (such as the military and the police force), communications networks (steamship routes, telegraph cables, and the circulation of newspapers), and markets constituted crucial horizontal connections between colonies as well as linking individuals to the metropole.

In his terms, this is a metaphor,

> a heuristic tool for conceptualising these networks and the various forms of cultural traffic they enabled within the empire ... [and whereas] most imperial historiography reduces the empire to a series of metropole-periphery binaries, the web reinforces the multiple positions that any given colony, city or community might occupy (Ballantyne, 2006:69).

What I want to do here is to adapt Ballantyne's model and to think of the world of Indian Ocean sailors as another of these global webs, intersecting with both the webs constituted by other diasporic populations and that constituted by imperial structures. Ballantyne's approach is helpful in a number of ways. It suggests how colonially created structures may nevertheless have provided the context for seamen's own manoeuvres in shaping their lives. Thus, it provides a basis for moving beyond a conception of the lives of the colonised as simply shaped by the impositions of colonial or capitalist power onto a subordinate society, restoring a sense of the agency of the seamen in shaping their world. Ballantyne's angle of vision also suggests the importance of looking closely at the interactions of varying segments of the colonial and colonised populations, and how these shaped particular outcomes. The world of British sailors can also be thought of as constituting another trans-imperial web, in constant interaction with the web established by the imperial communications system and that constituted by the Afro-Asian sailors. Ballantyne rightly emphasises the lateral connections between colonies, rather than simply fixating on colonial links to Britain. As he says, such 'horizontal' connections have been underplayed in the historiography, because they transgress the boundaries of metropolitan-focussed imperial history or studies framed within the boundaries of individual colonies. He might have added that anti-colonial nationalist historians have largely been equally reluctant to think outside the framework of metropolis–colony linkages and of national boundaries.

In sum, then, what I am proposing is that it is helpful to think of the British Empire as a set of overlapping webs, and for our purposes three of these are crucial: the webs of the shipping companies, of British diasporic labour and of Indian Ocean seafarers. The web metaphor enables us not only to capture how existing patterns constrained and directed certain flows of activity, but also to escape simple hydraulic models of domination and resistance. I will outline some of the features of these webs and attempt to show how African, Asian and British sailors shaped their world in interaction with one another and with the constraints and opportunities presented to them by imperial organisation.

The first layer of the web that I wish to explore is that created by the British Empire's shipping companies. The transition from sail to steam was not instantaneous. Although the first steamship to go from Britain to India around the Cape was as early as 1825, the original steam technology, with its paddle wheels and vast consumption of coal, was not a really viable basis for tackling the vast distances of the mid-Indian Ocean (Roff, 2000). It was only after ships using screw propellers and efficient engines had been fully developed that, around 1880, the sailing ship began to really give way to the steamship on a huge scale. Throughout the period from then to the Second World War, over half the tonnage of ships in the world consisted of British merchant marine vessels – the adoptively, but enthusiastically, British mariner Joseph Conrad (2004:159) recalled in later life that the 'red duster' flag of the United Kingdom's merchant fleet 'prevailed to such an extent that one always experienced a slight shock in seeing some other combination of colour blow out at peak or flagpole of any chance encounter in deep water'. This fleet was pivotal in holding together the global economy. Throughout the period, virtually all intercontinental transport of goods and passengers rested on it. Between 1850 and 1913 global per capita output rose by 90 per cent, but transnational trade grew sixteenfold (total carrying capacity grew by 279 per cent, but the greater speed of steamships meant that they could make far more voyages than a sailing ship in the same time) (Fischer & Panting, 1995).

It is also important to note that the relationship among shipping employees, capital and the British state was not one in which class and racial hierarchies were simply congruent. Small but significant pockets of Asian ship-owning capital existed under the empire. The young lawyer M. K. Gandhi was first brought to South Africa to represent the interests of the Natal-based steamship owners Dada Abdulla, part of a fairly substantial stratum of steamship owners from India that formed in this period. By 1939, 23 per cent of coastal shipping in India was locally owned (Desai, 1939:17). By the late 19th century the sultan of Zanzibar, the king of Burma, the Thai authorities and the Sultan of Oman had all bought steamships. The successful Straits Steamship Company was controlled by Singapore Chinese capital (MacKenzie, 2004:120). As such companies often employed British captains and engineers, this produced some complex reversals of imperial racial hierarchy. The Syrian-American traveller Ameen Rihani gave this rendition of the comments of the master of a ship on which he sailed, a Captain Hay, who was employed by a Parsi-owned company based in Aden:

> I was Captain of a Transatlantic liner before the war, and here I am now on one of Kawasji's tubs getting barely one-fifth of what I used to get from an English company, What's to be done? Kawasji's few rupees are better than idleness in Liverpool (Rihani, 1930:175).

The second web layer was that of the African, Asian and Caribbean mariners who played a major part in providing the labour that kept the steamships running. This was especially the case in the Indian Ocean, where South Asian, Arab, Somali, East African, Chinese and Malayan sailors were indispensable to the viability of the British merchant fleet. Syed Ali would, in his day, have been described by the British – and possibly by his colleagues and himself – as a 'lascar'. Technically, a lascar was specifically a seaman from India. But the inevitable mixture of sailors of varying nationalities in all ports meant that it was often used to describe all Asian and East African seamen (although generally not West Africans and Caribbeans).

In understanding where the crews of the steamship era came from, it is important to recognise the flows between the world of the steamship and the worlds that both preceded it and existed alongside it. Bose (2006) has shown how the economy of the modern British Empire was largely dependent for its penetration into the Afro-Asian world on the retail networks of Asian traders. In the same way, it may be suggested that initially there was a great deal of reliance by British ships on the existence of a pool of Afro-Asian seafarers. Although, for reasons to be explained, increasingly seamen were recruited from inland areas, men from communities with a tradition of seafaring participated in both sectors and moved between them in pursuit of their personal objectives. As late as 1939 over a hundred ocean-going dhows were operating out of Kuwait, and only the hostility of post-war African nationalist regimes to Indian and Arab commerce and the availability of cheap motorised technology seem to have brought this centuries-old trade to a final end (Villiers, 1969). Ewald (2000) highlights the persistence of dhow-borne African slavery in the north-west Indian Ocean into the 20th century, and the flow of ex-slaves into dock labour in the ports of that region and into steamship work. By the 1870s Africans were working on steamships out of Aden and in the same period members of an African community based in Bombay were working on steamships, many of them being freed slaves left in India by British patrol ships. 'Seedis', as the Africans were known, became especially predominant in the stokeholds of the P&O, the largest of the British Indian Ocean shipping companies, in the late 19th century. In his classic account of his voyage as a crewman on a dhow travelling from southern Arabia in 1938 and 1939, the Australian sailor and author Alan Villiers (1969:75–77) provides a suggestive anecdote. On board was a Seyyid (a descendant of the Prophet) from Mukalla in the Hadhramaut of southern Arabia, travelling as a passenger and following his commercial interests in East Africa. The Seyyid had not only spent eight years working in the stokeholds of British ships, but had also been an automobile worker in Detroit. Villiers discovered that although the Seyyid did not speak English, he had a good command of Polish, the prevailing language in the Detroit industrial suburb of Hamtramck, where he had lived. The story suggests both how the boundaries of dhow and steamship worlds were quite porous and how a sailor might be able to move along the networks of the web from a proletarian position across the sea to end his career in his home in a position of relative economic socio-strength.

Although southern African historians are well aware of the pre-colonial trade route connections with the east coast dhow trade in the region, it tends to be assumed that by the late 19th century this was no longer a factor. While the dhow trade never seems to have extended to the coast of present-day South Africa, it did reach the southern limit of Mozambique in the late 19th century. When the Durban mariner Alex Anderson (1925:18) sailed to the Mozambique coast in 1869, he found 'large Arab dhows' in port, which still made voyages directly across the Indian Ocean to India. Anderson (1925:20–21) also found dates, palm wine and Indian prints on sale, commodities likely to have been transported by dhows.

It is possible to identify a number of major 'nodes' where Indian Ocean seafarers were recruited to British steamships. Firstly, there were seafarers who primarily worked out of the three great subcontinental ports of Calcutta, Bombay and Karachi, although originating from a very wide range of localities on the Indian subcontinent (and beyond it). Secondly, Aden and, to a much lesser extent, Mogadishu were the centres for Arabian and Somali sailors and for sailors from the Swahili coast of East Africa. Finally, Malay and Chinese sailors came through Singapore. Indian sailors were supposed to sign distinct 'articles' (employment contracts) when they were recruited in India that differed from those under which sailors were taken on in Aden or Singapore, but regional demarcation was not so strict in practice. British officials were often too ignorant to assess the origins of sailors in foreign ports; for example, many Indian seamen signed on as 'Malay' in Singapore to take advantage of better pay or more flexible service conditions.

Accurate statistics on the size of this workforce are hard to pin down. An often-cited statistic is that in 1914 'lascars' constituted 17.5 per cent of all sailors on British-registered ships, something over 50,000 men (Dixon, 1980:265). In 1935 the number of Indian seamen was put at 59,000, the fourth-highest number for any country compared to Britain, which had just under 153,000 seamen (Desai, 1939). However, east of Suez the proportion was undoubtedly much higher than this, and one has to be sceptical about how accurate the figures are in such a complex realm. Dinkar Desai, a lawyer and writer involved with the trade unions in Bombay, pointed out in 1939 that, given the fluctuating nature of employment in the maritime industries, the actual number of people who were sporadically employed in maritime industries was much greater. He convincingly suggested that there were 140,000 seamen in Calcutta, 70,000 in Bombay and 25,000 in Karachi (Desai, 1939:18–20). (I have not found plausible figures for sailors in other parts of Asia or in Africa.)

Labour on steamships was divided into three 'departments': the engine room, the deck and the saloon. The engine room housed the great furnaces that produced the energy to power the ship. The main types of labourers here were the 'trimmers' who brought the coal forward from the bunkers in which it was kept, and the firemen who shovelled the fuel into the furnaces and ensured that they burned at the right temperatures. The engine room was an industrial hell. Trimmers and firemen were in constant danger of being burned by the furnaces; crushed by sliding coal; choked by dust, smoke and fumes; or overcome by heat exhaustion. Deckhands were chiefly occupied with the maintenance problems posed by a metal ship at sea – they were constantly scraping, cleaning and painting. They also had to perform much of the work of loading and unloading cargo. The saloon crew, very small on a merchantman, but huge on a liner, worked as waiters, cooks, cabin cleaning staff and the like. As in other colonial enterprises, labour recruitment was highly ethnicised, with a 'common sense' developing among employers as to which groups were 'good' at which jobs and local social networks being tapped for recruitment. Thus, in ships sailing out of India, typically the saloon staff were from Goa and Calcutta and from among Christians of the Madras presidency, and the firemen and trimmers were Punjabis, Sylhetis or people of other East Bengal districts, as well as some Pathans, Kashmiris and members of the 'Seedi' communities. Deckhands comprised a large proportion of Muslims from the Malabar coast, and Hindus from the Surat and adjoining districts (Hood, 1903; Desai, 1939; Colaco, 1955). It seems that people from inland communities in India often kept a foothold in agriculture in their home villages and worked as migrant labourers in a pattern not very different from that in southern Africa.

How did the 'lascars' understand their own political identitities? There is a strong tendency for labour historians to look for signs of insurgency, but this is not equally useful at all historical junctures. Certainly, by the end of the 1930s sailors were caught up in the anti-colonial sentiment sweeping the world. But this should not be projected back in time. The initial appeal of African and Asian workers for shipowners was that they were not highly mobilised. Moreover, there are indications that at least some sailors had a certain faith in imperial justice, which made their anger when it failed all the more bitter. Consider the following case. In February 1927 two seamen from

Bombay, Abdul Gani and Patrick Fitzgerald, the former of Punjabi origins and the latter the son of an Indian mother and a Liverpudlian father, wrote impassioned letters from Antwerp complaining that they had been illegally excluded from entering Britain at London as crew on the SS Australind. Their letters suggest a profound sense of moral outrage at the challenge to their identity as British. Gani pointed out that he served out of British ports in the Great War and had all his discharges.[11] Fitzgerald was mortified:

> I cannot see why they would not let me land as I am a British Subject born in Calcutta on 20 September 1902 and my father is an European and had served in the British navy during the war who also is in Liverpool ... and who is a member of the Buffalo Lodge .... Sir, I think it will be hard for me to stay here and find a job as we are dark people, and I am a respectable man and never been destitute ... where(as) in England I could get a ship and find employment soon.[12]

The two men were allowed to come temporarily to Britain, but their appeal speaks of a more than instrumental relationship to British identity. Lascars were very active agents in the world, but not at all times actively anti-colonial agents.

Finally, there was the social web of the British seafarers' labour diaspora, in which I would include the maritime workers of Australasia. In the 19th century British sailors lived truly appalling lives. Between 1830 and 1900 one out of every five British mariners died at sea – perhaps a quarter of them from drowning and the rest from the effects of disease, exposure or malnutrition. Ships were often loaded to unsafe levels. The possibility of being fully compensated by insurance for their losses tended to make owners indifferent to the dangers involved. Yet under the 1870 Merchant Shipping Act, sailors could be imprisoned if they refused to go to sea because they thought their vessel was unseaworthy. Most sailors did not live to the age of 45 (Jones, 2006:12–23). In port, the situation in which sailors were paid in advance laid them open to swindling by 'crimps' – unscrupulous boarding-house keepers (Jones, 2006:121).

Before the 1880s British marine officers exercised very effective control over their labour force. W. Caius Crutchley, who went to sea as an apprentice in 1863, experienced 'the power of the master mariner' as an 'absolute despotism' that was, however, fully accepted by the crew: 'There was seldom any attempt made to obtain redress for ill treatment at sea' (Crutchley, 1912:16). Crutchley's book, like many other accounts of British shipping of the mid-to-late 19th century, is full of references to captains and mates who used their fists on sailors, beat ships' boys with ropes' ends and locked up disciplinary offenders in irons, on bread-and-water diets. In the 1870s Crutchley (1912:158), now a first mate, made use of these methods himself, recalling that in Cape Town 'on sailing day it was no uncommon thing to be obliged to go uptown in a hansom cab, find your men half drunk, and then sit on them in the cab until you could get them safely on board and in irons until they were sober'. The social relations of this world were, however, seldom challenged by British sailors.

I now want to examine how these interacting webs generated a certain kind of racialised politics in the maritime world, which lasted throughout our period. I would argue that British labour had a strong initiating role in this phenomenon. I do not think that to make such an argument implies a naturalisation of racism. British sailors were indeed confronted by an economic threat, for there is no doubt that many employers did want to replace them with the cheap labour of people of colour. But the combination of an awareness of this with strong unions that were almost exclusively white and the prevalence of a virulent racial discourse in this period did produce politics that was undeniably racist in response. Labour historians who want to deny the racism central to British trade unionism in at least the era before the First World War come uncomfortably close to the argument of the Australian publicist Keith Windschuttle (2004), who claims to his own satisfaction that the White Australia policy was not racist, because the trade unionists who supported it were motivated by economic considerations.

In the 1880s there was evidence of a new unwillingness by British seamen to accept their conditions. This needs to be placed in the context of broader changes in British politics and society. The admission of the upper stratum of the male working class to the franchise in 1867 and its further broadening in 1884, the elaboration by Gladstone of a combative radical liberal ideology, the firming of the position of craft unionism and the rise of agrarian radicalism in Scotland and Ireland all militated towards a situation where questioning the legitimacy of established forms of authority became more possible for subordinate social groups. The 1880s saw J. Havelock Wilson found the organisation later known as the National Seamen's and Firemen's Union (NSFU), the first effective national trade union in its sector. Although Wilson's extreme patriotism and his penchant in his later life for cozy arrangements with management have made him something of a butt of mockery for labour historians, he was in his day an extremely effective leader. In 1888–89 the famous shift to the New Unionism occurred in Britain, when previously unorganised categories of supposedly unskilled workers – the dock workers and sailors to the fore among them – engaged in landmark strike actions. The next year saw the success of Samuel Plimsoll's long-running parliamentary campaign for the regulation of the loading of ships, and in 1891 Wilson got into parliament, where he was able to promote his union's policies. Over the next two decades the political context became more and more characterised by forms of working class self-assertion, with the consolidation of the trade union movement, the Labour Party's breakthrough to significant parliamentary representation in 1906 and the massive syndicalist-led strikes of 1911–12, in which sailors and dock workers played major parts (Wilson, 1925).

Ship's officers and owners had a palpable sense that their power over British sailors had been undermined. In the early 1890s, during his last years at sea, Captain Crutchley (1912:320) felt that the 'after-effects of the strikes' had generated a 'dangerous spirit of insubordination'. Thomas Wilson Sewell, the respected chief engineer of the *SS Majestic*, noted during the same period the 'falling off in good men' in the crews that could be found for steamships (*New York Times*, 14 April 1890 cited in Fox, 2004:323). By the beginning of the 20th century captains were commonly portraying British sailors as completely unmanageable. In 1903 an experienced officer, Captain W. H. Hood, published a book entitled *The Blight of Insubordination*, deploring the current behaviour of British seamen. In his rambling, but quite well-documented text, Hood (1903:39), raging against the seamen, wrote that 'in a merchant ship commonly enough voyages start with a crew who are at once both insubordinate and mutinous'. For Hood the rot had been encouraged by the weakening of the skipper's authority through recent reforms of marine law, soft-hearted magistrates and undisciplined trade unionism. Many other officers felt similarly. In August 1904 Robert S. Riley wrote in the *Marine Engineer* that on leaving port, the ship's engineer was not surprised to find his men 'half drunk and altogether unruly' (cited in Fox, 2004:324). The *Nautical Magazine* noted in May 1909 that although few engineers would acknowledge this, they were afraid of violence from their men (Fox, 2004:124). Labour relations were further complicated by political tensions between predominantly Scottish Protestant engineer officers and stokers who were often Irish Catholics (Fox, 2004:324).

The crisis in authority relations within the British maritime world produced a new interest among captains and shipowners in the possibility of employing the labour of African and Asian sailors, who were seen as a cheap and tractable substitute for demanding and uncooperative British sailors. Ultimately, it was the difference in access to political participation between British sailors and colonised subjects that made this possible. The unenfranchised lascars did not have the access to political resources that the newly empowered British and Australian seamen were acquiring. This provided the basis for massive wage differentials. As late as 1939, for example, a British fireman received £10, 2 shillings and 6 pence a month, whereas a fireman from Bombay received £2, 2 shillings and 6 pence, and a fireman from Calcutta £1, 14 shillings and 6 pence (Desai, 1939:93). In addition, employers could simply crowd more workers into the same space: the relevant British legislation until nearly the end of our period provided for 120 cubic feet of accommodation for each British sailor, as opposed to 72 cubic feet for each lascar (Desai, 1939:97). Employers could also more easily get away with skimping on the feeding of lascars, with the result that these sailors experienced serious malnutrition problems.

The introduction of a new workforce coincided with and was made easier by the triumph of steam over sail on the oceans of the world, a development that was, in a sense, the industrialisation of the sea. The work of a seaman on a sailing ship can be thought of as artisanal: to climb the masts and set the sails required agility, expertise and the initiative to meet unexpected problems. For all its dangers and hardships, it was a way of life in which sailors could, and did, take pride. For instance, Herman Melville, in his autobiographical novel based on his first ocean voyage in 1839, wrote of the 'delight' he took in furling the sails in a 'hard blow', of the feeling of 'mastering the rebellious canvas' and of the 'estimation' in which a ship's company held the knowledge of a truly experienced sailor who was 'an artist in the rigging' (Melville, 1986:173–75, 182). On the other hand, the work of the steamship had a grimmer character; the craft of the sailor largely disappeared. What this meant was that the skills that sailing-ship men took years to learn were replaced with skills that could be acquired fairly quickly and had relatively little specific connection with seamanship (Fox, 2004). This undermined the esprit de corps that was the hallmark of sailing-ship life; it was noted that men on steamships, unlike their predecessors, did not sing at their work (Fox, 2004:318). It also made them easier to replace with new workers.

Ship's officers and other marine experts who were opposed to the introduction of Asian and African sailors elaborated a discourse as to why it was crucial to prevent the replacement of British sailors by Asians on British ships. Prominent among their claims were that Asian and African sailors were poorly skilled and that they could not cope in a crisis at sea. Such issues were thrashed out in a public political controversy in Britain in 1896 at the hearings of a parliamentary committee looking into the manning of British ships. In their evidence to the committee, a number of captains, as well as company nautical experts, gave evidence for the abilities of the 'lascars'. Captain Almond, inspector of the P&O line, for example, testified that his company employed lascars because they were as efficient as European crews and more so as firemen in hot latitudes, and that 'under no circumstances of wind or weather' had he known lascar crews to fail him (Hood, 1903:7). The committee went on to accept the worth of the lascar as a sailor.

A major theme in the controversies of the era was the sailor's relation to alcohol. *The Liverpool Courier* of 2 July 1902, for example, carried a letter describing a scene in a South African port where three ships lay alongside one another, with a British, Chinese and Indian crew, respectively. Two-thirds of the British crew ended up in jail, while the other two ships sailed on time. The plausibility of such tales is hard to deny. Of course, British sailors had drunk from time immemorial, but the combination of drink and political radicalism and the possibility of drawing labour from cultures in which drinking was prohibited or disapproved of were likely to sway employers' approaches to hiring. The next ten years saw a series of parliamentary enquiries and initiatives on maritime questions.

J. Havelock Wilson and his union consistently stood for policies of racial exclusion. This was sometimes explicit, as when Wilson's enforcer, Edward Tupper, led a race riot against the Chinese community in Cardiff in 1911, of which he later openly boasted in his autobiography (Tupper, 1938:13–48). More subtly, Wilson was able to deploy formal rhetorics of equality and good management for inegalitarian purposes. He campaigned for the space allocated to lascars and British seamen, and the money spent on their feeding by employers to be equalised – laudable measures on the surface. But Wilson's call was clearly based on the assumption that if employers' savings in hiring sailors from the colonies were reduced, they would give preference in hiring to British employees. Similarly, he advocated a language test for sailors, supposedly to ensure that, for safety reasons, they could understand their officers, but in fact with a view to finding another mechanism to exclude African and Asian sailors from the labour market.[13] In reality, officers and sailors generally communicated quite effectively in a range of creole languages, especially an Urdu-based tongue known as Lascari-Bat. Manuals in this language were widely available from the 1890s onward ('Malem Sahib', 1892; Valenti, 1896; Harrison, 1905) and were extensively utilised by officers in the P&O and other lines (Valenti, 1896:2).

The 1919 race riots in British ports seem to have been precipitated largely by socio-economic tensions between African and Asian workers who had entered the maritime labour market and settled during the war, and returning white servicemen. While the NSFU cannot be charged with instigating them (as it could in the case of the 1911 events), it certainly did not do much to restrain its members from instigating racial attacks either (Jenkinson, 1987). In 1921 the NSFU demanded the repatriation of Arab sailors from British ports. In the following year the NSFU won the introduction of the PC5 card system under which a sailor had to get union approval for employment, which adversely affected Asian and African sailors, because local NSFU branches varied in their willingness to grant membership. When in 1925 the Home Office issued the Special Restrictions (Coloured Alien Seamen) Order, an actually illegal fiat requiring African and Asian seamen to register with the police, the NSFU supported this measure (Hirson & Vivian, 1992:41).

Australasia tends to be somewhat absent from all the existing accounts of Indian Ocean labour. But the action of the labour movement there in closing the maritime labour market to Asian and African seamen had important long-term implications for the spatial politics of the Indian Ocean. Australia was a major destination for British shipping, representing perhaps a tenth of all British seaborne trade at the end of the 19th century. Although the opening of the Suez Canal in 1869 drastically shortened the trip between Britain and Asia, it did not reduce the distance of the journey between Britain and Australia to anything like the same proportion – and Suez had its negative side in the form of high fees and congestion. The result was that a very large proportion of British trade and passenger traffic to the Antipodes continued to use the Cape route, sustaining Cape Town and Durban as significant ports. In addition, because of the inadequacy of inland communications in Australia, coastal shipping came to constitute a massive and strategically crucial sector in the Australian economy (Blainey, 2001). In the mid-19th century a substantial number of Chinese sailors were employed in this sector. But in 1878 the recently formed Federated Seamen's Union of Australasia struck against the employment of these men by the Australasian Steam Navigation Company and won, thus starting to establish a principle of racial exclusion in the local shipping industry (Broeze, 1998:204–5). In 1888 local mass movements in Melbourne and Sydney based in the labour organisations prevented the landing of ships carrying Chinese immigrants or manned with Chinese crews (Rolls, 1992:454–508), a key moment in the development of the White Australia policy that became such a crucial institution of the new pan-Australian state in the first half of the 20th century. The unions not only succeeded in totally pushing Asian sailors out of the local maritime labour market, but also continued to agitate with partial success for the exclusion of Asians from intercontinental ships calling at Australian ports. And this was true even in the radical left of the labour movement. In his definitive history of Australian communism, Stuart McIntyre (1998) shows that the party, which became quite dominant in Australian sailors' and wharfmen's unions, while formally opposing the idea of White Australia, in practice viewed and treated Asian labour as a threat to the existing unions.

Despite the emergence of significant trade unionism among the seamen of the major Indian ports in the interwar years and a major infusion of social radicalism into British seamen's politics in the 1920s, there was little sense of any major change in the racial politics of the Indian Ocean workforce in the interwar period. In 1925 there was an international strike of British seamen against an attempt by shipowners to impose a wage cut. Havelock Wilson, still at the helm of the NSFU, opposed the action, which was driven by the communist-led National Minority Movement and a breakaway union led by the radical Labour Party politician Manny Shinwell. This dramatic strike gave rise to major demonstrations in the port cities of South Africa, New Zealand and Australia, and paralysed the imperial transport network (Hirson & Vivian, 1992). In Australia, the strike coincided with a vicious struggle between the local labour movement and Prime Minister S. M. Bruce, who was attempting to deport two seamen's union leaders and change the legislative framework for the maritime industries. But for all its radicalism, the strike did not move outside the framework of racial protectionism. In fact, because of the exclusion of Indian seamen from the British unions, those same unions immediately had to cast lascars in the role of strike-breakers. In Durban, the local labour activist H. H. Kemp, who had been elected leader of the local strike committee, told an approving rally that he favoured the expulsion of all 'Asiatics' from South Africa and that if, as was then rumoured, lascars were brought from Bombay, he would join the white citizens of Durban in throwing them into the sea (Hirson

& Vivian, 1992:49). The political tensions provoked by the story of lascar recruitment for the South African ports were considerable, with both the Natal Indian Congress and the *Times of India* warning that such a move would be inflammatory, and Prime Minister Hertzog issuing a statement implying that such lascars would be deported should they arrive (Hirson & Vivian, 1992:49–50). In Australia, the local unions framed their conflict with Bruce in terms of their suspicions that he was conspiring with British shipping interests to reintroduce Asian labour into the Australian industry. Bruce was indeed a recently appointed director of the P&O and strongly anti-labour, but in the end there was no change to Australian racial policy in respect of shipping. The seamen's strike eventually broke. When it did, ships started moving again with crews drawn from white scabs, exhausted strikers – and lascars. The experience simply reinforced the racialisation of the politics of British seaborne trade unionism.

Trade unionism among seafarers in India began to gather momentum at the end of the First World War. But after an initial flare-up of conflict in 1920, the Indian-based union movement was rather quiet and ineffective in the interwar years. It suffered from high levels of fragmentation – separate unions clustering around each port – and factionalism – separate groupings being run by socialists, communists and different Indian National Congress groupings. In addition, sailors were under the thumb of the gat-serangs – recruiters who operated patronage networks that milked sailors for bribes in return for jobs. This system was one of the major grievances of unions and it dampened organisational possibilities by drawing sailors into patronage relationships that were inimical to the logic of unionism. Ethnic factors also played a part in limiting the appeal of the unions, with, for example, Goans tending to dominate the leadership of the Seamen's Union of Bombay, one of the better-organised groupings. For much of the interwar period this did not eventuate in major mobilisation, but by the end of the 1930s a new militancy started to emerge. In 1938 the Seamen's Union of Bombay launched a quite substantial strike protesting current hiring practices; this led to significant confrontations with the authorities in Bombay (Colaco, 1955). Within a week of the outbreak of war in 1939 strike action for higher wages on a massive scale spread among Indian seamen across the British Empire. The strikes apparently started in South Africa and then moved to Britain and elsewhere. British officials suspected communist involvement and, indeed, given the communist line at that juncture of opposing the British war effort, this may well have been a factor. However, it seems that the major impetus was that the sailors resented risking their lives for a pittance and were emboldened by the shaky political condition of the Raj. The strategic threat posed by such a strike in wartime galvanised the British cabinet to come down heavily on the shipowners. Wages more than doubled over the next few years and reforms of working conditions were undertaken (Balachandran, 2003:121–23).

Syed Ali's maritime world no longer exists. The Second World War marked the end of his era, for the massive losses of merchant ships in the war and the building of huge numbers of new ships to meet the crisis saw steam finally give way to oil burners, with their smaller crews. While we are still invisibly reliant on the ocean transport of goods for much of what we consume, that transport system has been working in a very different way since the container ship revolution of the 1960s. And, of course, air became the major means of transport for passengers and high-value goods. Syed Ali was at sea in the last years of the British steamship empire.

For a South African historian, what must be striking about the politics of the steam empire is that it bears remarkable similarities to the history of the gold-mining industry in South Africa and thus perhaps casts a new light on the vexed question of the 'exceptionalism' of South Africa. In both cases, the introduction of a new technology in the late 19th century generated a demand for cheap unskilled labour. In both cases, employers turned to colonised subjects for this labour. In both cases, white enfranchised labour saw this situation as a threat to their established position and used their access to political power to resist it. However, this chapter also suggests a major difference. To a much greater extent than in the rigidly policed mining industry, the multivalent web of transoceanic connections made it possible for workers to slip around or through the grids employers and officials set up to contain them. 'Lascars' like Syed Ali were often able to move and find their own way along the webs that stretched across the oceans.

3

Chapter

The Interlocking Worlds of the Anglo-Boer War in South Africa and India[14]

Pradip Kumar Datta

Internationalising national histories

The Anglo-Boer War was an international event. This statement may seem unstartling given the way global events, such as the invasion of Iraq or the attacks on New York and Washington DC on 11 September 2001, keep occurring today. The distinction of this war is that it is one of the first events of this kind. Symbolically straddling the last two centuries (1899–1902), as if it were foreshadowing the contemporary moment of our modernity, the war was notable, among other things, for actively involving people from five continents and for provoking debates in separate political circles, many of them located in countries that had no direct stake in its outcome. It was also international in the simple sense of providing a serious spectacle that was closely covered by newspapers of different countries. The course of the war was sensational. The British – the world imperial power, for whom the Boers seemed no match – surprisingly faced a series of reversals at the outset, a trend that culminated in the 'Black Week' of December 1899, when British forces were defeated in three important battles. They recovered, but after having defeated the Boer conventional armies by June 1901 they found the guerrilla tactics of the Boer commandos too difficult to handle by conventional means. British frustration inspired their deployment of catastrophic technologies of violence that included scorched earth policies and the use of concentration camps for Boer children and women, as well as African families.

In small or large measure, the Anglo-Boer War changed lives and histories in different parts of the world. Debates occurred among European socialists on the nature and implications of capitalist colonial transformation of pre-capitalist systems. What effect did colonialism have on capitalism? Was it 'progressive'? (Kaarsholm, 1988). More immediate quarrels were enacted in countries that participated in the war. Troops were sent from New Zealand, Canada, Australia, India and, of course, Britain, while a small international contingent of volunteers from Europe joined the Boers out of solidarity with their cause.[15] This sharpened political lines in countries that sent the troops. In Canada and Britain, for instance, it produced a gigantic wave of patriotism. In Britain, the volunteer movement mobilised participation in the war among the middle and working classes (Miller, 2005). On the other hand, many socialists and liberals supported the other side. Bertrand Russell, who later became a leading pacifist, recalled that he had supported the Boers (1991:136–38), while Keir Hardie, the Scottish socialist and co-founder of the Labour Party, sympathised with the 'unpolluted', 'pastoral' Boer world (Kaarsholm, 1988:49). Dissident Christian sects such as the Quakers, together with some socialists, however, mounted brave pacifist campaigns. We know, for instance, the strangely evocative story of Martin Butler, an artisan, pedlar, worker and newspaper editor operating in rural New Brunswick in Canada. A man with Catholic and socialist sympathies, he became convinced of the evils of imperialism after Canada had dispatched its troops and launched a newspaper to pursue his pacifist campaign, at considerable personal cost (Stiles, 2004). In India, British brutality inspired the angry poetry of Rabindranath Tagore that presaged, with uncanny prescience, the apocalyptic conflicts that nationalism promised in the new century.[16]

Indeed, there is sufficient material to write a global history of the Anglo-Boer War. However, my intention is comparatively limited – and somewhat different. I wish to look at the histories of South Africa and India and the ways in which these were shaped by the war. This is not a history formed by encounters of travellers that can then be explained by the framework of civilisational encounters. As a regional unit within the international, South Africa/India acquires its coherence and interconnectedness from being a part of the same empire. This is compounded by an inter-imbrication of large populations that is the consequence of the migration of large numbers of people who inhabit an international polity where population is increasingly equated with political power and cultural threat. Indian migrants occupied ambiguous political and social positions in South Africa and occasioned new initiatives in the war. In India, meanwhile, smaller numbers of politically dominant temporary migrants, i.e. the British residents, provided more immediate intensity to the war effort. At the same time, the South Africa/India region was differentiated by the fact that while South Africa was a settler colony, India was directly colonised. An interweaving thread to stitch together my narrative is provided by the career of the barrister Mohandas Gandhi – later to become the Mahatma – who worked for and with people in both contexts. He vigorously linked the war to the general conditions of the South African Indian migrant indentured labourers and traders, and campaigned for them in an India that, for its own reasons, was concerned with the outcome of the war.

Instead of a global history, I wish to write an interlocking history of the South Africa/India region. What I call interlocking history is in many ways an extension of the conception of connected histories that Sanjay Subrahmanyam has formulated. Like Subrahmanyam, my interest in comparative history is subordinate to a concern with the history of interlinkages between different spatial entities. Subrahmanyam appears to define connected histories in two ways. The first is in terms of an explanation of circulation and spread, which he charts out through the dissemination of millenarian beliefs in the long duration of the 'Early Modern' period that spans the period from the 15th to the 17th centuries (Subrahmanyam, 1997a:748). The second focusses on a history of encounters between two cultures/civilisations to work out the 'dialectical' relationship between them. This involves a comparison of mentalities and an elaboration of the complexity of the transactions (Subrahmanyam, 2005:11–12).

Interlocking history builds on Subrahmanyam's insights to make two distinctions. The first concerns the nature of the event. Although the Anglo-Boer War has been seen in terms of the circulation model, i.e. in terms of 'effects' and 'feedbacks' from contexts other than South Africa (the premise of histories of the war that I have cited above), the contours of the event itself pose a somewhat different challenge, that of conceptualising it as happening in several locations. The key point here is of the simultaneity – or, rather, near simultaneity – of the event and its extensions. The possibility of an event affecting a place outside that of its origin almost immediately, is of course, conceivable only from the late 19th century, after the introduction of the telegraph in the 1870s, which allowed the rapid transmission of information to newspapers, backed up by the ever-increasing familiarity of other spaces owing to the rapid development of transport technology.[17] The near simultaneity of transmission does away with the fundamental distinction between the originative space of the event and the space of its impact. The Anglo-Boer War became an international event not only because it disseminated itself, but also because the rapidity of its dissemination allowed 'outsiders' to participate in its unfolding; those outside South Africa responded to the war by using it to make sense of their lives. Obviously, the event does not produce a uniform habitation, for it works on and with separate configurations that possess different political, social and cultural elements. Some of these features may be common, some commensurable and some may or may not make sense in the context of the other. But the event interlocks these configurations, making them address each other, and in doing so changes the internal configuration of each 'national' space.

The specific supra-regional canvas of interlocking history allows us to attend to a paradoxical double movement of our modernity. What we have in our modernity is the parallel formation of national and international orders of social life. The rise of the national accounts for the idea of defined and bounded contexts: national histories define their embeddedness in the nation by placing boundaries around the context in which events are then located. Often overlooked in the privileging of the nation is the obvious fact that it develops with a sense of inhabiting the world of the international. Indeed, without the latter, there cannot exist a sense of the nation and the particularity of belonging that it signifies and enacts. It is true, of course, that a sense of hierarchy is maintained between the two, by which the nation acquires its privilege. But it is equally relevant to note that the international possesses its own sense of importance that allows the national to map out its needs, ambitions and particularities. This is especially true of the imperial world, where the international is critical to understanding the overdeterminations that shape the world of the colonial masters and which, in turn, hold out important consequences for the way the national condition is thought.

The general contour of this double movement may be understood through newspapers. While dominantly 'national' in their coverage, newspapers sometimes privilege international events over it. During the Anglo-Boer War, the balance of political reportage often shifted in favour of the international. Both colonial and Indian newspapers in English gave exhaustive daily accounts of the war, especially during the early months of surprising Boer successes. Anxieties about the outcome of the war, the experience of soldiers and debates about it saw the war become as significant as domestic events within the hierarchy of news space. The space of the 'other' became as important as one's 'own' preoccupations; it began to inhabit the imagination as much as the national. This deep sense of connection was consolidated by other forms of writing (and speaking), such as the poems of Tagore.

The intensity of this preoccupation produced a shared public world between India and South Africa. I should add some riders immediately, however. This public world – as is probably true for all internationalised publics, except those that are institutionalised as such – did not possess a consistency that is true of national publics. International publics like this one tend to be produced conjuncturally, through specific issues. The fact that the South Africa/India public produced through the Anglo-Boer War functioned coherently for a relatively long period is in large part due to Gandhi's initiatives. Indeed, once he returned to India, South Africa tended to become less important a preoccupation in India (although it never became unimportant, especially after the introduction of apartheid). I should also add that the constituent elements of this public were not symmetrically integrated. South African Indians were far more continuously engaged with events in India, as Uma Dhupelia-Mesthrie's story (2004) of Manilal Gandhi's editorship of *Indian Opinion* reveals.

I am not interested here in thinking through the wider nature of this public. Rather, I wish simply to examine its conjunctural interlocking during the war. I aim to focus on the idea of the 'imperial subject' – specifying its nature, practices and consequences – as the general organising principle of this public. In both countries, the 'imperial subject' determined the position and, in varying degrees, the self-definition of the colonised. The 'imperial subject' was a critical part of the political identity of the migrant Indians, given their small numbers, relatively uninfluential status and the escalating racist campaign that they faced. Indeed, even as late as 1913 Gandhi invoked loyalty to the 'imperial subject', although, after all his disappointments with the imperial authorities, he now visualised the Crown as a purely ideal entity. In India during the internally placid turn-of-the-century period, on the other hand, the idea of the 'imperial subject' remained, but its hold became progressively more tenuous. Within this constellation of trajectories of the 'imperial subject', the war was obviously experienced very differently and produced divergent effects. For South African Indians whose conditions were rapidly deteriorating owing to a slew of discriminatory legislation, the war was more than a matter of direct involvement in its battles; it was seen to hold the key to their future position in relation to other communities. For Indians 'back home', the event came in a discursive shape and hence could not have such serious, practical repercussions. But it did offer a powerful public preoccupation, crystallising an ambivalence towards the colonial authority that deepened scepticism of the Raj. In retrospect, it makes the advent of the Swadeshi movement in Bengal – the first mass movement against the British that was launched in 1905, three years after the war had ended – seem less surprising and sudden. Nevertheless, differences between these two nationalised spaces functioned with a sense of kinship, which came fundamentally from the fact of imperial domination and nationalist concern, with Gandhi a key link. This is an obvious, but enabling observation. Together with the recognition of the differences that mark the two historical worlds, it will allow us to explore the intricacies of 'imperial subjecthood' and the problematic configurations of nationalised communities within an internationalised world.

The Anglo-Boer War, Gandhi and the 'imperial subject'

Studies of Gandhi as a nationalist generally regard his period of volunteer service for the British during the Anglo-Boer War as an illustration of his loyalist phase that preceded his scepticism of British authority and subsequent turn to nationalism. While one cannot fundamentally disagree with this reading of his career, it reduces the idea of loyalism to a simple-minded belief that existed in an asymmetrical relationship with the many instances of discrimination he experienced in South Africa.[18] Gandhi's loyalist phase is more valuable if it allows us to observe how the norm of the 'imperial subject' functioned in the political, social and cultural world of South African Indians. What explains its necessity, and what forms of empowerment does it allow and curtail? These questions become more significant if we take into account the fact that Gandhi's loyalism had to make sense to his Indian followers, who did not always support his positions.[19] It is also relevant to note that the African leadership of this time supported the British and played a critical military role in countering the Boer guerrillas (Warwick, 1983).[20] Thus, I would like to begin my account with the experience of the Voluntary Ambulance Corps formed by the South African Indians, which gave visible proof of their loyalism by hard work. It also involved a substantial risk to their lives.

The work of the Ambulance Corps was a grind. After fairly rudimentary training, the volunteers had to work in rough terrain, sometimes without water. Frequently, they had to cover up to 100 miles in five days, usually with their stretchers and heavy baggage that included their water, food and firewood. Initially, the thousand-odd stretcher bearers had to sleep without tents. At times, they went beyond their brief to work at the front, with shells falling in very close proximity. The volunteers were divided into two groups. The first was drawn from indentured labourers, requisitioned from their masters by the army and the administration; they were paid 20 shillings per week, as against the 35 shillings paid to their white counterparts. The other group was the 'leaders', some 30 individuals drawn from professional classes and led by Gandhi, who volunteered their services free. The Indian traders declined active participation, but assisted with sizeable donations of money and rations. They even made a substantial contribution to the Durban Women's Patriotic League, a leading support organisation for the war effort, many members of which had earlier participated in anti-Indian demonstrations. The generosity of the Indians was therefore astounding. Despite this, their initial offer in October 1899 to assist the war effort in any capacity was declined; it was only in December, at the time of British military reversals, that General Buller, the commander-in-chief, accepted.[21]

The Indian involvement in the war dramatised a conspicuous display of loyalty, as demonstrated by the unconditional nature of their offer, the acceptance of discriminatory pay, the unremunerated service of the 'leaders' and the risking of their lives. Gandhi unequivocally declared that 'the English-speaking Indians came to the conclusion that they would offer their services ... unconditionally and absolutely without payment, in any capacity ... in order to show to the Colonists that they were worthy subjects of the Queen' (Gandhi, 1960c:129). The Indians appear to have had a point to prove, an anxiety to soothe. Gandhi called the act of involvement a 'privilege' (Gandhi, 1960c:114), a word that holds more meaning than the immediate context of its use here suggests.

Taken together, these acts and statements define the peculiar double location of the 'imperial subject'. On the one hand, it was based on the notion of separate nations, which it was the obligation of imperialism to develop. This was an international system that prompted Gandhi to express his trust in the empire as a 'family of nations' (cited in Gandhi, 1960c:viii). At the same time, 'imperial subjecthood' also allowed a placeless loyalty (bounded only by the empire) through which people located outside the originative space of their nation could claim a purchase on the land of their new habitation. And this was critical for the Indians, because the claims of the 'imperial subject' offered the only substantive ground for the Indians to residence in the new land that many were beginning to regard as their home. It must be remembered that Indians were migrants – consisting of indentured labourers, with a small number of traders and a handful of professionals – who in the 1890s were still newcomers to South Africa (Swan, 1985:1–9). They could not claim to belong to the land by virtue of prior occupation, like Africans; by the fact of settling on it and making it productive, like the Boers; or because they had mastered it, as the British had done. The vocabulary of independent nationalism was one that was not accessible to them. What they did possess was the claim to being an 'imperial subject': 'It was the Indian's proudest boast that they were British subjects. If they were not, they would not have had a footing in South Africa', proclaimed Gandhi eloquently (1960c:136).

This purchase had become critical at a time when a rapid offensive was being mounted to remove the South African ground from under the Indians. The threat to Indians was already palpable from the early 1890s, but it reached a climax on Gandhi's return from India in 1896. Ostensibly made to fetch Kasturba, his wife, Gandhi utilised the trip to mobilise public support in India, which was one of the aims of the Natal Indian Congress (NIC). He travelled across the country from Calcutta to Bombay, giving speeches and persuading the press, especially Anglo-Indian newspapers, to publish sympathetic articles. He also elicited support from Indian National Congress (INC) leaders, including Bal Gangadhar Tilak, the extremist leader who called for 'Swaraj', or self-rule, and the moderate Gopalkrishna Gokhale. Further, he wrote the Green Pamphlet, which summarised the injustices perpetrated on South African Indians. This article was misreported by Reuters and circulated internationally. The subsequent outrage in South Africa resulted in the setting up of two anti-Indian organisations in Natal and a campaign that mobilised railwaymen, shop assistants and bricklayers to demonstrate against the landing of the ship in which Gandhi returned. Only through the intervention of an English woman and assistance from a frightened administration (which had been stoking racist sentiment, but wanted control over self-defeating excesses) did Gandhi manage to escape from a crowd that had expressed the desire to lynch him.[22]

The demonstration gave impetus to the racist legislation, press campaigns and public statements by white leaders that had begun in earnest in the period that Natal acquired and consolidated responsible government. It provided the sanction of visible popular authority to government policies. Swanson (1983) has drawn attention to the importance of racism among administrators in Natal in explaining the popular onslaught. What probably needs more emphasis is the fear of a growing migrant population, some of whose members were prospering and providing business competition: there was a pervasive fear of being 'swamped' by Indian 'hordes' and traders.[23] The consequence was a multipronged attack on Indians. While the Franchise Bill sought to remove the claims of Indians to citizenship and political influence through the vote, indentured labourers were legislatively discouraged from remaining in Natal after the expiry of their contracts. The Wholesalers and Retailers Licensing Act curbed the commercial rivalry to whites posed by Indian merchants. A refinement of the Immigration

Restriction and Quarantine Act – and its strict implementation – sought to counter the spectre of Asian 'hordes'.[24] Running parallel in a mutually supportive movement were measures passed in the Transvaal. As early as 1885 the government there had passed Law 3, which excluded Asians from citizenship and ownership of land, in addition to placing them in separate locations for residence and business. For its part, the Orange Free State devised a more streamlined solution: it simply banned Indians from trading or owning land. It was a bleak decade for the Indians.

Gandhi was convinced that these measures were designed not merely to ghettoise Indians, but to ease them out of South Africa itself.[25] He could not discount the possibility of what we call 'ethnic cleansing' today. It was precisely for this reason that he welcomed the Anglo-Boer War as a 'blessing' for Indians (Gandhi, 1960c:215), for it allowed formal acknowledgement by the authorities that Indians could assist the empire and work with European subjects. It provided access to a sense of a shared condition, which was reflected in patronising acknowledgement of Indian services by normally anti-Indian settler newspapers.[26] The sense of sharing was clearly not based on equality, but nevertheless could be regarded as a precondition for the procurement of more rights. It is somewhat embarrassing today – but also interesting – to note Gandhi's delighted gratitude as he crowed over the 'enchanting' sound of the phrase 'British subject' (Gandhi, 1960c:110). His sense of doting wonder can also be read as an expectation of a more substantive promise than the simple satisfaction of knowing that Asians had gained recognition from their imperial master. What was it in the status of 'imperial subjecthood' that held out greater possibilities?

The 'imperial subject' idea involved ambivalence and paradox. It allowed a sense of anchorage in the dominion of the empire, but nothing prevented it from aspiring to a status on a par with that of British subjects living under a constitutional monarchy; it presented the promise of citizenship for the colonised subject. This ideal lay behind the many appeals that Gandhi made to British officials and the press, ranging from Christian notions of brotherhood to British standards of character and free trade. Of course, the major, recurrent appeal that Gandhi made was to Queen Victoria's proclamation of 1858 that had been issued to signal the change to imperial rule in India and which promised equality of opportunity and freedom from discrimination to all subjects of the queen in India. The proclamation was already regularly used in India to demand more jobs for Indians (Ray, 1979:93), but Gandhi treated it as if it were a regulating principle of a constitution.

The plurality of Gandhi's appeals may show the possibilities for the 'imperial subject', but it also underlines its inherent weakness. Clearly, Gandhi could not pretend that he was a British citizen: reverential treatment of Victoria's proclamation concealed the absence of any constitution guaranteeing citizenship rights, a fact that was ruthlessly underlined by the provisions of the Franchise Bill in South Africa. The 'subject' part was not interchangeable with the 'citizen' element of the 'imperial subject' appeal. At the same time, it was not ontologically divorced from it, for the 'subject' occupied a position on a shared continuum with the 'citizen'. In a letter to the *Times of India* on 20 December 1901, Gandhi called for Indians to assert themselves 'and to claim for her sons in South Africa the full rights of a British citizen'. This continuum was a temporal one. All cultures shared in the same history that was measured by the time lag of 'civilisation'. Some national civilisations were historically more advanced than others. This meant that the 'imperial subject' idea was premised on an internal hierarchy between those who 'represented' history and those who had to catch up.

As we know, this lag normally supplied the justification for colonial rule, for it allowed colonial rulers to claim legitimacy on the grounds that their rule was necessary to 'civilise' the colonised. But what is sometimes overlooked is that the pace of progress is never predicted, and neither does the logic of historical justification for imperial rule prescribe clear criteria for judging when and if 'civilisation' has been attained. It is precisely this lacuna that Gandhi – while attempting to expand the scope of rights and recognition – exploited. True, other nationalist figures did the same, but what is interesting in Gandhi's case is his notion of Indian civilisation. In contrast to orientalist-inspired visions, Gandhi saw it as an unfolding story of achievements that had not been interrupted by the medieval Muslim period. For him, Akbar, the great Mughal emperor who initiated a policy of religious tolerance and consolidated a mixed Hindu-Muslim culture, represented a major achievement. It was a civilisation that changed and absorbed outside elements. Consequently, it appropriated 'modern' British contributions such as electoral democracy and could boast of professionals who had reached the higher echelons of the British establishment.[27] This narrative of civilisation subsumes the imperial notion of learning from colonial culture within the assumption of an existing and dynamic civilisation. The process of 'learning' from the British was not so much a pedagogic act as a part of a longer history of cultural absorption and transformation. Consequently, the hierarchy is maintained, not as a fixed and unbridgeable chasm of standards from the British, but as the formal and pragmatic acceptance of distance. Thus, Gandhi argued the case for inclusion of Indians in the Natal franchise by simply reassuring the settlers that Indians did not have any political ambitions: it was really a matter of self-respect for them (Gandhi, 1960c:101). He did not need to make civilisational claims. In short, the assertion of comparable civilisational standing was accompanied by a self-deprecating acknowledgement of formal subordination, a position that prevented the hierarchical distance from being grounded on substantive, ontological difference.

The Anglo-Boer War and Indian hierarchies

I have explained the importance of the 'imperial subject' in claiming anchorage in South Africa. In the light of my discussion on 'civilisation', it becomes clear that the 'imperial subject' is a peculiarly high-modern phenomenon, in which a form of belonging is claimed by 'rootedness' in an internationalised territorial entity defined by the British Empire. What is also interesting is that this anchorage is not embedded in a system of immutable hierarchies. The hierarchies of civilisation are based on the modern principles of social mobility, for they allow access to both a shared and a dynamic schema of time through which the colonised could aspire, if not to equality, then to something akin to citizenship and symmetrical recognition. But it is precisely at this point, where 'imperial subjecthood' holds out a promise of acceptance, that it also withholds the offer. This contradiction in the 'imperial subject' idea became very obvious to Gandhi in 1903, following his return from India.

Gandhi had stayed in India for over a year, practising as a barrister and publicising the South African question by addressing the National Congress in 1901 and achieving a resolution from it. One possible reason for his prolonged stay was his confidence that South African Indians, after their contribution to the war, would acquire a better deal under the British. The Gandhian leadership had based its strategy on a fundamental distinction between the British settlers and the Colonial Office. There seemed to be sufficient justification for doing so. The two groups had come into conflict on several occasions regarding policy towards Indians. Further, the Transvaal situation opened an opportunity for Indians to identify with the condition of the disenfranchised, mainly British *uitlander* settlers,[28] to claim recognition for themselves.

The role of the ambulance corps in the war had been publicly well received and gave Gandhi renewed hope, but the British victory did not lead to the amelioration of the position of Indians. Instead, discrimination intensified. The British rigorously implemented discriminatory laws, whereas the former Boer republics had been relatively lax in this regard. They also inaugurated an Asiatic Department where there had previously been none. New discriminatory legislation, such as that which sought to place restrictions on the children of indentured labourers in Natal, was introduced.[29] What Gandhi had not considered was that the unification of South Africa, set in motion by the Anglo-Boer War, found initial common ground in racism. The 1902 Treaty of Vereeniging, which paved the way for the union, featured three elements: eventual self-government for the republics, safeguarding the Dutch language and the exclusion of blacks from political partnership (Selby, 1973:201). From the beginning there was consensus on racial discrimination – while agreement on the other points was sorted out only later.[30] Racism functioned as a surrogate nationalism.

In a fundamental sense, the contrary relationship between co-belonging and equality was replicated in the internal structure of the 'nation'. The imperial dispensation of South Africa structured a constant tension between the 'coolie' and the 'free' Indian. One of the key moves made by the settler governments was the attempt to elide the 'coolie' into the 'Indian/Asian'. The word 'coolie' was not only a term of contempt; it had legislative standing. Used by various laws in Natal since the 1860s to refer to indentured labour in order to deploy authoritarian measures such as the pass law, it was enshrined in Law 3 of 1885 to equate 'coolies' with non-British subjects such as Malays, Arabs and Turks (Gandhi, 1960c:8–10). The use of the term 'coolie' was of a different order from straightforward racist stereotypes. Its use normalised the possibility of a legislative reclassification of non-indentured Indians by which their 'imperial subject' status would be taken away.[31] It may be mentioned that its deployment overrode the use of the popular term 'Arab' used to refer to Indian merchants. 'Coolie' removed the possibility that Indians might attain 'freedom'. The threat of legislative reclassification was actually enacted in the Transvaal in 1898, when the Location Law transferred the residences and businesses of Indian merchants and traders to the outskirts of Johannesburg on the understanding that they were not British subjects – and this new place was called the 'coolie location'.

There has been an important debate on the subject of the relationship between Gandhi and the Indian elite. Swan (1985:44) has suggested that the elite were too concerned with distinguishing themselves from the 'coolies' to fight racism, while Parvathi Raman (2004) has pointed to the integrative elements that wove together the world of the Indians. It seems to me that both arguments have merit, but it may be more fruitful to locate the general subject within the context of the downward push exerted by the settler governments. The governmental move to elide the 'free' with the indentured intensified the desire of the Indian elite to draw on both class distinctions and caste prejudices to distinguish itself from the 'coolies'.[32] At the same time, the general move to institutionalise the discrimination of all Indians – of which this move was a part – appeared to have affirmed connections. Responding to the imposition of legislative restrictions on the freedom of labourers to complain against their masters, Gandhi described them as 'the kith and kin' of 'free Indians': by virtue of their position, Gandhi thought, the latter could take a 'dispassionate view' of the matter.[33] The letter sums up the paradoxical relationship of the elite to the unfree: it acknowledges the sharing of national bonds, but from the distance of the 'dispassionate view'.

Nevertheless, it is worth emphasising that the pressures of class distinction intensified by legislation had to coexist with national sentiment aroused by the settler offensive and the strong social and economic links between the two constituencies. Many ex-indentured turned to petty trade or kitchen gardening after completing their tenure. Swan (1985:11–13) observes that the new elite that emerged in 1905 included members from this constituency. It should also not be forgotten that they provided the basic market of the Indian traders, who were themselves closely interrelated economically. Consequently, while their interests may have been marginalised by the Gandhian leadership, they were not completely overlooked. To the legalistically minded Gandhi, the cause of the indentured was taken up only in conditions of legal freedom. Thus, the £3 annual residence tax that the ex-indentured had to pay if they elected to stay on was taken up regularly by Gandhi, who appealed to the principle of free trade. The NIC also defended the right of Indians to ply rickshaws in Durban (Gandhi, 1960c:108). Sometimes the petitions drawn up by Gandhi contained signatures of both the indentured and the free (see Gandhi, 1960a:161).

If Gandhi's relationship with the 'coolies' can be seen as a rudimentary practice of 'nationness', it is interesting to note that it was part of another set of hierarchies produced by the 'imperial subject'. Gandhi's notion of the 'national community' based on kinship and distance is posited on active reiterations of sharing through acts of intervention on behalf of labour, but without foregoing hierarchy – and this hierarchy too was not immutable, but permitted an incipient mobility. At the same time, the practice of 'nationness' also drew on the imperial map of civilisations to position itself internationally. Hence, Africans were treated as inferior by the Indians; the sense of co-sharing did not extend to Africans. This produced an additional pressure on Indians. In addition to the prospect of becoming 'coolie', the free Indians faced the pressure of another downward push, i.e. the prospect of being regarded as the equivalent of Africans. A major objection of Gandhi to the Transvaal's Location Law was that it would 'place [Indians], who are undoubtedly superior to the kaffirs, in close proximity to the latter' (Gandhi, 1960c:75–76). While the criteria of purity-pollution so important to caste hierarchies may be at play here, what is more important is that this adds force to civilisational distinctions. If the British marked the high end of the civilisational hierarchy, the Africans represented its lowest extreme, and these extremes stabilised the intermediate and mobile position of Indians within it.[34] Structurally, the 'kaffir' was more important to the maintenance of the position of the free Indian than the 'coolie'.

Hence, it is not surprising that Gandhi did not seek to build solidarities with blacks, even after his disillusionment with the 'imperial subject' project. This may have been precluded by the very terms of his disappointment, for, as I have shown, it stems from a reversal of the direction in which civilisational mobility was supposed to move for the Indians. In *Hind Swaraj*, an admirable text in many other respects, written towards the end of his stay in South Africa, Gandhi questioned the criteria of civilisation that the British offered and dismissed them as materialistic. He counterposed against them the moral achievements of Indian civilisation. Gandhi replaced the historical grounding of civilisation with a matter–moral divide: one hierarchical scheme replaced another, with the position of moral superiority being given to the Indians and the baser one to the West (Parel, 2009:35–37, 60–63). What remains unspoken of is the position of blacks. It is an absence that can be construed to indicate that, as in the other civilisational order, in this one too he exists outside its pale, made patiently to mark its outer boundaries.

What we are left with is a condition of irony. The diasporic, international world of the 'imperial subject' does not produce a corresponding openness to international solidarities. The 'imperial subject' idea does not do away with the nation so much as make it possible to be reconstituted in places other than its originative space of habitation. The 'imperial subject' may not provide an embedded sense of place, but it provides firm boundaries based on civilisation (and on political criteria that remove groups such as Malays and Chinese from the list of possible solidarities) that foreclose the limits within which a new world is to be made and remade in the work of habitation. This does not mean, however, that the nation was simply transportable and replicable, like other things in the newly internationalising world. The South African experience suggested a more complex movement, in which the nation of the colonised is internationalised even as it began to come into its own. What we have is something akin to a diasporic nationalism, something that was to grow and come into its own only towards the latter part of the 20th century. Having said this, it should also be added that this diasporic nationalism was very different from the clearly worked out pragmatic and affective system of distinctions between countries of habitation and of origin that marks it today. Gandhi's version of diasporic nationalism in particular was indeterminate. As Dhupelia-Mesthrie (2004) shows us, Gandhi appears to have settled for a segmented version. He migrated back to India and yet left behind his son, friendships, solidarities and the foundational part of his institutional life, especially the Phoenix farm. And he kept contact, giving advice and providing interventions, even as he pitched his battle camp firmly in the world of a spatially determinate nation that provided a more successful site for meeting the need for equality and self-respect that he so deeply cherished.

This is a story of the 'future'; but it also returns me to the Anglo-Boer War. I turn now to look at the way it shaped another configuration, one not dominated by a single figure and hence a much more internally contested space: the war in India.

The Anglo-Boer War in India

The Anglo-Boer War existed primarily as a discursive event in India, although not entirely so. The volume of coverage is surprising – indeed, astonishing. The main site of the enactment of the war was the news space of British dailies. Two elements stand out in the coverage. Firstly, the newspapers produced, through the multiple sources of the reports they carried, an internationally interlocking site. Reports were datelined from many places. In the absence of foreign correspondents, dailies carried news from international news agencies such as Reuters and reprinted articles and reports from other sources in Durban and Pretoria, but also from London and even the United States. Gandhi's reports as a participant witness played a significant part in the exposure. All these sources enacted out the war as an international event, especially since reports on European responses to the war were given on a regular basis.

The second element of the war news space was its saturating effect. A wide range of newspapers across the country carried daily reports under front-page banner headlines, particularly during the three-month period from October 1899 to January 1900. This was preceded by intermittent, but fairly extensive coverage of the crises leading to the war. What added to the power of the coverage – and this is something that happens particularly with war reportage – was that it took on a serial form. The progress of the war became imbricated into the everyday lives of the people of a foreign land precisely because its outcome was not known. It was not a finished narrative, which intensified the implications of the war and the questions it raised. Besides its immediate consequences for India's position in Asia and the stability of the Raj in India, there was also a muted, but recurringly enunciated possibility of the war becoming a European one (*Hitavadi*, 1899a). It is probably for all these reasons that the war moved outside newspapers into other discursive worlds. The most remarkable example of its spread was its circulation in women's journals. *Bharati* ran an article with an admiring tone on Boer women combatants (Bhattacharya, 1973:159), while *Antahpur* did a piece on the Boers.[35] Pro-Boer literature and anti-war books and pamphlets, such as W. T. Stead's *Shall I Slay My Brother Boer?*, were circulated.[36] As I have mentioned, the war even entered the verse of Rabindranath Tagore.

The war circulated in India on two levels. It did not remain confined to the discursive, but was transformed into the performative primarily through the campaign of the loyalists. The British settlers provided the lead through fund-raising activities; thus, Vinolia soap advertised itself to say that the purchase of each bar would contribute a halfpenny to the Vinolia war fund, apart from helping to improve the customer's complexion (*Times of India*, 17 February 1900). These were supplemented by morale-boosting events, such as a film of some of the battles shown in Bombay or the hosting of carnivals to raise funds (*Times of India*, 15 February 1900). The efforts of the British settlers were ably supplemented by two other groups, the titled and the orthodox. Titled dignitaries held meetings in support of the British in places as far apart as Jullundur (Punjab) in the north-west, Delhi, and Murshidabad (Bengal) in the east. Some princes decided to raise subscriptions to send 800 combat horses, while the Maharaja of Kashmir vowed he would equip the whole British army with putties (*The Bengalee*, 2 February 1900). Their efforts were supplemented by the Darbhanga Raj of Bihar, which initiated a 'Hindu Voluntary Fund',[37] while the Nawab of Murshidabad hosted prayers for the success of the British at the city *masjid* (*The Bengalee*, 3 February 1900). Indeed, hosting prayers for the British – by both Hindus and Muslims – became an established occurrence.[38] The role of the Hindu orthodox press, led by the *Bangabasi*, which was the highest-selling paper in Bengal with a circulation of 26,000, is significant. While it had run a campaign against the colonial administration for introducing the Age of Consent Bill (which had raised the marriageable age of girls) in 1891, it expressed full-hearted loyalty to the British during the war and appealed for funds and prayers. This change of stance may have had local causes related to the political marginalisation of the orthodox by the professional middle-class politicians of a reformist orientation, who dominated the elected bodies and whose main organ was *The Bengalee*.

Possibly the most interesting and intriguing way in which information about the war circulated was through popular rumours. *The Englishman* reported with some asperity that the lower classes of the crowded Chandni Chowk market area in Delhi had started to celebrate the defeat of British forces (*Hitavadi*, 1899b). Meanwhile, in Calcutta, just after the December reverses suffered by British forces in South Africa, the uncertain course of the war had led to the introduction of betting on its outcome. The correspondent also reported that rumours were circulating in tramcars and carriages, some claiming that one Boer had the strength of five men, with others reporting that the British had 250 detectives to spy out anyone extolling Boer valour (*Bangabasi*, 1899). Even more intriguing was the experience of Edgar Thurston, who carried out an anthropometric survey in South India. Just after the war, in his encounter with a community he called the 'Oddes' and who had 'Boyan' as their title, Thurston found that they were very scared that they would be mistaken for Boers because of the similarity of their names. They feared transportation to replace the exterminated Boers. Indeed, through a long tour of Mysore province, he appears to have repeatedly encountered a fear that he had been deputed to recruit natives for South Africa (cited in McLane, 1977:35). These rumours, it may be speculated, may have had something to do with news that came back from indentured labourers in South Africa (Madras was the major port of shipment for them), in addition to nuggets of newspaper information that were probably transformed in the process of dissemination. What is significant in all these cases of popular rumours is the suspicion and hostility towards the British and a sense of identification – if not kinship – with the other side.

These instances of not fully and uniformly pro-Boer, but certainly anti-British, sentiment were probably an important reason why much thought was given by the administration to the control, dispersal and repatriation of the many Boer prisoners of war who served out their term of detention in India. While most of the relevant files (and, judging from the list, there were a number of them) are no longer available at the National Archives in Delhi, the few that still exist are significant. They demonstrate official concern to place the prisoners in several isolated camps throughout India, and included plans to sequester groups in the Princely States[39] away from British-administered populations. It is also interesting that officials considered what they should do in case any Boer wanted to remain in India (it is intriguing to speculate if any actually did so) and came to a clear resolution that such Boers would be actively discouraged.[40] On the whole, the administration appears to have successfully kept the Boer prisoners from exercising any kind of influence on the public debates that sprang up around the war.

While understanding the entire subcontinent's involvement in the Anglo-Boer War would be an important enterprise, my interest is confined to Bengal, and primarily to its middle-class public. In general, Bengal offered many instances in which international events crystallised and impelled nationalist concerns and mobilisation. A few years after the war, Japan's victory over Russia electrified the Bengali middle class with the prospect of an emerging East and motivated various public events.[41] But the Boer War offered no such inspirational value. Instead, it did two interconnected things. It strengthened existing ambivalences about the 'imperial subject' and, in so doing, thinned out imperial loyalism to the extent that it came close to losing its purchase altogether. Of course, this did not happen uniformly across the social spectrum.

It has been remarked that the Anglo-Boer War, especially 'Black Week', saw a sense of despair in Britain that was not matched even by the worst of the First World War experiences (Miller, 2005:692). Given this mood, it is not difficult to imagine the effect of the war on the British residents of India who exemplified the 'imperial subject'.[42] McLane (1977:24–25) has argued that the 'doctrine of infallibility' that was ultimately based on the simple military superiority of the British had by the late 19th century replaced the pedagogic legitimisation of the empire through the exemplar of the 'imperial character'. Placed against this horizon of self-justification, the military reverses abroad produced a deep anxiety. The effects of this can be seen in two kinds of movements. The first was an irritable insistence on the limits to which the imperial cause could extract support from the settlers.

The tea planters, for instance, strongly protested against the move to extract repeated donations for the imperial cause.[43] Secondly, there were anxious attempts to elicit popular support for 'imperial patriotism'. A long article in the *London Times*, reprinted in *The Bengalee* (2 February 1900), tried to show that the *uitlanders* of the Transvaal were as discriminated against as the Indians (while explaining away the racism of the Natal government as the handiwork of settlers), in an attempt to prove a commonality of interests. Imperial 'patriotism' suddenly came into vogue. It was probably for this reason that Anglo-Indian papers such as the *Times of India* and *The Statesman* prominently ran Gandhi's comments, for his loyalties most closely approximated to what the empire needed at that dire time.

As I have shown, the success of loyalism among Indians was confined to the titled and orthodox. This was the consequence of an inherent problem in colonial policy. The government wished to demonstrate the hold of the 'imperial subject', but at the same time carefully regulate the participation of Indians in it. Thus, the Lord Bishop of Bombay, bidding farewell to the Lumsden Horse regiment, congratulated the princes on their loyalty, exclaiming: 'We are all imperialists now.' He then went on to define imperialism as based on the principles of 'justice, equality, freedom of thought and speech, intellectual progress, pure religion' and similar verities. He also took care to subtly disengage the princes from their co-imperialists by stating that these were the principles of the 'modern Christian world' (*Times of India*, 16 February 1900). Actually, the distinction that probably grated the most was the one made between the settler colonies of Australia and Canada, on the one hand, and India, on the other.[44] This hierarchy became evident in the fact that the British studiously avoided taking Indian soldiers to the front – despite the advice of some ex-India hands[45] and in spite of repeated criticisms from the Indian press that rightly spotted the long arm of racism at work. Whatever the colonial administration in India may have thought, non-whites were unwelcome to participate formally in the war. Warwick (1983:15–20) and others have shown that the participation of Africans was not acknowledged in the war because there was a formal consensus among the warring parties that they must not be involved. The Africans were, of course, (formally) ruled out because they had historically posed a military threat. This was not applicable to the Indians, who were regarded as peaceful, a recognition that Gandhi kept emphasising in his appeals to the authorities. There was, however, a more fundamental problem of racist legitimacy. British South African spokespersons were clear that the blacks had to be kept out, since they must not be encouraged to regard themselves as being necessary in any way to the government.[46] The rationale of white political self-sufficiency goes a long way to explaining the bar on Indian military participation. It also explains the even more absurd refusal to deploy Maoris who were a part of the New Zealand contingent.

The visible inbuilt incoherences of the 'imperial subject' renewed and deepened the general alienation. It should be noted here that the press was regarded as unfriendly by the government. In 1891 a government survey discovered that 14 out of 19 newspapers could be regarded as hostile (Ray, 1979:94). This characterisation does not do justice to the ambiguity of this press: many of its constituents freely criticised the administration while remaining committed to the belief in the providential nature of British colonialism. Nevertheless, the survey defines the generally critical orientation of newspapers during the Anglo-Boer War. Here the significance of *The Bengalee* and its editor, Surendranath Bannerjee, needs to underlined. Surendranath, a leading light of the INC, led the turn to constitutional opposition to the British, which at one point resulted in a stint in jail; but he also firmly believed in the providentiality of British colonialism and the gradual progress it offered for transition to self-government. Important British officials regarded him as someone more amenable to negotiation than others. The editor of the *Hitavadi*, Kali Prasanna Kavybisharode, had a similar career. An INC worker, he was also jailed for five months for publishing a treasonable poem. Both became leading members of the Swadeshi movement.[47] At this time, however, no agitation was in sight and these publicists were suspended in a state of semi-belonging to 'imperial subjecthood'.

What is of interest here is not just the public ambivalence towards the government, but the fact that the precise balance of elements that constituted this ambivalence changed. The Boers themselves provoked ambiguity. Their surprising resistance was compounded by the romantic framing of their lives, dominant in Europe, and in their own self-perception as a people who lived a tough, bucolic life tied to the land. In Europe, this image hosted a series of debates that worked on the contrast between a 'traditional peasant ... with firm hierarchical values confronted with an aggressive, levelling capitalist civilisation' (Kaarsholm, 1989:110). In India, on the other hand, the striking feature of the Boers was that, despite their 'historical' disadvantage, they had successfully challenged the apparently invincible British. This was compounded by the knowledge that the Boers did not have a regular army. For Indians, the Boers demonstrated the power a community could generate by a simple and strong desire for independence.

'The Boers are determined to lay down their lives for their independence, which is dearer even than life', exalted one newspaper, saying that their act was an even bolder one than what a madman[48] would have done (*Samiran*, 1899). Attachment to the land itself seemed to explain the Boer successes, as the *Hitavadi*'s contrast between the British fighting in a foreign country and the Boers struggling for their independence and their families suggested (*Hitavadi*, 1899b). The power of this image needs to be measured by the sedimentation of heroic figures resisting foreign invaders that had been in circulation in literary works and theatre from the middle of the 19th century. However, these figures normally acted in the past against Muslims, ending their careers in tragic failure. This layer of sedimented effects was no doubt stimulated by the Boers, but it now also carried new messages, since Boer resistance was carried out in the present, and very successfully. Naturally, the Boers stimulated a great deal of exemplification and, correspondingly, a sense of the lack of a comparable desire for independence (no doubt heightened by the absence of any major political movement at the time) in the Indians themselves.

This is an economy of effect that, in normal circumstances, may have motivated actual deeds. But the unrelieved story of racist discrimination by the Boers that Gandhi's newspaper articles publicised prevented them from emerging as an unequivocal source of inspiration. The *Hitavadi* (1899a) best summed up this ambivalence when it observed: 'The oppression of the Indians in South Africa has led us to hate the Boers, still we feel constrained to praise their bravery with a thousand tongues.' The word 'bravery' needs comment, since, more than anything else, it was the courage of the Boers that was insistently cited. For Indians, Boer heroism became a convenient way of summarising their impact, for it could simply celebrate a pure character trait and thereby sideline the problematic that the Boers posed between their inspirational resistance, on the one hand, and the realisation that, like other Europeans, their attachment to land made them control and render inferior the lives of other peoples, on the other.

Nevertheless, it was the ambivalence that was important. It produced an ironic version of the 'imperial subject'. The British military reverses appear to have narrowed down the 'imperial subject' to one of simple loyalism alone. Further, they focussed an obsessive attention on British military power, indicating that this was the real source of British domination. This structure of ambivalence was different from the understandable and simple paradox of criticising the government while swearing loyalty to it. Now the groundwork of political faith was getting hollowed out, making it seem more a travesty of its former state. This structure is best embodied in *The Bengalee*. Towards the end of the conventional phase of the war, it admitted that patriotism was an 'exotic' thing in India and that Indians were dependent on the British to weld together the many nations of India into one great nation. At the same time, it defined this dependence as dictated by self-interest, making it clear that the British served a pragmatic function for Indians. The practical uses of the 'imperial subject' status were even more tangible in thinking out what could happen internationally as a result of the war. The great fear was that Russia would be emboldened to strike at Afghanistan and invade India. This prospect made *The Bengalee* (11 March 1900) state that it would back the British, for it was better to have a known than an unknown ruler.

But *The Bengalee* (25 January 1900) was also clear about its attitude to the British involvement in the war. In response to the refusal of some tea planters to raise additional funds for the war, the paper declared that it was an imperial war that did not in any way involve Indian interests. It made a clear distinction between government and people by saying that the contributions to the war made by India were not given by its people, since they were not even part of the government in a 'metaphorical sense'. Other newspapers went further. The *Prativasi* (9 October 1899), a vernacular with limited circulation, ran a story unambiguously entitled 'Worship of force, pure and simple' that featured a satire based on the Kali *puja* (worship). It told of preparations for worship of the goddess of force made by a number of *pujaris* (priests) headed by Lord Salisbury, with the *uitlanders* as minor priests; the sacrificial goat was, of course, the Boers, who were told that they were being sacrificed not just because of their crimes, but ultimately for their own welfare. The way *Prativasi* wrote about the Boer War seems as if it could have been writing about imperial justifications for colonising India. The war provided a displaced site to think about the conditions of Indians themselves.

Gandhi's refashionings

I have said that the 'imperial subject' was both attenuated and hollowed out by the response to the Anglo-Boer War in India. It is interesting to note that Gandhi both played and did not play a role in this sharpening of this loss of loyalty. From what has already been said, it is not difficult to see that Gandhi's critical understanding of the 'imperial subject' lagged behind that of his compatriots in India, and clearly the position of Indians in South Africa had a great deal to do with this. This may have been one of the reasons why he did not make a significant impact at the meeting of the National Congress in 1901. He recalled that he was barely given five minutes in which to sum up what he had to say (Uppal, 1995:174), which was in striking contrast to the widespread interest in the war. At the same time, Gandhi brought a new ethic of leadership into the country that may not have been given any recognition in India at that time, but which later proved to be a decisive element in countering the elitist social ethos of the 'imperial subject'. This was expressed in his willingness to do sanitary work during the INC meeting, a job that was normally done by the low castes, and in his decision to travel third-class as a way of getting to know the people of the country (Uppal, 1995:174–77). It should be recalled that, just before this, Gandhi had for the first time come into close proximity with the poor and low castes through the stretcher bearers with whom he had served in the Ambulance Corps. Proximity to the generally silenced social groups of India would have motivated his desire to know people who could not easily claim 'imperial subjecthood' (Vahed, 2000:212–13).

At the same time, it is interesting to note that his intensified criticism of the 'imperial subject' on his return to South Africa – while it may have been necessitated by the severe governmental racism in the Transvaal after the British had taken over its administration – was framed by his visit to India. In this context, a significant development should be noted. The reports Gandhi generated in this period were often used for more radical denunciations of the British than he himself may have liked. For instance, his report on British racism was deployed to delegitimise British attempts to prove a similarity of status between the *uitlanders* and the Indians under the Boers. Thus, the *Hitavadi* questioned Lord Lansdowne's profuse sympathy for the Transvaal Indians by asking where his lordship had disappeared to when the Indians in Natal had appealed to Joseph Chamberlain, the colonial secretary, for protection (*Hitavadi*, 1899b). In short, the *Hitavadi* read the statement as an ideological one, in contrast to Gandhi's understanding of official statements as declarations of literal intention. Gandhi could go back to South Africa with the experience of his own knowledge of that country being radicalised in India.

Possibly the most important gulf was one that existed between Gandhi's critical reworking of the grounding idea of civilisation and its near disappearance in the popular discourses of the time. Critiques had started of the militarism of Western countries even before the war had begun. Regarding the peace conference convened by the Russian czar a few months before the outbreak of the Anglo-Boer War to discuss a ban on dumdum bullets, the *Amrita Bazar Patrika* (23 June 1899) talked about the futility of making choices between bullets when the essential 'horrors of war' were unaddressed. Indeed, the *Patrika* expressed scepticism about such conferences, since war was too profitable for the Europeans to give up (*Amrita Bazar Patrika*, 7 June 1899). By the time the war started, this anti-militarist critique was consolidated and generalised by being mapped on to existing counter-criteria to the 'civilisational'. This was provided by the spiritual–material divide. This divide – based on a self-definition of the East as spiritually rich – was already an established counter-schema to provide a position of distinction from, and possibly equality with and superiority to, the West. The most eloquent formulation of the intensification was provided by *The Bengalee* (11 March 1900), which talked of the relationship of East and West in terms of spiritualism versus animalism/materialism. The materialist ideas of the West, it claimed, had been so strongly reinforced by scientific ideas that it could think of nothing except its self-interest. And the evidence for this animalism/materialism was demonstrated by the rejection of the peace conferences. The war itself was shown to be based on British greed for the gold of the Witwatersrand. The strand of this critique strengthened over the course of the war. By the period of the last guerrilla phase, this denunciation of Western civilisation and its intimate connection with the culture of war became a firm conviction. Like the continental critics of the British, *The Bengalee* (24 February 1901) saw Kitchener's policy of burning down houses and farms and of throwing women and children into concentration camps as a throwback to 'old, barbarous times'.[49] Reacting to the war, Tagore went further to mount what was possibly the angriest denunciation of the culture of war. His volume of verse entitled *Naibedya* included a few poems that envisaged the new century as arriving from the West in an apocalypse of blood and destruction, savage with self-interest. A very significant feature of his understanding, for our purposes, was his figuring of civilisation as a hooded snake.

Nevertheless, the material–spiritual counter-schema revealed a kinship with its 'civilisational' other – a relationship that surfaced in Gandhi's discourse under the most extreme pressure of circumstances. This was the inferior positioning of Africans. They were routinely referred to as savages in the Indian press, suggesting that neither the 'imperial subject' idea nor its critique was prepared to unseat blacks from their position at the bottom of the hierarchical heap. Indeed, even a perceived equation of Indians with Africans led to a wholehearted embrace of the values of civilisation. Referring to the news that Zulus and Basutos were being used by the British army, the *Bangabasi* (1900) departed from its usual loyalism. It dismissed Africans as uncivilised and demanded to know from their colonial masters how they dare regard Indians as uncivilised, a people with an unbroken record of excellence stretching from the ancient Vedas to Babu Dwarakanath Mitter, a contemporary dignitary. Equally damning was the ironic recuperation of racist principles in pieces that critiqued the British use of civilisational criteria. Thus, British stigmatisation of the Boers as 'semi-barbaric' and savage was contested by newspapers that tried to prove that the Boers were very civilised, since they had wonderful cities and so on (*Hitavadi*, 1899b). It may be remarked that no such scepticism was shown about the classification of Africans.

Conclusion: The impossibilities of the 'imperial subject'

In this chapter I have looked on the 'imperial subject' as a political imaginary that welds together – however loosely – an international community. I should make it clear that it provides the conditions of possibility for an international imaginary: it neither engenders it nor exhausts the possibilities of the international even during the time of its dominance. But it does provide a fairly powerful mode of mapping the world, because it locates power in a temporal schema of development that allows for the prospect of internal mobility in its scale of achievement. The Anglo-Boer War allows us access to a point where the 'imperial subject' begins to disintegrate. Caught in the cleft stick of different kinds of migrations of the colonisers, supplying administrators, professionals and capitalists, on the one hand, and impelling the movement of colonised labour, trade and professionals, on the other, the imperial order gets split. It becomes globally divided between a downward push and an upward pull. The white 'achievers' invoke the simple world of white versus non-white to fix and immobilise the prospect of internal mobility within the scale of civilisation. This attempt enters into unresolvable tension with the steadily growing claims being made by the colonised on history. This breaks the identification of 'civilisation' with a clearly stable system of power supplied by colonialism.

But its power as a norm seems to outlive this crisis. What happens in substantive terms is that it becomes a conflicted category. But since it is a category that is meaningless without the international scheme of organising relationships among nationalised collectivities, the conflict over claims to civilisation involves reinventing hierarchies and imposing these on recalcitrant others. In the degeneration of the 'imperial subject', we can sense a darker threat. This may not have been immediately apparent, since the rise of nationalism and equality claimed and formally accepted between nations may have obscured its presence. But it remains, producing ways of mapping the world today – while the nation state enters its crisis – as a grid of civilisations, equal in the eyes of the members of each, but committed to producing a world order that will render inferior and forcefully 'develop' the other.

The Disquieting of History: Portuguese (De)Colonisation and Goan Migration in the Indian Ocean

Pamila Gupta

Introduction

> The diaspora is a society in which the absent are a constant incitement to discourse about things moving. We call the diaspora 'the society of the absent' as a convenience and a theoretical position because in it, discourses of mobility appear as both cause and effect and are inseparable from diasporic life, saturating its internal social space (Ho, 2006:19).

The reason why I use the word 'disquieting' in this chapter has everything to do with the way in which the Goan (diasporic and elite) community of Maputo occupied a position of 'disquiet' – a state of uneasiness – within the Portuguese colonial hierarchy of Mozambique. Their patterns of migration consist of three distinct waves within the Indian Ocean region: from Portuguese India (Goa) to Mozambique in the 1920s in a search for economic betterment; next between the 1950s and 1960s, the period that foresaw the beginning of the end of Goa's decolonisation; and, lastly, emigration from Maputo as a direct response to Portuguese decolonisation in 1975. Each can be characterised as 'disquieting'. Specifically, during all three phases of (potential) migration, these Goan elites occupied a precarious position – one viewed with uncertainty by both coloniser and colonised – within Mozambican society.

In the first phase (1920s), it was considered one's colonial duty as a 'good' Portuguese citizen to emigrate from Goa to help out in the 'Africa cause' and settle in Mozambique. This was largely a male phenomenon – many of those who emigrated were trained medical doctors – with very few Goan women enduring the journey, and one that allowed Goans to take full advantage of the instabilities of colonial rule and its 'ambiguities of difference' (Stoler & Cooper, 1997:4) such that they were 'almost' transformed from colonial subjects to colonial officers as a result of migration. The source of 'disquiet' here is the ease with which many of these former colonised subjects adapted to their new (relative) positions of power.

During the second phase (1950s–60s), many Goans chose emigration to another Portuguese colony in the face of Goa's imminent decolonisation and absorption into a culturally different Indian nation state; here, interestingly, migration was largely a female practice – many as the wives-to-be of Goan settlers in Mozambique. Migration in this case, in the face of decolonisation, can be understood as a 'disquieting' form of neocolonialism.

In the last phase (1975), many Goans chose to leave or, rather, were persuasively convinced to leave Maputo by outgoing colonial officials so as to help prove Portugal's point that independent Mozambique would devolve into 'chaos' and that Africans were incapable of ruling themselves without a colonial administration, one that conveniently employed many Goans in key positions of authority. That the majority of Goans *did* leave was seen as a 'disquieting' source of betrayal by the newly independent Mozambican government; that this same government had simultaneously pushed for the departure of all Asians, including Goans, is also a source of 'disquiet'. However, during this last phase of Portuguese decolonisation in Mozambique, other Goan settlers chose to stay, and remain today as part of a 'society of the absent' (Ho, 2006:19), still living with a sense of 'disquiet' in the face of Mozambique's troubled post-colonial history.

In this chapter I explore the many facets of this 'disquieting' of history on both a practical and ideological level, a disquieting that is reinforced on an analytical level by a lack of historiography associated with this series of Goan migrations (Gupta, 2007). Instead, it is through an ethnographic approach – specifically through the collection of life histories – that I am able to access these distinct phases of migration through the perspective of different Goan imaginaries of Portuguese Mozambique.[50]

I first set up both my theoretical and methodological investments, developing a way of looking at Goan Mozambicans historically as 'colonial elites', but of a specific kind, moving between sites located within the Indian Ocean region at the same time that they occupied positions as 'local cosmopolitans' (Ho, 2006:31), i.e. deeply local and transnational at the same time throughout the colonial period. This in turn allowed them – in the past, present and now in the future – to sustain contacts simultaneously with Mozambique, Goa and Portugal. I also briefly discuss the usefulness of a life history or 'biographical' approach for revealing unwritten histories and ideologies of migration, as is the case for the Goan community of Maputo. Next I look at the 'longings and belongings' of many different individual Goans living in the context of post-colonial Maputo, recounting their testimonies that attest and give voice to these different phases of migration

(1920s, 1950s–60s and post-1975), as well as their fragility and resilience as a historical community that was created out of the itinerant quality that characterised Portuguese colonialism more generally (Gupta, 2007).

Lastly, in my conclusion I allude to the next generation of Goans living in Maputo, suggesting both the reality in which they live – their continuing sense of 'disquiet' in the face of Mozambican post-coloniality – and the ways in which they are very much continuing the patterns of 'local cosmopolitanism' practised by their ancestors, some of whom experienced not only migration from one Portuguese colony to another, but two very different moments of decolonisation, Goan (1961) and Mozambican (1975). The members of this (next) generation of Goans are both deeply attached to Mozambique and looking elsewhere, with the analytics of diaspora and mobility that motivated their parents also circumscribing them in terms of movement to both new and old spaces, and in the process creating new kinds of post-colonial subjectivities.

Ambiguities of difference in the Indian Ocean

> The Manichaean world of high colonialism that we have etched so deeply in our historiographies was thus nothing of the sort (Stoler & Cooper, 1997:8).

In this section I attempt to build a case both for revisiting the anthropology of empire and that of elite literatures in order to suggest that we view the Goans of Mozambique as colonial elites, and for renewing a biographical or life history approach to writing historical ethnography in the face of a dearth of source materials. Here I argue not only that research on the Goan diasporic community in Maputo must necessarily build on these foundations, but that it also raises new questions by the very fact of its complicated history of migration; the lack of source materials to access this history; the many cases of exceptionalism that characterise Portuguese colonialism, which have historiographical and ethnographic effects; and, finally, its intertwining through migration between two distinct, but connected colonial contexts (Gupta, 2007). I conclude by first turning to the innovative works of historian Thomas Metcalf, looking to his discussion of 'webs of empire' for tracing horizontal movements of (colonial) migration within the Indian Ocean region, and then to anthropologist Engseng Ho, looking to his recent diaspora scholarship on 'local cosmopolitans' in order to suggest the potential of his work for better situating the Goans of Mozambique within a variety of matrixes and accessed through a wider range of source materials.

One of the most significant findings to come out of the anthropology of empire literature has been the breakdown of the hegemonic power of colonialism, and with it a call to look at the vulnerabilities of colonialism and at power as a process of negotiation, rather than taking it as a given (Stoler & Cooper, 1997). The next step in this focus on the instabilities of colonialism has been to study the coloniser–colonised relationship in specific historical contexts. As anthropologist Ann Stoler (1989:635) writes:

> Colonial authority was constructed on two powerful, but false premises. The first was the notion that Europeans in the colonies made up an easily identifiable and discrete biological and social entity: a natural community of common class interests, racial attributes, political affinities and superior culture. The second was the related notion that the boundaries separating colonizer from colonized were thus self-evident and easily drawn. Neither premise reflected colonial realities.

Thus, just as the 'coloniser' was not a uniform or stable group, neither was the 'colonised'. Instead, the reality was that different categories of people ('European', 'native', 'creole', 'mestizo', etc.), operating in specific colonial contexts, were always in process and changing in relation to other qualities, both biological and social, in order to suit differing colonial agendas at different moments in time. Nor were these categories of 'coloniser' and 'colonised' inherent; rather, 'difference had to be defined and maintained', often by way of discourses of race and culture, for each 'served to buttress one another in crucial ways' (Stoler & Cooper, 1997:7). Thus, I want to suggest that in Portuguese India the Goans more or less occupied the position of 'colonised'. However, in the act of migration to a second Portuguese colonial outpost, in this case Mozambique, the Goans took on a very different status within the colonial hierarchy, a positioning that had everything to do with colonial categories of race, i.e. the difference between 'Indians' and 'Africans'. Moreover, these racial distinctions were often disguised through an emphasis on cultural distinctions of 'breeding, character, and civility' (Stoler & Cooper, 1997:7). In other words, markers of class (here standing in for race and culture) played a key role in positioning Goan-Mozambican settlers as more closely aligned with their Portuguese colonisers than their colonised counterparts, the African Mozambicans, even as individual Goans experienced racism at the hands of their Portuguese colonisers. Thus, I want to extend Stoler and Cooper's emphasis on the 'ambiguities of difference' one stage further and apply it to my historical ethnography of the Goans of Mozambique.

In their class positioning within the Portuguese colonial structure of Mozambique, these settler Goans must also be qualified as elites of a certain type. Turning then to the anthropological literature on (colonial) elites, we first need to ask who becomes a settler in a colonial context, and why. Next, we need to ask in what everyday ways is a settler group given or perceived or defined as elite in status at a distinct moment in time. As Cris Shore (2002:6) points out, 'the proper study of elite cultures is the habitus, networks, and culture of elites themselves, including their informal and everyday practices and intimate spaces'. This is a crucial point – that we look at the 'habitus', following the work of Bourdieu (1995) on elite settlers in their everyday practices and spaces, something that I believe can be accessed through an ethnographic approach. Moreover, following Shore (2002:13), we must also attend to the diachronic ways in which settler elites remain elites; in other words, they need to be studied as dynamic groups with a changing membership rather than as a bounded entity. Subsequent to this point, we must also recognise the power and 'endurance of old elite families', particularly in colonial contexts, as shaping the context in which the next generations of proto-nationalist elites – largely their sons – still had 'privileged access to the machinery of the colonial state' while reproducing themselves in a newly independent context, as Jonathan Spencer (2002:95) has shown for the case of colonial elites in Sri Lanka. Here, Spencer's Sri Lankan situation parallels that of the Goans of Mozambique, for as a community of elites whose roots also trace back to the mid-19th century,[51] his argument is an important one: these Goan Mozambicans have not only endured, but prospered over time and reproduced themselves through the generations as elites by way of their cultural, symbolic and real capital, and in relation to other segments of post-colonial Mozambican society. Nor must we forget to think about elites in relation to, and very much dependent on, wider affiliations with elites abroad, as Stephen Nugent (2002:72) shows for the case of Amazonian elites. This is a particularly relevant point for understanding the settler Goans of Mozambique, for much of their elite status, both during colonialism and in the post-colonial context, is predicated on continuing ties with elites in Goa, Portugal and Angola, and even Brazil and South Africa.

To revitalise the potential of using the collection of life histories as a historical ethnographic method and an analytical tool is crucial, particularly when the researcher is faced with a dearth of written historical source materials, as in the case presented here. On the one hand, I adopt this methodology because it has thus far been proven fruitful for the particular case of undertaking research on historical periods in which there is a lack of extant sources owing to the vicissitudes of archival preservation over time (Subrahmanyam, 1995:9). On the other hand, I utilise life histories not simply as sources for the verification of history, but rather for their interpretive value (White, 1997:438).

Within anthropology, the 'life history' has been adopted as a popular methodology, starting in the 1970s. Vincent Crapanzano's *Tuhami: Portrait of a Moroccan* (1980) is groundbreaking in the sense that he further developed it as a research technique that had in many ways long been around anthropology in one way or another. In his study of an illiterate Moroccan Arab tile maker, Crapanzano (1980:xi) allows his subject to 'articulate his world and situate himself within it'. Subsequent generations of anthropologists have since relied on orally recorded life histories to access not only the past, but also memories and larger social patterns. Moreover, very often there is a disjuncture between historical and oral sources, as I have found to be the case for the Goans of Mozambique. Here, life histories take on even more importance for the writing of social history, as they attest and give shape to events and occurrences that have left no visible written records except perhaps as what I call 'ethnographic traces', particularly when faced, as I was, with the mortality of individuals who are keepers of unrecorded memories. This same approach also has much analytical value, particularly for historical anthropologists; a focus on people and personalities has the potential to provide more nuanced views of migration through very real voices and lived lives, grounded in specific contexts, as well as to act as a window onto larger patterns of culture, history and power. Moreover, a focus on the narrative shape of these life histories is also relevant; I looked for both the presences and absences in their testimonies as a way of accessing the multiple sources of their disquietude resulting from living in Mozambique.

Thus, in this chapter, it is not only 'landscapes of the sea' (Pearson, 2007:16) and history making in (and not of) the Indian Ocean region (2006:367), to follow historian Michael Pearson, that I am interested in exploring, but also how degrees and experiences of 'otherness' of a specific group of colonised individuals shifted in the act of migration from one Portuguese colony to another via the Indian Ocean – in this case between Goa and Mozambique during three different historical phases, the 1920s, the 1950s–60s and post-1975. This is a topic underdeveloped not only in the anthropology of empire and the anthropology of (colonial) elite literatures as evidenced above, but also in relation to histories of (colonial) migration and diasporic communities living within the Indian Ocean arena (19th–20th centuries). This is a topic that has recently been taken up in more depth by historian Sugata Bose (2006); his work in turn has invigorated Indian Ocean studies among a wide range of scholars and from varying disciplinary perspectives. Here I point to two specific case studies that are relevant to my own.

I first follow historian Thomas Metcalf who, in his recent book entitled *Imperial Connections*, makes a compelling argument for looking at 'webs of empire'; too often, he asserts, the history of a colony is written in isolation from its colonial neighbours – a historiography too often also inscribed in state archives – where in fact there was much movement both vertically and horizontally (Metcalf, 2007:9). Taking into account horizontal movements between colonies (and not just vertical movements between metropole and colony) thus allows us a window onto these alternative and lesser-known colonial narratives, experiences and subjectivities. As Metcalf argues for the case of connecting British India and British Africa through migration within the Indian Ocean region during the early 20th century, individual Indians caught up in this colonial matrix were able to imagine new identities for themselves in the African context; they conceived of themselves not merely as colonial subjects, but as 'imperial citizens' (Metcalf, 2007:2), an important distinction that allowed them the possibility of living outside the confines of rigid colonial categories of hierarchy. Metcalf's groundbreaking research opens up a space for my own, despite the fact that the Goan Mozambique case is very different from the British one owing to the distinctiveness of the Portuguese colonising experience.

It is also productive to turn to the writings of anthropologist Engseng Ho, who has developed the idea of 'local cosmopolitans' relative to a lesser-known and older diasporic community in the Indian Ocean region. I take his discussion of the Hadrami diaspora to suggest that some of his theoretical and methodological tools are applicable to the case of the Goans of Mozambique. Specifically, the analytical import of Ho's idea of 'local cosmopolitans' is situated in his very definition of them as 'persons who, while imbedded in local relations, also maintain connections with distant places. They thus articulate a relation between different geographical scales' (Ho, 2006:31). Ho sets up a useful analytic for looking at diasporic communities not only diachronically (as is the case with the Hadramis and the Goans of Mozambique), but also as less strictly defined by attachments to a homeland versus a host country; instead, local cosmopolitans escape this binary: they are motivated by travel and mobility, interpolating minimally between at least two different contexts and remaining 'itinerant across the oceanic space' (Ho, 2006:189). In other words, they are deeply local and transnational at the same time, and without necessarily being in conflict over these 'structures of feelings' (Williams, 1977). Ho's ideas are pertinent to the case at hand, for it became increasingly evident to me through the course of conducting fieldwork in Maputo that many of the Goans I interviewed were not only the product of much mobility among Goa, Portugal and Mozambique, but some had very little anxiety over being Goan, Indian, African, Mozambican and Portuguese. Instead, they embraced all and none of these categories, many without issue.

Ho also expands the corpus of source materials to access narratives of these historically dispersed diasporic communities. Instead of relying solely on archival materials that, for the case of the Hadramis, are scant, he productively and creatively turns to other source materials such as gravestones, textiles, biographies, genealogies, legal documents, poetry, novels and prayers (Ho, 2006:xxiii). While not all these source materials are available in the Mozambique case, his research productively suggests the potential of accessing historical narratives in more creative and, perhaps, personalised ways. For my own case study, again in the face of a paucity of enriched documentation, I have chosen 'life histories' as an analytical tool for accessing the experiences of Goan migration to Mozambique, including the shape of their biographical narratives. Moreover, it was this same life history approach that got me to the point of meeting Délia Maciel, who is engaged in writing her own life history as a Goan settler in Mozambique. Finally, Ho (2006:62) layers the historiographic with an ethnographic mode, adopting the perspectives of people now living in a specific place to access the history of its diasporic imaginings. It is this ethnographic perspective, one of developing the analytic of 'local cosmopolitans' and in relation to a very different history and context, that I adopt in my own ethnography of the Goan diasporic community of Maputo.

On longing and belonging

Migration has ambiguities of its own, based on what I would call the dialectics of 'belonging' and 'longing'. The theme of belonging opposes rootedness to uprootedness, establishment to marginality. The theme of longing harps on the desire for change and movement, but relates this to the enigma of arrival, which brings a similar desire to return to what one has left. These themes are often regarded as typically modern predicaments, but I am not so sure (Van der Veer, 1995:4).

Diaspora is of long duration (Ho, 2006:3).

I take my title for this section from diaspora theorist Peter van der Veer, whose theme of 'longing and belonging' is a fitting one in that it encapsulates, once again, a focus on the 'ambiguities of difference' of a specific migration process, as opposed to its certainties. Similarly, Van der Veer's development of 'longing and belonging' as a dialectical process over time allows me an analytical framework for getting at the sentiments of individual Goans living in Maputo, accessed through the prism of life histories. Finally, his focus on 'change and movement' as they are part of the diasporic experience over time and not just as a 'modern predicament' also echoes Ho's focus on travel, mobility and the 'long duration' of diaspora, thus reinforcing my viewpoint that the Goans of Maputo are best understood as 'local cosmopolitans' for whom acts of colonial migration shape, but do not necessarily determine post-colonial mobilities; i.e. they are often overlaid experiences that have everything to do with the history and itinerant character of Portuguese (de)colonisation (Gupta, 2007).

That the Goans of Mozambique are understudied is precisely because they are so well integrated into Mozambican society, as opposed to, for example, the Goan diasporas of the United States, Canada and the United Kingdom, where a wider disjuncture exists between the homeland and host country (Cahen et al., 2000:138). Sociological studies of Goan diasporas of (East) Africa are also extant, but are complicated by the fact that the Goans in this case were historically lumped together with other Asian and Indian migrants as 'stranger communities', or as 'the hyphen between Africans and Europeans' (Kuper, 1979:243), when in fact they were a distinct group with their own cultural patterns of migration, patterns that were very much imbricated in their history of colonial subjectivity under Portuguese rule. Jessica Kuper (1975:58) makes a case for the uniqueness and separateness of the Goan community living in 1970s Uganda: largely working-class clerks, cooks and tailors, these Goans regarded themselves as 'culturally European' rather than Indian. They also tended to see themselves as different from all other 'Asians'; as a result, they largely kept to themselves within Ugandan society and maintained strong ties with Goa, even in the face of its recent integration into the Indian nation state. This same idea of cultural distinctiveness will also come up in the Mozambican case, but in relation to a higher-status group of elite Goans (doctors and bankers), and with very unexpected and complicated effects. Thus, I undertake this study precisely because of how 'longing and belonging' are so very unusual in this particular diasporic case.

Empire builders, agency and the spirit of the times (1920s)

> Tropical doctors were best suited to treat tropical diseases among tropical peoples in tropical places (Bastos, 2005:27).

Since its inception in 1847, all the appointed directors of the Goa Medical School, a prestigious centre for teaching and learning medicine, were of Portuguese origin (Bastos, 2005:26).[52] When Rafael Pereira was appointed its first Goan director in the 1880s, he made the above statement in the context of urging other doctors of Goan or 'tropical' origin to emigrate to Portuguese Africa to help out with the larger Africa cause.[53] As Cristiana Bastos (2005) asserts in her case study of two Goan doctors – Arthur Gama and Germano Correia – who in fact did emigrate to the tropics of Mozambique during the late 19th century, these diasporic Goans occupied a peculiar and interesting position within the colonial hierarchy in Mozambique. She writes:

> Like the many Indo-Portuguese who served as colonial officers and doctors, Gama and Correia occupied an ambiguous, floating position in the hierarchies they described. Invited to participate in the inner circles of power and ideological formation, they were at the same time excluded from those circles as second-class citizens. As a group, they epitomized a feature of Portuguese colonialism: the production and segregation of particular groups that were allocated a key role in the colonial administration and at the same time banned from its upper echelons. Goan physicians illustrate the complex mutual constitution of colonizers and colonized, as the latter embrace the colonizers' political project and refine its ideology while serving as subordinate 'colonials', producing and reproducing from their limbo the racialized views of the world needed to govern empire (Bastos, 2005:25).

I quote Bastos in full here because she makes several key points when contextualising the Goans of Mozambique and their liminal position within the Portuguese colonial hierarchy. Even as they occupied an 'ambiguous floating position', they were alternately invited into the inner circles of power and purposely kept out. At the same time, as subordinate colonials, they promoted the ideology of colonialism and were part of its apparatus of colonial governmentality (Scott, 1995), a point reinforced by historian Sharmila Karnik (1998:99), who suggests that these Goan immigrants did in fact 'consolidate the administrative machinery of Portugal in Mozambique'. The viewpoints of Bastos and Karnik are thus extremely relevant for understanding how Goans functioned in colonial Mozambican society by providing a sense of (some of) their motivating factors for immigration not exclusive to its medical doctors. Perhaps Bastos's (2005:26) suggestion that these Goan physicians could be interpreted as 'colonial handmaidens' of a larger Portuguese system is potentially viable.

I first met Esmeralda, an anthropologist herself, on a sunny afternoon in Maputo. After meeting outside a well-marked popular grocery store, we walked to her apartment located on the sixth floor of a nondescript cement tower block. Ensconced in her apartment, surrounded by books and with her newborn daughter sleeping in a back room, she recounted the history of her father's migration to Mozambique from Goa for me.[54] Her father had been part of that same wave of Goan doctors who had come to work and live in Mozambique in the first half of the 20th century. Born in 1900 in Loutilim (Goa) to a Catholic Brahmin Portuguese-speaking family, he had chosen to go first to Portugal to continue his studies in medicine in the year 1920. After qualifying as a doctor in the metropole, he had worked in the north of the country before deciding to continue his studies in Paris. Newly married to a French woman, he arrived in Mozambique in 1928 to take up a prestigious medical post in Inhambane; according to Esmeralda, he was this region's first doctor. After his wife's sudden death five years later, he returned to Portugal to once again take up a post there. However, according to Esmeralda, by the 1950s he had found the 'Salazar culture' intolerable, so he returned to Mozambique, only now with his new Portuguese second wife. It was in Maputo that he created a life for himself; working as a medical doctor and producing a family of five children. Esmeralda recalled how her father, even though he did not feel part of the 'Goan community' in Maputo, went to the Goa Club regularly on Sundays to play chess.[55]

Fernandes, a father of two and married to a Portuguese Mozambican, recalled for me over coffee in his plant-filled sunny apartment, also located in a nondescript cement tower, but on the other side of town from Esmeralda's, how his Goan father came to Mozambique in 1927 at the age of 20.[56] He had been part of the colonial drive, the so-called 'spirit of the times', as a result of which a large wave of Goan men came to seek their fortunes and improve their economic situation in Africa (Fernandes, 2006:77). While many of these Goans were trained medical doctors, Fernandes' father was one of the many immigrants who had come to work as managers (*prazeiros*) of the landed estates located in the interior of Mozambique,[57] just as this had been the case for the fathers of Raul, Cesar and Filipe, three other Goan Mozambicans I met on this same visit to Maputo. This group of Goans were different from the upper-class privileged group that Esmeralda's father had intermingled with; instead, they were of largely middle-class standing, practising Catholics, both Portuguese and Konkani speaking, and with much closer familial ties to Goa. While Fernandes' father, after having established himself in Mozambique, returned to Goa in the 1950s to find a Goan wife who would be able and willing to live in Mozambique – once again, a typical pattern of diasporic communities – Raul's father had married the daughter of a close family friend also of Goan origin; not coincidentally, their respective families had known each other in Goa prior to emigration. Cesar's father, even though he returned to Goa regularly every four years (a practice also not uncommon for diasporic members) met and married a Mozambican-born Goan from Beira. Meanwhile, Filipe's father had followed the pattern set by Fernandes' father, of establishing himself in Mozambique before returning to Goa in the 1940s to find a wife. Interestingly, upon retirement, Filipe's father had chosen to return to Goa; the year was 1960, one year before Goa's decolonisation. However, finding a (suitable) wife was never as straightforward a process as this, for, as Filipe openly admitted to me, many of these same Goan men in the period between their arrival in Mozambique and their return to Goa to get married had lived with African-Mozambican women in relationships of concubinage, often producing children in the process. Typically, however, neither mother nor child was acknowledged after each man's return to Mozambique, Goan wife in tow. This was just one of the many ways of 'making empire respectable', to quote Ann Stoler (1989:635).

The story of Sandra's mother is a very different and perhaps unusual one. Sandra herself, in her eighties, had difficulties moving about, so I went to interview her in the family home that she shares with her daughter, Goan son-in-law and their children in a prosperous tree-lined avenue in Maputo not far from Fernandes' house. Interestingly, at the age of four her African-Mozambican mother had gone to Goa with a wealthy Goan family, which had employed her mother as the family servant. After living in Goa for 20 years, Sandra's mother returned to Mozambique at the age of 24 (roughly in the 1920s period); she first married another African who had also lived in Goa as the child of servants; as Sandra recalled to me, it was their love of the Konkani language and their shared experiences as Africans in Goa that brought them together. However, the marriage soon ended, producing no children during its short-lived tenure.[58] Her mother next met and married a Goan man, Sandra's father.

Sandra, having never visited Goa during her lifetime, but having seen Lisbon once, grew up speaking Konkani and Portuguese, and learning all the proper Goan dishes such as *sorpatel*[59] – Goan family recipes that had been passed down to her by her (African) mother. She herself married the son of a mixed African and Portuguese couple, producing a daughter, Carla, who was now married to Raul, whose father had also emigrated from Goa to Mozambique in the 1920s. Sandra's life history is so interesting because it reflects the other end of the spectrum from Esmeralda's, suggesting that there is no way to clearly categorise these histories of movement and mobility between Goa and Mozambique during the colonial period. At the same time, I believe the life histories of the parents of Esmeralda, Fernandes, Raul, Cesar, Filipe and Sandra all reflect the complicated diasporic histories that were created out of Portuguese colonisation, as well as individuals' differing ties to Goa, Portugal and Mozambique. Lastly, the telling of these life histories by their descendants (both sons and daughters) suggests a continuing interest in tracing genealogical pasts and an impulse to record history in the making on the part of this next generation of Goan Mozambicans.

Just as I would argue that Ho's analytic of the 'local cosmopolitan' is a productive one for characterising the Goan diaspora in Portuguese Mozambique, I would also reinforce Bastos's point that these Goans very much occupied 'ambiguous floating positions' within the colonial hierarchy and had the potential to go either way, as the cases of Esmeralda's father and Sandra herself suggest. That many Goan men of this generation chose to marry Goan women reinforces Bastos's (2005:32) point that this same 'floating position also risked being ranked lower than the members of his ethnic group considered proper'; hence the practice of abandoning one's African concubine and illegitimate children by the wayside in order to continue 'making empire respectable' (Stoler, 1989:635) through sexual unions and reproduction exclusively with Goans. Thus, even as the majority of them were working in the service of the state – they had been 'invited to build an empire', in the words of Fernandes – their respective individual ideological positionings within the empire were perhaps less clearly demarcated, a point that I take up in the next section, in which I look at the next generation of Goan Mozambicans, many of whom arrived during the period of Goa's decolonisation.

Goan decolonisation, liberation vs invasion, and neocolonialism (1950s–60s)

> The practice of ambivalence, interdependence, and hybridity was a necessity of the Portuguese colonial relation (De Sousa Santos, 2002:16).

> An appreciation of the fact of mobility itself attunes us to the narratives strung across the texts and to their slender threads across the ocean (Ho, 2006:29).

The period between the 1950s and 1960s also witnessed a phase of Goan migration to Mozambique, continuing a trend started in the 1920s. Thus, while many came as the 'wives' and 'children' of Goans already settled in Mozambique, as was the case for Filipe, who in 1954 at the age of 14 came with his mother to join his father, who had arrived 30 years earlier,[60] others arrived in the port city of Maputo for a very different set of ideological reasons having everything to do with Portuguese decolonisation in Goa. Specifically, in the period after India's independence from British colonial rule in 1947 and its violent partition into the Indian and Pakistani nation states, the 'Goa question' continually loomed on the horizon (Gupta, 1997); just as the French had Pondicherry, the Portuguese had Goa and Daman and Diu, both functioning as 'colonial enclaves' amid a larger British India and alongside several princely states. For newly elected Indian Prime Minister Nehru, however, the 'Goa question' was first put on the back burner in order to deal with what were considered more pressing issues, namely the bloody aftermath of partition. It was only in 1954, after the French peacefully handed over Pondicherry of their own volition that Goa's colonial future became a more pressing issue both within India and on the international scene (Gupta, 1997). In the period, from 1954 until Indian troops took Goa by force from Portugal in 1961 (a moment regarded alternately as a 'liberation' or 'invasion' by many Portuguese and Goans alike),[61] a number of Goans, realising – or, rather, foreseeing – the inevitable (i.e. that Goa would become part of India), chose emigration to another Portuguese colony – in this case Mozambique – for reasons of culture, language and religion. Thus, while many Goans located both inside and outside of Goa itself had very strong political views regarding the enclave's future, some vehemently refusing to believe that it could possibly be integrated into India, others living in Goa at the time saw this as a real likelihood and chose emigration as a direct response.

Délia's life very much reflects this tumultuous period in Goa's history. I had been told earlier that I had to meet Délia, for she was considered a real source on 'all things Goan' by many of my other Goan informants. An elderly lady who had just turned 80, she agreed to meet me in the early evening at her home, shortly after her afternoon nap.[62] As she recounted the story of her life to me, I realised that she was one of the few connecting – to return to my initial quote at the outset of this section – 'slender threads across the ocean' (Ho, 2006:29) through her writing. It turned out that she had in fact written and published her own life history, entitled *Fragmentos da Minha Vida* (*Fragments of My Life*) in 2003.[63] As we sat at her Indo-Portuguese-style wooden dining-room table sipping coffee, Délia stressed to me that she felt that it was extremely important to record this unwritten history for the other Goans living in Maputo in order to give future generations of Goans a better sense of 'community' (Ho, 2006:94). Délia herself was born in Goa in 1927 in a small *aldeia* (village), where her parents had been teachers in a Portuguese-speaking primary school. At this point in our interview, she recounted an incident from her childhood that had indelibly marked her, and which made an impression on me too. As a small child, not more than ten years old, she had been walking with her parents through the streets of Panjim, the capital of Portuguese India at the time. They had walked past what she only realised afterwards was a demonstration protesting against British colonial rule in India. She innocently started to join in, raising her right arm and crying out '*Jai Hind*' (Victory to India), the popular slogan that captured the hearts and minds of most Gandhi-inspired Indians fighting for self-rule. Instead of joining in, Délia's parents quickly slapped her, saying that her actions would get all of them into trouble if she did not stop participating immediately. I found her story remarkable, both at the time of its telling and now in the writing of this chapter, as an 'ethnographic trace' suggesting not only that palpable tensions were obviously in the air surrounding Indian independence, but also showing the extent to which Goa was affected during these tumultuous times in British India. Specifically, Délia's story signifies the ways in which Goans as a group were deeply divided (and sometimes ambivalent) in their state loyalties (Portugal vs India) on the one hand, and the ways in which (British) India's future was so surprisingly closely monitored by the Portuguese as perhaps setting a precedent for their own colonies' future, on the other hand. Similar points and positionings will be echoed in the testimonies of other Goan Mozambicans.

Délia's story also recounts the innocence of a child and the inculcation of moral values by parents. By 1954 the situation had worsened in Goa, at least for those who supported Portugal's continued colonial hold. Délia decided to follow in the footsteps of her two elder brothers – one of whom had been trained as a doctor at the same Goa Medical School decribed earlier – by emigrating to Mozambique. Délia arrived by boat in the port city of Maputo at the age of 26, a degree in nursing in hand. By 1960, on the eve of Goa's 'independence',[64] she had met and married a Goan Mozambican who had been born in Mozambique and who was in banking, a popular middle-class profession among many Goans of Maputo,[65] eventually setting up house in Maputo and producing four daughters. Next she recounted memories of Goans being 'poorly treated' by the Portuguese in Mozambique, although she could not recall a particular incident for me. At this point in the retelling of her life history, Délia paused to mention that if she had been single at the time of Goa's 'liberation' (her word choice), she would have definitely returned to her homeland, since her parents were in Goa and her ties to the enclave remained, while she was less connected to Mozambique. This last detail is a telling one, for it suggests the potential of migration both as a form of neocolonialism and as an (ideological) form of resistance, even when, as in the latter case, it was not put into practice by Délia.

The story of Edith, who, like Délia, came to Mozambique as a young woman, will by now be a familiar one;[66] however, there are 'ethnographic traces' that at the same time open up different research questions and point to different Goan genealogies and ideologies. Edith was 27 when she first arrived in Mozambique. The year was 1964, three years after Goa's integration into the Indian nation state. As she remarked to me during our very brief interview amid her painting-filled living room, she remembered Goa's 'invasion' (her word choice) by India very well, calling it a 'tragic' event in Goa's history. While her reasons for emigrating to Mozambique were never explicitly stated, I got the sense that the tragedy of Goa had much to do with her choice to emigrate. After living in the north of Mozambique for a period of 14 months, she left for Portugal, where she attended art school in Lisbon. It was here that she experienced racism first hand. She recounted an incident that had taken place early on in her schooling and that affected her quite deeply at the time. Identified derisively as 'Indian' in school (interestingly, her Goan-ness was a lost point to her largely ignorant art classmates), her immediate response had been to defend India, saying that it had an older civilisation than Portugal itself. One year later (1967) she returned to Mozambique. Very soon afterwards she met and married a Goan Mozambican, produced three sons, got involved in Mozambique's anti-colonial movement, and continued to live between Portugal and Mozambique. As Edith recounted her life story, I could not help but notice that her apartment was a shrine to Lusophone art, and she had interspersed many of her own beautiful pieces of artwork with more famous works by largely Indo-Portuguese and Afro-Portuguese artists. Interestingly, today Edith does not consider herself exclusively Goan, Mozambican or Portuguese, even though her base is Maputo. Instead, she considers herself a 'citizen of the world' with deep attachments to three continents: India, Africa and Europe. I ended my interview with this 'local cosmopolitan' with a tour of her apartment-cum-art-gallery, during which Edith told me an alternative life history through her paintings.

My interviews with both Délia and Edith suggest that one's ideological positioning often develops in relation to specific contexts and life experiences. Moreover, both their testimonies suggest that the cultural effects of colonisation do not simply end with physical decolonisation (Stoler & Cooper, 1997:33); instead, they live on and give birth to overlapping and sometimes contradictory practices (migration) and ideologies (neocolonialism) in the post-colonial, sometimes even within one individual. Lastly, the telling of their life histories on the part of Délia and Edith also reveals an impulse to record traces of the past that have gone largely unrecorded, be it through writing a personal memoir or creating a work of art through painting.

I end my discussion in this section by mentioning my conversation with Carla, Délia's daughter, whom I met quite by accident, as she had just arrived home as I was leaving her mother's apartment. Newly arrived from the United States after having completed a PhD in Linguistics, she had come 'home' for a visit, her future location uncertain.[67] We ended up talking informally for 20 minutes, comparing experiences of living in the United States, discussing the advantages (and disadvantages) of the American PhD system, and what it was like returning to Maputo after living in the United States for such a long time. Like mother like daughter, for Carla was a historian in her own right, giving me insights into the path of her ancestors and migration to Mozambique more generally. As she pointed out to me, the period during which her mother came to Mozambique – the 1950s – also witnessed the arrival of a large number of Portuguese peasants in the African colonies (Mozambique and Angola) as part of a wider state-sponsored campaign to enlarge the number of 'white' Europeans living in its overseas colonies. That they were simultaneously escaping (post-Second World War) poverty and dictatorial Salazarism only reinforced the potential of the African colonies as sites for immigration and improved living conditions. Interestingly, such had been the case for the parents of (Portuguese-Mozambican) Maria, who was married to the same Fernandes of earlier discussions and who will appear again in the next section on Mozambican independence.[68] That the majority of these peasants, according to Carla Maciel, were illiterate in comparison to the large number of Goan immigrants who were highly educated and skilled was not lost on the Portuguese colonial administration of Mozambique. They in turn purposely kept individual Goans apart, isolating them on arrival from one another in order to prevent the development of a politicised Goan community that could potentially resist colonialism and allow Mozambique to go the way of Goa.[69]

Mozambican independence: Chaos and dreams (1975)

They had had enough of the country, which was supposed to be the promised land but had brought them disenchantment and abasement. They said farewell to their African homes, with mixed despair and rage, sorrow and impotence, with the feeling of leaving for ever. All they wanted was to get out with their lives and to take their possessions with them (Kapuscinksi, 1987:13).

Historian Fred Cooper pinpoints the difficulties of tracing distinct patterns of decolonisation. He writes:

Patterns of decolonization are particularly difficult to unravel because we know the end point: the emergence of the independent state from colonial rule. It is tempting to read the history of the period from 1945 to 1960 [1975 in this case] as the inevitable triumph of nationalism and to see in each social movement taking placing within a colony – be it by peasants, by women, by workers, or by religious groups – another piece to be integrated into the coming together of the nation. What is lost in such a reading are the ways in which different groups within colonies mobilised for concrete ends and used as well as opposed the institutions of the colonial state and the niches opened up in the clash of new and old structures. Whether such efforts fed into the attempts of nationalist parties to build anti-colonial coalitions needs to be *investigated, not assumed* (Cooper, 1997:406; emphasis added).

This research is one such attempt to investigate how a specific diasporic group responded in very different ways to decolonisation, some reinforcing ideologies of colonialism through migration to the metropole, others opening up niches for themselves by aligning themselves with the newly elected authority, even as they faced the future with a sense of disquiet.

'It was chaos, but we had such dreams.'[70] This is the way Fernandes described the tumultuous events surrounding Mozambique's independence from Portuguese colonial rule in 1975. We were sitting in his apartment, talking over a cup of coffee, with Fernandes's Portuguese-Mozambican wife, Maria, by his side. They both described how it felt, as young Mozambicans barely 20 years old at the time, to get caught up in the politics of independence. They remembered feeling like they had a purpose, a reason for staying, although for Maria, upon reflection, it had been a more difficult choice to make, given that the rest of her family had chosen to emigrate to Portugal as a direct result of Mozambican decolonisation. For Fernandes, however, it had been a far easier decision to stay, as the majority of his family had remained in Maputo after colonial independence. In explaining his position within Mozambican society both currently and in the past, he poignantly described how he continued to feel 'Portuguese without a concept of race'. Perhaps Fernandes and Maria together, in some sense, represent a hopeful post-colonial Mozambique, with all its complicated histories of migration.

For other Goans living in Mozambique, the choice to stay or leave was one informed less by politics and more by age. As many of the Goans I spoke to from this 'society of the absent' (Ho, 2006:19) – including Fernandes – informed me, those who left consisted largely of elderly Goans, the majority of them leaving Maputo to retire (and in some sense die) in Portugal, a country and culture that for some was just as familiar as Mozambique, for others less so. Interestingly, and this was a point confirmed by my informants, fewer Goans chose to return to their so-called 'homeland', but perhaps this makes sense, given that many were even further displaced from it than from Portugal. Délia, whom I wrote about earlier, was one of the many Goans who chose to stay in Mozambique in the aftermath of 1975. She acutely described the situation for me, suggesting that those who left did so out of 'fear', whereas for those who stayed (including herself) it was a choice made out of 'strength' – a commitment to deal with the unknown and the 'new' Mozambique. Even as Délia perhaps oversimplifies the decision to stay or go by individual Goans by eliding age, class, race and gender politics – i.e. by removing these crucial factors from the decision-making process – the pride with which she made this declaration suggests the resoluteness of many Goans like herself who committed themselves to life in post-colonial Mozambique. Interestingly, one of the same brothers, whose path she had followed as a young woman by emigrating from Goa in the 1950s, had decided to emigrate from Mozambique in 1975 to nearby Angola (repeating, once again, the pattern of migration as a response to decolonisation) even as it too was experiencing its own chaotic decolonisation from Portuguese colonial rule.[71]

Other Goan Mozambicans, including Raul described earlier, explained to me that the divide between those who stayed and those who left had everything to do with race and class patterns of marriage. Simply put, if you were Goan and married to a Portuguese, then you undoubtedly left. If you were a Goan married to an African Mozambican, you more than likely stayed. Raul made this statement based on his own life experience, for he, a Mozambican-born Goan, and his wife Carla, who was of mixed Portuguese, African and Goan parentage, had actively decided to stay in Maputo for these very ideological and practical reasons.[72] Here it is important to reinforce sociologist Boaventura de Sousa Santos's (2002:16) point that the operation of class politics (and their racial configurations) in post-colonial societies is a topic that needs more research. The same Fernandes mentioned earlier echoed Raul's point, suggesting that decolonisation created even more serious cleavages within families, based on marriage patterns once again.[73] More often than not, older generations would choose to emigrate, leaving behind the next generation of Goan Mozambicans; however, in some extreme cases a set of Goan parents would leave, cutting off all ties with their host country and purposely not recognising the (impending) marriages of their children to African Mozambicans. According to my informants, this would not just happen between parent and child, but also among siblings. In other words, 'race' was always a fraught (generational) category for Goans caught between Portuguese and African Mozambicans. Finally, that the discourse of race became the pivotal point around which their personal narratives coalesced is also telling and confirms once again the 'ambiguous floating position' (Bastos, 2005:25) that these Goan settlers continue to occupy in post-colonial Mozambique.

Of course, these generalisations do not necessarily hold for all Goans; not only the experience of Goan-Mozambican Fernandes and his

Portuguese-Mozambican wife, but also that of Cesar and his Portuguese wife are cases in point: politics trumped race in their decision to stay in Maputo after decolonisation.[74] Moreover, the case of Esmeralda's parents is an interesting one, as it suggests that ideological divides existed within families, even between husband and wife. With Mozambican independence in 1975, it had been her elderly Goan father who had wanted to take the family and return to Portugal, whereas her much younger Portuguese mother had wanted to stay out of a political commitment to see Mozambique through its political transition. In the end, as Esmeralda recounted to me, her father died shortly afterwards in Maputo, 'a sad and broken man' who had lost his fortune from Mozambican nationalisation.[75] Esmeralda's mother quietly returned to Portugal after the start of Mozambique's civil war and still lives there today.[76] Of course, other Goans, like Edith, whom I discussed in an earlier section, chose to stay out of a political commitment to Mozambican independence. While she had been living in Portugal during Mozambique's moment of independence, she returned to Maputo with her family soon thereafter in 1983. Her husband had been actively involved in Mozambique's post-independence politics, tragically dying for his politics only three years later. Just as Edith's apartment had been a shrine to her art, it was also a shrine to her late husband, and thus to the political history of Mozambique.[77]

Lastly, it is important to contextualise all these migrations and movements within the context of Mozambique's political situation on the eve of decolonisation. Here I suggest that Goans occupied a position of 'disquiet', to return to the opening theme of this chapter; i.e. they were very much caught between the outgoing Portuguese colonial administration and the incoming Mozambican government. On the one hand, the Goans were never forcibly told to leave by the Portuguese in 1975; instead, they were given incentives to emigrate to Portugal in a bid to prove that Mozambique was incapable of self-rule, and interestingly, in much the same way that they had earlier been given incentives to move to Portuguese Africa in a bid to help out with the 'colonial cause'. However, just as some had been embittered on the eve of Goa's decolonisation, so too were they now on the eve of Mozambique's.[78] On the African side, the incoming post-independence government promoted a 'go back to Goa' slogan, telling them to return to where they had come from, suggesting that they had no place in the new Mozambique; it was now an 'Africa for Africans' situation. Interestingly, however, even as the newly elected government made the claim that Goans had no place in post-colonial Mozambique, they saw each Goan migration to Portugal as confirming their betrayal and collusion (as a group) with the prior Portuguese colonial government.[79] In some sense, the Goans were used as pawns in a large game of chess, each side claiming them as their own, or at the very least as being closely aligned with them. A game in which the details of each move were eventually lost in the political struggles of decolonisation and post-colonial transition. It is appropriate to end this section with Ho's point that this inability to situate oneself within new post-colonial states was not isolated to the cases of the Hadrami or the Goans; rather, it was a worldwide phenomenon. He writes:

> In the aftermath of decolonization, the identification of the new states with single nations made the creole transnational commitments of diasporic communities untenable. The new independent nation states broke the diasporas straddling them into two: citizens and aliens (Ho, 2006:305).

In other words, individual members of these creole, transnational diasporic settler communities had to make difficult choices, choices that had everything to do with history, culture and power.

Conclusion: The disquieting of history

If we think about diaspora at its etymological level as a 'scattering of seed' (Ho, 2006:xxiii), then the Goans of Mozambique are one such example. They scattered their seed(s) in multiple directions (Mozambique, Goa, Portugal) and at different moments in time (1920s, 1950s–60s, post-1975), creating diasporic communities with numerous ties elsewhere (Goa, India, Portugal, Angola, Mozambique, United States, etc.) along the way. By employing Thomas Metcalf's concept of 'webs of empire' and Engseng Ho's analytic of 'local cosmopolitanism' to understand the Goan diaspora in Maputo as part of a larger Indian Ocean narrative, we are not only allowed access to their complicated life histories and, for some, fractured identities, but also to rethink colonial and post-colonial migrations as they are tied to interconnected decolonisation experiences. Moreover, this case study, one that explicitly focusses on the 'ambiguities of difference', opens up a space for looking at the unexpected ways in which (colonial) categories of race and culture shift in the act of migration, with varying results in the post-colonial world. For the next generation of Goan Mozambicans, however, it will be a very different story, albeit one of both continuity and change.

Thus, while some of the children of this generation of Goan Mozambicans born after independence are following in the footsteps of their ancestors by emigrating to Portugal, others are renewing attachments to old places (Goa and Portugal) and/or creating attachments to new ones (South Africa, the United Kingdom, Brazil, Macau), while still other 'local cosmopolitans' are choosing to remain in Maputo, embracing their Goanness, Portugueseness and Mozambicanness simultaneously.[80]

I leave the reader with the 'disquieting' reflections of Paula, a Goan Mozambican born on the eve of Mozambique's independence, at present living in Maputo. She writes:

> I've never had enough to travel to Goa in order to know what belongs to me from that past … I'm thinking about write [sic] a story for a film on my family and some other family stories that cross the oceans and look after who they are … and I think I'm closer to a kind [of] answer, that moves me from the concept of not really having rotes [sic] to a place where I'm feeling comfortable with who I am, no matter from where it cames [sic].[81]

5

Chapter

Monty ... Meets Gandhi ... Meets Mandela: The Dilemma of Non-violent Resisters in South Africa, 1940–60

Goolam Vahed

> The time for personal contact with the great leader had now arrived. I
> [flew] to Wardha with Dadoo in order to receive more precise guidance in
> regard to future plans .... To be with Mahatma Gandhi was like the vision
> of a dream. I was not going to meet a stranger. His teachings had become
> part and parcel of my life. His autobiography had been my Bible, and in
> my leisure time I have been reading it over and over again .... Gandhiji was
> sitting cross-legged with the spinning wheel in front of him. We had come
> to meet the Father of the Indian Nation, and the welcome we received was
> naturally that of a dear father to his affectionate children. We will never
> forget the warm smile which lighted upon both of us – the smile of the
> hero we admired for thirty years. We gave him an account of the progress
> of the struggle, and were quite surprised to find that, in the midst of his
> multifarious activities, he had found time to keep in touch with the latest
> developments of our satyagraha movement .... Throughout our talk he kept
> on emphasising the central lesson of the satyagraha movement. He asked
> us always to remember that non-cooperation was not the weapon of those
> who found a shelter in a negative attitude of life; it was a most positive
> action leading straight to success if the principles were not compromised
> on the way. India recovered her freedom by clinging to the principles of non-
> violence. South African Indians, he said, would see the milky way if they
> followed the example of the mother country. He also advised patience.
> Success never comes in a flood, he said (Shukla, 1951).

Doctor G. M. 'Monty' Naicker's recollection of this meeting in April 1947
underscores his reverence for Mahatma Gandhi. Gandhi did not (re)appear
from nowhere. The new inheritors of the Natal Indian Congress (NIC) and
Transvaal Indian Congress (TIC) held Gandhi in the highest esteem and
paid homage to him at every opportunity. In some ways this marked a shift
from the 1930s, when the agents-general held sway in local politics and the
'moderates' held the leadership of the NIC and TIC.

This chapter focusses on Monty, as he was affectionately referred to by
contemporaries, as a Gandhian whose commitment to non-violent resistance

came to the fore during the campaign of 1946–48 in Natal. Monty was deeply influenced by Gandhi, whose philosophy of non-violent resistance shaped his thinking in the crucial decades of the mid-20th century when South Africans were debating how to overturn segregation and apartheid, a system predicated on and backed up by the use of state-sponsored violence.

Monty's ideas did find resonance in the early joint campaigns of the Indian Congresses and the African National Congress (ANC). But as the 1950s moved into the early 1960s, Monty had to confront the fact that the movement that he thought best exemplified Gandhian ideals was contemplating a new direction – a turn to violence. Many of Monty's closest comrades in the NIC were adamant that this was the way to go. Monty's adherence to non-violent resistance and the dilemma facing activists are the main substance of this chapter. The focus is on two key moments, the Passive Resistance Campaign of 1946–48 and debates around the ANC's turn to armed struggle in 1960.

Edinburgh

Monty Naicker was born in Durban in 1910, the year the Union of South Africa was established, signalling the coming together of 'old foes', the Afrikaner and British, in a common quest to ensure continuing white dominance on the southern tip of Africa. Monty was the son of P. G. Naicker, a fruit exporter and stallholder at the Indian market. He attended Marine College in Leopold Street and proceeded in 1927 to study medicine at Edinburgh University, where his contemporaries included two other 'coolie doctors', Yusuf Dadoo and Keseval Goonam (see Goonam, 1992). Their lives were to intersect not through their medicine, but through the interstices of political confrontation, all three cutting their teeth in the Passive Resistance Campaign of 1946–48.

Monty would not have anticipated the profound effect life in Edinburgh would have on him. It was there that he rubbed shoulders with the anti-imperialist fighters of India. He joined the Edinburgh Indian Association. Regular debates and lectures suggest that this organisation was also a hotbed of Indian nationalist and anti-imperialist agitation. A slew of speakers made their way through its doors, while regular discussions were held about the unfolding struggle against the British Raj in India. Doctor Goonam (1992:42), in her autobiography, mentions the visit of Srinivasa Sastri, who:

was very unpopular among Indian students and became even more so when he came to Edinburgh to receive the freedom of the city at a time when thousands of Indian freedom fighters languished in British jails. What were his views on British Home Rule for India, they heckled.

Marie

Monty returned to South Africa in 1934. Two years later he married Marie Appavoo from the Eastern Cape, whose two brothers, Shunmugam and Nadaraj, were Monty's contemporaries at Edinburgh. Even as Monty was establishing his practice and becoming domesticated, political divisions were continuing to fester. In Natal, the NIC and the Colonial Born and Settlers Indian Association amalgamated into the Natal Indian Association (NIA) in October 1939. While the majority of the executive were old moderates, the likes of Monty, Cassim Amra, George Ponnen, H. A. Naidoo and George Singh had strong roots among the Indian working classes and formed the (Natal) Nationalist Bloc within the NIA, which would later coalesce into the Anti-Segregation Committee.

Monty made his entry into local politics in 1940, as I. C. Meer (2002:47) recalls:

> On 11 February 1940, Dr. Naicker made ... his maiden speech in a packed City Hall. He took his stand clearly and forcefully against non-Europeans supporting the war, and vigorously attacked the NIA leadership for collaborating with the white authorities to enforce voluntary segregation on Indians.

Monty was 30 when he made this intervention. But it was in a sense a culmination of some five years of integrating himself back into the city of his birth. Important impulses in the development of progressive ideas were sprouting in the Indian quarter of the city. Pre-eminent was the Liberal Study Group (LSG), an important avenue to radicalise middle-class Indians. Monty and Doctor Goonam both joined the LSG, founded in 1937 by trade unionists and communists such as H. A. Naidoo, George Ponnen, Dawood Seedat, Cassim Amra, A. K. M. Docrat, P. M. Harry, Wilson Cele and I. C. Meer. The LSG held classes in English, political economy and public speaking. They discussed issues such as 'passive resistance', 'non-Europeans and the war', the socialisation of medicine, and the international situation (*Call*, February 1940), and laid the foundation for the political beliefs and actions of many.

Monty takes charge

By the late 1930s access to urban space in Durban was a contested issue. Africans with a precarious toehold in the city hugged the outer expanses, in particular Cato Manor. The ramifications of this 'squeezing' were to have dramatic and tragic consequences at the end of the 1940s. For the moment, though, the white city barons were most concerned about what came to be known as 'Indian penetration' of white areas. The sexual innuendo that could be read from this wording probably lent weight to the mounting hysteria. The Lawrence Committee, which included a number of Indians, was appointed in February 1940 to talk (Indian) purchasers out of transactions (*Call*, July 1940). Radicals tried to reverse this at a mass meeting on 9 June 1940, but failed, resulting in Nationalist Bloc members such as Monty, Cassim Amra, 'Beaver' Timol, George Ponnen, H. A. Naidoo and Manilal Gandhi being expelled from the NIA (*Call*, July 1940). Whites continued to agitate for legal segregation, even though the Broome Commission of 1940 concluded that there was no evidence that Indians were 'overrunning' whites. The Second Broome Commission was appointed in February 1943 and its report, published on 6 April 1943, led to the Trading and Occupation of Land Restriction Act of April 1943, which banned white–Indian property transactions in Durban for three years. It was called the 'Pegging Act', because the intention was to 'peg' Indian land ownership and occupation until further measures were introduced (Bagwandeen, 1991:50–57). Growing segregationist practices 'helped define the boundaries of identification between communities and also gave rise to oppositional political practices' (Raman, 2006:194).

The Nationalist Bloc saw this as the first step to racial segregation, and Monty, George Ponnen, Dawood Seedat, Billy Peters and M. D. Naidoo (re)joined the NIC executive to present a united front. The fragile unity collapsed when moderates agreed to the Pretoria Agreement of 19 April 1944 (Bagwandeen, 1991:142), which established a board of two Indians and three whites to license the purchase of property by members of a different racial group. Voluntary segregation (Lloyd, 1991) was the last straw for radicals, who formed the Anti-Segregation Council (ASC) in April 1944 under Monty's presidency. This was a broad front of intellectuals; trade unions; and sports, cultural, youth and farmers' associations that decided to work from within the NIC to effect change (Bagwandeen, 1991:142). The ASC hosted a conference on 6 May 1944 at which 29 organisations rejected the Pretoria Agreement and, beginning with a rally at Red Square, set about mobilising the masses. The ASC threw its resources into raising consciousness about the 'betrayal' in Pretoria and challenging the moderates (*The Guardian*, 14 July 1945). In the first three months of 1945, 31 meetings were held and the NIC's registered membership increased from 3,000 to 22,000 (*The Leader*, 12 January 1946). Most of these were members of trade unions. Workers came to form the core constituency of the political leadership.

The NIC's annual election was scheduled for 3 March 1945. The old guard under A. I. Kajee and P. R. Pather continued to delay the election until a frustrated Monty, B. T. Chetty and A. K. M. Docrat got a court order that elections be held by 22 October (*Indian Views*, 19 September 1945). Most of the office bearers resigned from the NIC (*The Leader*, 20 October 1945) and all 46 nominees of the ASC were elected to the executive of the NIC. Monty was president and Doctor Goonam vice-president – the first woman to hold an executive position (Roux, 1966:360). When Monty got up to address the animated masses at Curries Fountain, alongside him was a hybrid of communists, Gandhians and liberals. Monty's acceptance speech took a more decisive bent as he called for the unconditional repeal of the Pegging Act; the vetoing of the Natal Housing Ordinance; the rejection of residential zoning; the removal of the provincial barriers, which were a stigma on Indians; adult suffrage; and free education for Indian children up to Junior Certificate (*The Leader*, 27 October 1945).[82]

Passive Resistance Campaign, 1946–48

The first step was a meeting with South African Prime Minister Jan Smuts on 9 November 1945. There was great optimism, borne of their confidence to make a coherent argument and the fact that Smuts may have been keen to maintain his growing reputation as an international statesman.[83] The meeting proved an initiation into the hardball of politics, as Smuts made no concessions (*Indian Views*, 14 November 1945). In fact, with the Pegging Act due to expire in March 1946, Smuts announced in parliament on 21 January 1946 that the government would introduce the Asiatic Land Tenure and Indian Representation Act to regulate the occupation of fixed property by Indians. During March the NIC agreed to embark on passive resistance and the Passive Resistance Council (PRC) was formed (*The Leader*, 6 April

1946, in Cachalia, 1981:45). The day of 13 June 1946 was designated as Hartal Day to mark the start of the campaign. Monty's diary entry read:

> 13 June: Hartal Day. After 2:00 pm, 100% closed shop. Miss Asvat, Miss Chellan, Miss Nayager, Mrs Patel, Zora Bayat, and Mrs Pahad from Johannesburg; 5:30 pm march. 20,000 present [Red Square]. After march, left at camp. Police nearly used force.

Monty gave a powerful 20-minute speech at the rally. I. C. Meer (2002:95) recalls that he was 'unusually charged that afternoon, and the crowd cheered enthusiastically'. The historic mass meeting culminated in a great procession from Red Square to the corner of Gale Street and Umbilo Road. Under Monty's leadership, 18 passive resisters (including seven women) pitched tents on vacant municipal land in defiance of the Ghetto Act. Monty and Dadoo blamed compromise, 'a policy which has enabled the Government to introduce measure after measure of racially discriminative legislation', for the deterioration in the position of Indians.[84]

One problem that resisters faced was the violence of what they called white thugs. The Reverend Michael Scott, one of the few whites to join the campaign, provided an eyewitness account of the actions of white thugs at the Gale Street camp:

> Groups of European youths dressed in sports kit ... gathered in two's and three's on the opposite side of the plot to where we were standing .... Suddenly a whistle blew, and with shouts and catcalls the whole formation charged and bore down upon the little group of resisters who were standing back-to-back so as to face in all directions .... With their fists they struck the Indians in the face and about the body. No one retaliated but some tried to duck or ward off blows before falling down. On the ground they were kicked (Troup, 1950:128–29).

Monty recorded these events in his diary:

> 14 June: Quiet day. Three Europeans tried to damage tent. Applied Gandhian teachings successfully.
> 15 June: Same thing applied in the evening. Wild rumours about town. Met Dadoo at 10:00 am at Aerodrome.

16 June: 30 Europeans (organized) pulled the tents and dragged it away. This roused the determination of volunteers to unite and struggle; 11:00 pm put tent up again.

17 June: 5:30 pm meeting to appeal for non-violence and guards. 8:00 pm 150 Europeans expected and action; Cordon of passive resisters formed. Used women around outfield; 12 passive resisters replace tent.

18 June: Dadoo left for Johannesburg. 300 European and 500 Indians assembled on East side of camp. Only the leaders in camp. Having sent women volunteers to the footpath, Europeans brought women to molest our women. Very tense situation. Teach courage.

19 June: At appeal of Major Coetzee and Keevee decided to remove leaders from 5:30 pm to 10:00 pm and we decided to appeal to Indian supporters to keep away from camp for the period. 8:00 Europeans assembled. Completely out of control. One car burnt. One other car set light. Wife in same car. The few Indians present provoked and some badly assaulted – slept outside (no camp put up, was early in the morning – very cold). The ground. Asvat, Bhaba. Showed courage vindicated.

20 June: Today at 2:00 pm met European sympathizers – Satchel, Wormington, Paul Sykes. They considering forming an organization.

21 June: Last night, as the previous night, Europeans intent on assaulting us. Again cordoned. Isolated Indians hit and cars stoned. Ultimatum by Deputy-Commissioner Lt. Colonel Booysen to quit camp or charge for inciting public violence – refused. Cable from Tata and £100 from Henderson from Ireland who deeply sympathetic.

On 21 June Monty and the resisters were finally arrested for 'trespassing'. They were found guilty, but cautioned and discharged. They returned to the Gale Street camp, because they wanted to be imprisoned. They were again charged with 'trespassing' and the magistrate passed a suspended sentence of seven days' hard labour. Undeterred, the resisters made their way back to Gale Street and occupied the camp once more:

22 June: 7:30 pm District Police Johnson gave us notice to quit ground or else be persecuted for trespassing. Refused – were arrested and taken in to jail. One batch remained till 9:00 pm at B Court. M. D. and I left charge office at 12:00 am. (Tore all Edicts at 8:45.)

23 June: Went to camp at 4:50 in the afternoon. 5:30 arrested and taken to charge office. Released and set to appear in court at 9:00 am next day.

24 June: Went to court at 9:00 am. Great interest by Indian people. Two of the thugs present to observe. M. D. and myself asked to appear on the 1st July. The rest cautioned. Last evening the thugs really got going. 2nd batch released. 3rd batch Joshi and A[unclear] laid out unconscious. Spirit untainted. We were released at 1:30 am. Went to office. A[unclear], myself and M. O. decided to go in the next batch. Sympathisers begged us not to go as thugs still present in large numbers to keep us up. We went and were arrested immediately. Court at 9:00 am. Charged. Rowdy mass weekly. Enthusiastic. Money coming in. Went to camp.

26 June: Rowdy and Europeans great. Act read and arrested. Spent up till 2:30 in charge office, then in the cell. Condition very hard. Court on Tuesday – seven days hard labour suspended for three months.

27 June: Dadoo and next batch of fifty arrested. Appeared on Wednesday. Case remanded till Thursday.

28 June: Led batch with few more to occupy the land tonight. Expect to be imprisoned for long time. Sentence: six months hard labour.

For Gandhi, the aim of *satyagraha* was to eliminate the hostility of an opponent without harming that opponent. Gandhi contrasted *satyagraha* (holding on to truth) with *duragraha* (holding on by force), as in protest, which aimed to harass rather than enlighten opponents. Gandhi (1967) writes that 'if we want to cultivate a true spirit of democracy, we cannot afford to be intolerant. Intolerance betrays want of faith in one's cause'. Gandhi saw suffering as a means to a just society. Non-cooperation was a means to secure the cooperation of the opponent consistently with truth and justice (Gandhi, 1920).

The glimpses that we get of the attacks by whites and the preparedness of Monty and fellow resisters to endure those attacks point to these lessons having been absorbed. Its effectiveness in 'enlightening' whites was debatable, however.

When Monty and the resisters occupied the camp for a third time, they were sentenced to five months' imprisonment, which Monty served in Newcastle and Pietermaritzburg. After his release on 16 November 1946 Monty wrote of his prison experience:

When I was locked up in the prison of Newcastle, I spent my time reading *My Experiments with Truth*. I had read this book many times before, but inside the prison walls the words came to have a different meaning for me. It was in Newcastle that he [Gandhi] started his epic march with thousands of men, women and children; and somehow I felt that I too was in the crowd that marched past across the Transvaal border in serried ranks. I said to myself that if only the spirit that animated our people in those days could once again be mobilised, how nearer would we all be to the goal! It was true that Mahatma Gandhi was now in India and not in South Africa, but did it really make any difference? Had we not promised to be pure *satyagrahis*? And whether the master was in our midst or engaged in a bigger struggle elsewhere, we had to show the mettle of our pasture. It is to the credit of the South African Indians that in 1946, when we decided to take up the challenge, Gandhiji sent his blessings from India (16 September 1948, from Shukla, 1951).

The success of the non-violent resistance, aside from broadly supported moral principles, depended on widespread publicity. The mass rallies, the public garlanding of those who had served their terms of imprisonment, exposing the violent behaviour of the police through Indian newspapers such as *The Leader* and *Graphic*, and international publicity provided a sense of theatre. The PRC published *Flash* and the *Passive Resister*, which gave instant and widespread coverage to the campaign.

But the authorities were determined to break resistance 'by any means necessary'. They first used a 70-year-old law relating to trespass, then the Riotous Assemblies Act, handing down long jail terms. When this did not work, magistrates handed out fines of £5 each without the option of imprisonment. Resisters refused to pay the fine, leaving, in the words of the PRC newsflash No. 47, 'the headache on the other side'. Eventually, resisters were given one month in jail with hard labour.

By December 1947 support for civil disobedience was waning. There were 1,500 volunteers in the first six months and only 500 in the next eighteen. Statements by Monty and Dadoo suggest a recognition that outside intervention was necessary. For example, *Passive Resister* opined on 11 December 1947 that the 'most practical method by which measures may be inaugurated that could lead to a solution of the conflict remains a Round Table Conference between the Governments of India, Pakistan and South Africa'.

Recognising that the Ghetto Bill could not sustain the campaign, the May–June 1947 NIC conference resolved to challenge the Immigrants Regulation Act of 1913, which prohibited Indian interprovincial migration. This became all the more important because the movement was stymied by the fact that the police were not arresting volunteers at Gale Street. On 25 January 1948, 15 resisters from Natal, with Monty at the forefront and reminiscent of the 1913 March inspired by Gandhi, crossed the Natal–Transvaal border at Volksrust. They were met by Dadoo as they did so. Dadoo and Naicker were summonsed and sentenced to six months' imprisonment for violating the 1913 law. Monty was defiant as he read out a statement in court on 2 February 1948 on behalf of himself and Dadoo:

> The Passive Resistance struggle which we are conducting is based on truth and non-violence. It is associated with the name of one of the greatest men of all time, Mahatma Gandhi, on whose death in tragic circumstances just a few weeks ago the whole world wept. Among the millions of men who paid their last tribute to this great soul was Field Marshal Smuts, the Prime Minister of South Africa. Mahatma Gandhi was the father of our struggle. Gandhiji too defied the unjust laws of South Africa and suffered imprisonment during the 1906–1914 Passive Resistance Campaign. This is the man whom Field Marshal Smuts referred to as a 'prince among men'. This is the man – the pilot of India's march to freedom – who is the source of inspiration of our just struggle for democratic rights in South Africa.

The Passive Resistance Campaign ended in June 1948. The campaign was already petering out, but it was developments in white politics that occasioned a rethink.

Smuts's United Party was defeated by D. F. Malan's National Party in 1948. Malan was the self-same arch proponent of the idea of the Indian as 'alien' and advocate of repatriation as the solution to the 'Indian problem'. The policy of appeasement initiated by Sastri and the moderates had failed to quench his desire to rid the white man's country of the scourge of the 'coolie'. Despite this history, the NIC announced that it was suspending the campaign until the new government had made a clear pronouncement on the future of Indians (*The Leader*, 5 June 1948). Was this just a cover for the fact that sustained repression had slowed the campaign? It soon became clear that the new government was determined to make the old policies even tougher. The minister of the interior, T. E. Dönges, refused to meet the NIC, which he described as 'communistic in orientation', guilty of brazenly defying the laws of the country and constantly crying out for foreign help (Bhana, 1997:78–79).

Despite the campaign petering out, significant aspects are to be noted. One is the cooperation between 'communists' and 'Gandhians'. Many of the activists who initiated mass action against discrimination were communists who were influential in the NIC's cooperation with Gandhians such as Monty Naicker and Nana Sita. Gandhi dismissed letters from some South Africans who complained that Dadoo was a communist. On 27 November 1947 he wrote to S. B. Medh: 'The best way is not to bother about what any "ism" says but to associate yourself with any action after considering its merit. Dr Dadoo has made a favourable impression on everybody here.'[85]

The Passive Resistance Campaign was doomed to fail. It was naive to think that the government would repeal the Ghetto Act in the face of non-violent protest. Pitching tents on Gale Street in itself was not sufficient to build momentum, especially when the state ignored attempts to duplicate this elsewhere. While passive resistance had widespread support among Indians, even if large numbers did not volunteer for imprisonment, and the movement drew support from outside, it was unsustainable in the absence of clear time frames. When interest waned, the leaders had no alternative strategy of resistance. The campaign was played out in Gandhian terms: Monty's going to jail, his refusal to engage in violence despite the assaults by whites and his crossing of the border all reflected this. And in the midst of the campaign, Monty and Dadoo visited India.

Gandhi

Monty was aware of the importance of independent India to focus attention on South Africa. A trip to India during March and April 1947, at the height of the Passive Resistance Campaign, was crucial in terms of Monty's political outlook and in garnering the support of India in opening new fronts in the United Nations, and in the drive to unite the struggle of Indians with that of Africans in South Africa. Monty was already driving a closer working relationship with Africans as a signatory of the Xuma–Naicker–Dadoo pact in 1947 for cooperation between the ANC and the Indian Congresses. The Indian visit coincided with the 1947 Asian Conference, where Monty and Dadoo met delegates from 32 countries, including Tibet, Nepal, China, Egypt, Iran, Indonesia and Vietnam. They met Nehru, Gandhi and Jinnah, and a host of other leaders (*The Leader*, 7 June 1947).

While Monty and Dadoo had a great deal in common, including their veneration of Gandhi and the need to build a non-racial struggle, unlike Dadoo, Monty did not become a member of the Communist Party or embrace the armed struggle. Monty, while following the Gandhi template, probably did not realise that he was to take the struggle beyond the boundaries defined during Gandhi's South African years. In many ways, a combination of factors – the Passive Resistance Campaign, the 1949 Indo-African disturbances, the Defiance Campaign of 1952 and the realisation that there were limits to what India could achieve – pushed the Indian Congresses into a substantial working relationship with the ANC. But this did not cut off the link with the Indian nationalist cause.

1952 Defiance Campaign

For Monty, the riots of 1949 in Cato Manor reinforced the fact that he had to push more forcefully the idea of breaking racial boundaries around political struggles. This would crystallise in the non-racial struggle during the Defiance Campaign of 1952. While the riots cast a long shadow, Monty was willing to pursue non-racialism. Together with this, there was a move from 'passive resistance' to a more active form of resistance – defiance. While still seeking to avoid violence, the campaign aimed to be more assertive and this was reflected in its naming, according to Billy Nair.[86]

The Defiance Campaign began nationally on 26 June 1952, but in Natal it only started on 31 August. This was because both Monty and ANC head, Chief Albert Luthuli, were concerned about Indian–African cooperation so soon after 1949. Monty, according to Billy Nair, was also concerned that the Indian response would not be enthusiastic, given that the two-year Passive Resistance Campaign had taken a heavy toll. However, the NIC resolved to participate, according to Nair, 'because … for the African people this was a new experience'.[87] Luthuli also faced opposition from Africanists such as A. W. G. Champion and Selby Msimang.

A crowd of 4,000 attended a rally at Red Square on 31 August 1952 to initiate the campaign. Both Monty and Luthuli addressed the rally. Thereafter, led by Monty, volunteers entered the 'whites only' waiting room and were promptly ushered into police vans, and subsequently sentenced to one month's imprisonment with hard labour (Meer, 2002:146). Although there was much enthusiasm and large numbers attended rallies, only about 200 people had courted imprisonment in Durban by the time the campaign petered out in December. However, it did mark the emergence of the ANC as a mass organisation and created awareness for the Congress of the People in Kliptown in June 1955, where the Freedom Charter was adopted. The likes of Monty, Dadoo, Nelson Mandela and Walter Sisulu, as banned people, missed this historic occasion.

Monty pushed the non-racial alliance further than anybody before him. He invited ANC leaders such as Luthuli and Sisulu to open the annual conferences of the NIC and South African Indian Congress (SAIC) during the 1950s and he himself delivered the opening address to the National Conference of the ANC in Durban on 16 December 1954. Monty was not just leading the NIC, he was taking it in new directions and, while he might not always have carried the masses with him, symbolically he was signalling a new path. The personal price he paid, though, was high. During the early hours of 5 December 1956 activists across the country, mostly members of the ANC, Congress of Democrats, Indian Congresses and South African Congress of Trade Unions (SACTU), were arrested on allegations of treason (*Indian Views*, 5 December 1956). In all, 156 people were charged with 'high treason'. On 19 December 1956 the accused appeared in court to open preparatory examination. The first phase of the trial lasted until 17 December 1957, when allegations were withdrawn against 61 of the accused. On 6 December 1958 the state announced that new indictments would be framed against 91 accused. Charges against a further 61, including Monty, were quashed on 20 April 1959. The last 30 treason trialists were found not guilty in March 1961.

Monty had an especially healthy respect for Chief Luthuli. A large portrait of Luthuli, for example, dominated the lounge of his home. While Dadoo was Monty's great friend over these years, it really was Luthuli who was Monty's political beacon in the local context. In October 1961 Luthuli was awarded the Nobel Peace Prize. There was some irony in Luthuli's award, as the leading figures in his organisation were now committed to violence. But the non-violent strand still ran strongly through the Congress lines and Luthuli's popularity was incredibly strong. Politically and personally it was a very important moment for Monty. In driving the NIC into the Congress Alliance he placed great faith in the leadership of Luthuli. The Nobel Prize vindicated his own confidence in Luthuli.

Once the government, albeit reluctantly, granted Luthuli a visa, Monty organised a fabulous farewell for him as he made his way to Oslo. The NIC organised a mass meeting to honour Luthuli at Curries Fountain on 9 November 1961. The ground was packed to capacity as 15,000 people, mainly Indians and Africans, sat through a heavy downpour to celebrate the moment. According to one report, 'scenes reminiscent of the great meetings held in Durban during the Defiance Campaign were re-enacted'. Amid 'tremendous applause', Monty led Mrs Nokukhanya Luthuli to the platform, which contained a huge six-by-four-foot portrait of Chief Luthuli.

An application for permission for Luthuli to attend had been declined by the minister of justice. Speakers included Steven Dlamini of SACTU, Florence Mkhize on behalf of the Women's Federation, Vera Ponnen on behalf of the Congress of Democrats, C. K. Hill on behalf of the Liberal Party and M. B. Yengwa, former secretary of the banned ANC (*New Age*, 16 November 1961). Monty himself delivered a speech in honour of Chief Luthuli:

> The calm and dignified manner our Chief reacted to the campaign reviling and belittling him with violent, virulent and vicious words demonstrated to the democrats of the country and the world why our Chief – a devout Christian not caring about glory and whose character is not sullied by envy or arrogance – deserves the award .... Millions more South Africans than the handful who voted the Nationalists into power, admire, love and are prepared to follow our Chief. It is not accident or emotion that so many of us hold him so dear; it is not hero worship that so many of us admire him; it is not some kind of witchcraft that leads us to follow him .... The reason why so many respect and follow our Chief is because of his humility, his dignity, his service to better race relations through peaceful methods and his service to Mankind. The whole world, East and West, the 99.8 percent people acclaim him with this award. Only the 0.2 percent of White Nationalists are against this signal of honour to our country .... Where every avenue of peaceful negotiation is closed; where every Democratic leader is banned and banished; when the foremost organization of the African people – the ANC – is banned after 48 years of peaceful existence; when the clamour for other forms of struggle other than non-violence became louder and louder, our Chief was firm for a peaceful solution to the problem of South Africa .... When the ex-Minister of Defence said 'We are willing to shoot down the Black masses', our Chief sat at his home in Groutville armed with a ball point pen appealing in the hope of arousing the Christian conscience of the white people so that they might help him in finding a peaceful solution rather than a shooting solution.[88]

On 5 December 1961, the day of Luthuli's departure, lunch was served at the Himalaya Hotel, the main 'non-white' entertainment centre at the corner of Grey and Beatrice streets. Guests included Monty and Alan Paton. Over 4,000 people were outside the hotel (*New Age*, 14 December 1961). Luthuli's wife, Nokukhanya, remembers how, when they left the hotel, 'people picked him up onto their shoulders. They wanted to carry him all the way to the airport .... And what was happening to me? Well, while this was going on, I was trying my best to keep close to my husband, but those crowds!' (Rule, 1993:122). A cavalcade of a hundred cars accompanied Luthuli to Louis Botha airport in Habib Rajab's silver-grey Cadillac; the very car that took British Prime Minister Harold Macmillan around Durban during his 1960 visit. With Luthuli in the car were his wife Nokukhanya, daughter Hilda and Monty. The farewell was significant. The apartheid state was bent on crushing resistance, it had locked up thousands and yet the leader of the movement, with incredible local support, was off to receive a prestigious accolade for peace.

'The attacks of the wild beast cannot be averted with only bare hands'[89]

After the 21 March 1960 massacre of 67 Pan Africanist Congress (PAC) supporters protesting the pass laws, the government of Hendrik Verwoerd banned public meetings on 24 March, declared a state of emergency on 30 March, and outlawed the ANC and PAC on 8 April. Mass arrests followed. The force unleashed by the state marks this, arguably, as the moment when serious questions were raised about the viability of non-violent protest in the South African context. Gandhi argued that the use of force was immoral. One of the underlying principles of *satyagraha* was that the suffering of the *satyagrahi* would appeal to the heart and convert the wrongdoer. Gandhi saw non-violent resistance as dealing with oppression in a manner that allowed the oppressed to reconcile with the oppressor. It was thus a positive action aimed at reconciliation. By 1960 it was clear that the suffering of oppressed South Africans failed to affect the ruling class in this way. It also brought into question the other notion of satyagraha that 'a good result can only be brought about by good means' (Appadurai, 1969).

Activists such as Monty, Mandela, Nair, Sisulu and others were at a crossroads, because non-violence aimed at reconciliation had failed to yield the desired outcome. The dilemma is summed up by Gay W. Seidman (2000), who asked: 'What is the obligation of leaders to protect their supporters from serious physical danger when they know that peaceful protest may lead to their deaths?' The appeals to white conscience, peaceful protest and pleas to international opinion had all failed. The apartheid government had a powerful military machine, a sophisticated and repressive internal security apparatus, the support of Western nations, and mineral wealth at its disposal. While Gandhi's position was clear, i.e. that under no circumstances were individuals to resort to the armed struggle,[90] others were not so sure. As Rusty Bernstein (1999:232) put it, non-violence had always been a hard course to steer in a violent country. Now the tide was turning against it. Yesterday's non-violent activists were becoming today's trainees in sabotage and armed struggle. Yesterday's non-violent ANC had spawned today's armed struggle.

The adoption of non-violent resistance as a principle has been criticised by some activists. Monty's cousin, M. P. Naicker, who had been a key figure in the NIC and Communist Party of South Africa and who wrote for *New Age* and edited *Sechaba* in exile, came out on the side of violence. He credited Gandhi with 'moving millions upon millions of people into action for freedom and dignity against imperialism', but felt that

> while satyagraha had great potential ... the method also caused undue power to be placed in the hands of the leadership to curb and take away the initiative of the masses if they so wished .... To disarm the masses in the face of an enemy determined to rule by force is a problem Gandhi never really resolved (Naicker, 1969:57–59).

After the lifting of the State of Emergency at the end of August 1960, Monty, who had been on the run for five months, issued the following statement: 'Our people are to be congratulated on their tolerance and courage in bearing up with these uncalled for attacks by a Party at the head of Government, which has become power drunk and whose policy seems to be that "might is right"' (*Post*, 4 September 1960).

The next major event was the mass demonstrations on 29–31 May 1961 to protest against South Africa declaring itself a republic on 31 May. The Security Branch swung into action. Offices of SACTU, the Durban Residents' Association, and the NIC were raided and pamphlets confiscated, and the government mooted new legislation, the General Law Amendment Act, to strengthen its powers. Around ten thousand people were arrested in order to undermine the strike (Fullard, 2004). The stay-away was consequently not the success that organisers had hoped for. Monty was still holding out for discussions and dialogue, despite the brutal state response and its intransigence to overtures of negotiation and compromise. Within the leadership of the Congress Alliance murmurings were heard that a change of direction was needed. The call to armed struggle would be difficult to resist. Monty, according to Billy Nair, was one of the most implacable opponents of the armed struggle:

Now violence was a new form of struggle. Mandela made it quite clear and I agreed with him wholeheartedly ... not that I was violent and what-not, but because we tried all forms of struggle. The reaction of the ruling class was one of violence .... One has to just experience it for a few minutes, what they did. Or you get striking workers where a strike breaks out ... where they go into the factory premises, use the batons and their guns to crack the skulls of the workers. This was a common thing. So you had this form of repression, violent repression and that is why there was no alternative to violence. Mandela said there's a parting of ways now .... But, Monty and a few others in the NIC ... felt strongly that we should not depart from passive resistance.[91]

Around August or September 1961 the ANC executive met on Chief Luthuli's farm in Groutville, while the NIC executive met on Hurbans' farm in Tongaat. The NIC meeting was 'heated', according to Nair.[92] The dilemma was summed up by I. C. Meer (2002:225):

Were we contemplating a shift to violence as an easy way out of the hard task of mobilising the people in the face of repression? Would resorting to violence lead to the neglect of orthodox forms of mobilisation? It was a vigorous debate. By turning to violence would we not be giving the regime the excuse to come down on us even more heavily? Would we not be sacrificing the legal space that the Indian Congress, SACTU and CPC still enjoyed? On the other hand, if we did not shift to violent means, would we not be failing our people by not harnessing their rising militancy and providing them with the leadership needed?

Monty and Yusuf Cachalia especially were adamant that violence should not be adopted, as it would lead to the destruction of the whole movement. For Monty, non-violence was a principle from which he was not prepared to waver, and his opposition arguably had little to do with M. D. Naidoo's accusation that opponents of violence were afraid of going to jail. Monty remained consistent, like Luthuli, that non-violent resistance was a superior method of engaging the foe and in the long run would yield positive results. As Gandhi had advised him, patience was key. The NIC executive resolved that when they met with the ANC the following evening they would express the view that there was place for non-violent struggle, but if the ANC decided otherwise, the NIC would not be an impediment (Meer, 2002:223–24). According to Billy Nair, that meeting took place on the Bodasingh's farm on the North Coast.[93] While Luthuli and Monty spoke against the armed struggle, Mandela and Moses Kotane won the day. Mandela wrote in *Long Walk to Freedom* (1994:433):

> it was only when all else had failed, when all channels of peaceful protest had been barred to us, that the decision was made to embark on violent forms of political struggle. We did so not because we desired such a course, but solely because the Government had left us no other choice.

Thus was born Umkhonto we Sizwe, 'Spear of the Nation'.

Conclusion

The years following the adoption of armed struggle were characterised by the state turning to extremely repressive measures. This included listings, bannings and banishments, with many in the resistance movements going into exile or serving long periods of incarceration. These draconian measures destroyed personal lives and decades-old friendships, and cut off activists from their mass base. Talented people were rendered redundant and made to mark time as the years ticked by and memories of their exploits and leadership faded. Bannings allowed the government to circumvent the legal process. Anyone could be banned for promoting the aims of communism, which was so widely defined that even a staunch Gandhian like Monty was served with successive banning orders.

For most of the years from 1952 to 1973 he was either a prisoner awaiting trial, a detainee, 'on the run' or a banned person. He was served with a five-year banning order from 1963 to 1968, which, on expiry, was extended to 30 April 1973. The repeated multiple banning of leaders muted the effectiveness of organisations such as the ANC and NIC. Monty's ban expired at midnight on 30 April 1973. Much had changed in his absence. The NIC was revived on 25 June 1971 under Mewa Ramgobin. Monty did not play an active role in the NIC until the Anti-SAIC Committee was formed in November 1977 with him as chairman and Doctor Goonam as treasurer. The first of what was advertised as a 'series of countrywide meetings' was held on 26 November 1977 (*The Leader*, 18 November 1977), with a second meeting on 11 December 1977. Monty was the chief speaker on both occasions (*The Leader*, 16 December 1977). But just as his 'Second Coming' was gathering momentum, he took ill and died on 12 January 1978.

During his heyday, in Monty's mind the Passive Resistance Campaign was a re-enactment of the earlier movement of 1913: the Gandhi symbolism, the enthusiasm and the moral triumphalism. Going to jail, reading Gandhi's autobiography in prison, visiting India and crossing the Transvaal border were all examples of playing out the struggle in Gandhian terms. Some of the tactics of the struggle were adopted after consulting with Gandhi and Nehru, while the language often evoked images of 'Indian national identity with South African belonging' (Raman, 2006:202). But the period 1946–48 was a different political terrain, and the movement made little impact on the government. The earlier strategy of passive resistance was re-enacted in the 1950s, even if instead of 'passive' the word 'defiance' was used. The 1952 Defiance Campaign targeted laws that the liberation movement selected to defy, much like the Passive Resistance Campaign. The 1955 Freedom Charter flowed from this and the document was a broad statement of ideals, much as in the Passive Resistance Campaign. Other similar movements of the period had similar defining elements: pass laws, consumer boycotts, anti-removals, and so on.

In a sense, 1946–48 helped to project the SAIC and with it the ANC as 'peaceful' organisations, and this perception survived in the 1950s, even as the nature of the 'movement' was changing. For most of the 1950s the strategy was non-violent resistance, and it was largely the crisis in 1960 that tipped the scale in favour of those who said that non-violent forms of resistance were ineffective, since the government had closed all avenues of peaceful resistance. When the ANC eventually decided on a limited form of armed resistance (born out of necessity, since it was unable to mount an armed rebellion), it did not say that other forms of resistance should disappear. Many of the protagonists (including Mandela) who have written about it have introduced 'morality' as an issue – and indeed, some diehard Gandhians like Monty may have seen it that way, but it was mainly a question of the most suitable strategy.

Monty's dilemma raises questions about making moral judgements about the decision to embrace violence as well as essentialising the debate to one of violence or non-violence. Was moral justification needed to disobey an immoral system through armed struggle? Do people like Monty and Luthuli hold a higher moral ground for rejecting violence? Did their failure to publicly condemn those who embraced violence make them morally culpable? We should not box people neatly into absolute categories such as 'violent' and 'non-violent'. Those who found even this form of struggle objectionable recoiled and perhaps withdrew, but most understood the circumstances that made the change in strategy necessary.

Runkle has suggested that violence and non-violence are not always good or bad either intrinsically or extrinsically and that any action must be 'conscientiously examined' taking into account a 'whole complex of circumstances'. He acknowledges, though, that 'feelings, sincere and hypocritical, run so strongly against violence, [that] a resolve to do this is difficult to arrive at and to carry out' (Runkle, 1976:389). But did Monty's kind of politics disappear entirely? Some, like Gay W. Seidman (2000) and Stephen Zunes (1999), among others, suggest that it was not the armed struggle that ultimately forced the apartheid state to the negotiating table, but international pressure and new modes of non-violent resistance by black South Africans, such as mobilising students and communities to make the apartheid state ungovernable. To some, this may not be totally convincing, because it glosses over the strategy of making townships ungovernable, a strategy that included the gruesome act of necklacing 'collaborators'.

This form of resistance emerged in the 1970s and climaxed in the mid-1980s. The involvement of masses of people in opposition to the structures of apartheid was a form of resistance that Monty had always advocated. He would have been horrified by the necklacing of 'collaborators'. The international media latched onto it with the help of the apartheid regime, but it was a very small part of the resistance. More significant was the resurgence of communities, the kind that Monty would have loved in the 1940s and 1950s.

Socio-political Comparisons

chapter 6-11

Renaissances, African and Modern: Gandhi as a Resource?

Crain Soudien

Introduction

At the close of his *India: A Million Mutinies Now*, V. S. Naipaul (1998:517) says:

> What I hadn't understood in 1962, or had taken too much for granted, was the extent to which the country had been remade; and even the extent to which India had been restored to itself, after its own equivalent of the Dark Ages – after the Muslim invasions and the detailed, repeated vandalising of the North, the shifting empires, the wars, the 18th-century anarchy.

There is, of course, a certain irony in using Naipaul as a point of departure for this chapter on Gandhi and his significance for thinking about the African Renaissance. His positioning of Islam, as the opening quote suggests, as an un-Indian phenomenon is problematic. His reflections on Africa are perhaps even more so. His Africa, as opposed to his India, is signified by a profound, almost primordial, loss of meaning – 'nothing has any meaning', his main character, Salim, says at the close of *A Bend in the River* (Naipaul, 1980:281). Earlier, Salim describes the people in the prison in which he finds himself:

> Those faces of Africa ... I felt I had never seen them so clearly before. Indifferent to notice, indifferent to compassion or contempt, those faces were yet not vacant or passive or resigned .... They had prepared themselves for death not because they were martyrs; because what they were and what they knew they were was all they had (Naipaul, 1980:278).

In this reading of his fellow human beings there is nothing to redeem. But Naipaul, like Gandhi, and particularly those elements of Gandhi's approach to the question of racial discrimination in South Africa that appeared to seek for Indians a favoured position above Africans, is more than the sum of his parts. Naipaul's interest for this chapter lies in the powerful ways he presents India as a *remade* space, as a space that has been *restored to itself*. Significantly, he talks not of an actual restoration; it is not ancient India of which he speaks. As a concept, that is a modern idea. But, critically, he refers to an awareness that is about the self. This awareness has historical dimensions, even political ones, but, to put in place the thread of logic I use in this chapter, it is much more ontological. An important line in his argument demonstrating this is the phrase 'what they owe themselves'. It is this concept – to which I shall return – that is important in thinking about the ways in which Gandhi may be helpful in imagining an African Renaissance.

Are we able to say the same about the African continent after its own million mutinies, its own invasions and its own Dark Ages (not of its own making) that it has gone through? Clearly, there is a desire among Africans to restore the continent to itself, to take it into a glorious new renaissance. But has it, like India, as Naipaul claims for it, been able to *remake* itself? The argument will be made in this chapter that it has not, but that it can. What such a remaking might be, it is suggested, can now, in the 21st century, only be undertaken through a process of deliberate and critical reflection that centrally includes, as the Indians have done, a reappropriation of their pasts. Such a reflection, however, requires new lines of engagement with this past.

It is here that I draw on Gandhi. I look at a meaning of Gandhi in terms of what it might tell us about thinking into the future about the post-colonial context of Africa. I am aware of critiques of Gandhi that take issue with his understanding of African people and women. In terms of this, there are any number of directions one might take the discussion of Gandhi and his relevance for rethinking Africa. In working through these challenges, the most obvious approach is to focus on passive resistance and its historical provenance in the struggles against oppression (Reddy, 1991). Taking such a route allows one not to focus on passive resistance as a political strategy, but to understand the substrate upon which it rests and the kind of ethical identity or, to put it in my own terms, the humanness that it requires. In the discussion below I look at this substrate. Following this, the second section of the chapter looks at key developments in the African Renaissance discussion, and in a final section I consider what bearing our earlier discussion of Gandhi might have on the African Renaissance.

A remade India?

But let us return to Naipaul for a moment. What was this remaking, this restoration to which Naipaul addressed himself? It was essentially that 130 years after the 1857 Mutiny, India had set itself on the path towards a new kind of intellectual life: 'it was given new ideas about its history and civilisation. The freedom movement reflected all of this and turned out to be the truest kind of liberation.' Despite having begun with India's intellectual elites, Naipaul (1998:517) argued that the idea of freedom had worked its way down:

> People everywhere have ideas now of who they are and what they owe themselves .... There was in India now what didn't exist 200 years before: a central will, a central intellect, a national idea .... The Indian Union gave people a second chance, calling them back from the excesses with which, in another century, or in other circumstances (as neighbouring countries showed), they might have had to live.

There are, to be sure, many risks in using *remaking* and particularly *restoration* as hermeneutic registers in thinking about phenomena such as renaissances, not the least being the seductive epistemologies of ancient primordial essences lying buried and awaiting rediscovery. The ontological, however, is not a site of permanence or fixity. It is, as Zizek (1996:56) says, recounting the work of Schelling, an experience that in its unfolding 'fails in its endeavour to absorb the Real of the Thing without remainder ... every formulation [of the process of becoming] entails/produces a remainder'. Zizek here makes clear how 'radically problematic' the ontological – human emergence – is, marked as it is 'by a maximum gap between possibility and actuality ... man is in *potential* the crown of creation, yet his actuality is that of a shattering Fall' (Zizek, 1996:56). Here lies the significance of Naipaul's observations. The *restoration* to which he points is not an original and immaculate India, but an India seeking to reflect upon its own *fall* to explain the process of *becoming* human on its own terms. Central in this *restoration* is a consciousness, deliberately cultivated, of the self and its modes and manners of expression – the experience of Indian everyday life – as a resource for thinking about being human that operates in relation to, but is not dependent on, the hegemony of Europe.

It is this deliberateness that is at the heart of this chapter. How might Africa, or even parts of Africa – and, indeed, subordinate and dominated people anywhere – begin to think of themselves in rhythms, cadences, times, moods, and, critically, in their subjunctivenesses and alternativenesses that are not parodies of their dominators' or conquerors' modes, modalities and technologies of what it means to be human? How might it, without falling into the essentialist trap of looking to an unsullied and only glorious African past, *restore* to itself its right of imagining what it means to be a human being, of becoming a human being, that is not animated either by envy – the mimicking of its subordination – or by its obverse, revenge – the achievement of subordination of its subordinators? It is this desire that frames and in some ways requires the identification of a range of readings that addresses the question of subjunctiveness in Africa and which speaks against an idea of an essential Africa.

Gandhi's ontological experiment

An important biographer of Gandhi, Louis Fischer (1963:3), remarks at the very beginning of his *The Essential Gandhi* that '[t]o the end of his days, Gandhi attempted to master and remake himself. He called his autobiography *The Story of My Experiments with Truth*, an "experiment" being an operation within and upon oneself'. Gandhi himself explains:

> [It] is not my purpose to attempt a real autobiography. I simply want to tell the story of my numerous experiments with truth, and as my life consists of nothing but those experiments, it is true that the story will take the shape of an autobiography. But I shall not mind if every page of it speaks only of my experiments .... The more I reflect and look back on the past, the more vividly do I feel my limitations .... What I want to achieve – what I have been striving and pining to achieve these thirty years – is self-realization .... [As] I have all along believed that what is possible for one is possible for all, my experiments have not been conducted in the closet but in the open (Fischer, 1963:3).

Many commentaries draw attention to the style of Gandhi's writing, and particularly its directness (Mehta, 1976:4). Metaphor is absent from much of it. On occasion, this directness produces what appears to be immodesty. More important, however, is the complexity, not just of the words, but of the challenge that his candour precipitates. He is unsparing of himself and demands the same of the rest of us. The self-realisation that he talks about in the passage above is about being able to 'see God face to face' (Fischer,

1963:4). From this will come freedom from later incarnations, he says. But its implications for this earthly life are great: to see the 'Spirit of Truth face to face one must be able to love the meanest of creatures as oneself'. Most compellingly, he continues, what this demands is that 'a man who aspires after that cannot afford to keep out of any field of life' (Fischer, 1963:4). Free of metaphor or not, the point he makes is that he 'live[s] and move[s] and ha[s] [his] being in pursuit of this goal' (Fischer, 1963:4).

India was the canvas upon which Gandhi sought to conduct this experiment. He remained in regular contact with others who sought to follow the way of *satyagraha*. Writing the foreword to a pamphlet 'A discipline for non-violence' by Richard B. Gregg, he concluded: 'However admirable this guide of Mr Gregg's may appear as a well arranged code, it must fail in its purpose if the Indian experiment fails' (Gandhi, 1968a:14).

Presenting *satyagraha* as an experiment as opposed to a plan of action or even a manifesto is important in understanding Gandhi's significance. He was opposed to the process of the iconisation of himself – Gandhism – taking place in India and elsewhere, as even his most vociferous critics acknowledged.[94] What he and others were doing was not writing or exemplifying a script for living, but attempting to live to the limits of scrupulousness.

What this scrupulousness means in thinking about remaking and restoring to itself the colonial subject is what we now need to engage. What does Gandhi's insistence on an ethical life mean for us now, in the present? There is a great deal of debate about his usefulness for managing our lives in a hyperglobalised world suffused with all kinds of terror.[95] In his correspondence with a wide range of people, as can be seen in the large corpus of writing he left behind (Gandhi, 1968b:149), the question about the virtues of modernity repeatedly arises. For example, any number of implied and explicit doubts are expressed about the benefits of modern machinery. His responses are often inconsistent and contradictory (Gandhi, 1968b:97). As a result of this, he is on occasion projected as being against modernity and European civilisation (Connell, 2007:187). As a consequence, his relevance for thinking about how we might confront the complexity of modernity and construct authentic identities for ourselves is called into question.

Gandhi, however, understood the modern moment both viscerally and cognitively. He is caricatured as a rejectionist of the benefits that came with modernity and Western civilisation, but nothing could be further from the truth. He was clear about the good and the bad contained in it and was able to cut to the quick of its Janus-facedness. Talking about religious expression, for example, he says:

> I believe in the fundamental Truth of all great religions of the world. I believe they are all God given and I believe they were necessary for the people to whom these religions were revealed. And I believe that, if only we could all of us read the scriptures of the different faiths from the standpoint of the followers of these faiths, we should find that they were at the bottom all one and were all helpful to one another.[96]

In terms of this, and extending the argument, he was able to see the complexity of faith, culture and civilisation and to recognise how significantly, in their human manifestations, these systems of thought could not simply be reduced to timeless essences. Western civilisation, thus, was not intrinsically perverse. The British were also, by nature, not evil people. What their leaders did, to illustrate the point, did not encompass the complexity of who they were and the kinds of people they were. Thinking along these lines, goodness and evil were distributed in equal proportion everywhere in the world. No one group of people held either an excess or a shortage of particular kinds of moral values. Gandhi's own intellectual formation was profoundly eclectic. Tolstoy and Ruskin, for example, were as important to him as was the mythological repertoire of India. C. F. Andrews, an English priest, was one of his closest friends. It was how he used these resources that is important for us to pay attention to. He was, therefore, as important Gandhi commentators such as Hardiman (2003) and Nandy (1998; 2002; 2005) have argued, deeply invested in the present and the conundrums of contemporary life. He came to be, as Hardiman (2003:294) has put it, the proponent of an alternative modernity.

What does this alternative modernity consist of? Gandhi's experiment with life drew variously on Indian tradition, Western philosophy, and practical experience in the diverse contexts of India, South Africa and Britain. He remained in a dialogue with these different influences and experiences, and while he insistently tended towards the simplicity of the ashram, he constantly sought to evolve for himself a moral code that recognised the complexity of thought and life. His attitude to this complexity of thought and life was that he should always be alert to its violent inclinations. He thus, as Hardiman (2003:294) has argued, 'tried to incorporate subaltern politics into his alternative by purging it of its violent aspects, so as to give it a strong moral superiority as against the coercive and violent politics of both the colonial state and the indigenous elites'. Similarly, he separated from Western civilisation its violent and its peaceful, or, as Nandy (2005:49) describes it, the recessive elements of this civilisation, to show how congruent it actually was with Hindu and Buddhist thought.

It was this ability – that of separating the distinct and contradictory components of civilisation – that led Connell (2007:186) to argue that Gandhi was 'not the exemplar of any cultural or psychological pattern, but ... the person who cracked the code of colonialism, who discovered the way out of the dead-ends that had defeated all other Hindu reformers'. He became the person who worked towards 'the right state of mind, and made it not a secret defiance but a public ethic and a political program' (Connell, 2007:186). Gandhi's significance, therefore, lies not in the caricatures of non-violence that we have of him, but centrally in the resources he provides for understanding *how* we might step *outside* of the logic of dominance. Ahluwalia (2001:36), talking about Gandhi's arrival in South Africa in 1893, comments that an early theme of his was to break down the representations ascribed to Africans and Asians 'who were subjected to extreme levels of discrimination. It was here that the essence of his philosophy of civil disobedience and non-violence was developed'. This moment is crucial for the purposes of this chapter. It provides us with a *way* in which we might begin to develop an argument for thinking about the kind – or, indeed, kinds – of renaissances that an African future might consist of.

What does Nandy say then? His key point is that Gandhi offered 'an alternative language of public life and an alternative set of political and social values, and he tried to actualise them as if it was the most natural thing to do' (Nandy, 2005:85). Gandhi did so in two ways. Firstly, he challenged the complex of masculinised conceits of civilisation and what supposedly constituted it that supported colonial dominance, and, secondly, he took an approach to history that questioned its determinist teleology and the way in which it appropriated what it understood to be 'objective' truth.

With respect to the first, he recognised the ways in which colonialism had come to construct British hegemony as *manly* and Indian subordination as feminine and passive, and the deep habituation of this in the lineaments of everyone's thinking (see Hogan, 2000). It was from this that Gandhi wanted to liberate both the British and Indians: '[t]he panicky, self-imposed captivity of the dominant ... groups in their self-made oppressive systems' (Nandy, 2005:51). Colonial culture ordered sexual identities in the following hierarchy: manliness was superior to womanliness, and womanliness in turn to femininity in man. The Indian response to this was to attempt to beat the British at their own game. To do this, 'they sought a hyper-masculinity ... that would make sense to their fellow-countrymen ... and to the colonizers' (Nandy, 2005:51). The problem with this response was that it homogenised the multiplicity of Indian life around warrior ideals that were only partially and episodically valorised in its history. By invoking this presumptuous ideal, these interlocutors of India found themselves marooned. 'Gandhi's solution was different', explains Nandy (2005:51). This solution took its inspiration from the reality that women were central to the making of the everyday. As Gandhi (1968b:354) put it, 'I am quite conscious of the fact that in the villages generally they hold their own with their men folk and in some respects even rule them'. While there is in some of Gandhi's writing what one might call a biological essentialism in which women are accorded their place as ordained by 'the scheme of nature' (they ought not to earn their living by doing what is properly man's work), he saw women as the embodiment of a future marked by sacrifice that was counterpoised to the brute power of men:

> Whilst ... I would always advocate the repeal of all legal disqualifications [which make women unequal to men], I should have the enlightened women of India to deal with the root cause. Women is the embodiment of sacrifice and suffering, and her advent to public life should therefore result in purifying it, in restraining unbridled ambition and accumulation of property (Gandhi, 1968c:485).

Gandhi used 'two orderings, each of which could be invoked according to the needs of the situation' (Nandy, 2005:52). The first came from both the great and little traditions of 'saintliness in India' in which manliness and womanliness were equal, but, critically, the 'ability to transcend the man-woman dichotomy [was] superior to both' (Nandy, 2005:53). The second, specifically used by Gandhi as 'methodological justification' for the anti-imperialist movement, asserted that the essence of femininity was superior to that of masculinity, 'which in turn was better than cowardice' (Nandy, 2005:53). Compressing Nandy, the insight he extracts from this explanation pivots on the presence, not dominance, of 'some traditional meanings of womanhood in India', which suture power, activism and femininity together more potently – and, indeed, more dangerously – than power, activism and masculinity. Gandhi (1968c:490) said, for example: 'For the courage of self-sacrifice woman is any day superior to man, as I believe man is to woman for the courage of the brute.' The extension of this approach, furthermore, has it that a woman as an object of sexuality was inferior to a woman as an object of motherliness and courage. Nandy (2005:54) concludes this exegesis by arguing that activism and courage – *caritas* – could be liberated from aggressiveness and recognised as being 'perfectly compatible' with womanhood. This position negated the very basis of colonial culture, 'with its built-in fears about losing potency through the loss of activism and the ability to be violent' (Nandy, 2005:55). Out of this position emanates a logic of agency, the will to act and, critically, its content that are not actuated by a notion of physical superiority embodied in the sexual potency of manhood.

The second element to Gandhi's alternative lay in a critique of dominant historiography. What he does is to subvert the teleological nature of modern history. Tellings of this modern history present historical development as an inevitable narrative of progress that requires a pathway 'from primitivism to modernity, and from political immaturity to political adulthood, which the ideology of colonialism would have the subject society and the "child races" walk' (Nandy, 2005:55). In this dominant trope, understanding or public consciousness was seen as the *causal* product of history. The present emanated from an unfolding teleology of a long and unchanging past. For Gandhi, this past was anything but unchangeable. It was a variable construct. It was not, to use Nandy's terms (2005:59), one-way traffic that pre-empted where the future might go. It was, in its configuration as myth, a resource that one could use to widen rather than restrict choice and agency. Myths 'widen human choices ... by resisting co-optation by the uniformizing world view of modern science' (Nandy, 2005:59). At the core of Gandhi's critique of Western notions of history was the post-Medieval and Enlightenment era understanding of time that chose to place emphasis on causes rather than structures – *why* as opposed to *what* – and the rationality of constant adjustment to 'historical reality' – pragmatic behaviour – rather than the rationality of 'a fundamentally critical attitude towards earlier interpretations' (Nandy, 2005:59). He rejected the idea that 'historical societies' were the true representatives of 'mature human self-consciousness' and especially its corollary that the more human beings were able to historically objectify the past – through fact – the more control they would have over their consciousness or their egos. He inverted this argument by saying that the more one understood one's ego, the closer one would be to managing the complex processes of the id – 'brain processes'. His commentary on the *Gita* is important here. He writes to his people in his ashram:

desire is insatiable like fire, and taking possession of man's senses, mind and intellect, knocks him down. Therefore first control your senses, and then conquer the mind. When you have done this, the intellect will also obey your orders (Gandhi, 1968b:279).

Powerfully, in this argument lay the opportunity of individuals and the communities to which they belonged to be able to choose their own futures 'without', as Nandy (2005:62) argues, 'high drama and without a constant search for originality, discontinuous changes and final victories'. In this narrative of life, people impose 'dominion upon fact instead of surrendering to it' (Nandy, 2005:62).

A new Africa

What might one then do with this approach in thinking about a new Africa? The relevance of Gandhi for this question has, of course, been considered elsewhere (e.g. see Mazrui, 1991; Reddy, 1991). Reddy is useful, for example, in rebutting the critique that Gandhi had been disrespectful of African people during his time in South Africa. He quotes Gandhi himself, who said: 'Indians have too much in common with the Africans to think of isolating themselves from them. They cannot exist in South Africa for any length of time without the active sympathy and friendship of the Africans' (Reddy, 1991:11). Gandhi, moreover, repeatedly made the point to the end of his life that he was an Indian *and* a South African. In terms of this, argues Reddy (1991:13), Gandhi did not belong to Indian South Africans, but to all South Africans.

Similarly, Mazrui (1991) is extremely insightful and provides one with an immediate point of connection to the central argument about ontology introduced earlier and which I am seeking to develop in this part of the chapter. He explains that Gandhi developed a new approach to modern politics that sought its authenticity not in the logic of the imperialising project. This imperialising project, argues Mazrui (1991:13), echoing Nandy's discussion above, idealised the modern Western state form: 'In the total ideology of imperialism, the right to initiate violence became a prerogative which only civilisation and statehood could bestow.' But how is the discussion about the African Renaissance being developed now? What direction is the discussion taking and of what use to it might Gandhi be?

The discussion of a new Africa takes place, of course, in the context of the continent facing many challenges that manifest themselves across a range of areas of social life. Many of them are self-inflicted, but the blight of colonialism – and only the most blind will deny this – is deep and now wholly institutionalised as a structural and even psychological reality. Against this backdrop, the question of a new Africa is insistent, urgent and beyond the sensitivities of small-minded politics. How might we begin to think of Africa, not on its own terms – because isolation from the rest of the world is virtually impossible, as the argument I will present later will hopefully show – but critically seizing hold of its own destiny?

Interestingly – and I acknowledge that the conditions are not identical – we find ourselves in a similar position to where India was at independence in 1947. For India then, the question was how it might build the nation. For us now on the continent as a whole, it is slightly different. But the challenge of making an identity remains. The echoes across these last sixty years are strong. In the lead-up to India's independence a debate was taking place between Nehru and Gandhi about modernity, modernisation and the West. At the heart of the discussion, driven by an 'urge to establish a modernity of [their] own, one that differed from Western modernity', which was, therefore, also a critique of modernity, was the question of what the character of the new Indian nation state should be (Prakash, 1999:201). It was here that Nehru bent one way and Gandhi another. Different as their postures were, both found themselves asking hard questions about the relationship of India's past to its present: 'What was the India that was brought into view by the people in the villages and by their cries of "Victory to the Motherland"?' (Prakash, 1999:201).

Nehru's answer to what the modern India should be was 'science' (Prakash, 1999:207). He had no wish to live in a timeless Indian past, but he thought he saw in the people 'an urge driving the people in a direction not wholly realized' (Prakash, 1999:204). To fulfil this realisation, what the Indian people had to do, he felt, was to modernise Indian society – i.e. disavow religiosity and embrace science. Such a science, however, had to grow out of India's national roots and was different from that of the West, which had a long way to go in developing science as 'a method, an approach, a critical temper in the search for truth' (Prakash, 1999:209). At the same time, in his vision of building an India that was both national and international, he was quick to rule out imitation of the West (Prakash, 1999:208). The West – and here I am aware of how the notion of the West itself is homogenised – had come to science without being able to say anything about the purpose of life. In India lay the possibility for another road to modernity – its past was not dead, but alive, and ready to give direction to science, and so to modernity.

For Gandhi, as we saw above, it was quite a different matter. For him it was fundamentally about discarding the Western idea of modernity. This modernity represented conflict and competition, which were alien to India's tradition of village life, which stood for warmth and the intimacy of family. This intimacy was built on face-to-face relationships that bound people together in an ethical order in which mutual dependence enforced self-discipline. As Prakash (1999:219) says: 'Indians were to attain their freedom and become national subjects by discarding Western disciplines and returning to indigenous sources of self-subjectification.'

The eloquence of this debate is powerful and evocative as we ponder our own modernity and ask hard questions about our own choices as nations in the making or as nations attempting to locate themselves in the global order. But the challenge in Africa is, of course, more than that of constructing national identities. It was Nehru himself who had said: 'Reading through history I think the agony of the African continent ... has not been equalled anywhere' (Mazrui, 1991:11). He argued that the people of the continent had more to be angry about than other people. It is in this sense – of confronting the weight of historical injustice – that the challenge in Africa is greater than it might be anywhere else. Recognising the scale of this challenge, Nehru cautioned, however, that 'to the extent then that the black man [sic] had more to be angry about than other men, he would need greater self-discipline than others'. Gandhi, moreover, came to the conclusion by 1936 that 'maybe it was through the negroes [sic] that the unadulterated message of non-violence will be delivered to the world' (Mazrui, 1991:11).

But what are Africans themselves saying? I outline in the discussion below two schools of African thought that remain current in the debate about Africa's future, the first of which I call the Utopians and the second the New Modernists. There are, of course, more. These, however, are most eminent in the discussion.

The Utopians

There is an intense desire among many oppressed people in the world to 'escape' from the embrace of the globalised mainstream. This view is present in the African context in particular versions of Afrocentricism and roughly approximates to what Adams (1997) describes as the self-determination school of thought in the United States. This view emerged out of frustration with the mainstream establishment and sought to separate black people physically and socially from the majority society and to create an independent 'environment such as a state in which blacks can implement their survival strategies' (Adams, 1997:441). This frustration is also seen in the work of proponents of indigenous knowledge elsewhere in the world. An example is that of Brady (1997:421) arguing for restoring Aboriginal knowledge in Australia. She says that her ancestors had in place systems of education and social cohesion 'which sustained them for 40,000 years ... I believe that it is time we empowered ourselves to take back our education so that we can move with pride into the next 40,000 years'. African versions of this position, of course, are by no means new and go back to struggles waged by people all over the continent, many of which await proper analysis. In the South African context alone the struggles on the eastern Cape frontier await a serious revision to show how much the war between the Europeans and the Africans was not just about land, but fundamentally about values. What have been described as millennial uprisings, for example, can be reinterpreted. These perspectives continue in the works of writers such as Banteyerga (1994), who argues that '"modern education" is not satisfactorily addressing the problems of Africa to meet the needs and aspirations of the African people'. Supporting Banteyerga, Nekhwevha (1999:503) makes the point that Africans need to move away from 'their long academic sojourn' in the Western imagination and should struggle 'to make African culture and experience the primary constituent of our world view'. For Nekhwevha, this approach would be integrative, empowering and liberatory.

Central to all these critiques is a very specific description of the forms of globalising hegemony against which they are fighting. These hegemonies are predatory and have no respect for local culture and knowledge systems. In globalising the local, their instinct is to instantly displace or relegate non-Western forms of understanding and knowledge to the margin. Evident in the analysis of the Utopians is a serious and sustained critique of the hierarchalising and ranking, the dividing, and, indeed, the 'othering' proclivities of the West and its economic, cultural and social forms. The problems pointed to are real and deep.

What these challenges lose sight of, therefore, without wishing to diminish the importance of their critique of mainstream education, is how Africanisation or indigenous knowledge systems are *already* engaged in articulation with the global world. What, however, an appeal for reviving a *displaced* Africa underestimates is the extent to which African people are continuing to hold on to their own cultural practices, are taking these practices into modernity – into institutions and practices defined by ideas of rationality such as humanism, individualism, democracy, parliament, systems of justice, education and so on that emerged in Europe in the 18th century – and are, in the process, redefining modernity and, indeed, their own traditions. Globalisation in this situation is not a one-way process. Let us hold on to that last thought as we move to looking at the second vision embodied by the New Modernists.

Mbeki and the knowledge vision: The New Modernists

Part of the difficulty of the Utopian ideal is the challenge of how to live in and with modernity. In this regard, the contributions made by African leaders are important. Among these, former South African President Thabo Mbeki's contributions are critical, because he is, arguably, paying the most attention to these questions, having repeatedly expressed himself with respect to the question of Africa's relationship to the West. It is important to engage critically with what he has to say, however. Addressing the Third African Renaissance Festival in Durban in 2001, he opened his address with the following comment:

> As Africans we are faced with the urgent challenge of ending poverty and underdevelopment on our Continent .... The first objective we confront ... is that we must ourselves take on the responsibility to answer the question – what are the ways and means that we must adopt to ensure that we achieve these objectives? (Mbeki, 2001:1).

In framing his answer, he begins with the comment that

> it is necessary that the peoples of Africa gain the conviction that they are not, and must not be wards of benevolent guardians, but instruments of their own upliftment. Critical to this is the knowledge by these peoples that they have a unique and valuable contribution to make to the advancement of human civilisation, that despite everything we have said, Africa has a strategic place in the global community (Mbeki, 2001:1).

In so doing he presents himself, interestingly, as Nehru's heir. Here, India and Africa stand in a like relationship to the West – each with its own moral authority as it attempts to position itself to take on the task of modernisation.

Critically, however, Mbeki falters, much as Nehru did, as he seeks to explain how this moral authority might be translated into a manifesto for socialising the nation *through* its past and *into* an autonomous future. For a practical solution to the question of *how* the authority of Africa is invoked, Mbeki turns to the concept – more the imperative – of recreation and leisure, 'without which' he says, 'technological development will create the forces for its own destruction' (Mbeki, 2001:12). I am not going to rehearse the full argument here, but the climax that it reaches after sketching the full panorama of Africa's natural and human riches suggests that 'tourism should be treated as a critical corollary of modern scientific and technological development' (Mbeki, 2001:12). The argument, of course, can be read simplistically, but, significantly, the point needs to be made that we are still left with the difficulty of working out the bases on which we frame our values. Mbeki's solution leaves agency in the visitor-knowledge producer. It is through the ocular example of what Africa is all about that the fullness of its glory will be made manifest. The problem is, of course, that it is we ourselves who must determine what it is that we think is important. We therefore need to speak for ourselves, as opposed to being spoken for.

Towards a new space: Alongside Gandhi

Important as these two approaches are, difficulties remain. One might argue that the first group we described above, the Utopians, present us with the challenge of how individuals and people anywhere might *actually* extricate themselves from the globalising world. The New Modernists, while recognising the ubiquity of modernity, struggle with articulating a view of themselves that is not derivative. As Partha Chatterjee (1997:30; emphasis added) says about them, 'the imposition of high [European] culture on society' has the effect of having to work with a 'discourse ... which, even as it challenge[s] the colonial claim to political domination ... also accepts the intellectual premises of "modernity" *on which colonial domination was based*'.

This latter problem, I suggest, constitutes the central paradox for determining a future direction for any renaissance in Africa – and, indeed, everywhere else in the world. The paradox for many amounts to the abidingly complex puzzle of how they might engage with this 'high' road and still remain alert to the challenges of including all their people and the full repertoire of their own memories, traditions and histories (see Sen, 2000).

But do these two approaches exhaust or contain the possibilities for a new Africa? Is Africa's future only imaginable in these dichotomised views of the world? Emphatically not. There are several ways in which the challenge might be met. I would like, however, to suggest that a productive vein of possibility is opened up by bringing a careful reading of Gandhi, and especially his attempt to uncouple masculinity from domination and history from determinism, to the challenge of renewal in Africa.

What such a hard reading forces is an abandonment of the dominant monological discourse driving the idea of Europe and those particular Afrocentric analogues that operate in its wake. I am suggesting that discourses such as these, following Gandhi, have had the effect of profoundly limiting description, analysis and, critically, imagination. The consequence is that it is almost impossible now to tell the story of Africa, its people and the individuals inhabiting its spaces – and, indeed, any place in the world – outside of the limiting masculinised and teleological tracks of thought engraved into the dominant rules of exposition and analysis.

What a Gandhian reading of Africa might stimulate is a re-evaluation of our dominant tools of social analysis and social description, such as tribe and race, many of which find their origin in attempts to make sense of life only as social systems. As a post-structuralist, I would not for a moment suggest that these are insignificant categories of analysis or, even less, that we can do without them, but in the ways they have come to be shot through with compulsions of social reproduction that depend on *great man* tropes, they obscure how much history and life are always multidimensional. I am also not discounting the possibility that great men and women exist – Gandhi was, after all, a great man – but they exist alongside a multitude of experiences and imaginations that dominant historiographical traditions, in their hegemonic and now near universal versions, choose to *order* in particular kinds of ways. What I am suggesting is that our current modes of engagement with the idea of a renaissance, or even its possibility, are captured by regimes of thought such as these. The possibility of a renaissance might begin through a process of unmooring Africa, or even loosening it, as some Indians have, from the epistemological imperatives of this great man history and beginning to see in it completely new and, it is to be hoped, autonomous ways of talking about itself.[97]

What these new ways would be aware of is how occluded African history is. It would come to terms with the aggression prescribed for manhood and the privileged status that expressions of violence are accorded in ways of telling the story of what it means to be a human being. It would recognise the collusion between colonial and pre-colonial masculine hegemonies in displacing the complex stories of everyday life in Africa. And, critically, it would come to terms with the teleological ways these dominances have prescribed Africa's movement into the future. Hogan (2000:17–18), to illustrate the point, explains that one of the effects of colonial denigration of indigenous culture was to create a view of indigenous cultures as feminine or effeminate and the metropolitan culture as masculine. This, as Oliphant (2009) argues in a recent thesis on identity-making processes in Lesotho, had multiple effects. Working in towns in Lesotho or in the South African mining towns came to be associated with masculinity, while staying home in the rural areas in Lesotho was associated with effeminacy. Being employed, especially away from home in the rural areas, either in the South African mining centres or of late in the urban areas of Lesotho, is to fulfil a man's socially defined economic role. It is to be manly and therefore fatherly and fit for marriage, if one is unmarried. This stereotype, Oliphant (2009:53) explains, was and remains

> socially strong, sustained and promoted but controversial. A woman in Sesotho is 'Mosali', which literally means 'one who stays behind', especially in the home. It also has its usual suggestion of the effeminate one. If a man is unemployed and is always at home, he is derogatorily referred to as 'Mosali'. This is considered very demeaning and insulting to a man. Many women, too, despise such a man as not man enough. Some separations in marriage have come as a result of this phenomenon.

Reading across the grain of accounts such as these, we would need to recognise, as suggested earlier, the patriarchal collusions that take place between the modern and the traditional, and the new social settlements that are emerging as 'modern'. But we would have to read these as constructed, as opposed to biological assertions of who human beings are. Reading them literally, we would not see the experimental nature of life. It is to this that I now turn. I suggest that a Gandhian reading of Africa would be significantly more aware of the experimental nature of the past and the present, and the deployment of each within the other. Resisting dominant historiography's tendentiousness, such a reading would go in search of contradiction and ambiguity instead of disavowing it. It would open itself up to the possibility that another story is always available. Alternativeness, otherness, displacement, the *subjunctive* would always be permitted, as opposed to the pre-emptive rules of history that declare these – the 'what might have been' – as *unhistorical*.

Powerfully, in coming to terms with the significance of this argument, where might we begin to look for this experimental ontology in Africa's history? I would argue that important new evaluations need to be made of the stories of the last 500 years and of where we are in the present. Crucial as the heroic resistance of *men* might have been in the shaping of the story of Africa – and, of course, figures such as Shaka Zulu, Hintsa, Mzilikashe, Moshoeshoe and countless others stand out powerfully – they have to be seen alongside a multitude of ways in which what has come to be perceived as *feminine* qualities have played a role in shaping human behaviour. Important new recountings, therefore, are necessary for explaining who we are and how we have come to the point of the present.

What this approach makes possible is for us to come to the present with new ways of explaining our social reality, to see it not simply, or only, as a stage or a phase in the long cycle of European inevitability, but as a time and space in which human beings are, as they have been in the past, experimenting with their lives. We see, thinking like this, important new ways of reading the present.

The experimental nature of the present

Discussions of the African present, predictably, abound with anxiety (Makgoba, 1999). It is not preoccupation that concerns us here. More important are the range of ideas of moving away from the challenges that obviously animate this present. In the discussion that follows, I make the argument that amid the challenges of African political and economic life, we have in the everyday experiences of people, not the headline news about political and economic strife, but important illustrations of how people are already engaging critically with modernity. Out of these engagements, I suggest, have come powerful new ontological stances. Instead, therefore, of inventing new ways of explaining how individuals and groups of people might mitigate, overcome, and even transform the corrosive and exclusionary modes of operation of our dominant modernity, our challenge in contemporary society is how to make explicit the knowledge practices that are inside of these ways of living across modernity and that are already there, and to make those the deliberate subject of public debate and dialogue.

In terms of this everyday, what is already present in African engagements with modernity is not, as many significant commentators on the African Renaissance have attempted to show us, a singular approach to living and being a part of the process of change taking place on the continent. To surface the polarities, it is neither only a singular African identity that is being cultivated, one that seeks to preserve its pre-colonial social and cultural lineaments uncontaminated, nor, on the other hand, a wholly overwhelmed and overdetermined African identity that has no regard and respect for or self-referentiality to its past. It is, as Achille Mbembe (2001:33) has constantly sought to remind us, a myriad of diverse social practices that one ought not to be seeking a unitary origin for. What is there in front of our eyes is what we ought to be looking at sociologically and analytically. And in a deliberate and self-conscious way we ought to recover that which makes us better human beings.

It is at this point that recovery of Gandhi's two insights about the Indian experience is crucial. Gandhi has significance for us as an ontology of anti-heroism. In his view of agency and history – the two critical elements I sought to explain above – resided the belief that India, as an example, had available to itself a mode of recovering history that did not depend on a determinist and masculinist causal view of the present. There, I suggest, lie important new ways of recovering ontologies of the human experience that are far more inclusionary, much more aware of contradiction, and distinctly more complex around notions of our humanity that are less raced and less masculinised. In them is a whole other dimension of who we have *actually* been as human beings and which we can talk about empirically through the lived experience of individuals and communities everywhere in the world.

What this view does is to help us recognise, as happened in India, the profound significance for inserting new sociological and historical modes of description of the world that we inhabited and to seed these into public discourse. The analytic reflection to make here is that those forms of historical recovery of Africa that subsist in declarations of African purity, nobility of spirit and uniqueness, while interesting as strategic counters to chauvinistic, masculinist and raced accounts of an imaginary Europe, are in and of themselves problematic. They are problematic to the degree, as Prah (1999), Mzamane (1999), Mamdani (1999) and, indeed, many others say, that they remain trapped in the discursive web of Eurocentrism. Their inclination is to rebut the deep prejudice of Africa as an empty historical signifier. Important and, indeed, necessary as this move might be, it has the danger of reproducing the categories of oppression embodied in the European discourse and failing to recognise how Africa has been going through its own ontological experiment in relation to modernity.

Modern anthropological work on Africa, such as that of the Comaroffs and Fabian, provides us with important resources to understand the syncretic way in which communities everywhere in Africa are remaking their lives. In this remaking, they are taking elements of their contemporary existence, from the full repertoire of social experience at their disposal, and crafting new forms of social engagement. A critical move of *being* has taken place here that we have failed to understand precisely because of the dominance of European historiographical tradition. In the process of elevating the sphere of the formal – the great man in history – the pervasive significance of the everyday is occluded. Here in the everyday, I suggest, are to be seen the million mutinies of Africa that Naipaul could not see. In response to Naipaul's resignation, it is suggested that in the everyday lie possibilities for seeing the persistence of agency. I could describe this agency empirically in the modes of survival and flourishing that have emerged everywhere. But it is in the modes of consciousness that have emerged that we need to look for what Africa is able to teach the world.

To understand the possibilities here we have to recover an important theoretical move that has been made sociologically by Du Bois (1970:20) with his idea of 'double vision', psycho-socially by Fanon (1967:182–83) in his discussion of what he calls the 'occult zone', and in the field of cultural studies by people such as Lawrence Grossberg (1994) and Homi Bhabha (1994) talking about the 'third space'. I am suggesting here that much of the everyday engagement with modernity takes place in this 'occult zone' or 'third space'. This third space is neither inside nor outside modernity, but pivots across the meaning of being both inside and outside of it. Central to this third space, it is argued here, is the fact that it is already a deep feature of everyday life in many societies. It is already present, for example, as young Chinese people encounter the similarities and differences of the old cultures their parents remember and cherish with the Western world presented to them in film, song, text and social practice. It is also present, as an example, as young African people take the lessons of modernity – primarily school – with them into their initiation practices and overturn initiation so that it is not simply or only a test of masculine endurance, but, critically, one of social literacy (see Ngwane, 2003). Young people such as these, described eloquently by Ngwane in his study of Eastern Cape initiation processes, take the ancient practice of going to the mountains and give it new content. The example he provides is by no means the general trend, but it is an important illustration of the experimental nature of social practice.

Ngwane's example is one that I regularly refer to. What we have here is documented evidence of young people overturning the essence of their initiation into adulthood through the transformation of initiation from a physical encounter with hardship to a mental challenge of acuity. Less dramatically, and demonstrating the reverse direction of cultural flow, there is the mobilisation of tradition in managing the everyday through the frameworks of schooled forms of thinking in the creation of social networks that not only help people to survive within modernity, but, significantly, to thrive. It is the merging of knowledge forms. We have locally what Sen (2000) saw being used to great positive effect in places such as Japan, namely the recruitment of ancient cultural practices to help people establish very different corporate cultures in the workplace. Important about these examples is that they signify and carry embodied forms of learning. The past is always in the present. It is there, however, not as a script, but as a resource. Intense internal negotiation is therefore taking place in people's heads and also conversations as people effect these translations between their different cultural universes and create for themselves new – call it hybrid if you like – social cultures that are deeply rooted in their everyday worlds. This learning is implicit and informal, and simultaneously intensely straightforward and deeply complex. What is important about it is that it manages to work across the epistemological frameworks of the different worlds it inhabits.

An important and urgent task facing us in the social sciences is how we might begin to make these developments that have taken place explicit with the primary purpose of understanding the nature of the agency that is being expressed in these social transactions in order to inform our practice as cultural activists. I have elsewhere described the difficulty of attempting to put into words the nature of this translation and suggested that it amounts to what I call a crisis of representation (Soudien, 2004). This crisis, I say, presents us in the historical juncture in which we find ourselves with a moment of profound pedagogical possibility, because in it one comes face to face with the possibility that one does not immediately have the words to capture meaning. The importance of this recognition is great. Because it is so complex, we back off from it. Getting closer to developing a hold on it will be a powerful and critical moment for all of us.

Sociologically, in trying to seize this movement between the traditional and the modern, we will see that knowledge is never capable of being faithfully and completely reproduced. It is always in a state of interpretation. Looking at it in this way, all knowledge is provisional and vulnerable, and no knowledge is absolute. Modernity as a new universalism, and homogeneity and standardisation as new forms of totalisation are therefore problematic. Knowledge itself must therefore be made the object of inspection and not simply accepted or rejected because of where it comes from. Questions must be asked about its history, its objective and its scope.

Conclusion

Significantly, in taking this way, we have here a form of Gandhi's experimentalism practised in the everyday. At the core of the experience – and here this experiment of African ontology makes a contribution and begins a process of, as Naipaul would have it, *restoring itself to itself* – is how circumstances of the last few hundred years have required Africans to live across difference and in the process come to develop what Du Bois (1970:20) calls 'double vision'. What this double vision consists of is an ability to read dominance even as this dominance is being exercised over one. Fanon's (1967:182–83) 'occult zone' is also, famously, precisely about this. This, of course, is by no means a peculiarly African phenomenon. Bhabha (1994) describes it, as explained above, as a phenomenon of the encounter between the colonist and the coloniser. But it takes on added significance in Africa where, as we heard Nehru say earlier, the 'agony of [the] African continent' placed it in a distinct position and gave it a special role (Mazrui, 1991:11).

The added significance of Africa, against its agony, is fundamentally the necessity of living across difference that colonialism has imposed on it. For Africa, this difference is expressed most acutely and most crudely in the systematisation of race as an ontology and the humiliation of the African subject. It is experienced also in a whole range of other forms of difference, with that of citizen and subject being an important example, as Mamdani describes. The ways in which the African subject has come to manage these differences to produce a *way of living* – sometimes described as a burden by commentators in the United States because of its twoness, its schizophrenia – are a critical source of vitality and renewal. In these terms it is a gift Africans have in leading the world by showing how one might live across complexity. This vitality, however, is not, in and of itself, virtuous or constructed around a notion of public good. Given the conditions of its genesis, it is available for the full range of human inclinations, including anti-social behaviour. Crime as a social phenomenon needs to be reread sociologically, I would suggest, against these ways of understanding the African experience.

It is here that the great work of intellectual responsibility lies for us in the circumstances in which we find ourselves. Our challenge is how we might theorise this experience in such a way that its *virtuous*, as opposed to its anti-social, potentialities might be revealed. This is the moment where the 'agony' of Africa is turned around into its beauty and strength. We have intimations of such an intellectual response in our discussion of non-racialism and anti-racism. But even this is as yet insufficiently explicated. It remains, nonetheless, deeply significant. This message, and the way it has come to be articulated (almost unique in the world), was expressed as early as the middle of the 19th century, when the new African elite began to consider the place of Africa in the world, but it took off in the 1930s, when small groups of left-wing intellectuals in the Western Cape, profoundly conscious of their own subordination and simultaneously aware of the impending racial horror of the Second World War, made clear, at the same time as Aldous Huxley was beginning to write on race, how vacuous the concept of race was (Prah, 1999:43). Many features of this project need to be highlighted and brought into perspective in order to understand the distinctiveness of the theory as an ontology. Characteristic of much of the work of the movement is its simultaneous foregrounding and sublimation of the individual. At its core, the project was, and remains, inspired by the Enlightenment project and is deeply committed to the notion of the individual as an agent in his or her own history. In this respect, the movement is unequivocally modernist. It is the individual who must step into history. In this, the basic individual human right to the franchise is non-negotiable. Along with it have to come civil liberties. It is not sufficient, the argument goes, that people have the vote; they have to have the right 'to fight and organise to change their miserable conditions .... There [has to be] the deliberate and *conscious* abolition of inequality' (Mokone, 1982).

The perspicacity of this work as an ontological route marker for Africans lies in its attempt to provide a theoretical framework within which the 'burden' of twoness, of double vision, might come to be used as a resource. This perspicacity emanates from an engagement with the historical, scientific canon long before this kind of writing appears in the work of the world's most significant anti-racist scientists, such as Stephen Jay Gould. Its key interlocutors, such as Ben Kies, are not only familiar with the latest anthropology of the 1950s – for example, the work of the Leakeys in East Africa – but also with the emerging work of South African anthropologists such as Dart and Broome, who are beginning to talk of the southern African region as being the 'cradle' of humanity. But it is, critically, grounded in the experience of living across difference in Africa and realising how fertile this way of life is and how it anticipates the belief in and the practice of an idea of the commonness of the human race. Kies (1953:12), for example, explains:

> We are in no position at the present time to pronounce upon the weight of the evidence thus far produced by the newer line of research. It is *sufficient* for our purpose to say that we, the so-called 'children of Ham', together with Messrs D. F. Malan and Eric Louw,[98] derive from the same stock, *homo sapiens* .... The human race is now, as it was when *homo sapiens* evolved, one biological species, with the same number and formation of bones, the same brain and nerve structure, the same internal organs, the same four types of blood groups ... and the same capacity, in fact propensity, for interbreeding .... Geographical dispersal, isolation and diet, have not made the slightest difference to the biological unity of man as a single species, and provide no scientific basis for a division into what are popularly mis-called 'races'.

It is out of the process of a critical retrieval of ideas such as these, as theoretical complements to the experimental approaches to living across the differences of time, space and identity that are emerging out of Africa, that the lineaments of an African Renaissance might emerge.

7

Chapter

Democratic Deepening in India and South Africa[99]

Patrick Heller

Introduction

India and South Africa are arguably the most successful cases of democratic consolidation in the developing world. With the exception of a brief authoritarian interlude – the emergency of 1975–77 in India – neither country has experienced a serious challenge to democratic rule since transition, and the likelihood of democratic reversal or even destabilisation, especially when compared to Latin America, East Asia and the rest of Africa, is remote. Democracy, as in Linz and Stepan's (1996) famous definition of democratic consolidation, has become the only game in town. Moreover, democracy has made a real difference. In India, it has helped forge a nation from the most heterogeneous social fabric in the world. In South Africa, democratic politics and constitutional rule have managed a transition from white minority to black majority rule with minimal conflict. That this has been achieved against a social backdrop of extreme social exclusions (the caste system in India) and the worst maldistribution of wealth in the world (South Africa) only underscores the achievements at hand.

But if both have fared well in consolidating democratic institutions, including the rule of law, democratic deepening has proven much more elusive. Thus, even as formal constitutional democracy has been consolidated, there is little evidence of an increased capacity of subordinate groups to have an effective role in shaping public policy. More specifically, both the depth of social actors who enjoy effective political power and the range of issues over which democratic power extends have not expanded, despite both countries' formal commitments to promoting social rights. In many respects, of course, this simply reflects the classic dilemma of capitalist democracy: most investment decisions are made by private property holders and the power of the market simply trumps the power of the ballot box. But this argument is too facile and in any event fails to account for another, and in many ways more fundamental, problem, namely deficits in the democratic process itself. As many democratic theorists have argued, the quality of a democracy is not just about its formal institutions (as the consolidation literature argues), but also has to do with the capacity of its citizens (and especially the most subordinate) to engage in public life. I argue that in both South Africa and India, this problem can be grasped only by examining the relationship between political and civil society.

Following recent debates in sociological theory (Cohen & Arato, 1992; Habermas, 1996), I distinguish political and civil society by their distinct modes of social action. Political society is governed by instrumental-strategic action and specifically refers to the set of actors that compete for, and the institutions that regulate (in a democratic system), the right to exercise legitimate political authority. Civil society refers to non-state and non-market forms of voluntary association that are governed by communicative practices. If the telos of politics is power and its logic the aggregation of interests, the telos of civil society is reaching new understanding through the public use of reason. This distinction perfectly maps the divide in the democracy literature between aggregative and deliberative theorists. As Shapiro (2003:3) argues, aggregative theorists regard 'preferences as given and concern themselves with how best to tot them up' and hence focus on formal institutions and the rules of the game, while deliberative (normative) theorists 'are more Aristotelian in taking a transformative view of human beings ... [and] concern themselves with the ways in which deliberation can be used to alter preferences so as to facilitate the search for a common good'. For reasons I elaborate below, democratic deepening requires striking a balance between the aggregative logic of political society and the deliberative logic of civil society.

Working within this frame, the historical argument I develop in this chapter is that in South Africa and India, civil society is increasingly being subordinated to political society and that deliberation is being displaced by power. This is consequential, because a weakened civil society cannot perform three critical democratic functions: (1) providing a space in which citizens can meaningfully practise democracy on a day-to-day basis; (2) anchoring the legitimacy of political practices and institutions in vigorous public debate; and (3) serving as a countervailing force to the power-driven logic of political society. Viewed historically, this weakening of civil society is paradoxical, given that the democratic transition in both countries was driven to a significant degree by civil society, including the moral force of arguments based on inclusive and modern claims to democratic citizenship. This paradox alerts us to the fact that civil and political society, although frequently assumed to be in a mutually reinforcing relationship, are often in tension, and that how this tension plays out has significant repercussions for the possibility of democratic deepening. Indeed, when one juxtaposes the robustness of representative democracy in South Africa and India to the ineffectiveness of civil society, it becomes clear that consolidation may well have come at the expense of democratic deepening.

Why civil society matters for democratic deepening

The literature on the deficits of representative democracy is now very large and need not be rehashed here. In the context of developing world countries, the core deficit is what I would refer to simply as 'effective citizenship'. Classical and contemporary theories of democracy all take for granted the decisional autonomy of individuals as the foundation of democratic life. All citizens are presumed to have the basic rights and the *capacity* to exercise free will, associate as they choose, and vote for what they prefer. This capacity of rights-bearing citizens to associate, deliberate and form preferences in turn produces the norms that underwrite the legitimacy of democratic political authority. But as Somers (1993) has argued, this view conflates the *status* of citizenship (a bundle of rights) with the *practice* of citizenship. Given the highly uneven rates of political participation and influence across social categories that persist in advanced democracies (and especially the United States), the notion of citizenship should always be viewed as contested. But in the context of developing democracies, where inequalities remain high and access to rights is often circumscribed by social position or compromised by institutional weaknesses (including the legacies of colonial rule), the problem of associational autonomy is so acute that it brings the very notion of citizenship into question (Fox, 1994; Mamdani, 1996; Mahajan, 1999). A high degree of consolidated representative democracy such as we find in India and South Africa should not be confused with a high degree of effective citizenship. As Chipkin (2007) has argued, a democratic system is not the same thing as a democratic society. Closing this gap between formal legal rights in the civil and political arena, and the actual capability (in A. K. Sen's [1999] use of the term) to meaningfully practise those rights is what I mean by democratic deepening. In contrast to the consolidation literature's focus on electoral institutions, the problematic of democratic deepening calls for closer examination of actually existing civil society.

But how do we evaluate the actual character of civil society? I draw on the relational perspective (Somers, 1993), which views civil society as a contested historical terrain existing in dynamic tension with political society and the economy. To make sense of the extent to which civil society is actually constitutive of citizens (i.e. nurtures associational capabilities) and is differentiated from the political society and the market, we have to examine it in terms of a horizontal and vertical dimension. The horizontal dimension refers to the Tocquevillian view of democracy, which focusses on the internal qualities of associational life. De Tocqueville argued that democracies function well when citizens make use of their associational capacities and recognise one another as rights-bearing citizens. This then leads us to the sociological question of the extent to which pervasive inequalities within society in effect distort the associational playing field and produce a wide range of political exclusions.

The vertical dimension is essentially a Weberian problem: many new democracies suffer from poor institutionalisation and, in particular, weak forms of integration between state and citizens. The problem is twofold. On the one hand, there is the problem of how citizens engage with the state. State–society relations tend to be dominated by patronage and populism, with citizens having either no effective means of holding government accountable (other than periodic elections) or being reduced to dependent clients. In the absence of clear and rule-bound procedures of engagement, citizens cannot engage the national or – just as importantly – the local state qua citizens, i.e. as autonomous bearers of civic and political rights. On the other hand, there is the problem of where citizens engage with the state, i.e. the problem of the relatively narrow institutional surface area of the state. Given that local government is often absent or just extraordinarily weak in much of the developing world, there are in fact very few points of contact with the state for ordinary citizens. Taken together, the vertical problem of state–society relations and the horizontal problem of perverse social inequalities undermine the associational autonomy of citizens, the sine qua non of any effective democracy (Fox, 1994). Citizens can vote, but can they participate consequentially?

Democratic consolidation

The striking point of comparison between India and South Africa is that their respective transitions were driven by broad-based, encompassing, secular, pan-racial/pan-ethnic movements deeply rooted in civil society. Because political society was the domain of European elites, the liberation struggle in both countries evolved and mobilised through structures of civil society (unions, schools, communities, peasant associations, religious organisations) and relied heavily on rich, domestic narratives of resistance to unjust rule to make their normative and political cases for democratic self-rule. Both movements unified immensely diverse populations to forge a single, more or less cohesive nationalist block that in the name of democracy – but, even more specifically, in the name of an inclusive, rights-based citizenship – made peaceful transitions to democracy. Other characteristics of the transition to democracy and subsequent period of consolidation need to be highlighted, especially to draw the contrast with the much more troubled trajectories of democratic deepening that both countries have travelled.

The political elites that came to power in India in 1947 enjoyed enormous personal and institutional legitimacy and widespread popular support. From 1951, when India held its first national elections, until 1967, the Indian National Congress (INC) was dominant. In the first three national elections it won commanding majorities in parliament (over 75 per cent of seats) and 45 per cent of the vote (India's majority rule, first-past-the-post electoral system amplifies the seats-to-votes ratio), and ruled every state except Jammu and Kashmir, Kerala, and the tiny state of Nagaland. What came to be described as the 'Congress System' exerted deep and wide control over political life, creating a degree of stability and order that was famously celebrated by Samuel Huntington (1968) as an example of successful political modernisation in the developing world. Although the Congress System would soon unravel, it undeniably consolidated democratic institutions and forged a nation from what was the most diverse, centripetal and noisy society in the world.

The institutional achievements of the INC in the first decade of democracy are remarkable. Firstly, the leadership of the INC presided over the writing of a constitution that has been a bulwark of Indian democracy, enshrining not only fundamental rights of citizenship, but also effectively balancing powers. Secondly, in the first decade of democratic rule, the INC very rapidly consolidated the territorial and political integrity of the nation. Over 500 independent princely states were incorporated into the nation and the Congress System itself spread deep into the territories of this vast subcontinent, establishing an organised political presence throughout the nation. Moreover, the Indian Administrative Service was strengthened and expanded, creating a national cadre of highly competent and professional elite bureaucrats. Thirdly, the INC, and Nehru in particular, adroitly dealt with a range of secessionist and insurrectionist movements. Although it did at times resort to repression (e.g. its armed response to a communist-led insurrection in Telengana) or to high-handed tactics (dismissing the communist government of Kerala in 1959), for the most part demands for greater regional autonomy were accommodated within India's federalist structures by redrawing state boundaries along linguistic lines and giving local political elites – including INC bosses – significant leeway in managing provincial affairs.

After 1967 Indian democracy was increasingly weakened by what Kohli and others have described as deinstitutionalisation:

> Organizational weakness in the Congress party, in conjunction with its failure to provide for systematic incorporation of the bottom half of the population into the political process, has put a high premium on personal appeal, populism, and mobilization of 'primordial' loyalties as strategies for gaining and maintaining power (Kohli, 1990:386).

The decline of the INC was met with the multiplication of small, often highly personalistic regional parties, the rise of Hindu nationalism and the Bharatiya Janata Party (BJP), and, most recently, the formation of new lower-caste-based parties, most notably the Bahujan Samaj Party in Uttar Pradesh. But even as the Indian state has largely failed in its developmental project and the party system has become increasingly fragmented, even inchoate, the foundations of democratic rule and governance remain robust. Firstly, elections in India have resulted in alternations in power and, indeed, the recent trend at the national and state levels has been for incumbents routinely to be voted out of power. Moreover, the Indian polity has not only survived the rise to power of an illiberal party – the BJP – but has also successfully accommodated a range of ethnic parties that, despite fierce competition, have tended towards moderation once in power (Chandra, 2005). Secondly, the secular and inclusionary principles of the Indian constitution have been assiduously safeguarded. The rise of Hindu nationalism and the INC's own well-documented flirtation with sectarian politics (or 'communalism', as it is called in India) notwithstanding, Indian law and politics have proactively preserved the rights of minorities and even during the period of BJP rule have upheld the principles – if not always the norms – of secularism. Thirdly, despite the serious weaknesses of the state, including a widespread failure to impose its rational-legal authority, the Supreme Court has seen its powers increase. The court has safeguarded the integrity of the electoral processes and kept in check some of the more perverse effects of a fragmented party system. Even more dramatically, it 'has managed over the years to apply a more substantive conception of equality that justices have used to uphold rights to health, education, and shelter, among others' (Mehta, 2007:71).

The most important measure of the institutional robustness of democracy in India is the degree of legitimacy that democracy and the nation enjoy in public opinion. Survey after survey confirms that overwhelming majorities of Indians favour democracy over all other political systems (in contrast to declining support for democracy in Latin America) and that large majorities identify strongly with the nation, i.e. with a sense of being 'Indian' (Linz, Stepan & Yadav, 2006). These views, moreover, hold steady across all major religious groups and even in border regions where secessionist movements have been active. The most telling evidence of how deeply rooted democracy has become comes from voting itself. As Yogendra Yadav (1999) has famously documented, Indian democracy over the last two decades has witnessed a 'second democratic upsurge'. As Yadav shows, not only have rates of electoral participation climbed, but the social composition of participation has shifted decisively in favour of women and lower-caste groups. The rise of new parties making direct appeals to lower castes and Muslims is further confirmation that the masses, as it were, have entered politics.

The African National Congress (ANC) has played a similarly commanding role in the first 13 years of South African democracy. It has won every national election with overwhelming majorities (66 per cent on average) and has ruled continuously in every province except the Western Cape and KwaZulu-Natal. Given the circumstances of internal colonialism that characterised apartheid, the transition to democracy was a necessarily complicated process that required elaborate negotiations. This, in turn, produced a new democratic nation that was built on sophisticated, nuanced and carefully designed democratic institutions, including a constitution that is widely acclaimed as state of the art and highly progressive. The ANC, moreover, moved quickly to expand this institutional base by passing comprehensive legislation that, across a range of sectors (e.g. local government, administration, public housing, social services), prescribed careful and balanced processes for achieving transformative goals, most notably the deracialisation of state institutions. The judiciary in South Africa is highly autonomous and has played a proactive role in supporting the constitution (in particular, its social rights clauses), and disciplining and monitoring government, including a number of cases in which high-profile liberation struggle figures have been successfully prosecuted for abuses of power. The bureaucracy, from the national to the local level, has been strengthened and diversified, and in comparative terms is highly professional and effective (Heller, 2008). Most notably, the South African state has been able to significantly increase a historically high rate of tax compliance and introduce a comparatively progressive tax structure, with most of the tax burden falling on the wealthy white community (Lieberman, 2003).

And, as in the case of India, the nation-building project has been highly successful. Regionalist challengers to the ANC, most importantly the KwaZulu-based ethnic Inkatha Freedom Party, have lost much of their traction and politics in post-apartheid South Africa has for the most part been spared the territorial or ethnic contestation that bedevils so many democracies in the region. Although the ANC, and Thabo Mbeki in particular, have on occasion played the card of African nationalism, for the most part the party and the state have maintained their commitment to non-racialism. Politically, the ANC's position has been so dominant and encompassing that it has even successfully absorbed its erstwhile enemy, the National Party. And despite significant tensions and repeated predictions of its imminent demise, the ANC has been able to maintain the support of the labour federation (the Congress of South African Trade Unions, or COSATU) and the South African Communist Party, the partners of its ruling 'Tripartite Alliance'.

In summarising the state of democratic consolidation in both South Africa and India, three points can be emphasised. Firstly, the basic institutions and procedures of electoral democracy have been firmly entrenched. There are no significant social or political forces in India or South Africa that do not accept the basic legitimacy of parliamentary democracy, including in each case well-organised and ideologically committed communist parties, both of which, at it so happens, are aligned with the current (January 2008) ruling majority. Secondly, the basic principles of and institutions for the rule of law, including a forceful constitution and a sovereign judiciary, are solidly grounded and have acted as effective and significant counterweights to excesses of political power. Thirdly, the general rule of law environment has safeguarded and in some cases expanded the role of civil society. In both countries, overt state repression is rare (and when it occurs it is vociferously denounced), associational life has largely been free of state interference, the media are diverse and noisy, social movements are tolerated (although grudgingly in the case of South Africa), and there are clear indications of a dramatic expansion of non-governmental organisation (NGO) activity. I will substantially qualify this point about civil society below, but the point remains that by all the standard metrics of democratic consolidation, both countries have fared well.

In explaining the relative success of democratic consolidation in India and South Africa, some shared factors come to the surface. Most obviously, the transition to democracy and the initial period of consolidation were managed by an ideologically cohesive, unified and highly effective political elite that enjoyed enormous political legitimacy. Some have argued that both transitions were in effect hijacked by elites (Bond, 2000; Chibber, 2005), but even if elites did indeed play the central role in managing the transitions and ultimately answered to narrow interests, their efficacy was in large part based on the fact that they led and represented broad-based movements, enjoyed enormous moral standing and for a significant period received periodic electoral affirmation. This historically conferred legitimacy gave the two congresses – the INC and the ANC – and their leadership enormous leeway not only in laying the institutional foundations of democracy, but, just as importantly, in forging a nation from disparate ethnic, racial and regional identities. One has but to glance at their respective neighbours (Sri Lanka, Pakistan, Zimbabwe) to appreciate the significance of India and South Africa's inclusive, democratic nationalism.

Arrested democracies?

For all their successes in consolidating democracy, the problem of *effective* democracy – i.e. the degree to which citizens can actually and effectively exercise their civil and political rights – remains acute in both countries. As argued above, this is primarily a problem of civil society, because even where political society is well established, as in India and South Africa, it is still in civil society that opinions are formed and solidarities are generated, and the ethical dimension of a *democratic society* is cultivated. It is, in other words, in civil society that modern citizens make themselves heard by directly and freely engaging in political life in a meaningful manner. I argue that civil society in India and South Africa remains highly constricted, leaving little room for the practice of citizenship. The problem here can be traced along both the horizontal and vertical axes of democratic deepening.

Any discussion of civil society in India and South Africa has to begin with the simple observation that associational capabilities are highly uneven across social categories and that they have their roots in specific histories of inequality: the caste system in India and apartheid in South Africa. These have produced what Evelina Dagnino (1998) in the Brazilian context has called 'social authoritarianisms', i.e. deep-seated inequalities of not only income and property, but cultural and social capital as well that permeate social practices and govern social interactions. So deep are these fundamental inequalities that many would question whether such societies can be fertile grounds for a vibrant civil society, predicated as it is on a degree of civic equality. Indeed, this is precisely why Partha Chatterjee (2001) and Gurpreet Mahajan (1999) have questioned the very relevance of the notion of civil society in India, and why Mahmood Mamdani (1996) has so famously shown that the legacies of colonial rule pose significant obstacles to advancing citizenship in South Africa.

But even as we keep in mind the serious challenges that deep and durable inequalities pose to democratic deepening, we also have to acknowledge that associational inequalities in both countries have hardly been intractable. The nationalist movement in both countries produced rights-based discourses that were direct attacks on caste and race. The associational ties that both national-democratic movements created cut across class, race and caste, negating inequalities in practice and declaring that the new subject of the new nation was not a Hindu or a black, but a citizen. With the transition to formal democracy, both nations declared the fundamental equality in politics, law and society of all citizens. And both supported an array of affirmative state interventions that would correct historical injustices, i.e. the 'reservation' of government jobs and university positions for 'untouchables' (now Dalits) and 'tribals' (now Adivasis) in India, and an array of affirmative action and black empowerment schemes in South Africa. This, moreover, was not just a short-lived historical moment when national fervour created a sense of solidarity that aligned with ideas of democratic citizenship. These norms of democratic equality have also been sustained by a range of social movements and even subregional politics. As Gail Omvedt (1998:137) has argued, in contrast to the reformism of the INC leadership, the many anti-caste movements in India, both before and after independence, 'fought for access to "public" spaces of work, consumption and citizen's life'. These movements, in other words, sought to expand democratic civil society by actively removing barriers to participation. In the south, these movements fundamentally transformed caste relations, and Varshney (2000) even credits these movements with the better government performance and better social development indicators observed in southern states. Also, as I have argued elsewhere (Heller, 2000), the extensive social rights- and equity-promoting public policies that have been secured in the state of Kerala can be tied directly to its historical pattern of civil society formation. In this state of 32 million people, successive waves of social movements – a rich and competitive sector of civic organisations and citizens who know and use their rights – has kept political parties and the state accountable, producing India's most competitive party system and its most efficacious state.

Similarly, in South Africa, despite the perverse inequalities inherited from apartheid, large segments of the black population are well organised, most notably the labour movement, and have been able to secure significant redress such as labour protection and the deracialisation of formal labour markets. Moreover, a wide array of movements, from local civics (Heller, 2003; Chipkin, 2007) to single-issue campaigns and HIV/AIDS movements, have deployed a range of 'in-system' and 'extra-institutional' tactics to press both rights-based demands (HIV treatment) and more counterhegemonic challenges (opposition to neoliberalism) on the state (Ballard, Habib & Valodia, 2006).

The general point here is that although social inequalities are deeply entrenched and must be foregrounded in any discussion of democratic deepening, they have not, under the conditions of formal democracy and associational rights, precluded political practices and discourses that explicitly challenge these inequalities. In other words, despite pervasive social exclusions, subordinate groups have used the political space created by democratic institutions to make claims. Thus, it is possible to argue that democratic power in India continues to be concentrated in the hands of elites and intermediaries, while at the same time recognising that contentious politics played out in civil society has deepened India's democratic culture (Jayal, 2007). Similarly, despite the direct subordination of much of civil society to the party/state in South Africa, local grass-roots politics and social movements continue to press for the vision of participatory democracy that originally informed the anti-apartheid struggle (Heller & Ntlokonkulu, 2001; Greenstein, 2003; Chipkin, 2007).

The democratic deficit in India and South Africa lies neither in civil society per se nor in the formal character of the state. The state in both cases is a democratic one, and although social inequalities have proven resilient, they have not precluded even the most excluded groups from invoking their rights. The more intractable problem has been the vertical dimension of democracy. Despite the conditions of highly consolidated democracies and their having legally guaranteed rights, citizens from subordinate groups find it difficult to engage with the state effectively. There are two interrelated problems here. First of all, as we will see in a moment, the surface area of the state remains quite limited, especially when it comes to local government. Secondly, in both democracies, political parties not only monopolise the channels of influence, but also exert considerable power in setting the agenda, i.e. determining which issues, claims and even identities enter the political domain. As a result, the public sphere is shaped largely by forms of influence that flow directly from political or economic power (parties, lobbies, powerful brokers) rather than from the deliberation of reason-bearing citizens. It is in this sense that I argue that the problem of democratisation lies less in the institutions of democracy or the party system (which is dramatically different in the two countries) than in the political practices and channels that link civil society to the state.

This problem of state–civil society relations could be explored from many angles, but I want to make the argument by focussing on local democratic government and social movements. The first is significant because it is in local arenas that citizens are made and that the surface area of democratic government needs to be expanded. The second is important because social movements in any democratic society are not only a critical countervailing force to the oligarchical tendencies of political parties, but can also raise, define and politicise issues that political society is often insensitive to.

The institutional space for the exercise of local citizenship in India is highly circumscribed. The average population of India's 28 states is roughly 37 million. Indian states enjoy significant powers and play a central role in development. But local elected governments – i.e municipalities and *panchayats* (rural governments) – have few resources and very limited authority. The first chief minister of Kerala, E. M. S. Namboodiripad, made this point succinctly when he noted that 'if at the level of centre-state relations the constitution gave us democracy, at the level of state-panchayat relations the constitution gave us bureaucracy'.[100] Until the passage of the 73rd and 74th constitutional amendments in 1993, most states did not even hold local government elections on a regular basis.[101] The development functions of local governments were limited to acting as implementation agencies for line department schemes, and ordinary citizens were afforded few opportunities to directly engage in or influence decision making about public allocations. The insignificance of local government in India is readily summarised: annual per capita expenditure at the local level in 1990–95 was a paltry 45 rupees (about one US dollar) (Chaudhuri, 2006). The actual presence of local government has been so thin, both institutionally and financially, that it has not provided a usable platform for public deliberation or action. To the extent that local citizens interact with local government, they generally do so through the mediations of various brokers and fixers, often leaders of caste associations or landed elites. And when the state is present in a more robust form, it often becomes little more than an instrument of dominant interests, as in the case of local police forces that actively harass and prey upon lower castes (Brass, 1997:274). In sum, the form of the local state and the mode of its interface are so institutionally weak and so thoroughly permeated by social power and extra-legal authority as to prevent the actual practice of citizenship.

The South African picture is more nuanced. In rural areas, given the legacy of customary rule and the still formidable powers enjoyed by chiefs, Mamdani's (1996) characterisation of local government as a form of decentralised despotism is still probably apt. Recent legislative reforms have in fact buttressed the power of 'traditional authorities' and, as Lungisile Ntsebeza (2005) has carefully documented, reversed many of the democratic gains of the post-apartheid period. Institutional weaknesses, moreover, make most local and district governments largely dependent on provincial line departments. But the picture in urban areas is quite different. Here, South Africa is quite unique, having inherited municipal structures that, in comparative terms, enjoy significant governance capacities and fiscal autonomy, especially in the three megacities of Johannesburg, Cape Town and Durban. It is even possible to talk of a local developmental state (Van Donk et al., 2008). The democratic character of that state is another matter.

At the time of transition, South Africa's foundational development document, the Reconstruction and Development Programme (RDP), reserved a central role for community participation in promoting local development. Subsequent legislation mandated a series of participatory processes in local governance. But with the shift in 1996 to a more market-driven vision of development (the Growth, Employment and Redistribution plan, or GEAR), the government came to see the local state more as an instrument of delivery than a forum for participation. As many commentators have noted, over the past decade local government has become increasingly insulated and centralised (Van Donk et al., 2008). In the name of efficiency and more rapid delivery, the ANC has managerialised decision-making processes and reduced the quality and scope of participatory processes created under the RDP. A wide range of participatory institutions such as community development forums have been dismantled or hollowed out, and municipal governance has been centralised into unicity structures that have entrenched a bureaucratic and corporatist vision of urban governance (Beall, Crankshaw & Parnell, 2002). The privatisation or outsourcing of many government functions and increased reliance on consultants have virtually crowded out community structures. At the ward level, elected councillors and their hand-picked ward committees have been given a new role and new resources for coordinating local development. Because of the electoral dominance of the ANC and the very tight control it exerts over the selection of councillors, the new ward committee system feeds into ANC patronage. In interviews and focus groups I conducted in 2001, township residents complained bitterly that their ward councillors were more interested in advancing their political careers than in serving their communities. More broadly, as Oldfield (2008:488) remarks, this 'focus on development as a delivery process has framed the substantiation of democracy as a procedural policy rather than political challenge'. In sum, the local spaces in which citizens can practise democracy and exert some influence over South Africa's very ambitious project of local government transformation (i.e. deracialising the apartheid city and closing the service gap) have narrowed.

A second critical space of state–civil society engagement is the political opportunity structure for social movements. In both countries the broad institutional space is favourable to social movement formation and generally quite permissive of contentious action, yet at the same time largely immune to social movement influence. In India, there is a long and rich post-independence history of social mobilisation, but, with the possible exception of the farmer movement that emerged in the 1980s, few social movements have been able to scale up and affect the political arena. The farmer movement successfully mobilised relatively well-off farmers to secure significant rents from the state. But its agenda has been a narrow corporatist one, more lobby than movement, and certainly not interested in expanding social rights. Although landless labourers constitute by far the single biggest constituency in India and are overwhelmingly Dalit and lower caste, nothing even resembling a sustained movement has ever emerged, except in the state of Kerala. If anything, movements of the agrarian poor have taken place largely outside the democratic arena in the form of the various Maoist-inspired local insurrections that are currently active in a number of states. India's industrial labour movement has been especially weak. From the very beginning of independence, India's labour federations were dominated by the state and, as Chibber (2005) has shown, were outmanoeuvred into accepting an industrial relations regime that subordinated labour's interests to the imperatives of promoting capital investment. Operating in a highly bureaucratic and quasi-corporatist environment, the federations have for the most part become instruments of political parties, and it is telling that they have never expanded their presence beyond the confines of the protected organised sector, which accounts for less than 9 per cent of the workforce.[102] Other movements, including those of Dalits, Adivasis, women and environmentalists, have developed innovative and effective forms of contention and built strategic ties with transnational advocacy networks, so it is difficult to downplay the richness and the vibrancy of the social movement sector.

Yet none of these movements has developed effective and sustainable ties to political society and, indeed, many have taken an anarcho-communitarian turn, embracing communities and rejecting the state (Bardhan, 1999; Corbridge & Harriss, 2000). This reflects the degree to which civil society formations have come to distrust a political society increasingly characterised by corruption, personalism, short-term calculations, and concentrated and insulated power. Mary Katzenstein and Raka Ray (2005) point to a decisive shift in how the political opportunity structure shapes the character of social movements in India by delineating two distinct periods. In what they call the Nehruvian period, the state, political parties and movements were aligned around a left frame of democratic socialism, but since the 1980s these progressive movements have had to reinvent themselves with the 'ascendance of its [the Nehruvian period] institutional mirror image on the right, the similarly synergistic nexus of state, party and movement now organised, however, around religious nationalism and the market' (Katzenstein & Ray, 2005:3). Indeed, movement activity over the past two decades has been increasingly dominated by forces tied to the rise of Hindu nationalism, including various 'elite revolts' (Corbridge & Harriss, 2000) against the new electoral power of the lower castes. Insofar as these movements seek to affirm traditional privileges of caste, male authority and the Hindu majority, they are in effect deeply illiberal. And although they have not proven a threat to formal democracy – as evidenced by the BJP's tenure of and departure from power – they have arguably had a deeply perverse effect on civil society by stoking intercommunity violence; legitimising old and new exclusions; communalising schools, unions and associations; and, in general, reinforcing the involutionary logic of exclusionary identity politics.

In South Africa, social movements played such a critical role in the anti-apartheid struggle that they entered the democratic period with significant organisational capacity, enormous popular support and a lot of momentum. Following a well-established pattern (Hipsher, 1998), a certain degree of demobilisation was inevitable with the transition to democracy, especially considering the formal representation through various corporatist structures that the labour and civics movements were given. But the degree to which movements have been almost completely neutralised or sidelined requires some comment. Firstly, one needs to address the most complicated case, i.e. organised labour. COSATU's strength and cohesiveness stand in sharp contrast to India's fragmented and marginalised labour movement, and are a testament to the depth and breadth of labour organising that took place under apartheid. And despite its alliance with the ANC, COSATU has retained its autonomy, often voicing criticism of the state and staging broad-based and well-organised strikes across sectors to leverage labour's bargaining capacity (Habib & Valodia, 2006). COSATU has moreover shown itself to be a powerful kingmaker, having played a critical role in Jacob Zuma's defeat of President Mbeki for control of the ANC at the party's December 2007 Polokwane conference. Yet most assessments of labour's role in South Africa's corporatist structures, and specifically the National Economic Development and Labour Advisory Council (more commonly known as NEDLAC), are critical, arguing that the ANC has largely set the agenda. Most notably, COSATU failed to block or even modify the ANC's shift from the redistributive RDP to the quite orthodox neoliberal GEAR. COSATU itself recognises its political marginality. In a policy document, the federation complains that the ANC National Executive Committee contains no active trade unionists or social movement activists and goes on to say that 'once elections are over we go back into the painful reality of being sidelined for another five years' (cited in Webster & Buhlungu, 2004:241).

For other social movements in South Africa, one can paint a much simpler picture. The national civics movement – the South African National Civic Organisation (SANCO), which, next to labour, was the most important component of the anti-apartheid movement – has become little more than a compliant ANC mouthpiece. As has been argued elsewhere (Heller & Ntlokonkulu, 2001), local civics remain very active, are extremely critical of the ANC's policies, and often engage in contentious action. They also serve as vital and vibrant local public spaces. But with the dismantling of local participatory structures and the cooptation of SANCO, civics have very little influence over the public sphere, much less over government policy. Focus groups I conducted in Johannesburg with residents from townships and informal settlements consistently painted a picture of a distant and insulated ANC and a pronounced distrust of ward councillors, who are more beholden to the party than to communities (Heller & Ntlokonkulu, 2001). In recent years, the extent of dissatisfaction over the quality of local government and persistent unemployment has fuelled the rise of new social movements in urban areas, including anti-eviction campaigns and various forms of resistance to the commodification of public services. In 2005 the minister for provincial and local government reported that 90 per cent of the poorest municipalities experienced protests. The minister for safety and security put the number of protests in 2004/05 at almost six thousand (Atkinson, 2007:58). These movements remain largely local and inchoate, and have had little choice but to resort to contentious actions, many directed specifically at ward councillors. They have largely been met with silence or outright hostility from the government.

A third movement of note has been the Treatment Action Campaign (TAC), which has received international recognition for its resistance to the government's disastrous neglect of the HIV/AIDS epidemic. This movement, which enjoys a very high level of professional capacity and some very innovative leadership, has scored a number of legal and moral victories over the government, including a new commitment to roll out anti-retroviral treatment. But what is most telling in this case are the extraordinary challenges the TAC has faced in engaging the government. For years the movement was subjected to thinly veiled claims of racism, routinely denounced by government officials as beholden to foreign interests and often actively harassed, including the prosecution of grass-roots activists for providing anti-HIV transmission treatment to rape victims. That the TAC persevered and ultimately helped change government policy is a testament to its tenacity and efficacy as a movement. But it needs to be underscored that this is a tragic triumph. After years of ANC leaders claiming that HIV did not cause AIDS and completely ignoring the TAC and other HIV/ AIDS organisations, not to mention international pressure and COSATU's protests, South Africa has the highest per capita infection rate in the world.

Towards a crisis of citizenship?

As I have shown, the space for both local democratic practices and encompassing social movements has contracted in South Africa and India. While there is still plenty of room for vibrant associational forms and even contentious action, the nature of civil society's relationship to political society has severely restricted the impact that civil society can have on public decision making. This then leads to a critical question: if citizens cannot practise democracy, what happens to citizenship?

Local democratic government in India is very weak, and even non-existent in many states. For the urban and rural poor, sightings of the state (to borrow from Corbridge et al., 2005) are intermittent at best, and when they can or must engage with the local state, citizens work through intermediaries or powerful political brokers. The political party system has become highly fragmented, increasingly organised around regional and ethnically defined vote banks. On a day-to-day basis, then, the Indian citizen engages with the state either as a client or as a member of a group, but not as a rights-bearing citizen. Engagement is predicated on exchanges, not rights. Demands on the state are made through bribes, by appeals to caste or communal solidarities, or through the influence of powerful interest groups. The logic of these exchanges is democratically perverse, because it either privileges – and in the process reifies – primary identities or powerful lobbies, or is predicated on clientelistic exchanges that compromise political autonomy, as when labour federations become appendages of political parties.

It is hardly novel to remark that the Indian state, including and especially the local state, is fraught with corruption and clientelism. But what is more often treated as a problem of institutions (e.g. in the literature on good governance) must in fact be viewed as a problem of how *politics is transacted*. Politics in India has been increasingly instrumentalised; shorn of its normative and deliberative qualities; and reduced to little more than a competitive, mutually exclusive scramble for scare resources. This marks a significant transformation of political society. In the Nehruvian period, all classes, castes and regions in India, with the exception of the religious right, embraced the Nehruvian normative frame of secularism and promoting equality. The concept of the national was clearly and powerfully inscribed with the ideal of the democratic citizen, and underscored by a social contract in which an affirmative state would promote equality and inclusion. This democratic vision did not, as we have seen, bridge the enormous gap between the liberal urban middle classes and the more community-oriented rural masses, but it did allow for an inclusive, secular and democracy-enhancing definition of the nation and political life. Today, that definition is under threat, both from the revival of identity politics and market liberalisation.

By equating the nation with 'Hindu-ness', the Hindutva movement (which includes the BJP, Vishva Hindu Parishad [VHP] and Rashtriya

Swayamsevak Sangh [RSS]) has directly challenged the norm (if not the rules) of Indian secularism and, by stoking the politics of sectarianism and demonisation, has subverted the ideal of citizenship. This involutionary logic in which civil society is folded back into society and its myriad fragmented solidarities is not confined to Hindutva. As Jayal (2007:13) notes:

> Hindu nationalism and OBC [Other Backward Caste] politics ... are curiously similar in their strategy of deploying the political to entrench or transcend the social. The politics of Hindutva seek out the political domain to consolidate Hindu identity (BJP), while the backward caste assertions have been chiefly preoccupied with providing the people with *samman* [respect] and *izzat* [honour] through representation in governance institutions. Another important similarity between them is that they both reject the idea of a civic community that is not inflected by particularistic identities. The idea of universal citizenship enjoys little purchase within these political arguments, as cultural citizenship has acquired pre-eminence, and social citizenship is compromised.

If the reassertion of caste politics threatens civil society, so does the fragmentising logic of marketisation. Market liberalisation has empowered a new middle class (Fernandes & Heller, 2006) and opened room for a much more assertive and aggressive bourgeoisie (Chatterjee, 2007; Kohli, 2007). If the Congress System allowed for class accommodation, liberalisation has polarised class positions. The dominant classes, which benefitted the most from developmental investments of the Nehruvian state (especially in state employment and support for higher education), now actively reject the very notion of the affirmative, equity-enhancing state. Kaviraj (2000:114) summarises the resulting democratic conundrum:

> The more education and health are prised away from the control of the state in the process of liberalisation, the more unequal their distribution is likely to become. The political equality of democracy would then lose its capacity to exert pressure towards social equality.

South Africa's democracy is, of course, much younger, yet there are already troubling signs of a slide from civic to ethnic nationalism (Chipkin, 2007; Mangcu, 2008). Subaltern civil society in South Africa has also become estranged from political society, but through a different process. Civil society has become deeply bifurcated between an organised civil society that effectively engages with the state and a subaltern civil society that is institutionally disconnected from the state and political society. Business groups, professionalised NGOs and organised labour continue to be well positioned to engage with the state. But subaltern civil society, and especially the urban poor, has more or less been sidelined from the political process in South Africa. This containerisation has taken place through a complex set of institutional, political and discursive practices.

In institutional terms, the surface area of the state in South Africa has dramatically shrunk over the past decade. As noted above, participatory spaces in local government have been dismantled and state–society relations increasingly bureaucratised and politicised. At the national level, corporatist structures are all but defunct. The state still transacts significantly with civil society, but does so in a highly selective and controlled manner. Across a wide range of sectors, the preferred mode of intermediation has become 'partnerships' with professionalised NGOs that carry out contracted services. Conditions for engagement with the state are increasingly set by complex standards for meeting performance targets and accounting practices that all but rule out community-based organisations. Highly paid consultants, often working for 'non-profits', now occupy much of the terrain between the state and society. Katzenstein and Ray's (2005:9) characterisation of the shifting nature of state–civil society relations in India might well have been written of South Africa: 'Economic liberalisation has been accompanied by the massive NGO-ification of civil society arguably crowding out some of the more protest-oriented forms of organizing within the social movement sector.'

The political terms of engagement for civil society have eroded as a result of the ANC's increasingly centralised and dirigiste style of politics. After the ANC was unbanned in 1990, it moved quickly to assert its dominant role in the transition negotiations. The United Democratic Front – the umbrella organisation that had coordinated anti-apartheid struggles during the ANC's exile – was pressured to disband. Once in power, the ANC moved quickly to consolidate its hegemonic position, asserting its right as the agent of the 'National Democratic Revolution' to demand political subordination of mass organisations. Both ideologically and organisationally, the ANC has sought to assert control over civil society, and especially black civil society. As early as 1991 the ANC demanded that township civics recognise its role as the leader of the liberation movement and asserted its primacy in all political matters. At the 1997 national conference of the ANC, President Nelson Mandela delivered a speech (widely reported to have been written by then Deputy President Thabo Mbeki) in which he openly rebuked NGOs that asserted 'that the distinguishing feature of a genuine organisation of civil society is to be a critical "watchdog" over our movement, both inside and outside of our government' (ANC, 1997). Mandela called on official aid donors to shift their funding from civil society to government.

The ANC's view of civil society was made even more explicit in 1999, when, on the eve of local government elections, a key party theorist deplored the 'dichotomy between political and civic matters' that the very existence of SANCO represented, and called for ANC branch committees to supplant SANCO by engaging directly in civic activities (Makura, 1999:17).

Direct political control over civil society has been exerted through a range of mechanisms. Much of the leadership of the civics movement was recruited into ANC positions or government jobs. Control over ANC election list nominations has been streamlined and centralised, with provincial committees closely vetting lists of local ANC candidates. In some cases, local civil society organisations have been taken over by the ANC. Others that have questioned or protested government policy have simply been frozen out, or even subjected to harassment. At the grass-roots level, ANC ward councillors are often locked into very contentious conflicts with local community leaders, and in some cases have even resorted to violence (Heller & Ntlokonkulu, 2001).

Finally, the ANC's relationship to civil society has shifted frames, moving from a democratic conception of the citizen to a nationalist conception anchored in an essentialised African identity. The conception of the nation championed by the anti-apartheid struggle and popularised in the Freedom Charter was one populated by democratic citizens united by their opposition to apartheid. But during Mbeki's presidency there was a marked drift towards a conception of the nation rooted in 'racial nativism' (Mangcu, 2008). Not only does this mark a shift from what Habermas and Pensky (2001) call patriotism of the constitution (solidarity is constructed through shared ethical commitments to the rights of citizens) to a patriotism of the flag (solidarity is rooted in an essentialised identity), but it has also been clearly inflected with a political content. During the anti-apartheid movement, the term 'black' was a political term referring to those excluded and oppressed by the state. But as Chipkin (2007) and Mangcu (2008) argue, being authentically 'African' has increasingly become associated with being loyal to the ANC. In this logic, the ANC is the sole carrier of the National Democratic Revolution and any attack on its policies is construed as an attack on the latter's transformative goals. The ANC thus routinely denounces critics, including contentious social movements, as 'ultra-leftist' and 'counter-revolutionary', and in one notorious case denounced its alliance partner, COSATU, as being racist for opposing the government's economic policies (Mangcu, 2008:5).

Conclusion: Explaining the subordination of civil society

In this chapter I have tried to show that we need to understand democratic consolidation and democratic deepening as two conceptually distinct, but historically intertwined, processes. Firstly, the success of democratic transitions against all odds in both India and South Africa was the result of broad-based encompassing independence movements operating in the interstices of civil society that cultivated mass support for democracy. The subsequent process of democratic consolidation was underwritten by a cohesive political elite that enjoyed mass legitimacy. Yet despite these successes, which include national integration and the institutionalisation of the rule of law, the challenges of democratic deepening, and specifically of promoting effective democracy, have been hampered by the subordination of civil society to political society. But how do we explain the difficulty that subaltern civil society has had in engaging the political arena in the context of two robust, consolidated democracies? To answer this question, I want to point to two shared historical-structural factors.

The first is that the transition in both South Africa and India was marked by an imbalance of political and civil society. In the standard, evolutionary narrative of the development of Western democracy, civil society gave birth to modern democratic society. It was most notably the relative autonomy and increasing power of an ascendant bourgeoisie that gave birth to parliamentary reforms (if not universal suffrage). If, as Habermas (1989) has famously argued, the bourgeois public sphere played a critical role in promoting democracy, his critics have noted that subaltern publics were already quite active well before parliamentary regimes were introduced (Eley, 1992). The advent of democracy in Europe was thus predicated on what were already well-formed publics. The contrast with post-colonial societies is clear. The Indian independence movement did, as Chatterjee (1993) has shown, develop in civil society and produced a quite active and vociferous public. But it was largely limited to elites and, as Chatterjee argues, focussed for the most part on claiming the spiritual and the private as the domains of the Indian nation. Moreover, as has often been remarked, there was a clear disjuncture between the Indian constitution's assertions of universal rights and individual autonomy, and the segmented structures and community orientations of most Indians (Kaviraj, 2000). This disjuncture was, if anything, amplified in the Nehruvian period by the relative weakness of the urban faction of the dominant class that ruled the state. Because they could not extend their hegemony to rural areas where landed interests still prevailed, the Congress State adopted a strategy of accommodation, working through local power structures and, in particular, aligning with local dominant landed castes. This, to borrow Mamdani's (1996) phrase, created a form of decentralised despotism, reinforcing traditional caste hierarchies and leaving little room for the expansion of civil society.

A similar imbalance marked the transition in South Africa. Black civil society had certainly developed significant organisational presence at the time of transition. But it had emerged and developed in a context of extreme repression and absolute exclusion, and had as such little experience of transacting with the state. The transition to majority rule thus represented both a political and an institutional rupture. The vacuum of authority was quickly filled by the ANC. As an organisation in exile that was constantly threatened by the apartheid state, the ANC had developed extremely disciplined organisational structures, including clear lines of command, that proved far more effective in establishing its power in the transition period than the decentralised and flat organisational structures of civil society. Thus, when the ANC asserted itself as the exclusive representative of the black majority, it also by the same token became the only institutional conduit to the state. From the outset, then, South African democracy was marked by an asymmetry of power between political society and civil society. It should be emphasised that in both India and South Africa this general imbalance of power between political and civil society, although marked by specific national configurations, has its origins in the overdeveloped nature of the colonial state.

A second shared feature of the trajectory of democratisation in both countries is that this initial imbalance of power between political and civil society had a double-edged effect. On the one hand, it allowed for the relative dominance of a cohesive political elite that could go about the task of managing the transition and unifying the nation with little effective opposition. This provided political stability and time for institution building, and explains the comparative success of democratic consolidation in both countries. On the other hand, the very same process allowed a dominant class coalition to secure both its political and its economic position. In both cases, this has been marked specifically by the rise of a large, rentier middle class that is closely aligned with the bourgeoisie. In India, the primary beneficiaries of the developmental activities of the state were the urban, English-speaking, mostly upper-caste professional classes who benefitted the most from the expansion of state activities and a small industrial elite that was directly supported by subsidies and extensive protection. Similarly, in South Africa, the primary beneficiary of the state's various transformative projects, most notably affirmative action and black economic empowerment, has been a new black middle class occupying positions within the state bureaucracies and a new black bourgeoisie that has translated its political connections to the ANC into significant rent-generating alliances with white capital. In class terms, the significance of these configurations of state power in both cases is that they locked in dominant class coalitions that precluded more redistributive developmental trajectories (with the exception of some subnational configurations in India) and short-circuited the social incorporation of the masses. In political terms, the dominance of the INC and the ANC neutralised the electoral power of the poor majority. The combination of this balance of class power and political dominance in turn had the effect of bifurcating civil society. The term is apt, because it recognises that civil society is deeply divided and that although subaltern civil society is quite vibrant, it finds itself unable to impact political society.

In India, the rise of the BJP and Hindutva marks the involution of civil society. The BJP is in every respect a social-movement party, having risen from the trenches of civil society through the activities of the VHP and RSS to achieve electoral power. It is a direct response to the failures of the Nehruvian modernisation project. The resurgence of communalism and casteism in India is not as such the resurgence of deep, primordial loyalties but, rather, the result of a failure of political society to link up with the more democratic impulses of civil society. It is precisely this failure that has opened the space for the politicisation of identities, with parties constantly seeking the electoral edge through the formation of new, but inherently unstable, ethnic alignments.[103] The process is involutionary, because it pre-empts the formation of the type of stable, lower-class–caste programmatic coalitions that have been associated with the more successful redistributive regimes in Tamil Nadu, Kerala and West Bengal (Corbridge & Harriss, 2000).

To date, the dominant-party status of the ANC has pre-empted any such process of involution. Yet the problems of having containerised civil society are becoming increasingly evident. As discontent over increasing social and economic exclusion increases, new forms of resistance have emerged. On the positive side, new social movements that have inherited South Africa's powerful tradition of civic contention have emerged both to challenge the ANC's political dominance and to champion more participatory visions of democracy. More alarmingly, excluded and disenchanted segments of the population have forgone 'voice' for either loyalty (clientelistic ties to the ANC or local power brokers) or exit (rampant crime), a dynamic that has its own involutionary logic.

What lessons can we draw from this comparison of two of the most robust cases of democratic consolidation in the developing world? Firstly, a consolidated democracy is not necessarily conducive to democratic deepening. Although both democracies have provided the associational space for civil society, the actual pattern through which political society has consolidated has in fact impaired social movements, limited the spaces for effective citizenship and resulted in the increased bifurcation of civil society. While one can certainly understand the value that political scientists accord to stable political orders, especially in highly diverse and unequal societies, the trajectories of India and South Africa also suggest that democratic and national consolidation can come at the expense of developing more effective forms of citizenship. Moreover, this is not simply a problem of sequencing. The problem, as O'Donnell (1993) has already pointed to in the case of Latin America, is that the failure of political society to effectively embed itself in civil society and to make itself accountable to citizens and not just interests can severely undermine the legitimacy of democratic rule.

Secondly, the analysis provided here could be read as a version of path-dependent arguments, in which an initial imbalance of political and civil society, of elite and mass interests, has locked in a highly self-limiting form of democracy. In both cases, though, this lock-in should be seen more as a conjunctural balance of power than as a stable equilibrium. In India, the demise of the Congress System – once lauded as a model of democratic stability – was as rapid as its consequences have been unpredictable. The current involutionary trend in the direction of the politicisation of identities does not bode well for democratic civil society, but is one that is almost by definition incapable of becoming hegemonic, given the very malleability of the identities being mobilised. Subnational trends (e.g. Kerala) and new social movements (e.g. the Self-Employed Women's Association) suggest, moreover, that other, more inclusive and citizen-centred solidarities are possible.

In South Africa, the political dominance of the ANC appears absolute. But the very source of its ideological hegemony – its claim to represent the National Democratic Revolution – sets a very high standard. For large numbers of South Africans, the promise of a more just and inclusive society continues to inflect the meaning of politics with a transformative thrust that by definition leaves much to be redeemed.

In both cases, it is worth heeding Habermas and Pensky's (2001:112) reminder that 'social movements crystallise around normatively liberating perspectives for resolving conflicts that had previously appeared insoluble'.

8

Chapter

Local Democracy in Indian and South African Cities: A Comparative Literature Review

Claire Bénit-Gbaffou and Stéphanie Tawa Lama-Rewal

Since the 1990s the local level has become an important arena of development of democracy in most countries of the world – in a move sometimes described as part of 'the third wave of democratization' (Huntington, 1992), paradoxically encouraged by both progressive movements seeking a form of grass-roots democracy and by the World Bank as a new form of governance. India and South Africa are no exception, and both countries implemented reforms of local government in the mid-1990s with the objective of broadening and deepening democracy.

This chapter aims at comparing the political and academic debates that took place in South Africa and India concerning decentralisation and, more broadly, local democracy in an urban context.[104] We believe, with Hantrais (2009:72), that 'the definition and understanding of concepts and the relationship between concepts and contexts are of critical concern in comparative research that crosses national, societal, cultural and linguistic boundaries'. Through a literature review and a contextualisation of local democracy's history, institutions and practices, this joint chapter aims at identifying the commonalities and differences in the political and social stakes contained in the debates on 'local democracy'.

We define local democracy here as a set of democratic institutions and practices that are focussed on the local level (from the metropolitan level downwards to the ward and neighbourhood levels, for instance), and that can take two broad directions: *decentralisation* (local government authorities allow local votes to matter more than at a state/provincial or a national level, possibly leading to more accountability and a better adaptation to local needs by local politicians and officials); and *participation* (i.e. mechanisms for citizens to address the state between elections). These two dimensions do not necessarily coexist, even though, according to the World Bank, '[p]articipation and decentralization have a symbiotic relationship ... participation [can be] a means to successful decentralization [or] ... a goal of decentralization'.[105] Our assumption is not that local governments and participation are inherently more 'democratic' (as justly pointed out by

Purcell, 2006), but that they offer a potential for increased accountability and responsiveness by local politicians and officials to local citizens.

Our methodology is based on a review of the literature that we used in our previous research connected with the subject,[106] but also, in order to avoid the bias inherent in the collection of references thus accumulated over the past years, on a systematic search in new bodies of literature. In India, Tawa Lama-Rewal explored the archives of two Indian journals that reflect ongoing political and academic debates: *Economic and Political Weekly* (EPW)[107] and *Seminar*.[108] In South Africa, where there is no real equivalent for EPW or *Seminar*, Bénit-Gbaffou reviewed a number of multi-authored books published on local democracy in the recent years: a series on local government (Parnell et al., 2002; Van Donk et al., 2008); a series of *State of the Nation* (published yearly); and a multi-authored book on democracy and delivery (Pillay, Tomlinson & Du Toit, 2008).

The politics of decentralisation

In both countries, a brief genealogy of local democracy highlights how decentralisation has been favoured and resisted in turn; how it has served contrasting political agendas; and how, ultimately, electoral considerations of parties in power have determined its present form. One must note that in both national literatures a large number of authors are at the same time observers *and* actors of decentralisation. For instance, many Indian publications originate from the Institute of Social Sciences, an NGO close to the Indian National Congress (INC), which works as an observatory of decentralisation and continuously produces reports about various aspects of this policy.[109] In South Africa, academics with practical experience in local or national government were approached by political parties during the transitional period to contribute to social change.[110]

Decentralisation in India: A Gandhian dream implemented by communist parties

In the Indian context, the idea of local democracy belongs to the Gandhian political discourse (Mukherji, 2008). Gandhi, who led the freedom movement in the 1920s, was convinced that a new, independent India had to be built, politically but also economically, on the hundreds of thousands of Indian villages. He subscribed to the Orientalist myth of village republics as part of the Golden Age of India and conceived the new political system as based on a pyramid of rural communities economically self-sufficient and regulating themselves through discussions aiming at producing a consensus.

Even though Gandhi occupied a dominant position and was a moral reference for a large part of the nationalist movement, his views on local democracy were strongly opposed by Ambedkar (the leader of the untouchables and the architect of the constitution) who viewed Indian villages as a site of backwardness. The constitution finally reflected Ambedkar's position, as the subject of 'local government' is only mentioned in directive principles, which means that the ultimate decision on this matter remains with the states. Yet even though the INC from the 1950s onwards engaged in policies that were opposed to the Gandhian vision (i.e. state-driven industrialisation instead of developing cottage industries, and strong political centralisation instead of local self-government), this vision resurfaced at regular intervals, first within the INC, then out of it when major Gandhian figures left the party.

One can identify four major landmarks in the history of local democracy in independent India. The first one is the report produced in 1957 by the committee formed under the chairmanship of Balwantrai Mehta – a Gujarati INC politician and a staunch Gandhian – which popularised the phrase '*panchayati raj*'.[111] It is important to note that decentralisation at that time was not synonymous with local democracy: even though the report recommended the setting up of a pyramidal structure of locally elected councils at two or three levels (village, block, district), its main objective was to make the implementation of local development programmes more effective and it recommended that political parties should not participate in local elections.[112] As a result, in 1959 all states got a law organising *panchayats*, but the resistance of bureaucrats and elected representatives at higher levels to a true devolution of power combined to weaken *panchayati raj* institutions (PRIs) except in Gujarat and Maharashtra (Narain, 1965; Kumar, 2006).

The second landmark is the political comeback of Jaya Prakash Narayan (popularly called JP), a socialist leader soon converted to Gandhian ideas, who left the INC after Gandhi's death to practise Gandhi's ideals in his ashram. In 1959 JP had written a manifesto for a communitarian democracy, derided by many as completely utopian (Narayan, 2001). In the mid-1970s, when Indira Gandhi confronted a severe economic and political crisis, JP accepted the invitation by a student organisation linked to the Hindu Right to take the lead of the students' agitation in Bihar and to appeal for 'total revolution'. He denounced the centralisation of power by Indira Gandhi, which bred corruption, and advocated a refoundation of Indian democracy on the basis of villages: in his vision, universal franchise should be practised only at the village level, and the village council should be responsible in front of the '*gram sabha*', or village assembly (i.e. the sum of all adults in the village). This is the only moment when the idea of direct democracy found a national echo. In 1975 Indira Gandhi declared a state of emergency and arrested all her political opponents, including JP. When she lifted the state of emergency and organised elections two years later, the INC was, for the first time since independence, defeated at the national level by a broad coalition gathering all her opponents, from the communists to the Hindu Right, around the Janata Party, which considered JP as its guru.

The Janata government announced a new vision of development, based on rural communities, and under Ashoka Mehta (who was in jail with JP during the freedom movement) set up a new committee to review the functioning of PRIs. The Ashoka Mehta report, released in 1978, is the third landmark. It recommended, again, a three-tier structure of locally elected councils, but supported the role of political parties in local elections. It also recommended the formation in each village of a village assembly with a consultative role. While the Janata government soon proved unable to overcome its inherent contradictions, a few state governments started implementing the recommendations of the Ashoka Mehta report and became pioneers of decentralisation, especially West Bengal and Karnataka.

The fourth landmark is the decentralisation policy adopted in 1992 in the form of two constitutional amendments: the 73rd Constitutional Amendment Act (CAA) deals with rural India, the 74th with urban India. This policy, drafted in the late 1980s, pertains to Rajiv Gandhi's endeavour to modernise the Indian state. The policy draft incorporated most of the recommendations of the Ashoka Mehta report and it is often qualified as historic for two reasons: (1) it institutionalises locally elected councils as the third tier of India's federalism; local elections are now to be held under the supervision of newly formed State Election Commissions and no more than six months can elapse between the dissolution of a council and the new election;[113] and (2) it provides a substantial number of reserved seats for women, the Scheduled Castes (SCs), i.e. the lowest castes (ex-untouchables), and the Scheduled Tribes (STs). This policy draft was much discussed in 1989, but political turbulences (the INC lost the elections again in 1989 and Rajiv Gandhi was assassinated in 1991) explain why it started being implemented only from 1994 onwards.

Finally, which Indian parties are most interested in local democracy? Many of the parliamentary debates around the decentralisation policy in 1989 expressed suspicions vis-à-vis the INC, which so far had been characterised by a tendency to centralise power rather than delegate it: was decentralisation an electoral gimmick, meant to mobilise local 'vote banks' in support of state governments, which increasingly belonged to regional parties? Undoubtedly, what comes out strongly from a review of regional case studies is that both ideology and political culture make a difference in the implementation of decentralisation. Many studies of decentralisation focus on one state only, among which Kerala and West Bengal are studied most often.[114] These two states have been dominated by coalitions of communist parties (which alternate with an INC-led coalition in Kerala, but have not been defeated in West Bengal since 1977). Indeed, communist parties ideologically have consistently been favouring decentralisation and have a party structure[115] able to tap the electoral benefit of local mobilisation.

Decentralisation in South Africa: Implemented by apartheid; resisted by the ANC?

In South Africa, the central debates that one can relate to 'local democracy' have focussed on the reform of local government: the vast number of successive reforms from the 1980s onwards show the importance of the matter both in the late apartheid era and in the early post-apartheid period. One can broadly distinguish among the following periods:[116]

1. In the early 1980s the apartheid state started a policy of decentralisation – the design of a racially segregated society, reflecting the principles of apartheid, had so far required an important level of centralised control, as well as public funding that could only be raised by a powerful state. However, in the aftermath of the unrest in townships[117] spearheaded by the internationally famous 1976 Soweto uprising, black local authorities were created next to white local governments. The idea was to divide and rule, give black notables a stake in social stability and in the continuation of the apartheid regime, and enhance the rise of a black middle class able to resist and sedate the wave of youth resistance in black townships. However, the notion of 'democracy' could obviously not be discussed in this context – black local authorities were largely discredited and often the target of political violence from township residents. Many civic movements developed in the 1980s, calling for a boycott of elections and all services

and taxes raised by apartheid local authorities: their aim was to render the townships 'ungovernable'. Some of them joined the South African National Civic Organisation, a federation of civics. The power and dynamism of this 'grass-roots democracy' and popular resistance to apartheid (in a context where liberation parties like the African National Congress [ANC] and the South African Communist Party were banned) were epitomised in the development of the United Democratic Front. One of the famous slogans of the campaign was 'one city, one tax base', which called for a political and fiscal integration of municipal government.

2. From 1994 onwards the priority of the new democratic regime was to democratise local government, in particular in the sense of 'integrating' and deracialising municipal structures (Parnell et al., 2002). Until 2000 there was a period of 'transition' during which several local government reforms were enacted, reflecting hesitations between the objectives of redistribution and integration (requiring a certain level of centralisation, at least at metropolitan level), and the need to reflect a vibrant civil society (calling for a more decentralised type of local government structure). Interestingly, both civics and opposition parties (associated with white residents) called for decentralisation, while the ANC insisted on creating strong metropolitan governments (Cameron, 1999). The 1995 interim local government structure allowed for a two-tier structure (with one metropolitan government and several substructures), but the 2000 reform scrapped the substructures (which had proved to be dominated by opposition parties) and created what was called 'unicities' (one-tier metropolitan councils). The legacy of civics forms of direct democracy was sidelined, owing partly to the need for reconciliation and redistribution and the fear of recreating racially segregated local governments (reflecting the spatial structure of segregation in South African cities), and partly maybe to the perception that civics' legitimacy was now superseded by democratically elected local governments.

3. From 2000 and the adoption of the 'final' structure of local government, debates shifted to the notion of 'developmental local government'. This notion is in fact quite ambiguous, but supposedly emphasises the broad role of local government not only in terms of service delivery, but also in fostering the creation of sustainable settlements and communities; an effort to coordinate various categories of infrastructure and service

provision; a focus on local economic development (Van Donk et al., 2008); and, lastly, a focus on community participation.[118]

This debate has increased as mass urban protests have erupted around the country (Atkinson, 2007) and there is a rising perception of corruption and inefficiency in local government's ability to 'deliver' urban services – whether wrongly or rightly, as impressive numbers of houses and figures on access to urban services are published yearly by the South African government, but evidence also shows that some of these public goods are not adapted to local needs (McDonald & Pape, 2002; Charlton & Kihato, 2008). This pressure on local government takes two contradictory directions: on the one hand, legislative texts increasingly emphasise the 'developmental' role of local government, and the need to build 'sustainable' communities and encourage their participation in urban governance (Piper & Deacon, 2008), where the ward level is consolidated around the ward councillor and through the election of a ward committee, which is considered to be the main platform for participatory democracy. On the other hand, a rather hard line on local government 'efficiency' and 'ability to deliver' is adopted (Hemson & O'Donnovan, 2007; Van Donk et al., 2008) through 'performance targets' against which municipal officials and politicians are judged, following the lines of the neoliberal and technocratic principles of the New Public Management (how many houses, water and electricity reticulation systems, roads, etc. have been delivered; to what extent have costs been recovered; etc.?).

Contrasting roles of cities in constructing local democracy

One striking difference emerges from this parallel genealogy concerning the place of cities in the conceptualisation of local democracy. Cities are almost invisible in the Indian literature, whereas in South Africa the emphasis is on metropolitan areas (at the expense of weaker, smaller municipalities).

The idea that the natural location of local democracy is in *rural* India has been extremely widespread among politicians and scholars at least until the 2000s. Thus the decentralisation policy drafted in the late 1980s at first concerned only villages; the 74th CAA was drafted on the model of the 73rd CAA almost as an afterthought. Very few texts address precisely the urban dimension of local politics,[119] or the local dimension of urban politics, and many of them were written by American scholars in the 1970s (Oldenburg, 1976; Rosenthal, 1976; Weiner & Osgoofield, 1976). A prominent exception here is the literature on the Shiv Sena, a regional party built on the promotion of the 'son of the soil' in Bombay. The party has a dense network of local branches in the capital city of Maharashtra, on which it has been able to rely and which allows it to be a major player in both municipal and state elections (Kaviraj & Katzenstein, 1981; Gupta, 1982; Hansen, 2001a).

This rural bias does not exist in South Africa, a predominantly urban country with a strong sense that political avant-gardes develop in cities (and in particular in a few townships that have become symbols of resistance and mobilisation, nationally and internationally). The legacy of civic organisations has also grounded an ideal – if not of 'local democracy', then at least of 'power to the people' – in the major urban centres. Several authors argue that post-1994 local government restructuring and decentralisation works quite well for large, economically powerful cities and much less well for smaller urban municipalities, not to mention rural districts, which have huge needs, little wealth creation capacity and a chronic shortage of skills, and rely much more on centralised types of interventions (Makgetla, 2007).

The transformative agenda of local democracy

In both countries, debates on local democracy raise the question of the role of the state in the transformation of society (in post-independence/post-apartheid contexts). While the importance of the central state in promoting a progressive society is consistently stressed, the role of local government in this regard is more contested. On the one hand, there is an apprehension that the local level of democracy might lead to forms of conservatism – e.g. the supposed 'backwardness' of villages – or reactionary local or minority politics. On the other hand, local government is expected to provide an important arena of social transformation. Thus, in both countries, local government reform is seen as an opportunity, or even a key instrument, for building a more integrated society and addressing some of its inequalities, understood mainly as inequalities inherited from the past and from institutional structures, rather than other types of inequalities, e.g. current socio-economic inequalities. The meaning of 'transformation'/'integration' obviously varies.

South Africa: Reconstruction, integration, transformation

In post-apartheid South Africa, local government was a crucial arena of 'reconstruction', 'integration' and 'transformation'. Each of these terms has its own nuance, but has been used in relation to South African cities, urban policies and local government restructuring. 'Reconstruction' refers to both the institutional dimension ('reconstructing local government') and the spatial dimension ('restructuring' of segregated cities, in particular through an ambitious and modernist housing policy) of the post-apartheid project. 'Integration' asserts the necessity of getting away from apartheid ('separate development') and in particular racially segregated municipalities. The interim local government structure and the final unicity structure both made sure that former black and white areas were included in a shared administrative and political entity, not only for electoral and fiscal purposes, but also as a political statement putting an end to decades of separate development. 'Transformation' (a term that emerged later) euphemises the notion of deracialisation through affirmative action that brings about a progressive shift in leadership structure (political and economic) so that it becomes more representative of the country's (racial) demographics.

The centrality of the urban question in some of the civic movements developed in the 1980s (around the motto 'one city, one tax base'), the fact that cities were perceived as epitomising the contradiction of the apartheid system (racial segregation, but massive use of a black workforce by white-owned businesses and industries) made them a central object of attention in post-apartheid South Africa. The transitional period saw the blooming of ambitious plans of desegregation and integrated urban development (which never really took off, owing to their cost and the amount of local resistance to social and racial desegregation), and local government restructuring (which was achieved in several steps, as mentioned earlier). For the latter, the ANC clearly made the choice of a centralised form of local government, with strong metropolitan councils and no second tier of local government, but a number of electoral wards. There were obviously political considerations in this choice, with majority rule and the fact that elections work almost as 'racial censuses' guaranteeing the transformation of the face of local government.

India: Quotas as a social experiment/democratisation by inclusion

The 1989 issue of *Seminar* devoted to the decentralisation policy[120] (which was then being debated in parliament) displays the ability of concerned actors and academics to foresee the major hurdles that were to materialise after the policy had started being implemented, i.e. local authorities' lack of resources; the need to train newly elected representatives; and, more generally, an institutional context unfavourable to a true devolution of power. But this issue also reveals the great expectations attached to decentralisation, which in several articles appears as a way to reform Indian democracy at large; for instance, Rajni Kothari (1989:16), the seasoned political scientist, writes:

> A true vision of a decentralised polity and society involves transformation in the nature of the state both with regard to its institutional structures and its operating culture, as well as in respect of its relationship with civil society and the sources of its legitimacy and authority.

In parliament, the Indian central government justified decentralisation with two main arguments: (1) the traditional one that village councils, as nodal points of rural development, must be strengthened institutionally; and (2) a new argument emphasising democratisation as inclusion. Decentralisation was supposed to 'enlarge the funnel of representation' (Rajiv Gandhi, quoted in Sivaramakrishnan, 2000:17) by creating a large number of new, local, elected positions and by reserving a substantial number of seats for women, SCs and STs.

One of the most striking – and most studied – aspects of the decentralisation policy is indeed the mandatory provision of reserved seats for social categories hitherto politically marginalised: women (33 per cent of seats),[121] SCs and STs (the latter two categories benefit from quotas in proportion to their local demographic weight). Even though the sociological characteristics and the bases for the exclusion suffered by these categories are quite distinct, all electoral reservations clearly pertain to the same policy: they stem from a common principle (reparation), they aim at a common goal (including the excluded) and they work along a largely common institutional design (reserving constituencies). Yet a specific problematic is associated with each beneficiary category, i.e. the impact of electoral reservations on the stigmatisation suffered by SCs, the isolation characterising tribal societies and the 'glass ceiling' that limits women's political representation (Tawa Lama-Rewal, 2005).

Quotas for women stir the greatest interest (there are not so many studies on quotas for other categories – an exception being the study of Kumar and Rai [2006]), because they are the most substantial and because they do not exist at other political levels (unlike quotas for SCs and STs, which have existed in the national parliament and in state assemblies since 1952). In a society that remains strongly patriarchal, the prospect of about a million women suddenly being elected to local councils looked revolutionary. After the adoption of the decentralisation policy, the study of the implementation of women's quotas has become a subfield of studies on 'women and politics', but (in keeping with the rural bias) very few studies have been devoted to women in city councils.[122]

A major difference between the two countries is that in South Africa, social transformation is not about protecting and promoting minorities, but about making/helping the demographic majority to access positions of power. Yet one can also observe an important similarity in the two cases, i.e. the transformative agenda of local democracy is strongly linked to representative democracy. Indeed, in South Africa the democratisation of local government was first understood in the sense of including black (majority) voters and destroying 'whites only' administrative, political and fiscal entities (Cameron, 1999) at all levels of government, while in India the political representation of hitherto marginalised social categories is the focus of attention.

The conservative framework of local democracy

In both countries, local governments face several challenges in their endeavour to implement a transformative agenda. Indeed, the democratisation of local government gives rise to a double issue, i.e. the relationship between local bureaucrats and elected representatives (with the latter often criticised for their lack of expertise, experience or skill, whereas bureaucrats are often suspected of following a conservative agenda), and, more generally, the question of the place of politics in local democracy.

Bureaucratic inertia in Indian cities

The Indian decentralisation policy combines political and administrative dimensions. Urban local bodies are divided between an executive (i.e. administrative) and a deliberative (i.e. political) wing, and the dominant municipal regime empowers the commissioner, a top-level bureaucrat nominated by the regional state rather than elected councillors. In this context, one of the running themes of the Indian literature is the difficult relationship between officials and elected representatives. The idea that bureaucrats reproduce the attitude of colonisers vis-à-vis the population they are in charge of has almost become commonplace in India. The difficult relationship between officials in the local administration and locally elected representatives is not new – Oldenburg described it very vividly in 1976. However, it is probably exacerbated today by the fact that owing to quotas, a large number of local representatives are also newcomers in politics, which puts them in a dependent position vis-à-vis bureaucrats, who know the rules, but are often not willing to part with their knowledge.

Another strong limit to the transformative capacity of local government is the dual structure of Indian urban governance, which is shared between urban local bodies and the regional state (through the utility agencies that are dependent on the latter, dealing with planning, water, transport, etc.). Since local government is a state matter in the Indian federal polity, all states had to adopt conformity legislation before they could implement the 73rd and 74th CAAs. Wherever there was some scope for adaptation, states have interpreted the 74th CAA in a restrictive way and have attributed only limited functions to urban local bodies.

Moreover, as far as the implementation of the decentralisation policy is concerned, there appears to be an important discrepancy between the responsibilities delegated to local authorities and the human and financial means actually transferred to them. The financial crunch of (urban) local bodies is thus a central theme of the literature on urban governance (see, for instance, Mathur, 2006). The State Finance Commissions put up in the framework of the decentralisation policy have issued a number of recommendations, which are often ignored. Many studies discuss the tensions between the cities' financial resources and their assigned role in the delivery of basic goods and services such as water, electricity or housing (Sekhar & Bidarkar, 1999; Pethe & Ghodke, 2002). They scrutinise the extent and modalities of financial transfers to local bodies, and all of them agree that the gross inadequacy of such transfers in relation to the tasks assigned to local bodies (at least on paper) is a major reason for the limitations of decentralisation.

Fragmented power in South African cities

The relationship between politicians and bureaucrats is also a very important question in post-apartheid South Africa, as the 'sunset clause' (in the agreement between the apartheid regime and the rising ANC in the early 1990s) had agreed on not firing former (apartheid) state employees and officials so as to create a smooth transition. At local government level, however, the imperatives of transformation implied that (1) politicians be given authority over officials; (2) an affirmative action plan be adopted to appoint new officials; and (3) council policies and priorities be reconciled with new (ANC) policies (Van Donk et al., 2008). The successive local government reforms partly allowed for such a renewal in municipal staff, sometimes leading to a certain loss of expertise that has resulted in inefficiencies or in privatisation through the increasing use of consultants and independent agencies to draft urban policies or even by-laws. In some cases, the politicisation of the hiring of officials led to a high level of instability;[123] these crucial dynamics, however, so far seem to be under-researched.

In South Africa, local governments are responsible for many basic services (water, waste management, electricity reticulation, sanitation, roads, land and planning, transport planning). For these responsibilities, and perhaps unlike their Indian counterparts, the bigger municipalities are somehow well resourced (their income mainly taking the form of property tax; rates on water and electricity; until recently, tax on businesses; and national grants). Equally important is the responsibilities municipalities share with provincial governments: housing, health and education (and, in fact, also land management). However, this shared responsibility often creates problems of coordination,[124] as reflected in the debate on terminology. Legislative texts and academic literature sometimes define local government as a 'tier' (the lowest tier, under the supervision of higher tiers such as provincial and national governments); sometimes as a 'sphere' (i.e. democratic platforms in their own right, with interaction with, but not submission to other spheres of government). This hesitation is also captured in the debate around 'developmental local government', where development can be understood in a narrow sense (as captured in the sentence 'local government is the hands and feet of the Reconstruction and Development Programme', not 'the head or brain': its function is to 'deliver' according to a policy that has been decided elsewhere) or in a broader sense (encouraging residents to participate in the definition of their own needs and the allocation of public resources). While legislative texts – and the hopes they have given rise to (Parnell et al., 2002; Van Donk et al., 2008) – explicitly adopt the broader understanding, local government practices rather seem to lean towards the narrower, including participation more as a matter of exception and response to emergency/crisis than in their daily and normal working (Bénit-Gbaffou, 2008).

Politics is largely discredited in local government workings. In South African cities, ward committees, supposedly 'neutral' and non-partisan, are criticised as both inefficient and heavily politicised (Piper & Deacon, 2008). Politics is equated with either corruption or political violence, although the lack of political competition in a dominant party context is still being analysed as detrimental to local government accountability and leading to rising arrogance, corruption, and inefficiency within state and party.

On the whole, in both South African and Indian cities, the transformative potential of local democracy is severely constrained for reasons linked to the national and local political contexts. India's federalism allows some slackness in the interpretation of decentralisation principles, but the great competitiveness of its electoral scene ensures political interest for local democracy. In South Africa, on the contrary, the dominant party system is not conducive to a genuine adoption of local democracy principles; where electoral competition exists locally, like in Durban or Cape Town, it does not yet seem robust enough to have led to meaningful democratic debates.

Urban democracy: Missing links between local government and social movements studies

The literature on participation (both institutionalised and extra-institutional) in both countries is characterised by strong judgemental values and wide gaps.

Representative vs (institutionalised) participatory democracy

In India, local democracy is hardly participatory, especially in cities, despite the provision in the 74th CAA for ward committees to be a space where elected representatives, municipal bureaucrats, and civil society could meet and discuss local problems. This provision has been interpreted in a restrictive sense by most states, and Mumbai today is the only city where ward committees actually include civil society – in the form of three NGOs selected by the local councillors.

More generally in India, participation is usually discussed only as *electoral* participation[125] – Jayal (2006:7) has convincingly summed up this phenomenon as the 'fetishisation of representation'. Thus, observers of (local) democracy have been discussing the turnout of various social categories in local elections and have also, more broadly, paid attention to the participation of various categories of people as candidates and as candidates' supporters. The notion of participation as a direct form of democracy has so far been discussed mostly in the context of studies on Kerala, related to the recent experiment with participatory planning.

One can, however, expect more studies focussing on participation in urban governance in the near future, since there seems to be an expansion of 'invited' spaces of participation focussing on local affairs (Cornwall, quoted in Miraftab, 2006). Participation is the keyword of new schemes launched by state or municipal governments in the 2000s aimed at involving the middle class in the management of urban affairs and, more precisely, in the improvement of service delivery (Paul, 2006; Tawa Lama-Rewal, 2007; Zérah, 2007b; Baud & Nainan, 2008). Also, the "recently launched" Jawaharlal Nehru National Urban Renewal Mission (JNNURM), a central government scheme launched in 2005 to

> encourage reforms and fast-track planned development of identified cities [with a focus on] efficiency in urban infrastructure and service delivery mechanisms, community participation, and accountability of [urban local borders] ULBs/parastatal agencies towards citizens[126]

may evoke more interest in participation in the sense of 'consultation'. Indeed, the JNNURM includes a Community Participation Law whose content has been widely discussed by neighbourhood activists in the big cities. Thus, current studies focussing on ad hoc consultation procedures (Mitra, 2002; Thakkar, 2004; Ramanathan, 2007) might soon give way to a focus on the institutionalisation of such procedures and their engagement with local structures of political representation. However, participation here seems restricted either to middle-class groups – giving rise to the powerful critique of the notion of 'civil society' (Chatterjee, 2006a) – or to being used as a World Bank-inspired tool for managing urban poverty.

By contrast, South African local democracy has made ample institutional provision for participation at the local level, mainly through ward committees elected by local voters whose members are given specific portfolios and are supposed to help liaise between the ward councillor and civil society. However, numerous studies have shown the inefficiency and superficiality of such structures as platforms for residents' participation in urban governance.[127] Therefore, even though the institutions of local participation are much more developed than in Indian cities, the reality of residents' participation might not be all that different.

In both countries, and probably even more so in South Africa, no political party is really supporting residents' participation (in contrast with the experiment in local democracy in Brazil, for instance), because they have little political interest in doing so or limited capacity to implement it at the grass-roots level. The ANC is a dominant party in South Africa, like the INC was before the 1980s in India, and, unlike the Workers' Party in Brazil, it does not need to advocate for another form of democracy to gain support from the masses. Decentralisation could only provide a platform for opposition parties,[128] while participation is only seen as a 'nuisance', wasting time and resources by debating (and contesting) ANC policies. Opposition parties, and in particular the Democratic Alliance, have opposed the unicity reform and argued in favour of decentralisation (Cameron, 1999); they have also repeatedly criticised ANC-led metropolitan councils for not being participatory enough; but the Democratic Alliance is far from developing a programme on participatory democracy, not being a radical party and lacking the mobilisation resources at the local level to promote such a programme. Other opposition parties, more radical in their ideology and more likely to be sympathetic to the legacy of the civics and direct democracy (like the Pan Africanist Congress or the South African Communist Party), simply lack the necessary financial and human resources – they are not mass movements like the ANC.

This political context is very significant to explain the lack of progress of participatory democracy in South African local governance. Indian examples mentioned above (West Bengal and Kerala, where decentralisation and participation have been implemented by leftist coalitions in power) confirm the importance of political party strategies in explaining the implementation (or lack thereof) of participatory institutions. In most cases, promoting participatory democracy is not seen as an effective electoral strategy by political parties.

Invited and invented spaces of participation: Contrasted legitimacies

In South Africa, there is a gap between literature focussing on local government and local democracy (although, as mentioned earlier, the term is seldom used) and literature on social movements and civics, which rarely directly addresses the issues of urban governance and democracy (unlike issues of social justice, revolutionary potential, political resources and organisation). The link with local government and democratic institutions is underdeveloped, as social movements overall appear more confrontational than cooperative (Ballard, Habib & Valodia, 2006), even though the reality might be more nuanced (Oldfield, in Van Donk et al., 2008). Some address the issue of the alliance between civics and local politicians or officials, but often to deplore the decline of civics as a force of confrontation (Heller, 2003; Zuern, in Ballard, Habib & Valodia, 2006); others start to look at deeper linkages of clientelism at the local level (Staniland, 2008; Bénit-Gbaffou, 2010).

Indian literature seems even less focussed on developing the link between social movements and civil society, on the one hand, and local democracy, on the other. A large majority of papers focussing on the notion of civil society are theoretical and often normative in their approach. A few papers are more empirical, but they usually discuss the role of civil society organisations at the national level. Rob Jenkins (2010) clearly shows how the Indian discourse on civil society distinguishes social movements – supposed to be massive, altruistic and progressive – from NGOs, which are suspected of being too small to matter, opportunistic and reformist at best.[129] But the relationship of social movements to democracy, local or otherwise, is far from clear.

As far as cities are concerned, only a small part of the literature on social movements focusses on urban movements (Shah, 2002). Within this limited literature, the issue of class is prominent. Concerning the urban working poor, labour movements have traditionally been closely associated with trade unions that are themselves 'sister organisations' of political parties. But in today's India, 'informality [a labour practice that characterises more than 90 per cent of the workforce] poses serious challenges to both the theorists and the practitioners of class politics' (Roychowdhury, 2008:604). Collective action by workers in the informal sector is being documented (Sheth, 2004; Dasgupta, 2009), but there is usually no discussion of the links between these mobilisations and local democracy. An exception is Omvedt's (2002) account of the Dalit movement, describing how the short-lived Dalit Panthers' movement, 'born in the slums of Bombay' in 1972, engaged with electoral politics as it opposed both the INC and the Shiv Sena. This is not so surprising, since, contrary to the South African case (where activists, trained with a Castellsian vision of 'the urban question', have taken the right to the city as an object of struggle), the city in India is more a site than an object of struggles. It is the place where protests are being staged, but protests are usually not *about* the city.[130]

On the whole, urban activism in India today appears to be increasingly dominated by the middle classes, and one can distinguish two broad types whose relationships with institutionalised structures of interest representation are quite different. Firstly, there is activism by the middle classes, but on behalf of the poor: typically, NGOs whose main mode of action is lobbying authorities at various levels (Harriss, 2007; Roychowdhury, 2008). Secondly, one observes an increasingly assertive activism by the middle classes and for the middle classes (Fernandes, 2006; Ghertner 2008), typically through neighbourhood associations that frequently resort to press campaigns and judicial action (Dembowski, 1999; Mawdsley, 2004; Véron, 2006). In both cases, there appears to be hardly any connection between these types of activism and local authorities; indeed, several studies show that the major constituency of local representatives is not the middle classes, but the poor (Baud & Nainan, 2008; Ruet & Tawa Lama-Rewal, 2009).

Finally, in both contexts the marginal place of social movements in the academic field of local democracy reflects a different set of theoretical literature (political studies rather than literature on local government); but it might also echo a binary vision of urban governance, opposing the state (and its institutions) and civil society (in all its forms, including social movements); or at least the workings of institutions (including participatory institutions) and more informal (and often more oppositional) lobbies and movements. This theoretical opposition is also a political one that allows local authorities to discard mass urban movements (particularly when they become oppositional and violent) as part and parcel of local democracy. Here, similarities between the Indian and South African contexts tend to grow, as in both cases the most radical social movements and spaces of 'invented' participation (i.e. falling outside participatory structures and institutions) are increasingly criminalised by the state and the media.

In South Africa, it takes the form of movement leaders being put in jail and sued in court, a general discourse on a 'third force' trying to compromise the democratically elected South African government and its efforts to build the nation. (Ballard, Habib & Valodia, 2006; Miraftab, 2006).

In India, the unequal legitimacy of various categories of urban mobilisations is revealed by the implicit, but very strong, connotations of the various terms used to qualify urban dwellers. Indeed, all possible terms seem overloaded with meaning. To call them 'voters' (as much of the literature on local democracy does) suggests that urban democracy can be reduced to the local electoral process. 'Residents', in the Indian contemporary context, implies legality and thus excludes the squatters who form anywhere between one fourth and one third of the population of megacities. Moreover, 'residents' are now associated with 'resident welfare associations', which conjure up an image of middle-class colonies, as opposed to 'slum dwellers'.

The term 'citizens', too, postulates a series of rights of which a large number of city dwellers in India are deprived. It is much favoured in the framework of participatory programmes for the middle classes (Nair, 2006; Tawa Lama-Rewal, 2007; Zérah, 2007a); it has been appropriated by neighbourhood activists (as clearly shown by their numerous press statements) and, as a result, has come to evoke a combination of legality (of residence in the city) and legitimacy (of participation in urban governance). Indeed, Ghertner (2008:66), through an analysis of court cases related to slum evictions in Delhi, highlights the potency of 'discursive devices' in constructing a 'property-based citizenship'. Unlike in South Africa, 'community' cannot provide a solution to this lack of a neutral term, because in India it is a code word for 'caste' or 'religious group'. Two recent papers dealing with neighbourhood activism use the term 'bourgeois', which evokes more explicitly the combination of economic and political clout enjoyed by this social group (Chatterjee, 2006a; Baviskar, 2007).

By contrast, 'resident' has become a neutral term in South African urban society, although when referring to civil society, a more commonly used term is 'community' (for both low- and higher-income local groups of residents – otherwise differentiated into 'civics' for the former and 'ratepayers'/homeowners' associations' for the latter). It has not always been the case, however, as the right of residence in South African cities (considered ultimately 'white spaces' where black people had only a temporary right to stay under apartheid) was restricted to whites, and blacks with a permit. In post-apartheid South Africa, it is not politically possible to deny anyone the title of local 'resident' (even if they are living in an informal settlement, and even if they are an undocumented migrant). This also explains why residents of informal settlements do have rights in South African cities (notification of eviction, relocation, etc.), even though most of them are not aware of these rights, nor able to access them if they do not have political and social resources, which contrasts to the situation of informal dwellers in Indian cities.

Conclusion

Our comparison shows that some important concepts have different meanings in the two contexts. One of the most significant differences is the meaning of the term 'residents', which excludes the poor in Indian cities, which is a telling comment on the social "and rights" status of the majority of the urban population. A second notion whose meaning is significantly different is 'communities', which evokes caste in Indian cities, but is commonly used in South Africa to describe local groups of residents engaging in participation (although it often implicitly designates racially homogeneous groups). More broadly, some notions have different echoes in the two contexts. Decentralisation is linked to the Gandhian Utopia in India and, more ambiguously, to both the apartheid infamy in South Africa and post-apartheid global governance rhetoric. Local democracy is implicitly urban in South Africa, but rural in India; thus, cities figure prominently in the heroic narrative of the victory of democracy in South Africa, but not so in India.

But there are also important similarities. To start with, in both cases, local democracy has been considered mostly as a matter of 'more representative local government' (in the sense of a local government mirroring the society's demographics), but for different reasons. In South Africa, the non-white majority was for decades deprived of representation (in leadership in state institutions as well as in private organisations) – a fair representation is thus about promoting non-whites in leadership positions. In India, attention is paid more to marginalised groups. Thus, in both cases, local government is seen as a tool for social engineering – setting up a path towards more equality and more inclusion in the broader society. In other words, decentralisation is linked to socio-political experimentation. Lastly, the reinvention/deepening of democracy through decentralisation is limited by resistance to making local government more participatory, thus the question of the relationship with democracy remains open. Indeed, participation is the weak dimension of local democracy in both countries – although it is at least institutionally and rhetorically encouraged in South African cities, whereas it is largely absent from the legislative texts governing urban local bodies in India. If some forms of 'invited' participation are encouraged through different mechanisms (broader and more generalised in South Africa), 'invented' participation (generally more oppositional) is often demonised and seldom used by opposition parties.

This literature review points to the need for a more integrated view of urban democracy that would link up studies of (urban) social movements, civil society and urban politics in order to analyse democracy in the city. Such an endeavour would necessarily lead to discussing the nature and specificity of urban citizenship – in so far as it is constructed by the relationship between the political participation of city dwellers and the structures of urban governance. This seems to be all the more urgent today as another convergence appears that is born from the global dominance of a neoliberal agenda: poorer populations are being pushed out of city centres and new movements claim a right to the city, defined in different ways by different social groups. In this regard, Chatterjee's conceptual distinction between 'civil society' ('proper' urban citizens who have rights and are recognised as such) and 'political society' (the mass of the urban poor who, living in informality in one way or another, have access to the state only by stealth, through local arrangements and through favours, while simultaneousy being at the core of political parties' attention) can usefully be used in a South African context, even if, as we have stressed, the lack of rights on the part of the poor seems less acute than in India. An understanding of the politics of local democracy, in its noble sense of citizenship and participation, but also in its not less meaningful sense of clientelism and everyday political strategies and tactics to access urban resources, seems therefore crucial.

9

Chapter

Reimagining Socialist Futures in South Africa and Kerala, India[131]

Michelle Williams

Introduction

The collapse of the Soviet Union and the ascendance of neoliberal globalisation catalysed progressive forces around the world to re-examine their basic beliefs about whether an alternative to capitalism was possible. Many parties – such as a number in Europe and Latin America – shifted to visions of social democracy.[132] For these parties, the focus shifted from alternatives attempting to transcend capitalism to ameliorative projects within capitalism. Out of this reflexive journey, however, at least two parties deepened their efforts to find democratic *socialist* alternatives. The South African Communist Party (SACP) and the Communist Party of India (Marxist) (CPI[M]) in Kerala, India spent the greater part of the early 1990s *rethinking* their visions of socialism around radically democratic politics. In addition to the international challenges, both the SACP and CPI(M) faced domestic challenges – of an economic and political nature – that led them down this reflexive journey of ideological renewal. I use *socialist democracy* to refer to this new vision in which ordinary citizens play an increasingly important role through parliamentary and participatory democratic mechanisms.[133] While both parties envisioned alternatives, the CPI(M) has gone further in implementing its vision, while the SACP has largely failed to put into practice its new understandings of socialist democracy. Nevertheless, in this chapter I focus on their similar visions adopted in the 1990s.

Based on materials from archival fieldwork in both Kerala and South Africa between 2001 and 2005, I examine the efforts by the SACP and CPI(M) to rethink the content of their socialist visions. During the 1990s both parties held numerous congresses, workshops and conferences,[134] and also produced a plethora of documents in which they worked through their evolving theoretical positions. This chapter is based on a perusal of this material.[135] I argue that the SACP's and CPI(M)'s reflexive journeys provide important insight into democratic alternatives grounded in local conditions.

Rethinking alternatives: Socialist democracy in the 21st century

Since the 1950s Western scholarship on communism has painted a monolithic picture of the deleterious effects of communist parties, interested as it was in the Soviet Union's undemocratic and authoritarian control of the international communist movement (Arendt, 1951; Selznick, 1952; Talmon, 1952; Claudin, 1975). As a result, scholarship on communist parties has been dominated by accounts of authoritarian politics, overwhelmingly influenced by the 1950s generation of scholars. There have been studies on the authoritarian nature of 20th-century socialism (e.g. Jowitt, 1992; Courtios et al., 1999), on the causes and consequences of the demise of the Soviet Union (Slovo, 1990; Habermas, 1991; Hobsbawm, 1991; Milliband, 1991), and on the link between the fall of the Soviet Union and the expansion of neoliberalism (Eyal, 2002), as well as theoretical statements on the future possibilities of various socialisms (Amin, 1990; Blackburn, 1991; Pierson, 1995; Panitch, 2001; Wright, 2010). Studies have also been published claiming a new type of politics that moves beyond the conventional structures of unions and parties (Escobar, 1992; Holloway, 2002; Klein, 2004). In addition, Western scholarship that has looked at communist parties focussed on Soviet and European parties (e.g. Tarrow, 1967; Rabinowitch, 1978; Boggs & Plotke, 1980; Smith, 1983), largely ignoring those in the Global South.

These studies have resulted in an expansive body of literature, but have also left important silences, especially with regard to democratic socialist experiments. Why have these efforts received so little attention? There are two reasons for this lacuna. Firstly, Western scholarship on communism has tended to have an anti-communist lens in which the death of communism was accepted as an inevitable necessity owing to the inherent contradictions of communism (i.e. communism is equated to statism, which is equated to authoritarianism) (Selznick, 1952; Talmon, 1952; Jowitt, 1992). The idea of democratic communism is, in other words, antithetical to US scholarship on communism. Secondly, the existing literature on global alternatives has focussed mainly on social movements and global forums such as the World Social Forum and transnational networks (e.g. Klein, 2004; Mertes, 2004; Evans, 2005; De Sousa Santos, 2006), but has neglected the continued importance of political parties for transformative politics. Indeed, there has been strong scepticism about the virtues of political parties (e.g. Hart & Negri, 2001; Holloway, 2002). For much of their histories, the SACP and CPI(M) have challenged this rendition of communist parties and demonstrated the necessity of political parties especially in *envisioning* democratic, egalitarian alternatives that unite broad sectors of society.

The SACP and the CPI(M) in Kerala challenge this history by developing visions of socialist democracy.[136] Highlighting the importance of democracy was not unique to these parties, as there was a general trend among the Left around the world to place democracy at its centre. Few of these efforts, however, maintained a more extended and deepened vision of democracy that included not just the political, but also the economic and social spheres of life and sought the extension of ordinary citizens organised in class- and mass-based institutions. The SACP and CPI(M) were rethinking the notion of the developmental state and its connection to civil society. Civil society is a contentious term and warrants clarification. It is both a domain of social organisation that is separate from the state and economy, and an arena of contestation of discrete voluntary associations. As an arena of contestation, civil society includes a panoply of associations such as conservative religious groups, elite NGOs and working-class organisations. One of the paramount roles of political parties, especially communist parties, is to organise civil society around class-based issues. In this chapter, I focus on civil society as a domain of social organisation that is connected to, but analytically separate from, the state and economy.

By this point, some readers may have asked how it is that I can compare the CPI(M) in Kerala, a state within a nation, with the SACP, which functions at the national level. Reflecting the diversity of India, the organisational structure of the CPI(M) is largely a federal structure in which the state-level party has a great deal of autonomy. The CPI(M)'s constitution specifically outlines the division of labour among the tiers of the organisation: the state-level structures are responsible for developments within their respective states. This federal structure thus provides a great deal of autonomy to the state structures, allowing the Kerala CPI(M) the authority and power to respond to the conditions and demands of subaltern classes in the state. For the SACP, the 1990s were marked by a high degree of unity, from top to bottom, as the party was rebuilding its structures. The SACP's unitary structure, which has become even more salient in the new millennium, thus makes a comparison between the SACP and the CPI(M) in Kerala feasible, as the CPI(M)'s state structures have a similar distribution of powers as the national-level SACP.

These parties are particularly interesting because of their crucial differences and striking similarities. Both parties have unique histories of political mobilisation and class formation, and operate at different levels.

But these differences hide important similarities. The SACP and CPI(M) are among the few communist parties that commanded strong and growing bases of support during the 1990s and have regular access to state power. For the SACP, access to state power is through its strategic alliance[137] with the African National Congress (ANC), which is the dominant party in post-apartheid South Africa; for the CPI(M), state power is accessed through leftist electoral coalition governments in which the CPI(M) is the dominant party. Moreover, both parties share long histories of political activism dating back to the 1920s and were at the centre of political developments in their respective societies for the second half of the 20th century. For much of their histories, both parties have been crucial actors in oppositional politics, with limited or no access to state power. Nevertheless, both parties kept pace with the aspirations of subaltern classes and have persistently organised a range of interests into coherent class-based projects for social transformation. The SACP and CPI(M) have thus been central political actors in shaping the contours of their societies.

The ideological convergence of the CPI(M) and SACP

Kerala and South Africa have captured the imagination of peoples across the globe for the accomplishments in their respective societies. Late 20th-century Kerala defied Western development models by achieving indicators of physical quality of life that compare favourably with those of 'developed' nations despite its low per capita income levels and slow economic growth. For example, Kerala's adult literacy rate is 91 per cent, compared to the national average of 61 per cent, and life expectancy is 73 years, compared to the United States' 77 years and India's 63 (UN, 2004; Kerala figures from GOI, 2002). These achievements have been at the behest of communist party mobilisation around redistributive reforms. Despite these achievements in human and social development, between the 1970s and early 1990s Kerala suffered from economic stagnation, with industrial growth limping along at 3.48 per cent, while agriculture slumped into negative growth during the 1970s and 1980s (GOK, 1991:2; Heller, 1999:9). For the CPI(M), its 1987 election victory marked a turning point. Having been in and out of government and unable to increase its electoral support since the 1960s, by the mid-1980s the party was opening itself to new approaches to politics in its efforts to keep pace with the aspirations of the populace. It recognised both the need for economic growth and the need to develop programmes that involve mass participation and encourage local initiative and self-reliance. These external conditions played into the party's internal dynamics, shifting the balance of power within the party in favour of a grass-roots tendency that ultimately led the party away from state-led development based on mass mobilisation around redistributive reforms towards society-led development enlisting participatory organisation.

South Africa is perhaps best known to students of African studies for the impressive character of its near-century-long national liberation struggle and the relatively peaceful transition to a democratic South Africa, much of which was guided by, and under the organisational impetus of, the SACP. For the SACP, the 1994 ANC election victory marked a turning point. After forty years of clandestine activity the party now had access to power via the ANC. The SACP recognised the need for renewal and the importance of developing transformative politics. Thus, in the 1990s the SACP was realigning itself from a politics of protest to a politics in which it was a crucial actor in constructing new institutions and mechanisms for mass participation and nation building. The party prioritised developing policies and strategies for nation building and advancing democratic *visions* of socialism.

The two parties' ideological renewals grew out of an understanding that socialism could not be conceived of as a predetermined model of social organisation, but rather was an undefined process of extending democratic practices of collective decision making and the progressive empowerment of subalterns to participate in the development of society. Visions of socialism that could be reached through either revolution or reforms were abandoned and were replaced with visions of a continuous process of transformation that progressively eliminates forms of exploitation and oppression through the extension of civil society over the state and economy. Socialism, in other words, required a long transition consisting of many phases and multiple forms grounded in local conditions (SACP, 1995:13–15; CPI[M], 1998a:3–9). In short, the two parties shifted from a state-centred understanding of socialism based on the Soviet experience to a society-centred vision of socialism that found its moorings in radical democracy. This convergence centred on four themes: democracy, the state, the relationship of capitalism to socialism, and the extension of civil society. In the remainder of this chapter I look at the four organising themes of their ideological visions through the lens of each party's theoretical documents.

Deepening and extending democracy

The SACP's and CPI(M)'s visions of socialist democracy placed participatory democratic politics at their centre. It was a major theme for the CPI(M) in the 1990 Central Committee document 'On certain political-ideological issues related to developments in some socialist countries' and the 1992 Congress document 'Resolution on certain ideological issues', as well as the 1994 and 2000 Kerala conference papers. For the SACP, it is a central theme in its 1995 'Strategy and tactics' Congress document entitled 'Socialism is the future: Build it now', its 1998 programme 'Build people's power – build socialism now!' and its 1999 and 2000 Strategy Conference documents. It was also central to the heated debate at the party's 1991 Congress over the slogan of the 'dictatorship of the proletariat', which was abandoned in favour of language referring to widening and deepening democracy by the working class and poor. In these documents, both parties espoused a vision of radical democracy that extended the control of civil society over the economic and political domains (CPI[M], 1990:309; SACP, 1995:7–8).

As the CPI(M) searched for ways to define a programme for change anchored in the democratic roots of the socialist tradition, the more extensive understanding of democracy dominated the thinking of certain tendencies in the party. At this time, the CPI(M) combined its commitment to a multiparty parliamentary system in which political parties contest for state power through free and fair elections with more radical conceptions of democracy in which ordinary people are empowered to make and implement decisions in the political and economic domains of social life (Isaac, 1994). Learning from its own history,[138] the party understood that introducing democratic institutions into local politics without challenging the social and economic power of the landed elite meant that meaningful participation by subalterns was virtually impossible (in other words, political democracy in itself does not ensure the transformation of social relations). Thus, the CPI(M) argued that the institutions of formal democracy had to be underpinned by extending the role of civil society into the political and economic arenas, which requires constant struggle by subaltern classes to secure their right to participate and ensure the implementation of democratic decisions (CPI[M], 1990:302, 308). In order to democratise the political, economic and social realms, the CPI(M) looked to decentralisation as a primary mechanism for advancing this cause (Namboodiripad, 1994:5).

The vision elaborated in a 1992 Central Committee resolution clearly articulates the culmination of this line of inquiry:

[The] advance to socialism in any country must be accompanied by increased initiative of the masses both in running the economy and running the state. Lenin's statement 'every cook must learn to govern' must be a growing reality. A concrete form of these initiatives in the various stages of development embraces larger and larger numbers of people. Measures which free citizens from unnecessary restrictions and provide healthy dialogue within the limits of socialist society, strengthen the society (CPI[M], 1998b:128).

Statements to this effect, highlighting the importance of popular involvement in both economic and political domains, are found in numerous party documents throughout the 1990s. The participation of ordinary citizens would drive the transformation of society. For example, again quoting Lenin, in its 1990 resolution the CPI(M) (1990:309) argued:

Only when it enlists the vast mass of working people for this work, when it elaborates forms which will enable all working people to adapt themselves easily to the work of governing the state and establishing law and order ... is the socialist revolution bound to last.

The party further argued that a range of institutional changes were necessary in order to deepen and extend the possibilities for citizens to exercise democratic rights, calling for

the widest participation of the people in running the State, administration and oconomy ..., through self-government and work collectives. Advance of socialism requires reforms of the political structure aiid the institutions of the State which enrich and strengthen socialist democracy (CPI[M], 1990:309).

This new ideological orientation was not, it was emphasised, a substitute for class or political struggle against bourgeois-landlord policies. Rather, it was an attempt to continue the struggle within the concrete conditions that existed by extending the power and control of civil society over economic and political activity.

Similarly, for the SACP, while it always highlighted the importance of political and economic democracy, in the 1990s the nature and content of democracy was given more attention.[139] The party envisioned a socialism that was firmly anchored in deepening and extending democratic norms and practices as widely as possible. Beginning with SACP leader Joe Slovo's 'Has socialism failed?' (1990), the party launched itself on a journey in which it fleshed out the importance of democratic politics for the realisation of socialism. Democracy had always been treated in generalities and usually referred to either non-racial representative democracy, the 'dictatorship of the proletariat', or 'organs of people's power'. But what these slogans meant in practice and how they related to each other were largely left unaddressed.

The SACP's understanding of the role of democracy stemmed from its conception of the National Democratic Revolution (NDR) and Colonialism of a Special Type (CST). The SACP arrived at its analysis of South African society over a period of many years starting in 1928/29, when it adopted the Native Republic thesis, which called on the Communist Party of South Africa (CPSA)[140] to ally itself with the ANC, as well as other national bourgeois organisations (Bundy, 1991:17). The Native Republic thesis set the foundation for theoretical developments in the late 1940s and early 1950s linking race and class struggles, which culminated in the CST thesis, which was adopted in the 1962 party programme 'Road to South African Freedom'.[141] CST posited that blacks suffered dual oppression, as the oppression of the black majority was a necessary condition of the exploitation of black workers (SACP, 1963). Thus, to fight class exploitation required struggling against national oppression, and, hence, the SACP argued that the most appropriate response at this stage was national liberation (Slovo, 1989:34–35). Clearly, the SACP had an instrumental approach to national democracy and mass power – it was necessary for the realisation of socialism – but had not yet defined participatory democracy as a fundamental constituent of socialism.

Similar to the CPI(M)'s commitment to both representative and participatory democracy, in the early 1990s the SACP saw national democracy as not only necessary for the construction of socialism, but argued that a multiparty electoral system was an important mechanism for ensuring accountability and control by the citizenry (SACP, 1995:7–8).[142] The SACP went further to highlight that the logic and principles of democracy had to be deepened and extended into all other spheres of society – from the political, which included the government and administration, to the economic, social and cultural spheres (SACP, 1995:14). The party argued that

> a multiparty parliamentary political system is not, on its own, sufficient, it has to be supplemented by strong institutions and mass, independent

organizations – women, students, trade unions, civics and so forth – which can participate in the decision-making process (SACP, 1990:13–14).

Of course, the SACP had been committed to national democracy in so far as it fought for the NDR, the first goal of which was a united, non-racial democratic South Africa. It had not, however, taken such pains to articulate its socialism to be fundamentally about representative *and* participatory democracy (SACP, 1995:8, 14).

In the 1990s, however, the party developed a greater appreciation for democracy as a qualitatively important component of socialism. It was envisioning an extensive role for civil society in governance and over the broad direction of the economy. Participatory democracy became an end in itself and not just a means for achieving a socialist end. Linked to this was the idea that socialism had to be developed and defended by popular movements in civil society and not a bureaucratic state (or party) apparatus. For example, in the 'Reconstruction and Development Programme' (RDP), a deepened and extended notion of democracy was posited as a key thrust in the economic and political development of South Africa (ANC, 1994:120–21; Tripartite Alliance, 1994). In short, the SACP was envisioning both an extensive and a deepened role for civil society in which it increasingly shaped the political and economic domains of social organisation (SACP, 1995:6–8).

Thus, the CPI(M) and SACP similarly envisioned an extended and deepened notion of democracy as integral to a socialist democracy. This reimagining of socialist democracy to be fundamentally about participatory democracy had important implications for the parties' views about the nature and role of the state.

The new state

Espousing participatory democratic visions of political and economic organisation, therefore, also requires rethinking the state, its role in development and the party's relation to it. Both the SACP and CPI(M) had historically adhered to notions of an omnipotent state that did not empower people to deliberate, make decisions and implement their decisions through active participation in state institutions. In the 1990s, both parties abandoned notions of a hierarchical command-structure state with omnipotent powers and in its stead envisioned a state that plays an affirmative role (by which is meant a regulatory and redistributive role), is responsive to the demands of its citizenry and also provides institutional space for meaningful participation from below (CPI[M], 1990:307; SACP, 1998:49).

In their new visions, the state's pre-eminent role was to create institutions for popular participation and ensure the means through which the citizenry are adequately prepared to participate. This conception of a state differs from the one commonly found in the development literature. For example, Peter Evans (1995) defines the developmental state as bureaucratic, based on highly selective meritocratic rules and governed by a sense of commitment and organisational coherence.[143] It also presides over industrial transformation and is 'embedded' in concrete social ties to society (by which Evans largely means local capital) and 'provides institutionalized channels for the continual negotiation of goals and policies' (Evans, 1995:12). This vision of a developmental state prioritises accumulation and says nothing about the extension of civil society through the active participation in decision making and implementation by ordinary citizens. It is clear, then, that the CPI(M) and SACP were envisioning a 'developmental' state that was both more inclusive and more extensive in its societal project. In order to achieve this vision of a developmental state, the parties looked to participatory democratic mechanisms.

For the CPI(M), its thinking around the developmental state challenged the party's long-held view of the state. During its first term in government in 1957–59 it believed that holding state power translated into real power that could transform the economic and political power relations in society. It saw the state as the active agent of change, working at the behest of the lower classes, on whose support it depended. After its bitter experience in government in this period, when 'bourgeois'[144] and landlord forces flouted democratic norms and practices in order to destabilise the government, the CPI(M) came to hold the perspective that state institutions could only be used for agitation and propaganda. It formally articulated this view of the state in its 1967 Central Committee resolution 'The new situation and the new tasks confronting the party', in which it argued that the government was an instrument to intensify the people's struggles for land, higher wages and democratic rights, and against the policies of the central government (CPI[M], 1997). Implicitly – and perhaps unintentionally – the CPI(M) was advocating a position that took an instrumental approach to democratic institutions, arguing that they could be used to strengthen the opposition, proselytise the political perspective of the Left, develop popular consciousness and expand organisational networks (CPI[M],

1997:649–56). Underpinning this perspective was the view that gaining access to government office in the current conditions did not necessarily translate into real power, and therefore revolutionary confrontation was still the primary objective.

By 1987, although still officially supporting the 1967 resolution, the party recognised the need to adjust to new national and international conditions. For example, in Kerala and West Bengal the party regularly held state power, which placed particular demands on it to deliver concrete changes through state institutions. Thus, the party in government in these states had to find at least partial solutions to the problems faced by subaltern classes and could not simply use the state for agitation and propaganda. Rather, the state had to be used as an agent of change. The party began to recognise that participatory democratic institutions could help create conditions and institutional spaces for meaningful participation from the citizenry (CPI[M], 1990:307). Ultimately, the institutions of the state would be strongly affected by (and even subordinated to) civil society, which would not only give citizens the opportunity to direct developments that affect their lives, but would also ensure greater accountability of state institutions (both representative and bureaucratic) to civil society. These shifts resulted in a new understanding of the state, which was now seen to play a vital role in development, but would be subjected to the control of civil society (CPI[M], 1990:306–9). One way in which the party conceived the democratisation of the state apparatus was through democratic decentralisation (Namboodiripad, 1994:5).

For the CPI(M) in Kerala, this translated into practical efforts to transform the bureaucracy and state administration to play a vital role in empowering people to actively participate in the deliberation, decision making and implementation of development. This required the formation of new participatory bodies that intersected with local government institutions, as well as the transformation of local government structures in order for them to be open and accountable to civil society. The CPI(M) thus delineated six phases of development initiatives that connected local government bodies with participatory forums (e.g. *grama sabhas* or village councils) in every stage of the development process (Isaac & Heller, 2003:82–87). The development agendas of every locale were derived from an integrated process of people's participation and local government initiatives. Devolving funds to local government institutions as a first step forced the reorganisation of the bureaucracy and state administration to combine the state's role as an affirmative state with local government's role as a participatory institution by opening local government structures to meaningful participation from subaltern classes. The CPI(M) thus moored its developmental state in civil society through extending and deepening democratic institutions. Thus, the first two elements of the socialist vision were integrally interwoven.

The SACP's understanding of the eventual transition to socialism rested on a particular assumption about the omnipotence of state power. The party repeatedly explained that once state power was in the hands of the working class, the transition to socialism would occur almost inevitably, although it would still require struggle (Slovo, 1976:146–47; SACP, 1989:34).[145] The state was the citadel of power and, hence, the working class would have to win for itself the dominant role in the new government to ensure that the direction of the national democratic state was in accordance with the interests of subaltern classes (Slovo, 1976:148; SACP, 1989:40). This formulation of transition drew heavily on the classical Marxist-Leninist path to power in which the party was first to mobilise to attain state power and then to use state power to transform society, with both struggles led by a vanguard party (Wallerstein, 1990:30).

With the state *the* locus of power, other forms of power (e.g. 'organs of people's power') prevalent throughout South Africa were often viewed instrumentally – their utility was measured in terms of whether or not they helped capture state power or acted as mechanisms to ensure the accountability and effective functioning of representative democratic institutions. While the SACP acknowledged the importance of various forms of people's power and organisations, it had not arrived at a position in which it saw these forms as loci of power in their own right (SACP, 1989:34). Grass-roots, participatory politics was not yet seen as a qualitatively important component of democracy. Thus, in the late 1980s the SACP still adhered to a mechanistic view of state-led development strongly influenced by the Eastern European and Soviet experience in which priority was given to an omnipotent state in controlling, leading, and guiding the economy and development. This top-heavy view of the state provided little in the way of institutional channels for grass-roots participation.

In 1993 the party acknowledged its overemphasis on a state-led orientation in a Tripartite Alliance discussion paper where it argued that

> despite the Freedom Charter's broad social and economic perspectives, we tended to have a statist (that is, state-centred) approach to the NDR. The NDR would come about when an ANC-led National Liberation Movement ...

smashed the apartheid regime, assumed state power (which we tended to equate with the 'transfer of power to the people') and then implemented its programme (Tripartite Alliance, 1993:4).

By the mid-1990s the party had shifted its perspective and viewed other sites of power as significant and not just as a function of attaining or an auxiliary to state power (SACP, 1995:13–14). Power was no longer seen to reside only in the institutions of the state, but was seen to be diffuse, and therefore contesting it would occur in multiple spheres by multiple forms of movements (SACP, 1999:4). In other words, although the state continues to be a major locus of power, power does not lie solely with the state, and holding the reigns of state institutions might not translate into real power (Moleketi, 1993:16; SACP, 1999:3–4).

The party (along with its Tripartite Alliance partners) now saw the NDR as much more than the transfer of state power, and that it included the ongoing process of 'popular self-empowerment'. Forums for such involvement had to be developed at the various levels of government, and the transformation of the state itself was seen to be dependent on mass participation and had to be people driven (Tripartite Alliance, 1993:6). These shifts in its vision of the state are seen in the elaboration of the 1995 'Socialism is the future' document, the 1998 party programme and the 1999 Strategy Conference documents, as well as the RDP,[146] which became a major thrust in SACP thinking in the mid-1990s. For example, in the RDP a new vision of a developmental state with a great deal of emphasis on participatory institutional mechanisms was articulated. In all its documents, the SACP placed significant emphasis on the role of community-based organisations (i.e. organs of people's power) in development and formulated an economic and social programme to develop, expand and stabilise the economy through meeting the basic needs of the people (Nqakula, 1994:8). The state's role envisioned in the RDP and other documents was to facilitate and create institutional spaces for democratic action, while the main thrust of transformation was society centred (SACP, 1995:8). The institutional spaces created for such participation include standing, hearing and theme committees in parliament, the National Economic Development and Labour Council (NEDLAC),[147] local development forums, housing and electricity forums, and university transformation forums (Tripartite Alliance, 1995:10; SACP, 1998:49). In addition, the transformation of local government created institutional space for participatory governance (Carrim, 2001:33–35).

The role of political and community organisations was to capacitate, train and educate people to take advantage of these spaces created by the state and policy makers. Thus, the state was not to subordinate civil society, but rather would create institutional spaces and nurture conditions that would encourage popular participation in and ultimately civil society's dominance over governing and economic activity. For example, in its 1998 programme the party argued that the strength of the state was directly related to (and even dependent on) the strength of civil society and its ability to build social cohesion around a development programme (SACP, 1998:27).

This understanding of the state reflected the party's shift from a monolithic view of the state to an understanding of the state as a complex set of semi-independent (autonomous) institutions with multiple sites of power, as well as to a more inclusive understanding of social power rooted in myriad institutions in civil society and not simply the organised working class. The SACP saw local government as a crucial site for potentially deepening democracy. The transformation of local government shifted significant powers to it as a constitutionally mandated tier of government with original powers (i.e. not just a function of the provincial or national level) and hence provides tremendous potential for citizen participation through institutional channels (SACP, 1999:24–25). The SACP succeeded in consolidating a vision of the character of the state as developmental, by which was meant an activist state with institutional avenues for mass participation.

Coexistence of socialism and capitalism

Moving from issues of governance and the state, the CPI(M) and SACP also developed their thinking on issues relating to the economy. With their new commitments to participatory democracy and a developmental state moored in civil society, it is clear that both parties were, at least for the foreseeable future, jettisoning visions of revolutionary rupture with the capitalist system (CPI[M], 1990:293–94; 1998b:120–21; SACP, 1999:3). Indeed, both parties envisioned a transition in which capitalism and socialism would coexist for an indeterminate period of time. The parties were finding a route between the orthodox view of a revolutionary break with capitalism and accommodationist reforms within capitalism.[148] The parties similarly argued that the conditions for and transition to socialist democracy would have to be created on and through the terrain of capitalism by developing socialist logics alongside the predominant capitalist logic through democratic politics (CPI[M], 1990:293–94; SACP, 1995:13–16).

Both parties translated this element of their vision into practice through efforts at securing the necessary capitalist development to nurture economic growth, while simultaneously developing alternative logics of accumulation. In both Kerala and South Africa, the parties actively sought the creation and extension of micro-production units based on cooperative principles.

In Kerala, the CPI(M) married these efforts to the decentralisation campaign and provided backward and forward linkages for local-level production. While the party placed special emphasis on developing alternative logics of accumulation, given Kerala's rudimentary capitalist development, it also sought capitalist investment in areas in which Kerala enjoyed comparative advantage and those that tapped its high human development capacity, such as the information and technology sector (Isaac & Franke, 2001:32–33). Thus, socialism and capitalism, the CPI(M) envisioned, would exist simultaneously.

Protracted class struggle remained at the heart of its vision of transformation in which the transition to socialism would include the prolonged existence of both a capitalist and a socialist logic (CPI[M], 1990:293). While the two forms of social organisation would coexist, the period would be fraught with continuous confrontation 'between the counter-revolutionary forces which wish to preserve the exploitative capitalist order and the revolutionary forces that seek to liberate humanity' (CPI[M], 1998b:120). This marked a significant shift from its earlier position positing an imminent revolutionary break from capitalism. While the party still ascribed to the long-term objective of a revolutionary break, in the medium term (which could last a long time) socialism and capitalism would exist together. Indeed, it went even further to argue that elements of socialism must be constructed in the current conditions and through the process of transformation. Clearly, the CPI(M) was advocating a more processual view of socialist construction based on the specific conditions in India.

In South Africa, the SACP argued that under South African conditions a transitional phase of national democracy was necessary, described as a long transition in which the foundations and capacity for and elements of socialism must be built from within society through a process of revolutionary reforms (replacing the 'political economy of capital' with the 'political economy of the working class') (Zita, 1993; Cronin, 1994:39–41). This view of the coexistence of capitalism and socialism was further articulated in the early 1990s (SACP, 1995:13–14). Thus, a noticeable feature of its formulation, and similar to the CPI(M)'s vision of the simultaneous existence of capitalist and socialist logics, was the processual construction, through revolutionary reforms, of the conditions for socialism.

The SACP was explicit about the absolute interrelation between the NDR and socialism. At its 9th Congress in 1995, the SACP clarified that the attainment of state power provided the conditions for developing socialism in the current context. While the 1994 democratic breakthrough indicated a strategic defeat of CST and a political defeat of the apartheid regime, class exploitation continued to characterise South African conditions. The NDR was, therefore, conceived as a protracted struggle that included the continuous and simultaneous struggle for both democratic and socialist transitions in which capitalist and socialist logics would coexist for an indefinite period (SACP, 1995:13). Thus, the SACP highlighted the importance of delinking,[149] to a degree, from world capitalism, but acknowledged that socialism was a long-term, historical struggle to shift the balance of class forces in favour of the subaltern sectors (especially the working people) and would have to be built on a terrain dominated by capitalism (SACP, 1995:5–6; 1998:60). While the SACP developed a vision about South Africa's place in the international system, it was slow to develop its ideas on economic transition within the national context. It was only in the new millennium that the party addressed such questions. For example, in the 2001 Gauteng Provincial Congress document 'Building a people's economy in Gauteng' and the 2005 Central Committee Special Congress document 'Class struggles in the National Democratic Revolution: The political economy of the transition in South Africa, 1994–2004', questions about capital's hegemony over the transition and building alternative logics of accumulation were addressed. During the crucial years of the 1990s, however, the party paid too little attention to the contours shaping the economy in favour of big capital's interests. Nevertheless, both the CPI(M) and SACP envisioned a period in which capitalism and socialism coexisted.

Fundamentally related to the coexistence of capitalism and socialism are issues concerning the character of economic activity, which is the fourth element to the two parties' vision of socialist democracy.

The role of civil society and the state in the economy

For many people, socialism is primarily about the central role of the state (and state ownership) in production and distribution in the economy.[150] The failures of this 'statism' (and state ownership) have forced a reinterpretation of the role of the state in economic activity. Faced with many new challenges in the economic arena, both the CPI(M) and SACP turned their attention to clarifying their understandings about the transformation of the economy from one dominated by economic (or political) elites to one dominated by civil society. There are two dimensions to their thinking on economic activity (i.e. about the way economic resources are allocated, controlled and used). One concerns the extension of civil society over economic activity and the other concerns the state's control over economic activity.

With regard to the first dimension, and linked to their vision of deepening and extending democratic decision making into the economic domain, the parties supported the increased role of civil society in determining economic activity and thus sought the creation of cooperative forms of economic organisation, work collectives, democratic management and decision making in production (CPI[M], 1990:308–9; 1998b:136; SACP, 1998:42–43, 50). For the economy to be organised to serve the needs of ordinary people rather than political and economic elites, it must be controlled to a certain extent by ordinary people. The CPI(M) and SACP thus elaborated the importance of various forms of ownership that challenged the binary contrast between socialism and capitalism where state ownership is the alternative to private ownership of the means of production. The parties continued to support the idea of social ownership of the means of production and socialised production as among the primary ownership forms, but, they insisted, these were not the only forms of ownership. The CPI(M) and SACP argued that under socialism at least three forms of property would exist: state, cooperative and collective, and individual ownership (CPI[M], 1990:315–16; SACP, 1995:15; 1998b:70).

In terms of the second dimension, the state was also to play a crucial role in determining economic activity. It was to ensure redistribution; facilitate alternative logics of accumulation; and regulate the management, control, distribution and use of economic resources. Hence, the state was to be actively involved in the economic arena and nurture the increasing control of civil society over economic activity. Both parties were clear that any vision of anti-capitalist economic activity had to take into consideration the role of markets, but argued that markets had to serve the needs of the populace, which could be secured through the decommodification of certain services (e.g. health and education), the promotion of cooperatives and a degree of state intervention in the economy (CPI[M], 1990:314–16; 1998b:138–40; SACP, 1995:15–16). Both parties saw the failures of the Soviet Union's planned economy (CPI[M], 1990:298) and the deleterious effects of the free market system in the West, and thus argued for a system that combined the strengths of each (SACP, 1995:15). Markets were necessary, but had to be regulated to ensure that they served societal needs and not just profit maximisation (CPI[M], 1990:138–40; SACP, 1998:39–46, 49–50).

For the CPI(M), the failure of the Soviet economy, together with the fact that the Indian capitalist economy had grown over the previous forty years, forced the party to rethink and nuance its approach to economic development. In its 1992 ideological resolution the party acknowledged that it had overstated the likelihood of capitalism's imminent collapse and had underestimated the tenacity of the system and the potential of technological revolutions (CPI[M], 1998b:120). The party had to acknowledge that in India capitalist development had achieved significant economic growth since independence. The party now argued that it had the responsibility to try to achieve economic growth within the capitalist system in the most democratic and egalitarian way possible while simultaneously struggling to transcend capitalism through establishing alternative logics of accumulation (Isaac & Franke, 2001:33). Challenging the increasing penetration of the market, the CPI(M) envisioned a socialist economy in which ordinary citizens would play a central role through organising various aspects of economic activity and not just shaping the deployment of economic power (CPI[M], 1998a:142–43; Isaac, 1994:59). Hence, it promoted cooperatives and production for human needs, not simply profit. For example, in Kerala the CPI(M) has promoted small-scale cooperative production units, pushed for the decommodification of social services such as health and education, and established an extensive public distribution system of ration shops that provide subsidised staple foods to all households.

The party supported the idea that markets were pivotal, but insisted that planning is necessary to coordinate the management of the national economy into a single whole to meet social needs and to properly direct markets for social ends. Left on their own, markets produce immense negative effects such as economic irrationalities and negative externalities ranging from the failure to provide adequate public goods to the inability to reproduce the labour force, environmental degradation, regular economic crises and the increased suffering of large numbers of the world's population (Wright & Burawoy, 2004:1). In order for markets to play a positive role, however, they have to be properly regulated, which requires state intervention (CPI[M], 1990:315). In other words, the CPI(M) (1990:314) envisioned an integration of planning and markets:

socialistic planning pursues the aim of increasing the socialised productive forces so as to ensure increasing goods and welfare services of the citizens. Within this framework, the central plan and market relations should not be seen as opposing principles of regulation. The plan should utilise the market relations and regulate them for the immediate economic goals corresponding to the stage of development.

The party was, thus, directly challenging free market dogma that advocates a minimal role for state intervention in the economy. At the same time, the party was also challenging the idea of centralised planning of the economy. It maintained that state intervention and markets have positive roles to play in the economy, but at the same time civil society had to play a greater role in shaping economic activity.

In South Africa, the SACP was also aware of the urgent need to formulate alternative economic proposals to the hegemonic neoliberal development models that permeated thinking in the early 1990s.[151] Such proclamations notwithstanding, when the SACP and ANC returned in 1990, the liberation movement had not worked out an official economic policy. While both organisations were committed to a mixed economy (outlined in the late 1980s), by 1990 neither had developed a coherent economic programme. The 1994 democratic breakthrough meant that the Tripartite Alliance had to confront the complexities of translating popular aspirations for economic transformation into concrete policies. Over the course of the 1990s a number of articles appeared in *The African Communist* indicating serious reflection about the nature of economic development.[152] Like the CPI(M), the SACP pushed for both the increased role of civil society (especially the working class) in determining economic activity and the importance of active state involvement in shaping the direction of the economy (SACP, 1995:15–16; 1999:7; Satgar, 1997:68–73; Carrim, 2001:39–41).[153]

The party rejected arguments against state involvement in the economy and argued that 'there is no example of a developing country achieving high growth, let alone improving human development, on the basis of a minimalist state' (SACP, 1998:44). While the SACP was clear about the pivotal role the state had to play in the economy (especially in redressing the extreme inequality and poverty generated by the apartheid economic and social system) in order to put the economy on a new trajectory of sustainable development, it was careful to qualify the state's role.[154] The party argued that state intervention in the transformation of the economy had to be policy driven (e.g. by the formulation and implementation of industrial, sectoral and labour market policies) (SACP, 1999:14). The SACP summarised its understanding of the active role of a developmental state to include the provision of essential services (e.g. health, education and welfare), the creation of conditions for a developmental growth path (including human resource development, democratisation and participation), the promotion of redistribution (of income and wealth), and countering the effects of market failure (e.g. unemployment and jobless growth) (SACP, 1998:45). This included strong state intervention when necessary, and in some cases the state might have to go beyond facilitation and support and act by 'pressuring and cajoling capital, as well as taking active steps to transform ownership patterns' (SACP, 1998:41). In short, the state was to act as a catalyser and strategic coordinator and, when necessary, actively intervene in the economy in order to realise the nation-building, democratic, social and economic objectives of the NDR. Transformation, however, was to be society centred, with civil society increasingly making inroads into the political and economic realms.

In addition to the importance of state involvement, the SACP also articulated the need to maintain anti-capitalist class struggle by transforming economic power relations. The deracialisation of capitalism was only justifiable within a broader transformation programme that extended democratic control to the working class. It therefore indicated the importance of structural reforms that help shift the balance of class forces by undermining the core of capitalist power. Among the top priorities were redistribution and restructuring production, which included production for social needs, the democratisation of management, broadening the empowerment of workers and a labour-intensive (rather than capital-intensive) emphasis (SACP, 1995:17).

Building socialism in the current conditions included the social-isation of a predominant part of the economy, the decommodification of essential services, freedom and equality, and participatory planning (SACP, 1995:16–17;1998:69). Thus, the party envisioned a fundamental role for ordinary people in economic activity, which had to be strengthened in order to ensure that the socialisation of the economy would extend beyond formal ownership to become real empowerment of working people (SACP, 1995:14–15). The SACP supported the development of cooperatives as an attempt to shift the vector of power from economic elites to ordinary people through democratic principles of production, ownership and management (Satgar, 2001:64). To be clear, the SACP envisioned a cooperative movement that challenges the dominant structures of accumulation; if they fail to challenge capitalist accumulation patterns, cooperatives simply become shock absorbers for the poor and unemployed (SACP, 1999:46–47).

Like the CPI(M), the SACP saw the importance of markets and argued for their regulation in order to ensure that they served societal needs and not simply the profit motive (SACP, 1995:15). Markets have an important regulating and distributive function in the economy, but significant areas of society, such as health care, education and public housing, cannot be left to market forces (i.e. they have to be decommodified) (SACP, 1995:16). In short, the party defined its economic vision as consisting of a society in which

the socialized sector of the economy is predominant, democratic, rational planning is increasingly possible, a democratic culture and practices reach deeply into every sphere of social life, and there is a substantial equality of income, wealth, power and opportunities for all its citizens, and thus a growing freedom for all (SACP, 1998:71).

Thus, in their ideological visions both the CPI(M) and SACP pushed for the subordination of the economy to civil society and the state.

Conclusion

There are two important implications of the SACP's and CPI(M)'s ideological journey for our understanding of democratic egalitarian alternatives. Firstly, the way in which these parties envisioned socialist alternatives challenges the pervasive understandings about communist parties. While the anti-communist genre of literature has lost its salience in recent years, scholars such as Selznick (1952), Duverger (1974) and Courtios et al. (1999) asserted that communism was inevitably authoritarian, thus confining much of our thinking about the nature and character of communist parties. Yet the political reimagining of the SACP and CPI(M) highlights the existence of another tradition that not only challenges the inherently authoritarian rendition, but also exemplifies the democratic potential inherent in socialism. Secondly, the reimagining of the SACP and CPI(M) reflects a striking convergence in the thinking of two parties located in vastly different places, each with unique histories of liberation movements, class formation and national development. Confronted by the failures of 20th-century socialism, the

SACP and CPI(M) arrived at remarkably similar visions of socialist alternatives anchored in participatory democratic practices in the political and economic domains. In other words, these parties envisioned similar responses to the question of how to deepen socialist practices: rather than the dominance of the state or economy, they sought the dominance of civil society over the institutions of the state and economy. Indeed, both parties *envisioned* a social transformation that shifted power from the state to the people.

What does this mean for the parties' practices? Despite having developed similar visions, the CPI(M) and SACP pursued two very different political projects in practice in the years following their ideological renewal. In the case of the CPI(M), the party attempted to pursue all four themes, resulting in a politics that shifts the vector of power from the state and economy to civil society. For the SACP, the party focussed primarily on state-led development initiatives, resulting in a politics that subordinates civil society to the state and economy. Thus, the ideological reimagining that took place in the 1990s was an important first step in developing a transformative politics. It did not, however, guarantee that the parties would reorient their practices in line with their new visions. Reimagining socialist futures is a necessary preamble to any attempt to implement radically democratic socialist experiments in practice, but it is not a guarantee that this will take place.

10
Chapter

Labour, Migrancy and Urbanisation in South Africa and India, 1900–60

Phil Bonner

Migrant labour, or, more specifically, the migrant labour system, has been identified by a broad spectrum of liberal and radical social scientists as the core institution of South Africa's 20th-century political economy. It has been credited with underpinning white prosperity and white supremacy alike: white prosperity in the sense that the ultra-cheap 'bachelor' wages that could be paid to oscillating African labour migrants who left their families behind in the African reserves guaranteed impressive profits for both gold mining and later other industries, which were, by various mechanisms, spread across most sectors of white society; white supremacy because migrancy prevented Africans from settling in the bastions of white power in the towns and allowed the denial of political rights to virtually all Africans outside the reserves. In the majority of these accounts labour migrancy has been pictured as being either constrained or coerced. Land alienation, finally ratified by the 1913 Land Act, confined Africans to 8.7 per cent of South Africa's land, thereby precluding or inhibiting the independent reproduction of families in the reserves. The poll tax, which eventually climbed to £1, 10 shillings a year in 1925 and could be paid only in cash, forced Africans on the migrant labour market to earn wages, and a host of mechanisms such as the recruiting monopoly instituted by the Chamber of Mines in the early 20th century; the maximum average wage system by which members of the Chamber of Mines agreed to place a ceiling on the aggregate African wage bill; the labour contract system, which imposed criminal sanctions for breaches of it; single-sex compounds to accommodate migrants; and passes capped migrant earnings and prevented them from creeping up over time (Wolpe, 1972; Johnstone, 1976; Legassick, 1977). As a result, as Francis Wilson (1972:46) famously observed, African gold miners' wages remained static in real terms between the early 1900s and the late 1960s.

This somewhat stark and instrumental view of the role of migrant labour in South Africa's political economy has been given greater nuance in important respects in the last twenty or so years. Scholars have traced the emergence of partly self-sustaining migrant cultures whereby migrancy acquired a positive moral valency in the societies that gave it birth and was propagated as a life goal among youth who were about to follow that path (Stichter, 1985:12–18). At no point, nevertheless, did these scholars minimise the significance of the overarching institutional structure that gave labour migrancy in South Africa its peculiar cast.

The challenge that the Indian comparison presents to South African scholarship is that it discloses an equally entrenched migrant labour system, but shorn of its characteristic logic and institutions. Single-male migrancy dominated the Indian labour market during its formative phases and was set in place without the complex political apparatus and range of coercive interventions that were the apparent prerequisite of its South African counterpart.

This chapter will focus its attention on India's premier industrial cities, Bombay (now Mumbai) and Calcutta (now Kolkata), and South Africa's conurbation of the Witwatersrand. A number of excursions will also be undertaken into the urban milieus of India's Delhi, Madras (now Chennai), Nagpur, Bangalore, Ahmedabad, Surat and Pune, and South Africa's Durban. It builds on and overlaps with a previous study of mine published in the journal *Studies in History* (Bonner, 2004a).

Labour migrancy in India

Indian nationalist historical orthodoxy of the mid-20th century saw the movement of labour to cities as the outcome of the inexorable processes of underdevelopment and exploitation set in motion by British colonial rule. In this view, land taxes, deindustrialisation and a measure of commercialisation combined to expel impoverished artisans and peasants to the cities in a relatively uncomplicated and one-way fashion (Patel, 1952). From this perspective, migration was an interim phase. Increasingly, permanent urbanisation was assumed to be the outcome, much as had been the case in Europe and the United States (Joshi & Joshi, 1976:1–17).

This view came under challenge in the 1950s and 1960s, following the mass rural–urban migration of the decade 1941–51. Rural pressures underlying the movement were now seen as being located at least as much within the complex internal dynamics of Indian village society as in external impositions (e.g. Breman, 1974; Kumar, 1989). At the same time, migrancy came to be understood not just as an interim phase, but as a semi-permanent condition.

A near deluge of studies in the 1960s and 1970s showed the working population in India's two leading industrial cities, Bombay and Calcutta, as still consisting overwhelmingly of migrants – 84 per cent in the case of Bombay in 1961 – with other major urban centres displaying the same characteristics (see, for instance, Sen, 1960; Zachariah, 1968). Moreover, the highly skewed sex ratios exhibited by both the leading industrial cities suggested that a large proportion of these migrant workers had left their wives and families at home in their villages, and had little inclination to opt for a permanent, settled urban way of life.[155]

Labour migrancy in South Africa

Labour migrancy passed through at least three stages in late 19th- and early 20th-century South Africa. Prior to conquest, taxation and large-scale land alienation, young men migrated more or less voluntarily to work in South Africa's employment centres, particularly the mines. A second phase followed in the 1890s and early 1900s when the costs of deep-level mining spiralled upwards and demanded that wage levels be forced down to under half their former level; that huge drafts of unskilled African labour be continuously supplied; and that this labour be disciplined, mainly in compounds, to ensure that it worked a constant eight-hour day, thereby providing an adequate return on investment (for Indian examples, see Alexander, 2007). At some point following or overlapping the imposition of this apparatus of coercion and regulation, a third phase was reached whereby the supply of migrant labour reproduced itself without any further intervention.

One material factor contributing to this outcome was population growth. African society, including that part of it located in the reserves, was gripped by growing morbidity from diseases such as tuberculosis, syphilis, malaria and many others, but in a shift largely unrecognised in the literature, rates of mortality declined. Why this was so has still to be adequately explained, but the end result is clear: population levels inexorably mounted, pressure on land increased and spells of migrancy became an inescapable feature of black South African rural life (Beinart, 1994:202, 354).

At this stage, if not before, African societies themselves became active collaborators in the exercise. A spell of migrancy became incorporated in the typical life cycle of young African men. The critical role of such cultures of migrancy was only fully recognised at the beginning of the 1970s, when the Mayers published their path-breaking study *Townsmen or Tribesmen?* and pointed to the singular contribution that could be made by the discipline of social anthropology, with its preoccupation with culture, to the comprehension of social change in black South Africa (Mayer & Mayer, 1971). Within a decade, a clutch of pioneering historical studies by young revisionist historians of South Africa had begun to break out of the straitjacket of structuralist Marxism to document the role of African agency in the perpetuation of migrant labour systems. As these studies revealed, migrant cultures demanded submission to a migrant moral code that required migrants to encapsulate themselves in 'homeboy' networks in the urban employment centres and to insulate themselves as completely as possible from the corrupting influences of the towns. The central injunction of this moral code was that migrants *should return home*, and regularly at that. What such studies exposed was a yawning gap in prior analyses that had never been satisfactorily answered: why did migrants go back home? (Harries, 1994:81–108; Delius, 1996:21–24).

Accessing these cultures (as well as those of groups and individuals who left the land and settled permanently in the towns) became prime goals of South African social historians, as well as a number of anthropologists and ethno-musicologists. The main means by which they sought to illuminate this subject was through the collection of oral testimonies, above all in the form of life histories, that shed light on a wide spectrum of life experiences. Among the reasons for their ready – indeed, enthusiastic – resort to such sources were a prior 'Africanist' phase of collecting oral traditions and the comparative dearth of written texts documenting from an African vantage point a deep, as well as a more recent, African past (although African vernacular newspapers remain strangely unexplored). Another crucial route to tapping otherwise hidden or buried migrant (and immigrant) experiences and culture was that offered by the discipline of ethno-musicology in the form of music, song and dance. Erlmann (1996:84–87) and Clegg (1984) investigated changing dance and musical forms to illuminate the way in which successive generations of youths refashioned migrant cultures in Zululand and Natal (today KwaZulu-Natal). Coplan (1985) and Ballantine (1993) examined a multiplicity of musical forms and verses to plot a proliferation of migrant and immigrant subcultures in the towns.

The moral codes of migrant cultures were instilled through elders, families, peers and, above all, through the rite of initiation. A fascinating example of the importance of this *rite de passage* can be found in the hills of Makgabeng in the north-west of today's Limpopo Province. In shelters scattered along gorges, initiation schools were held. Initiates were instructed in the need to go out to labour, to return and reinvest in their homes, and to avoid urban women. A central visual symbol painted on countless shelter walls in these gorges was the train, packed with migrants, puffing its way south to the Rand. The moral load of this image was both the necessity and extreme dangers and vulnerabilities of migrancy. It was an image initiates would never forget.

So effective were these cultural silos that encapsulated migrant worlds that migrant youth cultures persisted in the single-male migrant hostels of the Witwatersrand up until the late 1990s, when research that Vusi Ndima and I conducted revealed that youth deference to elders and migrant moral codes were still so deeply embedded that youths handed over their entire wages to the elders for safe keeping (thereby rendering inaccessible the corrupting influences of the towns) (Bonner & Ndima, 2008).

Labour migrancy in India: Some causes

Labour migrancy to Bombay and Calcutta is similar in several ways. Early arrivals on the labour market tended to be drawn from the immediate hinterland of each city, while long-distance migrants made a significant entrance into the workplace of either city in the late 19th century only. In both instances, the bulk of the new arrivals hailed from the Eastern United Provinces (subsequently Uttar Pradesh) and Bihar, both situated deep in the interior. In the case of Calcutta, an additional source of long-distance migration was the state of Orissa to the south (Zachariah, 1968:50–55; Chandavarkar, 1994:129, 146–48; De Haan, 1994:92, 96).

What drove these rural populations to undertake such journeys to the towns? Firstly, as a number of path-breaking studies have now made clear, it is necessary to problematise the notion of migrancy as well as to deepen our historical time frame. As Ajuha (2002) states, most writings on the colonial period tend to disconnect India's pre-colonial from its colonial past. The pre-colonial period is pictured as harmonious, self-sufficient and communitarian, as well as anchored in particular localities, thereby denying any strong sense of mobility and change. As Ludden (1996), Kerr (2006) and Breman (1985) have pointed out, however, this picture is fundamentally misleading. Ludden (1996:109) asserts that half of India's population in the 18th century would have been made up of mobile people, ranging from seasonal migrants to hunters to herders, living out lives in 'a terrain of perpetual movement'. Kerr (2006:93–96) remarks on the activities of construction workers (known to the British as tank diggers or *wudders*), who were the most numerous group of migrant workers since pre-colonial times, travelling repeatedly from countryside to town or town to town. Washbrook (1993), who subtitles his article 'The golden age of the pariah?', contends that spatial mobility was as prevalent as sedentarism in pre-colonial India. Such itinerant groups, these studies agree, were perceived as actual or potential threats to social stability and political security in colonial India, and a variety of legal mechanisms were instituted to settle and 'peasantise' them (Osella & Gardner, 2004:xiii–xvii). Since access to rural resources was invariably inadequate to sustain family life, such a pre-existing life of 'circulatory' migration had to be replaced by oscillatory migration to centres of colonial employment, something more predictable and less threatening than itinerancy. From this perspective, the very process of sedentarisation in colonial India yielded some of the sources of colonial labour supply.

Other forms of migration and mobility also pre-dated colonialism in India or arose in the early period of colonial rule (i.e. up to the mid-19th century). De Haan (1994) believes that the principal streams of migrant recruitment to the jute mills of Calcutta (specifically Titagarth) followed previously established routes or had earlier precedents. The Bhojpur region of Uttar Pradesh and especially the Saran district, for example, which provided one of the earliest and most consistent sources of labour supply for the Calcutta mills, had contributed massive numbers (10,000) of sepoys to the British East India Company armed forces in the first half of the 19th century, while, subsequently, large numbers of residents migrated each year to cut crops in East Bengal for several months of the year, both long before the first jute mill was erected in Calcutta (De Haan, 1994:102, 105). Similarly, the Gurundi area of Ganjam in Orissa, which contributed another substantial and concentrated stream of migrants to Calcutta's mills, had furnished the bulk of the militias to the rajas in pre-colonial times in another instance of pre-colonial labour mobility or migration (De Haan, 1994:107).

Other factors, no doubt, induced or impelled such flows of migration to Calcutta's jute mills or other centres of colonial employment, of which more will be said below, but since none of the prime supply areas was noticeably poorer or more weighed down by landlessness than its neighbours, it seems that this pre-history to industrial migration must weigh significantly in the balance (De Haan, 1994:102, 106; see also Breman, 1996:62 for Ganjam dominance over Orissa migrants to Surat). A similar exercise of plotting pre-colonial patterns of mobility might well open up rich new analytical perspectives on the roots of labour migrancy in southern Africa. Much the same tendency is present in that the literature also pictures 18th-century African societies as localised, isolated and anchored. Yet long-standing processes and patterns of mobility may have been built on to construct the earliest migrant networks, only to be subsequently obscured from view.

The mounting privations experienced by rural households were equated in several studies published in late colonial and early post-colonial India with the rise of the landless rural labourer. Patel (1952) claims, on the basis of census records, that the number of agricultural labourers in village India soared from 13 per cent to 38 per cent of the rural population between 1871 and 1931, prompted by deindustrialisation, ruralisation and population pressure. Both Krishnamurty (1993) and Thorner and Thorner (1962:76–81) subsequently subjected the census categories to more rigorous scrutiny and concluded that the increase in the number of landless labourers was insignificant in this period, a view that now seems broadly accepted. Nevertheless, even a figure of 20 per cent landless is large and suggests a prima facie explanation for the ever-expanding streams of labour migrants from the rural areas to the cities. Common sense in this case, however, conceals and misleads. As a substantial corpus of historical writings now show, the totally landless and the most abjectly poor were the least likely to join the streams of migration to perform industrial labour. 'Tribals' such as those on the Chotra Nagpur plateau, who were dispossessed of their land rights in the mid-19th century, and already landless outcasts were incorporated in the lowest categories of agricultural societies (Bhattacharya, 1993; Chandavarkar, 1994:145; Breman, 1996:24–189).

This is not to say that urban industrial employers did not wish to exploit the vulnerable conditions of the poor and landless, or that they did not desire to set in place the lineaments of a migrant labour system analogous to that which subsequently developed in South Africa. Joshi (1985) shows how factory managers in Kanpur actively sought to recruit cheap labour from communities described as 'habitually criminal' under the Criminal Tribes Act of 1871 and campaigned for state intervention to help identify potential labour 'catchment' areas and prevent the absconding of new recruits (particularly those from 'criminal tribes'). Such efforts ended only in the 1920s when migrant labour became routinised. Joshi (1985) also records that managers possessed the legal power to prosecute workers for breach of contract under an 1859 law, which the Bengal Chamber of Commerce and the Jute Manufacturers Association sought to have extended to themselves (S. Sen, 1999:38), but they were unable to enforce this. Joshi then alerts us to an absolutely critical variable in this regard distinguishing India from some other colonial societies. Unlike the West Indies (to which one could obviously add South Africa), 'the state did not respond enthusiastically to management pleas for intervention' (Joshi, 1985:77–78). The old South Africa's structural Marxist preoccupation with the nature of the relationship between capitalism and migrant labour in this context thus acquires renewed salience, raising questions about why the state was so much less accommodating to capital in India (for South Africa, see Bonner, 1993:36, notes 4 & 5).

As a clutch of studies assembled and edited by Prakash (1993) demonstrate, landless labourers by no means encompass or exhaust the category of rural poverty. A common feature of all of the migrant-labour-exporting regions was what Banaji (1993) describes as the formal subsumption of labour in rural areas through the exploitation of the small peasantry by money-lending and land-owning capital from the mid-19th century. Such 'depeasantisation', to use Chaudhuri's (1993) term, whereby peasants continued to operate land (via sharecropping, for example) over which they had lost occupancy rights, allows us, as Prakash (1993:23) contends, to open up the category of agricultural labourers to include penurious, indebted small peasants. A further pressure driving rural populations into agricultural labour and migration, to which Chandavarkar (1994:146), among others, draws attention, was the decline of handloom weaving and other forms of artisan production, such as pottery, in the face of the onslaught of factory-produced textiles and imported metal goods, which became especially fierce in the last quarter of the 19th century. It should be noted, nevertheless, that the prime casualties of this process were Indian women who did not migrate (S. Sen, 1999).

It was these partly proletarianised peasants who retained ownership of inadequate parcels of land or some access to land via other means that made up the bulk of the stream of migrant labourers to the towns. Their conditions, as De Haan (1994:118) notes, varied enormously, with some people 'who seem to be proletarian in the city are often not'. Status, caste and material resources combined to provide a cushion of social and material capital that secured access to the most prized industrial jobs (the most prized of which was a permanent contract). The worse-off an individual was in the country, the worse-off he/she was in the town (see Breman, 1996:43).

A bewildering diversity of local circumstances, local tenurial arrangements, and local relationships of authority and subordination render risky almost any generalisation about the changing states of rural India. Two will, however, be ventured here, since they were influential in both India and

South Africa and underlay many of the changes previously noted. These are the commercialisation of agriculture (dealt with above) and population growth. Across India, the population climbed steadily from the early-19th to the mid-20th centuries. Between 1820 and 1872 the population of the Ratnagiri districts of the Konkan, from which most of Bombay's labour was extruded, grew from just under half a million to over a million. Massive subdivision of agricultural holdings ensued. Similarly, in the Deccan, the population climbed by 27.5 per cent between 1891 and 1941, while the cropped area grew by a meagre 6.6 per cent only, with similar results (Guha, 1985:86–87; Chandavarkar 1994:47, 141). Rowe's (1973:227) case study of the village of Senapur in eastern Uttar Pradesh reveals a similar pattern, with its population doubling between 1910 and 1970, leaving agricultural land overworked and giving lower yields. The conclusion thus seems inescapable. It was the *longue durée* of demographic growth that caused India's rural population to spill over in ever-increasing numbers to the cities.

Two broad reasons can be advanced for this steady upward trend in population growth. Firstly, although famines devastatingly struck India in the 1870s and 1890s, and bubonic plague repeatedly ravaged the continent between 1891 and 1911, the truly massive famines and epidemics all but vanished from view over the next fifty years (the last major Indian famine prior to the Bengal famine of 1943 struck in 1919) (Ghurye, 1974:185; De Haan, 1994:109, note 54). Secondly, urban employment and urban wages supplemented village subsistence and cushioned peasant families from periodic agricultural disasters. This, of course, presumes a pattern of seasonal migrancy and the retention of the migrants' links to the village. It was the prevalence of this pattern of seasonal migrancy that led Rowe (1973:226) to conclude that 'in direct contradiction to the claim that "the city will destroy the village", it is our finding that, in economic terms at least, the city makes the continuance of the North Indian village possible'. Famine, more so than its converse, sufficiency, also affected labour migrancy in one other way. Famines were frequently the trigger initially propelling groups of workers into oscillating migrancy, thereby establishing the first bridgeheads to the towns (De Haan, 1994:108–9; Breman, 1996:641; Joshi, 2003:81).

Labour migrancy in India: Some dynamics

Our core question nevertheless still remains: why, in the absence of institutional compulsions or controls such as those that existed in most of 20th-century South Africa, did Indian workers devote so much energy to sustaining a rural base? Low wages, job insecurity, irregular work, and a shortage of adequate and affordable accommodation all contributed towards this inclination. Chakrabarty (1989:208–9) records 'short-term service' punctuated by regular periods of unemployment to be the standard pattern in the jute industry of Calcutta. Chandavarkar (1994:73–123) shows casual labour as being common in all sectors of industry in Bombay, along with intense competition for what employment there was, as a result of a large surplus labour pool in the city (for Calcutta, see S. Sen, 1999). It was in this context, as a number of writers have observed, that it became imperative to maintain the safety net offered by rural connections. As Patel (1963:37) notes of Ratnagiri in the 1960s, a base in the village provided 'an invaluable security in times of unemployment, severe economic distress, old age and the like'.

However, the safety net offered by rural connections was not woven exclusively of rural threads. Rural kin, caste and village connections were also transposed into the city where they were deployed to find jobs and accommodation for new migrants and to provide various kinds of support or credit for those temporarily unemployed. A key component of this network was the labour recruiter or subcontractor known as the *sirdar* in Calcutta, the *mistri* in Kanpur and the jobber in Bombay. He recruited groups of workers, usually on a kin, caste or village basis, either at the rural base or in an urban working-class neighbourhood. He was responsible for delivering workers to the factory and for supervising and disciplining labour at the point of production. In some instances he rented out rooms to migrant workers in his group. Generally, he shared a common rural origin with the workers he hired (Newman, 1981; Joshi, 1985:252–54, 265–66; Chakrabarty, 1989:907–1115).

The practice of urban leaseholding in Bombay and Calcutta – which bears comparison to that operating in the inner-city slum yards of Johannesburg in the early decades of the 20th century (Koch, 1983) – encouraged rack renting by leaseholders and an escalation of rents. Rentals for single rooms were commonly a third more than ordinary workers could afford (Chandavarkar, 1994:176). This in itself constituted a strong incentive to remain migrant, since the only way for workers to afford accommodation was through various forms of sharing (see Bulsara, 1964:64–65; 1970:283–90; Gore, 1970:75; Breman, 1996:51; Joshi, 2003:106).

Surplus labour, irregular employment and low wages made kinship, village and related urban neighbourhood solidarities indispensable for migrants. One unemployed 'upcountry' worker told the Royal Commission into Labour in 1931 that he would live for months in working-class slums with the support of relatives and on credit from the *sirdar* until he ultimately found a job (Chakrabarty, 1989:210). Other sources of credit were the local *bania* (grain dealer) and in the final resort the feared Pathan (who are now known as Pashtuns) (Chandavarkar, 1994:189–92). These same constraints also dictated residential distribution. A common pattern across all of India's industrial cities has been residence close to the place of work. For these reasons, slums became an increasingly conspicuous feature of Indian cities as the 20th century wore on (Sen, 1960:158; Gore, 1970:110; Breman, 1996:51; De Haan, 2004:193). The location of slums was closely related to the distribution of employment opportunities. Here, the urban geography of India was strikingly at variance with that of South Africa. As Sen (1960:161) remarks of Calcutta: 'The slum areas are not concentrated in separate areas like the East End of London. They are to be found scattered all over the city, fashionable houses and *bustees* [i.e. slums] side by side' (see also Namibiar, 1970:182–98, 201–9, 219; Majumdar & Majumdar, 1978:1–611; Lewandowski, 1980:44–45; Kumble, 1982:9–44; Rao, 1990:22–28).

Breman (1996) observes that such abject conditions and shortages of houses acted as a powerful disincentive to workers bringing their wives and families to the town or even to visit. As one of his interviewees put it, 'where would she have to sleep?' On this issue Breman goes further, offering an interesting parallel perspective to some of the dominant lines of interpretation of South African migrancy. 'The refusal to implement a housing policy [by the government and municipalities]' he sees as 'a conscious effort to keep the lowest ranks of the urban economy mobile and to shift their reproduction cost as much as possible to the rural hinterland' (Breman, 1996:40–41).

One notable parallel and one striking difference between Indian and South African urbanisation stand out from the foregoing review. The first is that a low-wage migrant labour system evolved and reproduced itself in the Indian context without the benefit of the institutional apparatus evident in South Africa. The second is that residential segregation, which with few exceptions was the rule for 20th-century South Africa, was largely absent in Indian cities; a difference that reflected the different places in the colonial order occupied by India and South Africa. In contrast to India, South Africa was a colony of white settlement. South African governments always saw the cities as likely sites for the subversion of white supremacy, either through racial mixing in slums or through so-called black 'detribalisation' (Jochelson, 2001:21–66, 98–166). A near constant theme in South African urban governance was the desire to regulate movement to the towns through influx and efflux controls, and to assign a large section of the African workforce the status of migrants (Davenport, 1970; 1971). It was the absence of any similar kind of endeavour in India that allowed for large surpluses of urban labour and the proliferation of urban slums, which in turn provided the material and social underpinnings of migrant labour. In South Africa, by contrast, the requirements of white supremacy and particularly the quest to keep towns white meant that an elaborate institutional apparatus was needed to complement or substitute for the social and economic forces present in Indian villages and cities.

South Africa: Culture, gender and urbanisation

South Africa has a relatively foreshortened history of urbanisation compared to India, as well as a less-complex and graduated rural social structure. Initially, it was educated converts to Christianity who settled with their families in the towns. Like Tamil migrants to Pune, they went there in search of better-paying, white-collar jobs or self-employment and practised a culture of what Bozzoli (1991:122–228) and Goodhew (2004:199) term 'respectability' (see also Bonner with Nieftagodien, 2008:chapters 1–3 for Alexandra Township examples). In the 1920s and 1930s these relatively sedate early residents were overlain and overwhelmed by a second surge of black immigration issuing mainly from white farms, which carried with it markedly different cultural baggage and constructed a strikingly different cultural milieu.

The growing exodus of farm labourers/labour tenants from the farms was prompted by two developments. Firstly, greatly reduced access to land for labour tenants, whether for agriculture or for stock, and steadily mounting labour demands by the white owner were problems. This obviously bears comparison with the Indian experience. Secondly, a series of searing droughts that scoured the countryside between 1927 and 1934 and then after the Second World War exacerbated the situation, these were not paralleled in Indian agricultural history.

The 1932–34 drought shook rural society to its foundations, loosening bonds of servitude and dependence. Refugees from drought swarmed into small rural towns, where few found work, and then in many cases drifted on to the major industrial centres. Once the drought broke late in 1933, farmers likewise sought to recoup their losses by increasing their output and placed intensified demands on their tenants. Many tenants, having been shaken loose from the land over the preceding drought period, refused to comply and sought work on a permanent basis in the towns. In 1936 official reports estimated that out of a hundred aspiring workers arriving in Johannesburg each day, twenty were from the farms.

What is particularly striking about the pattern of migration is its generationally skewed character, which is not nearly so evident or well documented in the Indian case. Generally, young men and women moved first. The most common first step outside the farms for the sons and daughters of labour tenants was to seek temporary domestic work in the neighbouring small towns or local mines. As the 1930s progressed, these short-haul moves were followed by more distant and protracted visits to the main industrial centres. At this point the labour of the sons and daughters of the labour tenant was often permanently lost to both the family and the farmers they served (Bonner, 2004b:87–114).

Reserve society and migrant culture were still holding largely intact at this point, but in some areas they were fraying at the edges. The principal victims and most marginalised sections of the reserve population were African women, above all those living in the most impoverished reserves of the Ciskei and Basutoland (now Lesotho). Ciskei was an area distinguished by extreme shortages of land. There, polygamy became increasingly uncommon, while high rates of bride wealth paid in increasingly costly cattle meant that even monogamous marriages were difficult and had to be delayed. As Mager (1999:75) remarks, 'reduced cattle numbers meant that men and women endured a protracted liminal period between youth and adulthood', one index of which was the rising average age of marriage for both women and men between the 1890s and 1940s (19 to 23 for women; 24 to 30 for men).

These developments, which were reproduced in several analogous rural contexts such as Basutoland, had a profoundly corrosive effect on rural life. Firstly, young women were encouraged to elope or, more seriously, were abducted (Bonner, 1990:234–37), all too often to be subsequently abandoned (Mager, 1999:70) by the man. Secondly, the expanded gap between sexual maturity and marriage increased the scope for illicit sexual liaisons, leading to growing numbers of single mothers and illegitimate children (Mager, 1999:139). Thirdly, such single and abandoned women, along with widows, were denied access to or inheritance of land and lived an increasingly marginal existence 'on the fringes of patriarchal society'. Fourthly, and critically, these and other women came to be valued, in Mager's telling phrase, more for their sexuality than their fertility (*Mager, 1999*:87) and also became highly vulnerable to sexual exploitation and abuse (Mager, 1999:75, 87, 128, 193–94). Fifthly, the numbers of widows skyrocketed, partly as a result of the growing age discrepancy between husbands and wives (Mager, 1999:181).

Pressure on rural subsistence, matched by unprecedented bursts of industrial expansion in the 1930s and 1940s, drew a huge number of men into industrial employment. Many brought their wives and families to the town, but a large (if indeterminate) proportion of the urban female population continued to consist of single (if previously married) women. Between them, these were responsible for the numbers of urban women climbing by 79.95 per cent between 1936 and 1946, compared to 46.8 per cent for men, resulting in a seismic shift in urban sex ratios (Posel, 1991:24), which began to level off. The scale and composition of the inflow constitute one of the major differences between the pattern of Indian and South African urbanisation, which asks intriguing questions of both the South African and the Indian literatures.

Drought and the various vicissitudes experienced by white farms also expelled increasing numbers of poor whites into the urban areas. First to leave were *bywoners* (tenant/sharecropper families) displaced by disease, drought and the South African War of 1899–1902. These bear a close resemblance in several respects to early migrants to Indian towns. The scale of the movement grew in the 1920s and 1930s, when farm owners came under increasing pressure from commoditisation, rising farm prices and drought (Bonner with Nieftagodien, 2008). Poor white farmers would often dispatch their young daughters to the cities first, for whom growing numbers of low-paying jobs were available in the expanding light industry sector (Hyslop, 1995:61–64). Poor white men and women alike would congregate in the mixed-race inner-city slums, prompting a rising tide of moral panic about physical and mental degeneration, thriftlessness, and sexual profligacy, and a generally 'demoralising and corrupt intercourse with non-Europeans' (cited in Chanock, 2001:204–5). Venereal diseases, Jochelson (2001:22–31) writes, 'encapsulated anxiety about the physical and mental deterioration of the nation'. The slums, or 'racial borderlands', were perceived as especially threatening and the Achilles heel of white supremacy and 'civilisation' (Jochelson, 2001:50–55, 130). Accordingly, a policy of urban racial residential segregation was increasingly urgently implemented, beginning with the Natives' (Urban Areas) Act of 1923 and gathering momentum in the 1930s, when economic depression and savage drought drove increasing numbers of poor whites and poor blacks to seek refuge in the urban slums (Parnell, 1993).

A further peril associated with unregulated urbanisation in general and the urban slums in particular was African 'detribalisation', which posed additional social and political threats to white domination. As Jochelson (2001:112–28) notes, the entire process of urbanisation for Africans was defined as pathological and needing to be arrested or reversed. Thus, the presence of a settler society and more so of a large number of poor whites imposed radically different constraints on, and opportunities for, the processes of migrancy and immigration to those experienced in an Indian context. It is to this that we can ultimately attribute their different trajectories.

India: Culture, migration and urbanisation

Migrant cultures have not been the subject of such close attention in India. This seems to be partly owing to a greater divorce between urban and rural studies in India (although the same dichotomy was also a conspicuous feature of much South African scholarship), and partly to the different preoccupations of social anthropologists working in the two countries, something that in itself warrants explanation. Beyond this, however, one distinctive feature of South African historiography since the late 1970s, as was noted earlier, has been its reliance on oral testimonies documenting a wide spectrum of life experiences. The use of oral testimony (above all in the form of life histories) is a far less pronounced feature of Indian historiography and social sciences. One major reason for this, as Sumit Sarkar (2007) explains, is the abundance of vernacular texts that are available to illuminate India's past. But beyond that, Bhattacharya (2006) suggests a question of proclivity. Referring to subaltern studies, he observes a preference for written sources, which he feels cannot reveal the full picture. 'The sources used by cultural historians', Bhattacharya claims, 'emanate from literate elite groups, and "reading against the grain" does not take one very far. Features attributed in this elite discourse are aggregated in "popular culture", disregarding internal diversities.' 'Little work', he concludes, 'founded on historical evidence has emerged in the area' (Bhattacharya, 2006:14–15). The anthropologist Arjaan de Haan (2004:190, note 2; 192) amplifies these propositions. 'In the absence of a lively oral history tradition', he asserts, 'few anthropological or sociological studies of labour exist'.

One distinction widely noted in the literature is between northern and eastern Indian cities, where single-male migration predominated, and western and especially southern Indian cities, where family migration was far more common. Rowe (1973:233) follows Muckherjee (1961) in suggesting that one important reason for this variation is the extent to which northern Indian cities were primarily colonial creations. Muckherjee specifically proposes that southern India was least touched by colonialism and most closely corresponded to the traditional model (see also Prakash Rao, 1983:9–15). It is a short step from here to suggesting that the more traditional social structure and culture of India's southern cities are in some way responsible for more family-based migration and more even sex ratios, a pattern also apparent in southern migration to cities elsewhere in India. The city of Pune, for example, attracted large numbers of Tamil-speaking migrants during and after the Second World War – 64.8 per cent of one sample of these immigrants were single or unmarried on arrival. Ten years later, 66 per cent were married and living in nuclear families (Nair, 1978:23). The bulk of south Indian migrants to Pune were educated and involved in white-collar work. In other Indian cities, a close correlation existed between higher-income occupations and more settled urban family units, and this may be another example of the same pattern (e.g. see Kumar Bawa, 1980:65; Joshi, 2003:95, 102).

In the southern city of Bangalore, however, a different kind of family migration was evident. Here, a phenomenal rate of urban growth between the 1940s and 1960s was propelled by Tamil-speaking pariah (untouchable) immigrants from Madras state. Like poorer migrants in other Indian cities, they lived in slums located close to industrial sites. Unlike other north Indian cities, however, they arrived in nuclear families or soon brought their wives (Rowe, 1973:235–39; Prakash Rao, 1983:49–50, 227–44; for Madras, see Lewandowski, 1980:52, 93). Finally, in Calcutta and Bhilai, De Haan and Parry observe almost exactly the same pattern. De Haan (2004:200) notes: 'Telugu from Andrah Pradesh and South Orissa tended to move with their entire families ... to [take] up work in the factories' in the Titagarh industrial suburb of greater Calcutta. Likewise, Parry (2004:225) documents southerners (especially Tamils and Telugus) very quickly bringing their wives and children to Bhilai, with northerners only sometimes following suit considerably later, a trend that he claims, following Crook (1993), to have been visible as far back as the census of 1911.

Various reasons have been advanced to account for this pattern, such as unfavourable economic conditions and the oppressive nature of rural society for those from pastoral and agricultural castes. These, however, do not in and of themselves offer a complete explanation, since impoverished untouchables in northern India did not evince a similar inclination. Parry (2004:225) suggests that the divergent patterns may have been born of different features of industrialisation in northern and southern India, south Indian industries having been generally 'light and evincing more of a demand for women's labour', but also considers 'different gender norms' to have possibly been instrumental. Rowe (1973:241) likewise concludes that the most plausible explanation is likely to reside in social structures and cultural systems, i.e. '[t]he different family systems, the degree of authoritative strength held by the extended family ... ties to other castes in the rural social system and ties to the land'. Rowe suspects, for example, that the Bhayias in northern India were more linked or cemented into the north Indian social system compared to pariahs in the south, who were demonstrably more marginal. Breman (1974) provides solid evidence of the same in his study of *jajmani* (patronage) in south Gujarat. Both groups of untouchables encountered problems in escaping the rural social mesh, but southern pariahs were more inclined to try, and when they did leave, were more likely to make a decisive break, taking with them their wives and families, who, in contrast to higher-caste Brahmins and others, were expected and allowed to engage in remunerated work. We might conclude, then, that those retaining rights in land were most likely to engage in seasonal (oscillatory) migration, while those stripped of these rights would not initially have possessed the resources or freedom to engage in such a practice, but would ultimately be most likely to cut their moorings from the rural social order.

Migrant labour, urbanisation and social stability

In South African historical and social science scholarship, oscillating labour migrancy is widely credited with the responsibility for chronic family instability and a host of associated social ills, both in the countryside and in the towns. The male migrants' increasingly extended absences from home, their failure to remit money and their occasional reluctance to return to their rural families have all been factors prompting single but married women to migrate to the towns. There, the absence of employment opportunities for women, together with hugely unbalanced sex ratios and the sub family subsistence wages paid to mainly migrant males, encouraged them to engage in serial relationships with men, the illicit brewing of liquor and sometimes prostitution. Children born in such circumstances were largely schooled on the streets and turned in growing numbers to juvenile delinquency. By the 1940s the ubiquitous *tsotsi* was making his presence felt in most South

African towns, fuelling a rising incidence of violence and criminality (Glaser, 2000:20–183).

The contrast between this and the literature describing social life in India's main industrial cities is stark. There, male migrancy was equally pronounced, but family life survived relatively intact. On the one hand, the overwhelming majority of the wives of Indian male migrants to the towns remained firmly locked in the bosom of their joint families and rooted in rural homes. So unappealing were living conditions in the towns that, as one Calcutta labour historian writes, 'the choice was seen as one between family life in degrading circumstances or separation from their families for lengthy periods of time' (S. Sen, 1999:132). In northern and western India, at least, the latter decision was invariably taken. Few married men took their wives to the urban areas and few single women of the sort so visible in South Africa were sufficiently headstrong or desperate to undertake the risky venture to the towns. Nevertheless, and on the other hand, from the earliest days of the cities a proportion of urban job seekers settled permanently in the towns, increasingly so after 1961 (Mukerjee & Singh, 1961:52). Immigrants from southern and eastern India, as has been discussed earlier, featured prominently in this move and either migrated as family units or soon brought their spouses to join them. Once again, single women did not migrate. Right across India, it was 'unthinkable for rural women to come alone and earn a livelihood' (Prakash Rao, 1983:34). In Lucknow, to take one example, only a tiny number of females migrated independently to town (Mukerjee & Singh, 1961:71). In Kanpur, to take another, only a miniscule number of widows and divorcees, who had lost their rights in rural areas, sought employment in the mills in the town (Joshi, 2003:13).

In general, sexual behaviour among men and women who ended up in the towns is depicted in the urban literature as restrained. Gore's (1970:17) study of Bombay records very few casual 'illicit' relationships between men and women. Desai and Pillay's (1972:171) account of a Bombay slum contrasts the relative stability of family life that they observed there with the high levels of social disorganisation and family breakdown in Latin American slums. Other Indian urban centres exhibited more or less the same characteristics. In Pune, for example, declining social observances are recorded alongside the breakdown of taboos, with the outstanding exception of marriage (Gadgil, 1952:184–222). In a number of slum areas, desertion, clandestine prostitution and the occasional illicit relationship are recorded, but on an unexpectedly circumscribed scale (Majumdar & Majumdar, 1978:26, 147–49; Desai & Pillay, 1972:160, 171, 221–22; Department of

Economics, 1970:173–75; Prakash Rao, 1983:93, 100, 145–46, 153; Sinha, 1972:93, 96).

Yet such perspectives, as Amita Sen (1999) in particular shows, have been inscribed and have survived in the historical record largely by default. A male academy, with few exceptions, has produced a blinkered and culturally conditioned view of Indian women in colonial society and history. Through such lenses, Indian women typically emerge as bystanders, lacking agency and mute, their behaviour or their abscence not requiring serious explanation. In the urban context, as A. K. Sen (1999:4) observes, 'it has not even been asked why the Indian working class became overwhelmingly male'. By contrast, Sen sets out to highlight and interrogate the largely unstated assumptions that have served virtually by default to explain why so many Indian women remained rooted in rural homes. The core elements that she identifies are brahminical prescriptions about the seclusion of women to domestic space (*purdah*), child marriage, an insistence on chastity and a related recoil from pollution, and a prohibition on widow remarriage. These served both to confine Indian women within their homes and to render them utterly beholden to dominant men. They were thus simultaneously imprisoned, and imprisoned themselves.

On closer examination, however, as Sen and others show, these social practices and cultural prescriptions turn out to be in no way primordial. Sen cites O'Hanlon and others to show that the 19th century witnessed a gradual brahminisation of Hindu society. Castes that had never practised strict *purdah* or child marriage and had permitted divorce, remarriage and widow remarriage now adopted them with a vengeance, mainly to assert a higher social and political position. As striking and significant, dowry replaced bride wealth in marriage transactions. Such shifts in behaviour, Sen argues, mirrored a progressive devaluing of women's work and hence women's status in rural Indian society. Thus, a number of the seemingly eternal verities of Indian society turn out to be constructed and contrived, and lacking the authority of an unchanging tradition (A. K. Sen, 1999:64–88). This, nevertheless, made them in no way less potent. Moreover, as Sen shows, such changes explain why men controlled decisions to migrate to towns, why men migrated rather than women, and why women's labour and status continued to diminish as men earned the critical cash needed for rent and to pay debts, and women's work was domesticised and leached of all economic value. Indeed, as Sen's work shows, the steady slide of Indian women's positions in rural society, especially its lower orders, underscores the power of invented or appropriated social conventions and traditions.

Indian women, above all widows (who constituted an astonishing quarter of all rural Indian women in 19th-century Bengal), faced increasingly dismal and hopeless conditions (A. K. Sen, 1999:181). In reality, indeed, they had more and more incentive to flee to the towns. Most did not, but as Sen again remarks, a minority did. These generally highly marginalised women often abandoned their rural households in the company of men. These men, however, were rarely their husbands, and such women were at best able to construct what A. K. Sen (1999:199) calls temporary marriages. In instances where such men occupied the better-paying jobs of spinners and weavers, they sought to lock their temporary and highly insecure wives into 'a new form of purdah' (De Haan, 2004:20), which generally took the form, so A. K. Sen (1999:39) notes, of 'incarceration in tiny airless cubicles' in the mill town. Often they were dumped when these men returned 'home'. Otherwise women sought various kinds of employment, such as working in the mills, but also prostitution. Since such women, in the words of A. K. Sen (1999:186), could not 'live or in many cases work without male protection', they entered liaisons with them. As a consequence 'jute women became symbols of infamy and depravation', and were placed in the same bracket as prostitutes. So indeed were virtually all urban working women, ranging from domestics to cooks, needlewomen and laundresses, stigmatised as engaging in 'clandestine prostitution' (A. K. Sen, 1999:197). Elite male commentators saw them as purveyors of disease, practitioners or associates of crime, and generally as the scourge of the city (A. K. Sen, 1999:177).

This snapshot of Calcutta is not so far removed from the picture presented earlier of the Witwatersrand's multiracial slums and black townships. The main difference on the Witwatersrand is that white women laboured, while black women were confined to informal income-earning activities. In Johannesburg, the worlds of the (white) Afrikaner women factory worker and the African women beer brewer, childminder or laundress are curiously intermingled. What is so radically different in each case, however, are the numbers involved: a massive movement of women in the case of South Africa; a miniscule movement in the case of most Indian towns. The contrast is striking and still needs to be more adequately explained. How typical Calcutta is or is not of other towns also warrants further investigation.

Juvenile delinquency, which is often regarded as a key marker of social instability, has been far less conspicuous in Indian cities than in South Africa. In 1930 an educational commentator remarked that 'thousands of children' in Bombay were born into homes in which parental control and guidance were almost completely lacking. Their primary education was that of the streets. They got from it a certain superficial sharpness, but little knowledge that could be of service in the business of life and less than no discipline (cited in Chandavarkar, 1994:170). This observation could have been repeated word for word about many South African cities in the 1940s. In the case of India's cities, nevertheless, it does not seem to have produced large-scale juvenile delinquency, along with the massive sexual violence that became increasingly pervasive in South Africa's towns. The reasons for this are entirely opaque; India's social historians and sociologists are largely silent on the subject. They recognise that urban families have become pared down to their nuclear core, as compared to their extended counterparts in the countryside (Joshi, 2003:102, citing RCLI, 1931), but they then broadly make the assumption that this unit is stable and natural. The issue of explaining stability simply does not arise. Beyond that, generational discussions are rarely the subject of 20th-century Indian urban studies.

It is possible that a growing literature on crime may embrace – and mask – some of these issues. Joshi's seminal study on the northern Indian cotton-milling town of Kanpur, for example, highlights the activities of *goondas* in that town. Officially defined as 'hooligan, bully, rogue or *badmash*', *goondas* led gangs that were involved in a variety of money-making and often criminal activities. Youths were presumably members of such gangs, but, in the absence of any close analysis or explanation, figure as exceptions to the non-delinquent rule.

In Bombay and Kanpur, gymnasia (*akhadas*) provided an important social and sometimes political focus for urban youth and, as Chandavarkar (1994) notes, they also provided the basis for street gangs. His next remark that the youth were often pulled into more general political (and communal) activities typifies the slide that occurs in most Indian studies, where they feature as an integral part of the history of communal violence, but rarely as a social force in their own right. In Calcutta, gymnasia and *goondas* combined into a fearful force. Their criminal enterprises expanded to such a point that the Bengal government passed a 'Goonda Act' in 1926 in an effort to rein them in. *Goondas* were concentrated in Calcutta's *bustees* (slums) and controlled liquor and gambling dens, prostitution, drugs, and pickpocketing and burglary rings. Studies of the history sheets of *goondas* compiled by the Calcutta police show many *goondas* to be migrants to the city who had lost their fathers in their youth, but one gets little sense of dislocated urban families providing an important conduit into their ranks.

In India, the insecurity of urban life sustained high levels of single-male migrancy, especially in the north. Only in the 1960s and 1970s did a trend towards more permanent settlement begin to assert itself. Even then, migrancy remained widespread. Housing shortages and job instability required single male migrants to seek intermediary mechanisms through which to enhance their access to both resources or to cushion them in times of unemployment and other kinds of distress. A wide range of patrons emerged to fulfil these needs. The jobber or *sirdar* was the most prominent of these, but grain dealers (*banias*) and neighbourhood bosses (*dadas*) also played similar roles. The networks that they constructed were almost always rural village/neighbourhood/caste or communally based. In this way, both occupational categories and urban residential areas became colonised by groups from particular regions (Chandavarkar, 1994:172–200).

In part, this represented cultural continuity, since particular jobs had historically been performed by specific castes. However, there are too many examples of occupational drift as castes decoupled themselves from inapposite job categories within a more diverse and fluid urban setting for this to be considered the main cause (e.g. Bose, 1973:29). More important were the general exigencies of urban life. It was because of these that Bose (1973) found employment in Calcutta concentrated by regional origin and described the city as an archipelago of 'cultural islands'. Much the same could be said of Bombay. Joshi and Joshi (1976:134) identify 'differential corridors of migration' to Bombay and 'the specialisation of migrants from different areas in different industries and occupations'. Rowe (1973:228) writes that it was 'almost as if a map of North Indian districts was reproduced within the wards of (Bombay) city'. Bombay and Calcutta were admittedly the most heterogeneous cities in India (Gore, 1970:228), but even in less diverse northern cities such as Kanpur 'the struggle for jobs often took the form of community cohesion', while 'the authority of the *mistri* or jobber tended to solidify such loyalties' (Joshi, 1985:22).

Such regional, communal or even caste patronage networks were not solely the preserve of single male migrants in northern and eastern industrial towns. In Madras, where family settlement was common, a self-conscious 'simulation' of the regional culture of origin occurred within the new urban setting. Nair (1978) goes so far as to claim that simulation was 'fullest' where family migration was the dominant pattern and that the length of residence in urban areas tended 'to strengthen ethnic identity' rather than the reverse. Here, in contrast to Western urbanisation, he sees 'integration without assimilation'. Barnett (1976:16–25, 314–27) introduces a significant variation on the same theme. She suggests that southern towns, particularly Madras, presented unequal opportunities to different castes, resulting in a comparative loss of status for 'non-Brahmins', as opposed to Brahmins, which in turn led to a recrafting, even invention, of a non-Brahmin Dravidian and later Tamil identity.

In Johannesburg, and more generally in the urban agglomeration of the Witwatersrand, some significant similarities and differences to this pattern can be discerned. Like Bombay, this was the most ethnically/regionally heterogeneous urban centre in South Africa. Like Bombay, migrancy and more settled urban life existed side by side. Like Bombay, Calcutta and other Indian cities, a measure of ethnic occupational clustering occurred among its black population. Richards' survey of pass records for the late 1930s and early 1940s, for example, shows that Johannesburg's building workers were drawn disproportionately from the Transkei, municipal workers from East Griqualand and Tembuland, commercial workers from the Orange Free State farms, and industrial workers from Basutoland and particular parts of Zululand (Bonner, 2004a).

Here the similarity ends. Patrons, who were indispensable for individual or group survival in Indian cities, were barely visible in South Africa. Migrants were recruited through centralised recruitment agencies, or alternatively found jobs through relatives or friends. No jobber needed to intervene. The practice narrated by Majumdar and Majumdar (1978:120) in respect of Delhi, whereby jobs rotated among men from the same village, was even more typical of South Africa (where for many years such men would even illicitly rotate the same pass). White South Africa's endeavour to curb African migration also meant that black employees were channelled into state-managed and state-licensed housing. This again meant that no intermediary patron was required. A partial exception can be made of Johannesburg's inner-city slums, but here housing stock was accessed through white slumlords who had no vested interest in sustaining an ethnic or regional patronage network. The only times a situation similar to those typical of Indian cities arose were during the bursts of unregulated urbanisation that occurred in the 1940s and 1980s, when invasions of public land were initiated by black immigrants to the city. At these points, classic patron-type figures, often heading ethnic networks, emerged, the best known of whom is the founder of modern Soweto, James Sofazonke Mpanza (Bonner & Segal, 1998:20–28). For the rest, state-regulated urbanisation closed down the space that such figures could occupy. One possible intriguing consequence of this was the phenomenon of 'detribalisation', in which a common black urban culture was forged, of which *marabi* music was the icon. If that could be more conclusively established to be the case, the value of this comparative exercise would be affirmed.

Conclusion

This comparison of patterns of Indian and South African urbanisation suggests that both literatures might benefit from an interrogation informed by a knowledge of the other. The South African literature needs to be re-examined above all in relation to the dynamics underlying its migrant labour system and the purported social consequences of labour migrancy. For its part, the Indian literature needs to problematise family stability and pay closer attention to the neglected issue of generation. Both would benefit from a further comparison of cultural contexts. Beyond the scope of this investigation, but also hugely important, are the different political implications of these similar but divergent patterns of urbanisation – not least, the critical issue of communalism, which only really reared its head in South Africa in the late 1980s and early 1990s.

Conclusion

| Conclusion | # Cricket Ethics:
Reflections on a
South African-Indian Politics of Virtue[156]
Eric Worby |

A post-colonial encounter on ethical grounds

A reader of the foregoing chapters in this book might be excused for wondering why they ought to be considered part of a common scholarly undertaking. It is not easy to draw India and South Africa into the same frame of inquiry, nor, on the face of it, are there obvious and compelling reasons for doing so. 'Comparison' as a project might seem misconceived or misplaced. Contemporary India has a population of over a billion people. If one were to take the entire territory once encompassed by pre-partition India as the relevant unit, one would be obliged to add to this already unimaginably large number the further three hundred million inhabitants of Pakistan and Bangladesh. By contrast, South Africans number roughly fifty million. If South Africa were one of India's 30 states, it would rank only tenth in population, behind Karnataka and Gujarat. Contrasts intuitively outweigh similarities in vast proportion: from religious practices to household forms, musical styles to staple foodstuffs, it would seem that one might as well compare South Africa with Ecuador or India with Sweden.

Nor do the 'connections' seem, at first glance, to be remarkably dense or significant. At just over a million, the diasporic presence of people of Indian descent in South Africa is certainly substantial, but it is no greater than that in the United Kingdom or United States, and far less in absolute number and proportion to the overall population than in Saudi Arabia. In any case, these latter countries count 'Indians' among their immigrants as a result of relatively recent post-colonial migrations that have grown in intensity toward the end of the 20th century. By contrast, the major population flows from India to South Africa are much further removed in geopolitical time – an outgrowth by and large of the 19th-century British imperial labour and trading economy that has long since vanished from any living person's memory. In the imagination of most people who are designated as 'Indians' in the vernacular sociology of South Africans, India as such figures as a distant Bollywood fantasy rather than as a desired destination or a daily preoccupation.[157] And in India, South Africans of Indian origin can hardly be a matter of much interest or concern to all but a few, while actual South African immigration *to* India is too insignificant to bear mention. Are we not trying too hard to force the case here? Have we inflated – or, worse, merely invented – a scholarly agenda out of relatively thin air?

I want to argue otherwise. We can indeed find compelling justification for drawing these two places into common conversation, and we can do so, above all, on *ethical* grounds. I do not mean that as scholars we are somehow morally obliged to engage in such a project. Rather, I want to suggest that these two large socio-political formations – I use this expression to signal the relatively recent geopolitical zoning of the modern Indian and South African nation states – have long been mutually implicated in a common ethical field, even if that mutual implication is often suppressed or forgotten. One need only consider the pivotal moment in the late 1940s when inclusive Nehruvian nationalism triumphed in India and the Afrikaner exclusionary nationalist project triumphed in South Africa to see how, in effect, they created the crossroads where the great ethical questions of post-colonial modernity were posed for all of humanity.

To put it somewhat more precisely, I want to argue that what principally motivates both scholars and inhabitants of these two places to take an interest in one another – to make comparisons as much as to actively recall or forge connections – derives from a shared preoccupation with civic virtue and private ethics. By 'civic virtue' (or, alternatively, a 'politics of virtue') I mean an abiding concern with how to create a just society in which all people can live well – a society whose members are disposed to care about the well-being of others, even those unknown to them.[158] By 'private' or 'personal' ethics I mean the project of living a fulfilling life – one that is deemed to be worthy and virtuous in the eyes of others, especially those to whom one feels tied by obligations of kinship, friendship and community.[159]

The distinction I am making between the domain of civic virtue and that of private ethics is primarily a heuristic one. In lived experience, they bleed into each other continuously; indeed, they often mirror each other in ways that are constitutive of the political field. The media preoccupation with the private lives of public figures in both countries today makes this abundantly evident. And we should not forget that it was, after all, Mohandas K. Gandhi who exemplified – perhaps more effectively than anyone else in the 20th century – the political and ethical traction that could be gained by investing the most intimate and corporeal forms of self-conduct with public significance. Moreover, to make a distinction between ethics in the socio-political and private domains is to take for granted the long and complex histories that have made such a distinction meaningful, some of which are shared between South Africans and Indians and others of which are not.[160] I have no intention of exploring those histories here. Instead, I merely want to indicate some of the ways in which the contributors to this book, or the subjects about which or about whom they have written, have implicitly been situated in, and motivated by, a common domain of ethical concern and debate.[161] To that end, my discussion of ethics will wend its way through a consideration of matters interrogated by the contributors themselves: communism and democracy, imperialism and nationalism, non-violence and social protest, marriage and migration, social distinction and cultural belonging, and printing practices and reading publics. But for reasons that I hope will be apparent, I want to make an extended digression into a field where personal ethics and civic virtue dovetail in performance – the field of post-colonial cricket.

Cricket ethics

As I write this chapter in Johannesburg, the South African cricket team is playing the first match of a test series against Bangladesh at Mirpur ground in the northern suburbs of Dhaka. It is February – late winter in Bangladesh, late summer in South Africa – a time when both countries are graced by cool morning air and an ethereal pale yellow light. The match blares from TVs suspended in the tea stalls of Dhaka and the shopping mall cafes of Johannesburg – two nations, an ocean apart, temporarily occupying a common emotional space in the global ecumene. I came to cricket late in life. But having lived in both Bangladesh and South Africa for several years, it is not difficult for me to inhabit this mediated space with considerable passion as much as with divided loyalties.

In the world of test cricket, South Africa, like India and Pakistan, occupies the place of a perennial contender, while Bangladesh plays the part of a young and hungry upstart. With the test series against Bangladesh a fairly minor contest in the scheme of things – at least from the South African point of view – the South African sports press has nevertheless fastened onto the question of the racial composition of the national team selected to make the journey to the subcontinent. With only four out of 14 players coded as 'black',[162] the team falls two short of the target mandated for representation in the national team. By contrast, a look at the Bangladeshi squad yields an apparently natural picture of demographic uniformity – all Bengali, all

Muslim – in which the bloody past of nation making is all but forgotten and in which questions of representation or inclusion (say, of members of the Hindu or so-called 'tribal' minorities) do not even arise.

Are Bangladeshis interested in the South African debate over racial transformation in their national sports teams? If they are, as the Bangladeshi press coverage would suggest (see *Daily Star*, 2008), it is because they share with black South Africans a history of British imperial subordination based on race. If the wounds of that history are hardly fresh in South Asia, citizens of the subcontinent are acutely aware that South Africa remains traumatised by its iniquitous history of racial injustice – and to witness that trauma is to be called upon to remember the scars of their own past, as well as to question the persistence of a racialised distribution of power in a post-colonial world.

Although it does not merit a mention in the foregoing chapters, the relation of race to cricket is perhaps the most enduring source of common interest, enthusiasm, knowledge and public deliberation uniting citizens across the British post-colonies (Manning, 1981; James, 1993; Appadurai, 1996; Desai et al., 2002; Murray & Merrett, 2004; Vahed, Padayachee & Desai, 2010). Cricket is a game that foregrounds a preoccupation with ethics – and that sediments a history relating ethical behaviour to class privilege – in ways that other sports leave implicit.[163] As C. L. R. James (1993) observes, in common with all team sports, but in a fashion that is more self-aware, the fascination generated by cricket derives in large part from a set of meta-ethical concerns: What constitutes justice, good conduct, fair play? Who has the right to decide these questions and according to what cultural standards, what criteria of judgement? It does not take much effort to project the questions posed by the ethics of play onto larger political terrain. *Who* is permitted to play and (forgive the pun) on what grounds? Cricket – to the extent that it was explicitly used in many contexts to put on show the very fact of a male participant's membership in a Victorian imperial ruling caste – became a public and privileged site for the contestation of that fact in the colonial context, and thus for mounting a challenge to the legitimacy of the imperial project as such.

But a cricket match does more than stage a competitive or comparative performance of ethical principles. It also persistently addresses questions of culture and cultural belonging in relation to race, community and nation.[164] Like low tea and high table, cricket appears as a cultural practice that served as a marker of aristocratic blood and breeding, and, equally, as a masculine arena in which a tacit knowledge of Victorian morality – including such virtues as amateurism, fair play and puritan self-containment – could be appropriately embodied and put on display. Sustaining this picture requires forgetting that in the mid-19th century cricket was also played by largely working-class paid 'players' who were pitted against amateur 'gentlemen' (Williams, 2001:26). Cricket thus became the explicit staging ground for the contestation of class-based cultures of virtue that were played out both on the pitch and beyond the boundary – not only in the stands, but in society at large.[165] In British colonial culture, playing cricket served as an expression of entitlement on the part of the rulers, just as it served as an object of imitation and experimentation with elite colonial values and modernity on the part of the ruled (James, 1993; Appadurai, 1996; Desai et al., 2002). In its post-colonial incarnation, and especially with the amplification of its value as a televised spectacle and a commercial enterprise, cricket's erstwhile function of ethical formation has given way to one or other version of agonistic nationalism (Manning, 1981; Appadurai, 1996).[166]

The articulation of race and nationalist politics in Indian cricket markedly contrasts with the South African experience. In a subtle historical sociology of cricket's transformation under the Raj and after, Appadurai has shown how the formation of an 'Indian' national cricket team was not an outgrowth of a nascent nationalist movement, as one might expect, but rather its antecedent. It was conjured into being by the English, whose national team required an equivalent 'national' unit against which to compete when touring the subcontinent:

> Thus when English teams began to tour India, the question was how to construct an 'Indian' team that was a fitting opponent. In the early tours, in the 1890s, these Indian teams were largely composed of Englishmen, but as more Indians began to play the game and as more patrons and entrepreneurs began to organize teams and tournaments, it was inevitable that the full pool of Indian talent be drawn on to construct a first-rate Indian team. This process, whereby Indians increasingly came to represent India in cricket, follows not surprisingly the history of the evolution of Indian nationalism as a mass movement. Cricket in the Indian colonial context thus casts an unexpected light on the relationship between nationhood and empire (Appadurai, 1996:98).

Although there are parallels in South Africa, things ultimately took a rather different trajectory. As Desai et al. (2002:36) argue in relation to the development of cricket in Natal, the commercial and educated elites among Indian South Africans in the early 20th century

> imbibed the message of colonial administrators that sport was a means to discipline the population, entrench a healthy value system and teach social values such as teamwork, allegiance to fellow players, respect for rules and authority, and fortitude in the face of adversity.

More than this, they 'saw a close relationship between sport and politics. Through sport Indians could honour Victorian ideas of "civilisation" and "fair play", and become "civilised" so that they could rightfully demand equal rights' (Desai et al., 2002:37). The complement of this effort to instil a common ethical sensibility through cricket was just as vigorous an investment in making social distinctions. Such distinctions were based on race in the first instance – there was no effort on the part of elite Indian organisers to embrace African, Coloured or Malay players. But they also played up differences of religion and region of origin in India. And from the beginning, cricket in Natal was, by and large, a preoccupation of elites and a cultural vehicle for elite formation.

The South African Cricket Board of Control was created in 1947 – just one year before the National Party with its apartheid policies came to power – precisely in order to organise play among separately constituted African, Indian and Coloured teams. As Vahed, Padayachee and Desai (2006:66) have observed, '[i]n South Africa, cricket came to represent British class ideology in relation to Afrikaners, and racist exclusion in relation to blacks'. In this manner, cricket became yet another administrative means by which rigidly imposed racial categories were adopted by players and spectators as primary terms of identification: 'Membership in racially segregated cricket communities reinforced the notion of being white, African, Indian or Coloured' (Vahed, Padayachee & Desai, 2006:66). The 22-year moratorium on South African participation in international cricket was lifted in 1991 with the endorsement of the recently unbanned African National Congress (ANC), despite the fact that the first legitimately 'national' South African squad to be dispatched abroad was made up entirely of white players. Notably, India was the destination chosen for its first tour.[167]

Victory on the cricket pitch by the 'black' teams of India, Pakistan or the West Indies over the erstwhile colonial power (England) or its settler colonial outposts (Rhodesia/Zimbabwe, South Africa, Australia and New Zealand) was long tainted by murmured accusations that the victors were somehow pretenders – that they were culpable of cultural inauthenticity or, less charitably, of mimicry. It is probably fair to say that these forms of psychological compensation for imperialist nostalgia have faded. Nevertheless, over a half century after the decolonisation of British India, one finds at the heart of the ethical debates aroused by cricket the legacy of racism itself as a mimetic cultural practice – a pernicious colonial hangover in which those once victimised by the discourse of race now become the victimisers. How otherwise to interpret the crisis precipitated by Herschel Gibbs – a black ('Coloured') player for South Africa – being suspended for three games after making allegedly racist comments about Pakistani fans in 2007? Or by Indian player Harbhajan Singh, who was briefly suspended for allegedly uttering a racist slur towards Andrew Symonds, Australia's star all-rounder of mixed British and West Indian heritage?[168] Abolished long ago as an instrument of legal discrimination, the memory of racism is instantly recognisable as a feature of the colonial past that periodically resurfaces from the post-colonial unconscious to haunt the present.

An ethics of comparison

I have spent some time reflecting on race and cricket as a way of introducing a prism through which to reconsider the disparate themes and topics dealt with in the foregoing chapters and to suggest what new lines of inquiry they might make available. In the transnational ethical field constituted by cricket, it is fairly easy to see how personal morality is persistently mapped into arguments about public values, as well as the political institutions and practices that sustain them. It is not so difficult to see how the same applies to other domains of transnational conversation and comparison. After all, when South African political activists have looked across the Indian Ocean towards India and when Indians have looked back, they have been moved to pose comparative questions about political ethics and civic virtue: Does discrimination based on caste constitute the same affront to principles of justice as does discrimination based on race, and, if so, are there common remedial measures to be taken? What are the political means – legislative, educative, social activist, personal – by which intolerable inequalities in wealth and opportunity can or must be addressed? Is it through a vanguard party charged with seizing the state and steering the economy? Or is it through the devolution of the capacity and responsibility for redistributive activism to 'civil society' – a move towards what both Williams and Heller call the 'deepening' of democracy?

In view of the evidence provided by the studies in this book, it would be a mistake to overrate the nation state as the crucible in which a politics of virtue has been forged in either the Indian or the South African case. In reviewing, with Michelle Williams, the recent ideological convergence of South African and Indian communist parties, one is immediately struck by the extent to which both draw upon a shared *global* archive of variants in social democratic and communist political philosophy and practice that goes back nearly two centuries. It is an archive that was inescapably subjected to *local* reinterpretation both before and after the fall of the Soviet Union in 1989, with the major shifts in the global organisation of industrial labour it brought about, together with the corresponding emergence of a global coalition of 'anti-neoliberal' social movements.[169] At the same time, we might well see these variants as taking shape through what Isabel Hofmeyr calls an encounter between 'diasporic universalisms', whether they be based on ideological formations of the Left (anarchism, socialism, communism); pan-religious identification; or the commitment to a 'colour-blind, rights-bearing imperial citizenship'.

The comparison of communisms makes us think about the temporalities of liberation – of self, nation and humanity – that are so deeply embedded in communist secular eschatologies and the ethical positions that underpin them. Death through self-sacrifice and national or human liberation here converge on a common redemptive vanishing point that lies on the horizon of the future (Benjamin, 1968; Anderson, 1991). Yet in making comparisons and identifying connections between liberation movements, it is crucial to acknowledge that South Africa's day of deliverance arrived nearly half a century after India's, and under radically different conditions of global communication. India's independence came before television; South Africa's came just as the World Wide Web was becoming known to a globally interconnected public.

In South Africa, 1994 was a moment of punctuation so saturated with the expectation of deliverance that it was as if time were suspended, if not abolished altogether. The Truth and Reconciliation Commission (TRC) was, of course, like a protracted Day of Judgement within a socio-religious formation that was predominantly informed by Judaeo-Christian narratives of redemption. As an intensely mediated event, the TRC hearings constituted both the nation and global humanity as subjects of ethical refashioning after a century of carnage – including colonial regimes of forced labour, two world wars and several genocides – founded on the fetishisation of difference. If, as Patrick Heller argues, it is pre-eminently in civil society 'that the ethical dimension of a democratic society is cultivated', then it surely must be a conception of civil society that is understood to transcend national boundaries over both the short and the long term.

Yet differences in the pathways charted by Indians and South Africans through colonial subjugation into a democratic dispensation clearly influenced the divergent shape of the actual democratic institutions and practices that were to emerge. Claire Bénit-Gbaffou and Stéphanie Tawa Lama-Rewal have noted in their chapter that the imagined relationship between civil society and participatory democracy in post-colonial India differed markedly from that which emerged in South Africa. In India, Gandhi's romance with the rural village as a potential reservoir and wellspring of democratic purity still carries force – as expressed in the greater effort to decentralise power and to fine-tune representative democracy in retooled village institutions (the *panchayat*). In South Africa, whatever political virtue might be held to have been obtained in rural society was tainted during the struggle for democracy by the legacy of collaboration by leaders in the apartheid-constituted 'homelands'. Even though the current leadership is more inclined to stress its rural roots and values, it is the cities, towns and townships that constitute the key arenas where civil society engages the state in democratic experimentation and contestation.

Jonathan Hyslop's study of seafarers who manned the steamships of the British Empire in the first half of the 20th century provides an especially apt illustration of what might be called civil society under the antecedent condition of imperialism. Indeed, his investigation reveals a less salutary dimension of transnational associational life among British sailors in the form of a labour movement that promoted exclusionary practices based on racial citizenship and privilege. As Hyslop observes, there were remarkable parallels here with the anti-democratic ethos of white South African miners who similarly found their jobs at risk from a disenfranchised and more easily exploited black migrant labour force. The perils of reading a democratic ethics backwards into the history of organised labour here become apparent.

The narrow pursuit of self-interest by white sailors and miners, who counted as citizens rather than subjects of empire before the Second World War, alerts us to the ever-present conditions under which ethical particularism can re-emerge as a dominant feature of public life. In the mid-1940s, Indian South African workers, defeated in trade union struggles and facing increased competition from African workers and returning white servicemen alike, acted no differently: many came to see 'voluntary segregation as a solution to their material problems' and mobilised 'to protect what they saw as specifically Indian jobs' (Raman, 2006:200). The tension between universalist aspirations and a more pragmatic particularism carried on into the period of republican democracy. As Heller so acutely points out in his chapter, adherence to the superficial *forms* of electoral democracy without a concomitant effort to secure the means by which substantive claims for redistribution or inclusion can be redeemed by civil society has led to what he calls a process of 'involution'.

The unequal impact of economic liberalisation in both India and South Africa has, paradoxically, created conditions whereby class, race, religion and caste-based identities can re-emerge to organise and dominate the political imagination. In both countries, the universalising humanism that we associate with the ethics of Gandhi and Mandela seems to be in danger of losing its moral force. But this is nothing new. A dialectical movement between the expansive dreams of an inclusive universalism and the narrower, expedient choice of ethnic or racialised chauvinism has been the story of nationalist and diasporic movements everywhere.

An ethics of connection

The very possibility of making these kinds of comparisons between India and South Africa in the domain of ethics was always prefigured by the existence of very substantive connections, to a greater degree than I rhetorically allowed for at the outset of this chapter. The British Imperium, in providing for the mobilisation and regulation of workers – as well as of soldiers, traders, missionaries and administrators – provided the frame. The transoceanic ebb and flow of people between India and South Africa over the past century and a half – first on ships, more recently on aeroplanes – is well enough attested by the contributors to this volume. So is the movement of ideas, first borne by letters, pamphlets and newspapers, and now by the Internet. But one figure literally embodied ethical ideas and practices in transoceanic motion that were of disproportionate consequence. That person, of course, was Mohandas K. Gandhi, and it is to be expected that he figures centrally in many of the chapters in this book.

Gandhi must be regarded as one of the first public intellectuals to have an authentically global presence. The trace of the ideas that he has left for posterity through his published writings alone is indelible, although sometimes subject to overvaluation. Still, there is no one individual in the past century who better exemplifies the effort to craft a politics of civic virtue through the relentless revaluation of a personal – indeed corporeal – ethics. If nothing else, the endlessly circulating photographic archive of his sanctified, ascetic body makes apparent his iconic relationship to the modern political ethos (with its roots in much older religious traditions) of sacrificing the self in the name of human universality. Without doubt, it is Gandhi's life and work that have provided the most durable ethical link joining Indian with South African projects of political modernity.

In thinking about the flow, influence and local imbrication of Gandhian political morality and practice in South Africa over the course of the 20th century, two themes predominate. One concerns the aspiration to human universality – signalled in different ways by the collective figure of 'the nation', by the ethical goal of 'equality' and by the claim to inclusion that goes by the name of 'citizenship'. As I have already suggested, this aspiration has always carried with it, as its constitutive negation, the tense and contradictory residuum of internal hierarchy, difference and exclusion. The other theme concerns method – the point at which Gandhi's cultivation of the self (his valuation of manual labour, his vegetarianism, his determined celibacy, his minimalist modes of dress) informed and amplified his most enduring contribution to the politics of virtue: the method of *satyagraha* – 'holding onto truth' – rather than responding with violence, even in the face of the patent injustice and ruthless exercise of violence by the oppressor.

Gandhi's evolving project and its legacy – especially in South Africa – is explored from different angles by several of the contributors to the present volume. Isabel Hofmeyr's reflections on Gandhi's initiative to launch a printing press – first in Durban and then at Phoenix – focusses on the ethical dimensions that Gandhi attributed to printing as a project of virtuous labour, as well as to practices of reading as a moral imperative. In the first case, Hofmeyr documents how the work of operating the press and that of composing type and translating texts was understood by Gandhi as the embodied enactment of an ethical stance: one that embraced manual labour, on the one hand, while showing disdain for status distinctions and social hierarchy, on the other. In so doing, he was critically addressing the way in which caste belonging was sutured to obligations and prohibitions of work, among other dispositions of the body, back in India. Yet he was in South Africa, not India, and Hofmeyr points out that his inability to recognise and acknowledge his own reliance on cheap black African labour marked the limits of his moral compass. Indeed, it marked his own circumscribed vision of how far and to whom a project of civilised imperial enlightenment might extend.

One can only be struck by the originality of Gandhi's moral injunction that one ought to read and reread methodically, and take responsibility for disseminating texts to others. This was buttressed by a pedagogy of ethical technique – clipping, indexing, conserving, distributing – that mirrored what he saw as the inherently virtuous skills of typesetting and printing. Hofmeyr observes that Gandhi's project also constituted an ethical critique of the commodification of ideas, rejecting copyright and viewing the purchase of a book as a *moral* contract, rather than an impersonal one, with the community that had produced it. It was through the publication and circulation of print media that Gandhi helped to establish and invigorate an Indian Ocean public sphere, contributing to what Hofmeyr suggests was a utopian mode of sociality and a cosmopolitan sense of community.[170]

Hofmeyr also makes the provocative argument that the South African readers of *Indian Opinion* provided an experimental audience through which Gandhi eventually imagined, in *Hind Swaraj*, an Indian national identity yet to come. Yet one would be mistaken to draw the conclusion that those who printed the newspaper, or those who read it, were merely actors in a dress rehearsal for a performance that was always intended to unfold elsewhere. This much is clear from Pradip Kumar Datta's contribution to this volume. The Anglo-Boer War began in 1899, only two years after Gandhi's International Printing Press was launched in Durban. Datta shows how the war provided Gandhi with the occasion to mount an argument in favour of granting South African Indians full status as 'imperial subjects'. This political claim was simultaneously a moral one and, as Datta shows, it was established as much on the grounds of loyalty – duly demonstrated through an unqualified dedication to service – as it was on an acceptance of the necessity and inevitability of British tutelage and trusteeship.[171] Gandhi accepted the principle of a hierarchy of civilisations in which Indians of all social ranks were understood to be absorbing what the British had to teach them (including liberal democracy). African 'natives', however, remained at the bottom of a hierarchically ordered social array that Gandhi neither questioned nor challenged.

Datta's discussion of the role played by Gandhi as the organiser and leader of the Ambulance Corps indicates more than an interest in making a visible gesture of loyalty to empire at a time when Indians were threatened with forced repatriation. One cannot help but notice that the recruitment of labour into the Ambulance Corps mirrors the organisation of cricket in England at the same time, with working-class members drawn to participate by the offer of scanty pay and gentlemanly elites such as Gandhi conspicuously volunteering their services. The aspirant 'imperial subject' is in this way revealed to be one that embodies the same spirit of courage, selflessness and amateurism displayed by the Victorian middle classes back in the metropole and their white counterparts in the colony of Natal itself. This desire to be a good imperial subject, in Datta's memorable formulation, was grounded in a 'placeless loyalty (bounded only by the empire) through which people located outside the originative space of their nation could claim a purchase on the land of their new habitation'. Yet it was soon proven to be in vain, as Indians of all social classes were subjected to more severe forms of legal subjection and exclusion after the war than before it. This disheartening experience secured Gandhi's adherence to a very different politics – the project of Indian self-rule (in India) that was to be articulated in *Hind Swaraj*.

In the third of a century that elapsed between Gandhi's final departure from South Africa for India in 1913 and India's independence in 1947, the major contradictions of Indian society in South Africa – and indeed of Gandhi's own emergent politics of egalitarian universalism – were played out. As Hart and Padayachee (2000:687) have acutely noted, 'what made the situation in Natal unique was the juxtaposition of Europeans and Indians of similar class and in similar numbers'. Once indentured Indians ended their contracts, most gravitated towards the towns, where they came into direct competition with whites in small retailing and unskilled labour markets:

In consequence, the race problem in Natal was at the beginning mainly one of whites versus Indians. Experiments in racial segregation pioneered there later became the basis for more thoroughgoing national legislation aimed principally at blacks (Hart & Padayachee, 2000:687).

The internal social distinctions that Indians brought with them to Natal were in some ways effaced by their collective subjection to discriminatory laws and their deprivation of full citizenship. Yet in other ways they reflected an emergent set of class distinctions that took clearer shape during the period between the outbreak of the First World War and the end of the Second. Gandhian political ethics and the nationalist project back in India were not universally embraced. Indian merchants during this period were largely cooperative with the colonial administration – they were less concerned with citizenship and more preoccupied with retaining trading rights in white neighbourhoods. The Indian working class in Durban fought for rights to housing, even in segregated neighbourhoods, hoping to secure a permanent home in the city. Meanwhile, a more radical nationalist politics with a utopian diasporic dimension had emerged from the largely Tamil-speaking Hindus and Christians who were children of indentured labourers. They constituted an educated, aspirant lower-middle class that sought upward mobility into the professions through education, and it was members of this class who formed the Colonial-Born Indian Association in 1933. As Raman (2006:197) tells us, they published their own newspaper, *The African Chronicle*,

> the pages of which were filled with issues affecting Indians in South Africa. It also followed every twist and turn of the Indian independence movement: it is apparent that Indian national heroes loomed large in the imagination of the paper's white-collar South African Indian readership.

In pursuing a politics organised around the attainment of the rights of citizenship, their ethical stance was simultaneously grounded in a discourse that defended 'Indian honour' and objected to any 'slur on the mother country'. Yet when threatened with the actual prospect of repatriation, 'imaginings of India took on a less attractive aspect: a memorable picture in the *Leader*, a Natal Indian newspaper, of a windswept village hut during the Indian monsoon bore the caption: "Do you want to be sent home to this?"' (Raman, 2006:200).

An avowedly Gandhian politics of virtue and, more specifically, a resolute commitment to non-violent resistance remained central to the political creed of radical South African Indians from the end of the Second World War right into the 1970s. G. M. 'Monty' Naicker, leader of the Natal Indian Congress (NIC) after 1945, was an exemplary and in some ways tragic figure. As Goolam Vahed's rich political biography in this volume reveals, Naicker's identification with Gandhi was so complete that 'in Monty's mind the Passive Resistance Campaign was a re-enactment of the earlier movement of 1913: the Gandhi symbolism, the enthusiasm and the moral triumphalism'. In a reversal of their earlier position as sympathetic witnesses to India's struggle for independence, members of the NIC now sought to publicise the struggles of South African Indians among an Indian public with whom they presumed to share common moral principles as much as a common history of resistance. It was an effort to enlist the interest of that distant public in an unfolding dramaturgy of suffering and sacrifice. As far as Naicker was concerned, the same moral narrative that Gandhi had initiated and then carried from South Africa to India was now being replayed again at its point of origin.

An ethics of intimacy

What happens if we take questions of identity, justice and the good life into the more intimate realm of private ethics – of kinship, family, sexuality and reproduction? Or, alternatively, what happens if we bring the ethical structure of intimate life into the realm of political virtue and public life? This latter move shaped the core of Gandhi's distinctive political imagination. For Gandhi, as Crain Soudien argues in his chapter here, the Indian village was structured through face-to-face relationships that 'bound people together in an ethical order in which mutual dependence forced self-discipline'. In this way, the ethical life of the village provided for Gandhi a model through which to recover the virtuous expressions of self and sociality that had been eroded by the competitive and materialistic ethos instilled by colonial modernity.

Gandhi's view of the Indian village was in many ways a highly idealised fantasy – and this very simplification and idealisation made it possible for him and his followers to engage in the kind of prescriptive building of what sociologists would now call 'intentional communities', first at Phoenix farm outside Durban and then in ashrams across India. Here, indeed, is a South African–Indian connection of some historical import. But in thinking through such connections in terms of the interlaced ethics of intimate life as it is actually lived – rather than as it is prescriptively made – the approach needs to be both elastic (spatially) and elongated (temporally). It is telling that in Hyslop's discussion of the African and Asian 'lascars' who manned the steamships of the British imperial economy, nothing is revealed about their kin networks or, indeed, their sexual, reproductive and domestic lives – only a tantalising hint that some who hailed from inland India might have maintained agricultural enterprises at home even as they went to sea. But the 'webs of empire' they created were surely also webs of kinship and friendship, extended through sexual and economic partnerships, however fragile and ephemeral (although, for obvious reasons, these facets may be the most obscured from the historian's gaze). As it was for migrant South African miners, the workplace and place of residence (the ship) were virtually congruent for much of these sailors' everyday existence – yet surely they sustained some semblance of family life, however transitory, and there can be little doubt that some of them did so in more than one port. The private side of ethical life – the aspiration to realise a vision of a worthy career as a man, a lover, a father and even a husband – must certainly have guided their choices and movements as much as the conditions governing their insertion into an imperial labour market.

The motives that drive individuals to forge these kinds of connections constitute what I mean by the domain of 'private' or 'personal' ethics. Pamila Gupta's oral historical account, traversing three key moments of Goan migration into – and out of – Mozambique, provides an appropriate set of examples. As each of her informants contemplated the choice of migrating or staying put, the encompassing question must have been an ethical one: How and where can I best pursue a worthy and reputable life? More specifically, as her interviews reveal, potential migrants had concerns about the arc of their lives in terms of alliance and descent: With what kind of person shall I live and have children? With whom shall I contract a legal marriage? Where shall I die and be buried? In pondering these large concerns, migrants considered matters of status and reputation: How would their choices bring shame or dignity upon themselves and upon others for whom their actions had moral implications? Of course, such questions have always been situated within a larger set of unfolding political contexts and futures in which their status as citizens, Catholics, Portuguese speakers and ethnic 'Goans' were immensely consequential. So, of course, was their status as racialised subjects occupying an intermediate and sometimes indeterminate location on a scale of racial hierarchy. To me it seems essential to recognise the way in which these considerations, in the life course of any individual, may be pitched at highly variant scales – from a neighbourhood in Maputo to a network of kin spanning three continents. Equally, they may take into account apparently incommensurable temporalities: the certainties of aging and death, on the one hand; the uncertainties of future political and economic entitlements in the aftermath of decolonisation (in Goa) and liberation (in Mozambique), on the other.

Phil Bonner's review of the scholarship on migrant lives in South Africa and India makes the point about private or personal ethics at least as well, while opening up important questions about what is assumed and what is overlooked in the historical sociology of each region. For African male migrants in South Africa, the question has long been how to situate the compulsory phase of urban or mine labour into the arc of one's career as a worthy person – where work itself might have a value in the register of masculine rights of passage, but where the accumulation of assets, wives and children, and the establishment of an independent home are held to be paramount or ultimate goals (Moodie, 1994). African women in the region have had to endure a different set of pressures, but have been no less agentive in seeking to construct moral lives – as mothers, wives, traders, urban domestic workers and so on – often under appalling conditions of deprivation, while bearing responsibility for the care of children and the elderly (Schmidt, 1992). Variant practices of Christianity and Christian ideologies of personhood have, over a period of two centuries, deeply informed their own moral life narratives – as they did those of white men and women, but under conditions of possibility that were normally very different. For Hindus, Muslims and Christians of Indian descent, an attachment to moral scripts that in principle extend to believers in distant lands becomes a way of framing personal choices in light of a more universal ethics.

An ethics of universalism and difference

We should not forget that it is ordinary South Asians and Southern Africans themselves – and not just academics and World Bank policy analysts – who also make the comparisons and the connections between these two regions. I have always been struck by the high regard that people from the subcontinent have for the standard-bearers of the black world: Mohammed Ali, Pelé, Martin Luther King, Nelson Mandela. But this is combined with a striking ignorance about the history and cultural complexity of the African continent, and a kind of casual racism that reduces the continent to a jungle replete with fictive primitives. There are, of course, competing narratives of civilisation at stake, and ones that are largely, but not exclusively, born of the British imperial project, with its distinctions of status anchored for a long time in a mix of social Darwinism and Christian pastoral duty. The great paradox of British imperial ideology – perhaps its animating contradiction psychologically – was the overwrought assertion of its own commitment to an ethics of equality and humanity that denied the culture and society of the colonised other. Africa was seen as the terrain of despotic chiefs and dissolute or victimised women (Comaroff & Comaroff, 1991); in India, the culture of inequality was inscribed as a leitmotif for all social interaction and as a limit on the potential for achieving a rational political modernity. 'Caste' was the conceptual keystone in India, 'tribe' in Africa (Vail, 1989;

Dirks, 2001); both denoted the conjuncture of cultural commitment and political form that supposedly stood in the way of post-colonial development and economic modernisation.[172]

Few doubt the lasting damage that this history of essentialising difference has done and a sea of legislation and institutional renovation in post-colonial India and South Africa has been devoted to making it obsolete. But should one therefore deny 'difference', dismissing it as an artefact of academic simplification and political bad faith? That would be sociologically fatuous. No one would suggest that India is moving merrily down the road to the realisation of universal citizenship, ever nearer to realising a homogeneous distribution of rights and entitlements. Nor would anyone agree that South Africa is happily creating the conditions for the realisation of a singular national identity.

In any case, while acknowledging the lasting import of colonial forms of knowledge and culture (Cohn, 1996; Dirks, 2001), one must take care not to overplay either the capacity or the legacy of the colonial state in constituting the field of socially meaningful differences in a deterministic way.[173] Social and cultural identity is most usefully understood as a historical process rather than as an essence or a product – as *identification*, in the double sense of 'identifying with', on the one hand, and 'being identified by', on the other. In the first sense, identification mobilises and enables mobility, livelihood, marriage, reproduction and claims to assets; in the second, it signifies an act or imposition of others, whether one's neighbours or the state, and therefore canalises through law or social sanction certain kinds of movement, residence and occupational activity, while becoming a key vehicle for the reification or idealisation of certain kinds of cultural norms.

The political expression of identification – 'communalism' in India, 'tribalism' in Africa – was brought into being through processes of cultural formation, often enabled or incited by state knowledge production at multiple levels and scales (Worby, 1994; Cohn, 1996; Scott, 1998). As a result, while state institutions allocate voting and residence rights, families themselves police marriage, schooling and the socialisation of youth. Neighbourhood *goondas* or *dadas* in India or gang bosses in South Africa do the same among urban male migrants, mobilising for their own political and economic purposes at flashpoints of political volatility – 1947 or 1998 in western India, 1991 in South Africa (Hansen, 2001b; 2005).

There is another sense in which difference cannot be wished away, even as South Africa and India mutually engage in globalised cultural forms such as Bollywood films or in expanded trade. After all, for an 'Indian' South

African, a visit to the homeland can feel like a trip to another planet, despite the threads of language, cuisine, dress, and even religious practice that would seem to suggest cultural commonality and continuity. Consider the experience of the city and the geography of urban economy and residence that underpins it. The hawking of goods such as vegetables and fish, as well as services – from shoe repairs to knife sharpening – is an invariable part of the sound and streetscape of South Asian cities. By contrast, South African city centres and residential areas still seem haunted by an almost puritanical silence, the blare of taxi horns and radios excepted.[174] The spatial segregation or integration of residence by class and race, and the corresponding cultures of domestic labour, are equally distinct. In India, one might speak less accurately of the premise of inequality – Louis Dumont's famous 'Homo Hierarchicus' (1981) – and more precisely of a premise of social interdependence and socio-spatial proximity. In South Africa, social separation by class still rules, even as a rising black bourgeoisie and super-elite join their white counterparts in gated communities and securitised shopping malls. This difference, as Bonner points out, is also due to South Africa's 'relatively foreshortened history of urbanisation compared to India'. But it is also the result of a very deliberate and aggressive policy of urban purification that persists, even as it recalls the guiding ethos of apartheid planning.

The emergence of the so-called 'black diamonds' (the most visible beneficiaries of black economic empowerment) is an intriguing development that generates its own charged ethical field, and the question arises as to what their emergence portends for South Africa's future. The accompanying emotional and moral ambivalence may already be glimpsed in the nostalgia for township social life well known in elite black culture, as well as in the tension between fast-rising urban professionals and their rural relatives whose socio-economic prospects remain comparatively dim (Dlamini, 2010; Stauffer, 2010). The reactivation of networks linking suburb and township, or city and village, is often instigated by life-cycle events – especially marriage and death – and the processes of property transfer (often sharply contested) that they bring in their wake.[175]

An ethics of identification and belonging

The question of what it means to be an 'Indian' in South Africa – of why one might or might not want to foreground such an identity claim and to whom – must be situated in relation to shifting historical regimes of law and citizenship, to shifting practices of political mobilisation around identity categories, and to shifting moments when a recoding of personal identity intersects with efforts to rescript the South African national narrative. The disjunctures between who one wants to be and who one is perceived to be can be painfully disquieting. Consider, for example, the account that Rehana Vally provides of her first trip to India in 1990, the culmination of a decade when apartheid categories were stridently refused by many of those jurally classified as 'Indians', among others subjected to apartheid discriminatory legislation, and proudly dissolved under the common banner of being 'black'. In India, such an identity claim had no traction whatsoever. 'Despite my protestations of being a black South African,' she writes, 'my Indian interlocutors saw me as a "foreign" Gujurati. I had, despite myself, become locked into the Indian diaspora' (Ebr.-Vally, 2001:26).

This is merely one example of the use of ethnic 'shifters' (Galaty, 1982; Worby, 1994; 1995) in which the ethnic or racial name attributed to oneself or attributed to one by another has the force of reconstituting a social category. Today, such shifters sometimes challenge and sometimes reconstruct even the most durable walls of apartheid race classification that mark off 'Indians' in South Africa from those once called 'Natives'. Nothing could illustrate this process more poignantly than the dust-up over the 2007 Miss Teen India South Africa beauty pageant – an event that seems to concentrate with particular force the ethical dimensions of comparison and connection, of difference, identification and belonging in democratic South Africa.[176]

In July 2007 the regional leg of this national contest was held in the Eastern Cape city of Port Elizabeth. Both the panel of judges and the audience were almost entirely composed of 'Indian' South Africans, but when the winner was announced, the audience burst into an uproar, hurling insults at the judges and forcing them to escape through a back door under a security escort. As it happened, the newly crowned 'Indian' teen queen was a Xhosa-speaking 'African' girl. The judges were in unanimous agreement that the winning contestant, 15-year-old Anelisa Willem, was the best among the competitors, arguing that there would have been no outcry had she been 'an Indian girl'. 'She was really good', said one judge. 'She had the poise, personality and the talent'. Another added that '[i]t all boiled down to [her] race'. Ms Willem, for her part, expressed surprise and disappointment at the crowd's hostility to what she felt was a well-deserved victory based purely on merit: 'I love Bollywood movies and I have a flair for dancing', she remarked, adding that 'I have been entering pageants and competitions since I was six .... But I did not expect this kind of reaction from Indians because I have many friends in the community' (Govender, 2007).

This is a story that will bring a wry, uneasy smile to any South African's face. It seems to test and find the limits of the politics of virtue promised by a constitutionally driven non-racism – of the extraordinarily demanding promise to realise a new society 'after race' (Gilroy, 2000). Both Willem and her judges boldly attempted to enact this promise, and for that they remained unapologetic. But the audience – perhaps a better synecdoche for South African society as a whole – failed the test. What does it mean for the crowd to have asserted that an 'Indian' identity is reserved for those who conform to some imagined racial essence – an essence based on an exclusive claim to descent from the inhabitants of geographical India? The cancer of apartheid social theory here seems to have returned and metastasised with a vengeance. Then again, perhaps the audience at the pageant protested too much. Perhaps their irrepressible outrage may be read as a symptom of their own deep insecurity – of the tenuousness of their own claim to have a 'natural' mastery of presumably 'authentic' Indian cultural practices and appearances. Or perhaps they were registering their own fear that they do not fully belong in the 'new' South Africa – that the future of their attachments lies with the global Indian diaspora or, indeed, with India itself. Either way, weren't they openly betraying the politics of virtue to which all South Africans – especially those marked as 'black' – had committed themselves in the process of overthrowing the old apartheid order?

This question becomes more difficult to answer, even as the highly publicised political and commercial ties between Indians and South Africans proceed to deepen apace.[177] Consider the intriguing whirlwind of controversy surrounding Atul Gupta, the Indian-born South African computer tycoon who stepped forward recently to fund the *New Age* newspaper, a thinly disguised 'good news only' media outlet for the ANC. While some may have seen the arrangement as a happy interlacing of South African and Indian elite business cultures, others saw mutual complicity in a deepening culture of political corruption. After all, Gupta's brother, Rajesh, and President Jacob Zuma's son, Duduzane, are business partners with substantial share ownership in the South African branch of Arcelor-Mittal, the Indian-originated multinational steel giant. But when in late September 2010 Atul Gupta was arrested and detained for refusing to allow policemen to search his car, he charged that the police had abused him with racist language. His spokesperson said the policemen asked Gupta 'if he was Indian and told him that he should go back to his country, India' (*Mail & Guardian Online* (2010).

Although the racial identity of the policemen alleged to have made these remarks is unspecified in the news reports, it may not matter. It is hard to miss the echoes here of the shouts of the white workers who threatened to lynch Gandhi in 1897 as he returned to Durban after making a tour of India to publicise the mistreatment and disenfranchisement of Indians in South Africa. Over a century later – if policemen are anything to go by – the thickening of ties between ruling and business elites in India and South Africa may fail to find resonance with the people further down the class ladder.

Coda: Cricket's new ethical ecumene

The year 2010 saw the commemoration of 150 years since the arrival of the first shipload of indentured labourers from India at the port of Durban. The many and diverse events organised to mark this anniversary illustrate how memory can be made, mobilised and brought into play to suit diverse agendas in the present. Yet whatever the importance attributed to the connections of the past, cricket is clearly a preferred staging ground for connecting the two countries in future. One of the main instruments of the moment for making such a connection is the Indian Premier League (IPL).

The IPL burst upon the international cricket scene in 2008 – an enterprise hatched the year before by media mogul Lalit Modi, who had worked his way inside the Board of Control for Cricket of India (BCCI) and secured broadcast rights along with the right to auction teams for the proposed new league. The birth of the IPL perfectly expresses the spatial reordering of capital and consumer markets that began in earnest two decades ago after the fall of the Berlin Wall. The shift has given rise to a novel set of transcontinental alliances that pointedly exclude North America and Western Europe: BRIC, BRICSA, IBSA ... and so the list of acronyms designating new trade partnerships proliferates. Predictably, when the IPL schedule was announced, it conflicted directly with that of English county cricket, and the upstart league had no difficulty drawing away English players with salaries they had never before dreamed of. Indian big business had thrown down the gauntlet before the former imperial power on behalf of post-colonials everywhere.

The IPL pits eight Indian teams – each composed of handsomely remunerated international stars – against one another in a Twenty20 format tournament that lasts six weeks. Presenting the moral antithesis of test cricket, it is fast, loud, colourful and deliberately tawdry – complete with scantily clad cheerleaders in the style of the United States. After only a single season, the new league – which had, without question, succeeded financially and won a huge international following – fell foul of politics: the first phase of the Indian national elections were scheduled to coincide with the IPL tournament and the Indian government refused to guarantee security for the players, who were thought to be vulnerable to terrorist attack. In a miracle of commercial savvy and diplomatic dexterity, the entire tournament was moved, only weeks before the first match, to South Africa, on the assumption that cricket-crazy South Africans – and *Indian* South Africans in particular – would provide an instant, commercially viable fan base. These assumptions proved to be spot on (see Brett, 2008; see also Tomlinson & Singh, 2008). But after a third season played back in India, Lalit Modi, the league's founding entrepreneur, found himself at the centre of allegations of misconduct and was ejected from the BCCI. Inevitably, cricket ethics had again moved well beyond the boundary.

In drawing upon the manifold insights of the contributors to this volume, I have tried to suggest that we are a long way from the Gandhi of 1900, who longed for Indian South Africans and Indians to receive equal recognition as loyal subjects of empire. I might add that we are equally distant from another diasporic personality of that era – K. S. Ranjitsinhji, British India's most celebrated and most loyal representative on the cricket ovals of England. In a speech to young cricketers in Poona in 1910, he averred that '[c]ricket is one of the great boons the Government and English people have presented to us, and let us make the best of it …. It is because this game brings forth the best virtues of a man that it is worth playing' (Williams, 2001:31).

As the IPL's commercial and popular triumph on both sides of the Indian Ocean demonstrates, even the shared cultural memory of British imperialism is no longer necessary to bring Indians and South Africans together into a common ecumene of commerce and cricket. A century after Ranjitsinhji's acceptance by England's cricket elite as a well-mannered 'oriental' of elite bearing and exotic technique, South Africa's national cricket side has at last selected a player of Indian descent and he is fast becoming an international superstar. Hashim Amla, South Africa's modest, affable and devout Muslim all-rounder, is the son of a doctor and the grandson of immigrants from Surat (in Gujarat) who arrived in Durban with a shipment of farm labourers in 1927. He wears a full beard – 'one fist long', in line with Islamic teachings – prominent enough, along with his name, to have induced an Australian television commentator to refer to him as 'the terrorist' when he thought the microphone was on mute during an internationally televised test match between South Africa and Sri Lanka. Reflecting on the incident in an interview with a *Guardian* correspondent, Amla remarked:

> I don't think it's racial, I don't know what category it falls under ... but [in South Africa we're] very sensitive to that kind of stereotyping, so it was a big thing back home .... Nonetheless, the teaching of Islam has always been that when somebody apologises, you forgive them. The lesson for everybody [is that] we all have some inward prejudices that we need to address ... whether it be of colour, race or religion. I think if we all want to develop into good people and perhaps develop as a humanity, I think we have to address it (McRae, 2008).[178]

That same beard led fans of the Essex county club, for whom Amla played in England as a short-term overseas player in 2009, to call him 'WG', thereby identifying him with the heavily bearded W. G. Grace – indisputably the greatest player of the 19th century and, some would say, of all time. 'I have seen pictures of his beard but mine is definitely shorter', Amla has commented. 'If you go back many years the beard is a tribute to all the faiths stemming from the biblical Abraham – or Ibrahim, as we say in Islam .... We see it as universal.'

At a time when international cricket, and especially Indian cricket, seems to be coming into its own as a brash and sometimes tawdry form of mass popular entertainment, Hashim Amla had made a claim to a more restrained and virtuous universalism. It is a universalism that is not only made through the eloquence of reason, but borne demonstratively on his face and articulated through his bat. He provides, in his person and in his play, a riposte to a century of orientalising judgement – the tenacious legacy of empire that was reborn and twisted into the fanatical othering promoted by the US administration of George W. Bush and its allies after the 9/11 attacks on the World Trade Center and Pentagon. But for the time being, Amla remains visibly and irrevocably an 'Indian' South African, however shifting and slippery that signifier may be. In this way, his story encapsulates what I have tried to do throughout this chapter: to signal the dilemmas of ethical judgement and action connecting India and South Africa in ways that are perpetually in motion, as both countries carry along a closely linked past while fashioning a more closely intertwined future.[179] In doing so, I have tried to show how Indian and South African experiments in remaking post-colonial society have often served as mirrors and models for one another. For individuals, they have sometimes constituted a common field of possibility through which to realise a meaningful life, a sense of cultural belonging and sometimes even a sense of utopian social vision. The history of these conversations and connections is already centuries long, yet in many ways it is clearly only just beginning.

Notes

Introduction – South Africa-India

1   <http://www.http://cisa-wits.org.za>. The chapters in this volume have been selected from special issues and books that emerged as part of this research project. These are the *Journal of African and Asian Studies*, 44(1), 2009 on 'South Africa–India: Connections and Comparisons'; *South African Historical Journal*, 57, 2007 on 'South Africa–India: Re-imagining the Disciplines'; *Historia*, 54(1), 2009 on 'South Africa and India: Towards Closer Scholarly Links'; *Scrutiny2*, 13(2), 2008 on 'Cultures of Circulation in the Indian Ocean'; and Gupta, Hofmeyr and Pearson (2010). This introduction is a reworking of the piece that prefaced the *Journal of African and Asian Studies* special issue. It also incorporates a section from Hofmeyr (forthcoming).

2   This point is at times confused with the claim that the Indian Ocean trade was entirely peaceful, one that is now rejected (Wink, 2002:439).

3   Literally, 'holding on to truth', which was the philosopshy behind his passive resistance campaigns.

4   In 2008 India's gross domestic product grew at 9.1 per cent, while South Africa's grew at 6.1 per cent (World Bank, 2009a; 2009b).

5   This is a rough comparison only and does not take into account the vastly greater purchasing power of a US dollar in India compared to South Africa.

6   This could involve an attempt to reconcile the extensive scholarship on Indian Ocean security and international relations with more cultural and social forms of analysis such as currently characterise the new Cold War studies more generally.

Historical Connections

Chapter 1 – Gandhi's Printing Press

7   This information surfaced in an ongoing legal wrangle between two descendants of the ship's original owners, the brothers Abdul and Abdullah Zaveri of Dada Abdullah and Co. (*Southern News*, n.d.; *Deccan Herald*, 2004; *Times of India*, 2006).

8   For reports on Gokhale's 'protracted' arrival and departure, see *Indian Opinion* 14 September 1912; 9 November 1912; 21 September 1912; 28 September 1912; 26 October 1912; 2 November 1912; 14 December 1912; 11 January 1913; 25 January 1913.

9   Material by or on Erasmus runs in *Indian Opinion* from 14 April 1906 to 30 December 1905. For biographical details, see the edition of 5 November 1904.

Chapter 2 – Steamship Empire

10   I am grateful to Professor Liz Gunner for drawing this to my attention.

11   British Library, India Office Collection L/E/&/1494, File 27, Abdul Gani, Antwerp, to 'Indian Consulate', London, 11 February 1927.

12   British Library, India Office Collection I/E/7/1494, Patrick Fitzgerald, Antwerp, to 'Indian Consulate', London, 11 February 1927.

13   On these issues, see Wilson's numerous contributions to the debates in parliament on the Merchant Shipping Acts Bill; see Parliamentary Debates: First Session of the Twenty Eighth Parliament of the United Kingdom of Britain and Ireland, 6. Edward VII vol. CLXIII, 12th vol. of Session 1906, throughout.

Chapter 3 – The Interlocking Worlds of the Anglo-Boer War

14   I wish to express my thanks to Sumit Sarkar and Tanika Sarkar, with whom I first discussed this project; to Jon Hyslop and Lakshmi Subrahmanyam for help with articles; to Preben Kaarsholm for both articles and suggestions; to participants in the South Africa/India conference held at the University of the Witwatersrand in May 2006; to Uma Dhupelia-Mesthrie and the anonymous readers of this essay for their suggestions; and especially to Isabel Hofmeyr for pioneering the new Indian Ocean studies that opened opportunities for this research.

15   Boer prisoner-of-war camps in India included American, Danish, French, German, Greek, Dutch, Hungarian, Italian and Scandinavian people (Government of India [GOI], Foreign Dept., External A, Progs, March 1903, nos 173–97; Letter from Secretary, Foreign Dept, GOI, 16 July 1902).

16   Originally published in the Bangla volume entitled Naibedya, edited and translated versions of these poems appeared as *Sunset of the Century* and were included in Tagore's Lectures on Nationalism (London, 1918).

17   For summaries of transport improvements and migrations, see Pearson (2003:200–24).

18   A good illustration is the preface to *The Collected Works of Mahatma Gandhi, vol. 3, 1901–1903* (Gandhi, 1960c). Goolam Vahed's work (2000) is an exception that has helped me to formulate my ideas, although he also sees Gandhi's loyalism as a straightforward belief that dictated his involvement in the war.

19   The path-breaking work of Maureen Swan (1985), which makes a distinction between Gandhi and his followers, informs my assertion here. This is also true of later 'official' biographies of Gandhi, such as the detailed work by Uppal (1995).

20   It may also be mentioned that 116,000 blacks associated with the Boers were removed to concentration camps by the British and over 14,000 of them, possibly more, died (Warwick, 1983:4).

21   I have drawn on 'The Indian Offer', 'Indian Ambulance Corps' and 'Indian Ambulance Corps in Natal' in Gandhi (1960c:113–46).

22   For a vivid description of the event by a contemporary, see Doke (2005:51–62).

23   This is what a contemporary reported about the popular beliefs of the colonists (Swanson, 1983). The Indian population in Natal was 4,000 and the white 40,000 in the early 1890s (Brown, 1990:46).

24   For details regarding the debates and court cases around these, see Uppal (1995: 130–42).

25   In a letter to Dadabhai Naoroji, Gandhi said that the real reason for the Franchise Bill was to insult the Indians so much that they would be unable to stay (Gandhi, 1960a:174).

26   For details, see 'Indian Ambulance Corps in Natal' (Gandhi, 1960c:139–46).

27   'Open Letter' to members of the Legislative Council and Legislative Assembly of Natal, 19 December 1894 (Gandhi, 1960b:193–209).

28.   *Uitlanders* was the Dutch term used by the Boers in the Transvaal to describe foreigners.

29   The children of indentured labourers had to either go into indenture on attaining maturity or pay an annual tax of £3. There were, however, a few court decisions that favoured Indians (see Uppal, 1995:190–94).

30   Lord Milner, who first governed the Transvaal after the British victory and who was also appointed native affairs commissioner, declared that the reason the 'white man must rule is because that is the only possible means of raising the black man, not to our level of civilisation – which is doubtful whether he would attain' (cited in Selby, 1973:203–4).

31   Gandhi appears to have recognised the danger in his analysis of discrimination when he said that the use of the word 'coolie' prepared the grounds for legislative disabilities (Gandhi, 1960b:201).

32   This strand was startlingly revealed in Gandhi's publicly expressed wish that 'betterclass' settlers come to South Africa, for that would make the race problem disappear (speech at Calcutta Congress, 12 December 1901, in Gandhi, 1960c:215). It may be said that the 'better class' tends to be drawn overwhelmingly from upper castes.

33   Letter to C. Bird, colonial secretary, Pietermaritzburg, 18 May 1899 (Gandhi, 1960c:72).

34   Gandhi complained that the use of the word 'coolie' indicated the general desire to 'degrade the Indian to the position of the kaffir' (Gandhi, 1960b:229; emphasis added).

35   *Bharati* was a journal edited by Swarnakumari Debi, and was the second one to be edited by a woman. *Antahpur* was run by women and only featured articles by them. It published 'Boerjatir Bibaran' ('A description of the Boers') in its Magh 1307 (1901) issue. I am grateful to Rimli Bhattacharya for the last reference.

36   A newspaper advertisement for 'Transvaal War Books' says these were published between November 1899 and January 1900 and were priced quite cheaply, generally

at Rs.1 or less. It lists Stead's book at the less-affordable sum of Rs.8 (*The Bengalee*, 10 March 1901).

37 The meeting, consisting mainly of local pleaders, also hoped that the policies of the present ministry would be stopped by the British public.

38 The *Hindu Ranjika* of 20 December 1899 reported from the relatively obscure Rampur Boalia that during the eclipse of the moon hymns were chanted in honour of the goddess Chandi and prayers offered for the victory of Queen Victoria at a local temple by the orthodox Dharma Sabha there (National Archives of India, 'Report on native newspapers, no. 52 of 1899').

39 'Proposal to locate 5 000 Boer prisoners in Mysore', Foreign Dept., External B, Progs, nos 93/95, March 1901.

40 The government did concede that those burghers who had taken an oath of loyalty and had means of making a good living could be permitted to stay on (Offg. Secy, GOI, Military Dept. to quartermaster general of India, Foreign Dept., External A, Progs, nos 173–97, March 1903).

41 Pro-Japan rallies were held, while Saraladebi Chaudhurani, a powerful public figure, formed an association of young boys for developing the physique of Bengalis (Ray, 1979:141).

42 Anxiety occasioned laughter. A cartoon sequence features an English administrator imposing a fine on a clerk for reading reports on the war (*Bausmati*, 1899).

43 The opening speech of the proceedings of the India Tea Association complained that its members had already contributed to sending the Lumsden Horse and it was now the turn of the government to defray other costs (*The Bengalee*, 25 January 1902).

44 In the context of the differential treatment, *The Bengalee* (25 January 1902) observed that there was a clear distinction between these two sets of colonies, for one was based on 'self-governing communities', while India was a 'despotically governed community'.

45. General Kitchener himself approached the government to send an Indian cavalry regiment, while the English press canvassed for the use of Indian troops, which the government refused (Warwick, 1983:23).

46 Sir Gordon Sprigg declared that it should be shown that the 'rights and liberties' of the settlers were not dependent on the 'Natives' (Warwick, 1983:16).

47 *Sahitya Sadhak Charitmala*, vol. 7 (Kolkata, n.d.).

48 'Madman' has connotations both of the inspirational and of taking on an impossible challenge.

49 The assault on property, women and children was vividly reported through the testimonies of witnesses (see *The Bengalee*, 13 February 1901).

Chapter 4 – The Disquieting of History

50 Much of the data presented here comes from interviews and the recording of life histories with Goans living in Maputo during March 2007. This research is restricted to the (middle- and upper-class) elite Goan settlers of Maputo and does not include the Goan fishing community of Catembe or the Goan community of Beira, both of which are also sizeable and have very different (classed) histories. This ethnographic research was made possible through a humanities research grant from the Graduate School at the University of the Witwatersrand. I would also like to express my gratitude to Dirce, Brigitte and Celso for putting me in contact with members of the Goan community in Maputo. In the capital city itself, I found a social network of Goans, many of whom were interrelated through marriage. In a sense, they decided whom I would speak to; i.e. who was an appropriate 'Goan' to interview. Most of these interviews took place either in public spaces – restaurants and hotel lobbies – or in people's homes. Most of the Goans I interviewed were passionate about the subject at hand and had very strong viewpoints about this disparate community; colonial racism; their in-between status between coloniser and colonised; leftist politics; generational ideological shifts; and their identification of 'being Portuguese, but without a concept of race', as one informant described it. I thank them for their generosity and candidness. I have changed the (first) names of my informants to protect their privacy, excepting public and published figures.

51 While archival records suggest the presence of isolated Goans in Mozambique as early as 1560, the first wave of large-scale Goan immigration to Mozambique took place between the years 1800 and 1850. For some elite Goan families during the 19th century, the first son typically became a priest, the second a doctor and the third sought his fortune in Portuguese Africa. For more details on the history of this earlier wave of Goan migration that both underwrites and is connected to the later set of migrations under analysis here, see both Sharmila Karnik (1998) and Pamila Gupta (2007).

52 According to Bastos, the Goa Medical School was started in 1842, was recognised by the Portuguese colonial authorities in 1847, and operated until 1961, closing only with the demise of Portuguese control in Goa.

53 This is what was considered the 'third wave' of Portuguese colonialism (Brazil, India and now Africa). For an extended discussion, see Malyn Newitt (1995). Cristiana Bastos also notes that it was in the aftermath of the Berlin Conference (1884–85) that the Portuguese developed an active Africanist colonial policy and that 'the Goan doctors acquired a visibility on the map and in the ideological project of Portuguese colonialism' (Bastos, 2005:27).

54 Interview with Esmeralda, 22 March 2007, Maputo.

55　The formation of Goan or Indo-Portuguese clubs came up frequently in my conversations with the many Goans I interviewed. They all made the same point: that they were very popular under Portuguese colonialism as places of sociality for Goans, but were disbanded with Mozambican independence. The history and role of these Goan social clubs obviously needs further ethnographic and historical elaboration.

56　Interview with Fernandes, 19 March 2007, Maputo.

57　The system of *prazos* or 'leased properties' had been initiated in 1675 as part of Portugal's expansion into the interior of Mozambique. However, a lack of available (Portuguese) women for intermarriage and the general withdrawal of Portuguese settlers from Mozambique, which was considered as 'unfavourable land', starting in the 18th century saw the immigration of Goans into the colony to fill this particular niche and their practice of intermarriage with the Portuguese, forming a community of *prazeiros* (Prinz, 1997:112).

58　It was unclear whether he had died or they had divorced.

59　*Sorpatel* is one of the most typically 'Goan' specialties and is a spicy pork curry served on rice; this dish also serves as a defining identity marker for Catholic cuisine in Goa.

60　Interview with Filipe, 20 March 2007, Maputo.

61　These alternating viewpoints were evidenced in interviews I conducted with Portuguese citizens in Lisbon, Portugal in 1998; Goans in Goa, India in 1999; and Goan Mozambicans in Maputo in 2007.

62　Interview with Délia Maciel, 21 March 2007, Maputo.

63　At the beginning of the interview she tentatively and somewhat guardedly showed me her manuscript. By the end of our discussion two hours later she had lent me one of her few precious copies so that I could make a photocopy. Also included in her manuscript are poems written by her, another form of history writing, following the ideas of Ho (2006). I thank Délia for her generosity.

64　Interestingly, different Goans (depending on one's ideological positioning and having to do with the fact that Goa became a Union Territory of India only and not an independent nation) refer to 1961 as either the year of Goa's 'liberation' or its 'invasion' by the Indian government. I prefer to use the more ideologically neutral term of 'independence' to suggest its decolonisation from Portuguese colonial rule.

65　Here I am reminded of a point made by Ho (2006:223) that women were required to return to their origins in a genealogical sense, in and through marriage, while sons were encouraged to return in a geographical sense as part of the journey of education and the inculcation of moral virtues. Just as medicine had been a popular profession among the Goan migrants of the 1920s, banking was a popular profession among the Mozambican-born Goans of this next generation coming of age in the 1950s and 1960s.

66　Interview with Edith, 22 March 2007, Maputo, Mozambique.

67   Interview with Carla Maciel, 21 March 2007, Maputo. She addresses this same point in her recently completed dissertation (2007).

68   It was also during the 1950s that a large number of Portuguese emigrants arrived in South Africa, some via the colonies, others directly (interview with Fernandes and his Portuguese wife, Maria, 19 March 2007, Maputo).

69   Here it is important to remember that there was always a potential for political organisation on the part of the Goans of Mozambique, particularly since they experienced forms of racism, as Cesar recounted to me. As a child growing up between the late 1950s and early 1960s in Maputo, he remembers being one of the best students in his school, yet he never received any of the annual school prizes, since, as he recalled, they were implicitly reserved for the Portuguese students (interview with Cesar, 20 March 2007, Maputo).

70   Interview with Fernandes and Maria, 19 March 2007, Maputo.

71   Délia's brother was not the only one to follow this pattern of migration from Mozambique to Angola. According to Ana van Eck, a Portuguese Angolan and Portuguese-language teacher now living in Johannesburg, there was a small exodus of Goans who in fact moved from Mozambique to Angola, joining the already established Goan community in Luanda (conversation with Ana van Eck, 7 March 2007, Johannesburg).

72   Interview with Raul and Carla, 21 March 2007, Maputo.

73   Interview with Fernandes, 19 March 2007, Maputo.

74   Interview with Cesar, 20 March 2007, Maputo.

75   Interview with Esmeralda, 22 March 2007, Maputo. According to Esmeralda, her father, an extremely wealthy man at the time of decolonisation, lost all his properties from Mozambican nationalisation. Similarly, the Goan clubs that he had frequented were also closed down; there were no longer specially allocated spaces for Goan sociality.

76   Esmeralda herself reflects as much this history of 'local cosmopolitanism', having been raised in Mozambique, but with frequent visits abroad while growing up. She has memories of experiencing racism at the exclusive Portuguese school she attended as a young girl. As an adult, she lived for a long time in Paris, married a Portuguese citizen, and returned to Maputo to live. She frequently travels to Portugal to see her mother and one of her two brothers.

77   Interview with Edith, 22 March 2007, Maputo.

78   These were all points made to me by different Goan informants. I have combined them in one narrative for simplification.

79   This suggests a disjuncture between theory and practice. In theory they wanted all non-Africans, including Goans, to leave, but in practice they wanted the Goans to stay to show their commitment to Mozambique and to allay their fears that the Goans had always been aligned with the Portuguese throughout their colonial history. See Kuper

(1979:243) as a comparable example of the complicated position of Goans living in Uganda during an era of expulsion.

80   It is interesting that there has recently been a revival in celebrating one's Goan-ness through events such as 'Goa Day', which takes place annually on 20 August in Maputo and coincides with other 'Goa Days' celebrated throughout the Goan diaspora (United States, United Kingdom, Portugal, Brazil).

81   Email exchange with Paula, 7 March 2007.

Chapter 5 – Monty ... Meets Gandhi ... Meets Mandela

82   Accessed at University of Fort Hare Archival Collections, <http://www.liberation.org. za/naicker_president>.

83   Monty's delegation included George Singh, M. R. Parekh, B. A. Maharaj, B. D. Lalla, I. M. Bawa, E. H. Ismail, B. Goordeen and M. D. Naidoo.

84   Joint statement by Dadoo and Monty Naicker after a meeting of the PRC (*Passive Resister*, 11 December 1947).

85   <http://www.anc.org.za/ancdocs/history/congress/passive.html>.

86   Interview with Billy Nair, 25 February 2008.

87   Interview with Billy Nair, 25 February 2008.

88   Part of the speech is quoted in *New Age*, 16 November 1961. The full speech in Monty's handwriting is part of the Monty Naicker Collection kept by his son, Kreesan.

89   Quote from Mandela (1994:321).

90   Gandhi offered *satyagraha* non-violence as a method of combatting oppression and genocide, stating: 'If I were a Jew and were born in Germany and earned my livelihood there, I would claim Germany as my home even as the tallest Gentile German might, and challenge him to shoot me or cast me in the dungeon; I would refuse to be expelled or to submit to discriminating treatment. And for doing this I should not wait for the fellow Jews to join me in civil resistance, but would have confidence that in the end the rest were bound to follow my example. If one Jew or all the Jews were to accept the prescription here offered, he or they cannot be worse off than now. And suffering voluntarily undergone will bring them an inner strength and joy ... the calculated violence of Hitler may even result in a general massacre of the Jews by way of his first answer to the declaration of such hostilities. But if the Jewish mind could be prepared for voluntary suffering, even the massacre I have imagined could be turned into a day of thanksgiving and joy that Jehovah had wrought deliverance of the race even at the hands of the tyrant. For to the God-fearing, death has no terror' (M. K. Gandhi, 'The Jews', *Harijan*, 26 November 1938, in *The Collected Works of Mahatma Gandhi*, vol. 74, p. 240, <http://en.wikipedia.org/wiki/Satyagraha#cite_note-16>). When Gandhi was criticised for these statements, he responded in another article: 'Friends have sent

me two newspaper cuttings criticising my appeal to the Jews. The two critics suggest that in presenting non-violence to the Jews as a remedy against the wrong done to them, I have suggested nothing new .... What I have pleaded for is renunciation of violence of the heart and consequent active exercise of the force generated by the great renunciation' (M. K. Gandhi, 'Some Questions Answered', *Harijan,* 17 December 1938, in *The Collected Works of Mahatma Gandhi*, vol. 74, pp. 297–98, <http://en.wikipedia.org/wiki/Satyagraha#cite_note-16>).

Anticipating a possible attack on India by Japan during the Second World War, Gandhi recommended *satyagraha*: 'there should be unadulterated non-violent non-cooperation, and if the whole of India responded and unanimously offered it, I should show that, without shedding a single drop of blood, Japanese arms – or any combination of arms – can be sterilised. That involves the determination of India not to give quarter on any point whatsoever and to be ready to risk loss of several million lives. But I would consider that cost very cheap and victory won at that cost glorious. That India may not be ready to pay that price may be true. I hope it is not true, but some such price must be paid by any country that wants to retain its independence. After all, the sacrifice made by the Russians and the Chinese is enormous, and they are ready to risk all. The same could be said of the other countries also, whether aggressors or defenders. The cost is enormous. Therefore, in the non-violent technique I am asking India to risk no more than other countries are risking and which India would have to risk even if she offered armed resistance' (M. K. Gandhi, 'Non-violent Non-cooperation', *Harijan*, 24 May 1942, in *The Collected Works of Mahatma Gandhi* vol. 82, p. 286, <http://en.wikipedia.org/wiki/Satyagraha#cite_note-16>).

91 Interview with Billy Nair, 25 February 2008.
92 Interview with Billy Nair, 25 February 2008.
93 Interview with Billy Nair, 25 February 2008.

Socio-political Comparisons

Chapter 6 – Renaissances, African and Modern

94 See <http://www.ambedkar.org/ambcd/41L.What%20Congress%20and%20Gandhi%20CH>.
95 <http://www.gandiserve.org/cwmg.html>.
96 <http://www.gandiserve.org/cwmg.html>.
97 See Nandy (2002) for new ways in which the globalisation discussion is being managed.
98 Key politicians in the National Party who, at the time, were propagating the basic racial principles of separate development.

Chapter 7 – Democratic Deepening in India and South Africa

99　I am grateful to Michelle Williams and Amrita Basu for extensive comments, as well as to the anonymous reviewers for the *Journal of African and Asian Studies*.

100　As cited by V. K. Ramachandran at the International Conference on Democratic Decentralisation, Trivandrum, 27 May 2000.

101　The 73rd and 74th amendments to the Indian constitution in 1993 significantly strengthened the formal democratic character of local government. In some states, significant progress has been made, but by all accounts the problems of local democracy remain acute.

102　The exception here is Kerala, where the Confederation of Indian Trade Unions (the Communist Party of India [Marxist]-affiliated federation) has made significant inroads into the informal sector (Heller, 2000). In a very different pattern, new non-aligned movements have emerged in the informal sector, most notably the Self-Employed Women's Association and small but significant organising efforts in the construction and bidi (hand-rolled Indian cigarette) industries (Agarwala, 2006).

103　One of the more telling examples of this process came in the 1990s, when in response to the BJP's mobilisation of upper-caste Hindus, the Janata Dal recalibrated caste identity by creating the OBC (Other Backward Caste) category (Chandra, 2005:45).

Chapter 8 – Local Democracies in Indian and South African Cities

104　This work is part of a larger collective project comparing the forms and impact of political participation in the governance of South African and Indian cities (cf. <http://www.cisa-wits.org.za>).

105　<http://web.worldbank.org/WBSITE/EXTERNAL/TOPICS/EXTPUBLICSECTOR ANDGOVERNANCE/EXTDSRE/0,,contentMDK:20246049~menuPK:390249~pagePK: 148956~piPK:216618~theSitePK:390243,00.html>.

106　Tawa Lama-Rewal has previously researched reservations for women in municipal corporations, urban governance and the political mobilisation of neighbourhood associations in Indian megacities. Bénit-Gbaffou has researched local government, redistribution and local participation in South African cities.

107　EPW is a generalist weekly journal that includes all kinds of articles, from short commentaries on news items to long scholarly essays in social sciences ('special articles'). The authors who publish in EPW are journalists or scholars, students, or well-known intellectuals. The index of EPW issues since 1999 is available online; our search was restricted to the 'special articles' published between 1999 and 2008.

108　*Seminar* was founded in 1959 and publishes monthly thematic issues inviting comments by a variety of specialists (actors or observers) from all political opinions. The articles in *Seminar* are never longer than five pages, but each issue is built so as to reflect the current state of the political and academic debates on various subjects. We found seven issues in *Seminar*'s archives that deal with local democracy and/or urban governance: 'Panchayati raj' (no. 49, 1963), 'Decentralization' (no. 156, 1972), 'Grassroots democracy' (no. 234, 1979), 'The panchayati revival' (no. 360, 1989), 'Our urban future' (no. 372, 1990), 'City nostalgia' (no. 379, 1991) and 'Grassroots governance' (no. 438, 1996).

109 An example is K. C. Sivaramakrishnan, one of the few authors writing about the political dimension of urban governance, who is a retired, top-level bureaucrat who participated in drafting the decentralisation policy in the late 1980s.

110 For instance A. Mabin, S. Parnell, E. Pieterse and M. Swilling, who were involved in civil society organisations challenging the apartheid regime and who have worked directly or indirectly for post-apartheid local government. Some of them are still involved today as government consultants on urban policies.

111 'Panchayati raj' means (in Hindi) 'government of the *panchayats*', with 'panchayats' historically being councils of elders who are in charge of arbitrating conflicts in a given community (the caste or the village). The phrase was invented by Gandhi, who even before independence advocated a political system where village councils would play a major role ('gram swaraj', i.e. the self-government of villages); it has come to be synonymous with local self-government.

112 Here is another feature of the Gandhian view of democracy: Gandhi viewed parties as feeding on people's divisions and suggested that after achieving independence the INC be disbanded and its members engage in social work.

113 This is a major break from the past: before 1992, local councils could be superseded by the state administration and local elections could be, and were, postponed for years.

114 Decentralisation is also considered successful in Karnataka, where the local branch of the Janata Dal inherited from the Janata Party a strong commitment to 'grass-roots democracy'.

115 They are mass-based parties, with strongly committed cadres and a strong presence at the local level.

116 We will focus here only on metropolitan areas (the biggest cities), as it is the focus of our research programme and issues are slightly different for smaller municipalities.

117 Townships refer to residential areas that used to be reserved for non-white residents.

118 The Department of Provincial and Local Government lists four broad objectives of local government: '(1) build sustainable human settlements to address spatial and economic distortions; (2) support viable and robust local economies; (3) provide access to a package of free basic services to grant every household a minimum of services; (4) create meaningful opportunities for participation in municipal affairs' (quoted in Van Donk et al., 2008).

119 In the two issues of *Seminar* devoted to urban issues ('Our urban futures', 1990 and 'City nostalgia', 1991) there is no mention at all of local democracy or politics or

participation. On the other hand, all five issues devoted to decentralisation ('Panchayati raj', 1963; 'Decentralization', 1972; 'Grassroots democracy', 1979; 'The panchayati revival', 1989; and 'Grassroots governance', 1996) deal exclusively with rural areas. As far as EPW's treatment of decentralisation is concerned, we identified 34 articles dealing with rural India and 14 dealing with urban India.

120 'The panchayati revival', *Seminar*, no. 360, August 1989.

121 The 73rd and 74th CAAs prescribe that at least one third of seats be reserved for women, but recently states such as Bihar and Chattisgarh have increased this proportion to 50 per cent of seats.

122 An exception is the study of Ghosh and Tawa Lama-Rewal (2005).

123 It is the case in Cape Town, where political leadership is highly volatile and contested between the ANC and a coalition of opposition parties; or in Durban, where factionalism is rife and is expressed in particular in conflicts between the provincial government and the metropolitan council.

124 Institutional fragmentation is aggravated by the adoption of the principles of New Public Management, which creates parastatal, but autonomous departments, agencies and corporations to run different municipal functions on a cost recovery basis.

125 As a keyword, 'participation' leads to either electoral studies or studies of development programmes, especially with a focus on community management of natural resources (water, forests); see Manor (2004) and Puri (2004).

126 Mission statement: <http://jnnurm.nic.in/nurmudweb/toolkit/Overview.pdf>.

127 See the special issue of the South African journal *Transformation*, 66/67, 2008.

128 It was the case under the transitional local government system with two-tier municipalities, where submetropolitan structures were sometimes captured by the political opposition.

129 This distinction does not seem to be that operational in South Africa (perhaps a less globalised society in this regard), where emphasis is rather put on the difference between social movements (supposed to be massive, altruistic and progressive as well, but also having a radical political agenda) and civics (more local in their constituency and objectives, restricted to pragmatic, 'bread and butter' issues).

130 A recent exception is the series of protests evoked by the implementation of the new Master Plan in New Delhi in 2006.

Chapter 9 – Reimagining Socialist Futures in South Africa and Kerala, India

131 I would like to thank Michael Burawoy, Jennifer Chun, Vishwas Satgar, Sarah Mosoetsa, Jackie Cock, Devan Pillay, Kim Voss and Isabel Hofmeyr, for their comments on various drafts of this essay.

132 For my understanding of social democracy, I draw from Esping-Anderson (1990).

133 I use 'socialist democracy' rather than 'democratic socialism' or 'radical social democracy', as both parties insist that, for them, democratic socialism was tainted with the Eurocommunist experience and social democracy referred to the Scandinavian experience in which parliamentary democracy was the primary means.

134 The SACP held congresses in 1991, 1995, 1998 and 2002, as well as three strategy conferences in 1993, 1999 and 2000. The CPI(M) held congresses in 1992, 1995, 1998 and 2002, as well as two conferences in Kerala in 1994 and 2000.

135 For a discussion of their practices in relation to their ideological visions, see Williams (2008).

136 For example, the SACP held its 8th National Congress in 1991 and the CPI(M) held its 14th Congress in 1992, where fundamental questions about socialism, Marxism and democracy were asked.

137 After it returned to South Africa in 1990, the SACP formed a strategic alliance with the African National Congress (ANC) and the Congress of South African Trade Unions (COSATU), which was later broadened to include the South African National Civic Organisation.

138 Through the 1957–59 CPI(M)-led ministry, the party learned the importance of simultaneously dismantling power relations and securing democratic mechanisms beyond the political.

139 Notwithstanding its own transgressions in its internal organisational structures, the party had from the 1920s committed itself to political and economic democracy in society.

140 The original name of the party was the Communist Party of South Africa. In 1950 the CPSA was disbanded in response to the apartheid regime's Prohibition of Communism Act. In 1953 the SACP was reconstituted clandestinely. The change in nomenclature was partially a legal manoeuvre to clearly distinguish the SACP as a separate entity from the CPSA.

141 The ANC adopted a similar analysis at its 1969 Morogoro conference (Slovo, 1976:161).

142 Such a commitment to a multiparty system was not universally accepted within the ranks of the SACP. At an SACP–COSATU meeting in March 1990, a caution against ruling out the short-term necessity for a single-party system argued that 'while a one-party system cannot be ruled out in principle – particular conditions may make it

necessary – nevertheless in general the multiparty system provides one of the favourable conditions for democratic participation' (SACP, 1990:13–14).

143 Evans (1995:12) juxtaposes a developmental state to a predatory state. Predatory states 'extract at the expense of society, undercutting development even in the narrow sense of capital accumulation'. Such states lack the ability to prevent individuals from pursuing their own goals and thus individual maximisation comes before collective goals. Ties to society become ties to individuals, 'not connections between constituencies and the state as an organization'.

144 The term 'bourgeois' is not really applicable to Kerala, as there was no developed indigenous bourgeoisie at this time, but it is often used to describe the wealthy and conservative non-landlord class.

145 In the 1989 programme, continued struggle was outlined as follows: 'In the period after the seizure of power by the democratic forces, the working class will need to continue to struggle against capitalism. It will need to strengthen its organizations and build the bases of working class and popular power in the economy, in all sectors of the state and in the communities where the people live. A deliberate effort will have to be made to prevent attempts by the bourgeoisie and aspirant capitalist elements – and their imperialist supporters – to dominate state power and divert the revolution' (SACP, 1989:39).

146 The RDP was a common Tripartite Alliance programme for economic reconstruction and development of South African society. It was formulated by leftist intellectuals, COSATU, the SACP and the ANC. In 1996 it was replaced by the neoliberal macroeconomic policy Growth, Employment and Redistribution strategy (GEAR).

147 NEDLAC was formed in 1995 by an act of parliament (no. 35 of 1994). NEDLAC is a statutory body with considerable power and membership consists of representatives from business, labour, community and development organisations, and government. It is a consultative forum for all proposed labour legislation and social and economic policies (Gostner & Joffe, 2000:78). The power of labour and community organisations, however, is contingent on broader power relations and organisational capacities.

148 They were also sidestepping the old debate of 'revolutionary' versus 'reformist' strategies to socialism (CPI[M], 1990:311; SACP, 1999:4–6). Reformists believe that working through an affirmative state can ameliorate severe economic inequality, eliminate poverty and offset market irrationalities (such as the negative externalities in public goods, labour reproduction and the environment). Moreover, reformists argue that wholesale rupture with capitalism will not necessarily produce the desired alternative, but more likely will result in societies with new forms of inequality and economic irrationalities. The revolutionary camp argues that reformist efforts at change are merely cosmetic and do not challenge the destructive properties of

capitalism. Instead, they argue that a completely new society could be built through smashing the old system (Wright & Burawoy, 2004:1–2). The CPI(M) and SACP were attempting to move beyond this debate as both camps ultimately placed primacy on the central role of the state in transformation. Both parties, by contrast, were developing a society-centred vision of social change that sought to increase the capacity of civil society to engage both the state and the economy.

149 The party was adopting Samir Amin's (1990) notion of delinking in which popular national demands are placed before market demands and the market is engaged on terms beneficial to national development.

150 This understanding of socialism attempts to posit socialism as a negation of capitalism, which is characterised by the private ownership of the means of production. Thus, in the 20th century socialism was often reduced to state ownership of the means of production (Wright, 2006).

151 Indicating the need to elaborate viable alternatives, SACP leader Rob Davies (1991:38) argued: 'If socialists and communists are to regain more of the initiative in the national economic debate, we need to produce more substantive answers about what it is that distinguishes the vision of socialism we are defending from that which failed in Eastern Europe....The kind of policy which emerges in the stage of national democratic construction will significantly affect the prospects of a socialist project in the future.'

152 See, for example, Malinga (1990), Ramaphosa (1993), Marais (1994), Cronin (1995), Gomomo (1995), Erwin (1996), Marais (1996), Nondwangu (1996), Nzimande (1996), Satgar & Mantashe (1996), Dexter (1996), SACP (1997), Satgar (1997), Carrim & Kondlo (1999), Netshitenzhe (2000) and Pape (2001). In addition, the SACP and COSATU held a 'Socialist Conference' in November 1994 to further clarify their thinking.

153 For example, it was argued that 'a coherent transformation will require state ownership; policies that influence private investment; changed rights of access to and use of natural resources (e.g. land, water, minerals, forests, marine resources); and a range of regulatory and supervisory dispensations' (Tripartite Alliance, 1997:17).

154 In 1995 the SACP provided a series of state interventions necessary to transform market power relations that included: 'develop active labour market, state subsidies (e.g. housing subsidies for the poor), progressive government tendering policies that, for example, compel companies to implement worker training, encourage community banks, use public sector corporations to democratise the markets, mobilise worker provident and pension funds, democratise relevant financial institutions, establish consumer negotiating forums (e.g. rent boards), mobilise mass opinion to influence the market (product-specific boycotts) and regulate markets' (SACP, 1995:17).

Chapter 10 – Labour, Migrancy and Urbanisation in South Africa and India, 1900–60

155 More detailed studies confirmed these findings. For Bombay, see Zachariah (1968:14), Chandavarkar (1994:125), Gore (1970:56), and Bulsara (1964:11); for Calcutta, see Sen (1960:2, 16–17), Chattopadhyaya (1987:377–446), Das Gupta (1976:245–49), and Chakrabarty (1989:8–10); and more generally, see Bulsara (1964:10), Prakash Rao (1983:vii, 47–49, 235–36) and Rastogi (1996:14, 89).

Conclusion – Cricket Ethics: Reflections on a South African-Indian Politics of Virtue

156 This chapter considerably revises and amplifies the version published in the special issue of *The Journal of Asian and African Studies* edited by Isabel Hofmeyr and Michelle Williams that prefigured this book and that bore the title 'Cricket ethics and Indo-Xhosa ethnics: Towards a politics of virtue along a South African–Indian axis'. I have made these revisions mainly in order to take into account the five chapters in the present volume that did not appear in the journal, but also to remedy certain earlier deficiencies in my understanding of the history of cricket. I have chosen to retain the temporal frame in which the original essay was situated – early 2008 – and I refer to subsequent events, where relevant, in the concluding section and endnotes. Warm thanks to Keith Hart and Isabel Hofmeyr for their very thoughtful comments, both critical and encouraging, on the earlier version that have aided me in this revision. Thanks also to Michelle Williams for her extraordinary forbearance and to Shireen Ally for transoceanic moral support.

157 One of the best illustrations of the kind of self-conscious effort it takes to retroactively constitute connections of diasporic South Africans to India as 'natural' is provided by the Sunday morning television magazine *Eastern Mosaic*, currently aired on Sunday mornings on SABC2, in which South African Indians are instructed in the appreciation of contemporary Indian fashion, film, popular music, philosophy, cuisine and desirable tourist destinations. Commercial breaks feature Bollywood stars hailing South Africans (the 'Indian' heritage of the viewing audience is implicit) in a gesture of acceptance and welcome.

158 I have in mind the use of these terms that prevailed in the public discourse of 18th-century France, but which, as Linton (2001) argues, continues to have broad global relevance today. See also Kelly (1991).

159 Apart from this distinction, my general view of ethics here is largely indebted to Paul Ricoeur (2007). Ethics for Ricoeur unfolds at the intersection of a rule – an ought – that is taken to be obligatory, on the one hand, and a subject capable of perceiving itself as accountable for conforming to such a rule, on the other. Of particular interest is his notion of 'imputability' – the human capacity 'to recognize ourselves as

accountable (*computable*, from the Latin root *putare*) for our acts in the sense of being their actual author' (Ricoeur, 2007:2). I have also found the methodological approach advanced by Pandian and Ali (2010:9) for the study of ethical life in South Asia to be highly suggestive – indeed programmatic – and worthy of quotation at length: '[We] seek to move away from an understanding of morality as a matter of rules and principles, texts and codes alone: we call attention instead to the moral dispositions at work in lived experience, and the embodied practices of ethical engagement through which such dispositions may be cultivated and shared. One durable name for such practices is "virtue", and … we seek to open up an engagement with the quotidian pleasures of – and desires for – a virtuous life, as they resonate with diverse traditions of moral thought and exercise. At the same time, we also seek to account for the social and historical conditions under which such ethical pleasures and desires arise. We aim to work toward a history of the moral present in South Asia, an account of how individual lives and collective forms in the region came to assume their moral valence and tendency.'

160 For India, see the thesis brilliantly developed by Partha Chatterjee (1993) to the effect that the Indian middle classes resolutely preserved what he calls a 'spiritual' domain outside of the reach of the colonial public sphere, which served as the crucible in which a nationalist project could be nurtured. See also Anupama Rao's (2009) illuminating reconsideration of the place of 'caste' in constituting the subjects, form and substance of political modernity in India. A comparable effort for South Africa is ripe for the undertaking, especially as a way of getting past the simplistic and ahistorical opposition of 'African *ubuntu*' ethics to 'Western' ethics that characterises much public – and arguably too much scholarly – debate.

161 It should go without saying that Crain Soudien's essay foregrounds the example set by Gandhi's ethical discourse and practice explicitly, as he considers its potential for guiding South Africa's – and all of Africa's – future.

162 The term 'black' in South Africa, as a practice of demographic classification for legal purposes, comprises people formerly categorised as 'African', 'Indian' and 'Coloured' under apartheid. These older terms persist as everyday terms of reference.

163 For an exception, see the classic essay by Roland Barthes (1972) on the meta-ethics of theatrical wrestling.

164 See also the considerable body of scholarship by J. A. Mangan (e.g. 1986; 1992) on the link among sport (especially cricket), ethics and culture in the unfolding of British imperial culture over space and time.

165 I am grateful to Keith Hart (personal communication) for suggesting this way of reading the received post-colonial historiography against the grain. In *Beyond a Boundary*, James (1993) argues that cricket was eventually dominated in Britain by members of the rising Victorian middle class who were only too happy to have their

earnest, moralising ethos inculcated into their children in the public schools and equally eager to export it to the colonies via the imperial army and civil service: 'The class of the population that seems to have contributed least [to cricket's development] was the class destined to appropriate the game and convert it into a national institution. This was the solid Victorian middle class. It was accumulating wealth. More than most newcomers it was raw .... Its chief subjective quality was a moral unctuousness. This it wore like armour to justify its exploitation of common labour and to protect itself from the loose and erratic lives of the aristocracy it was preparing to supplant' (James: 1993:159). In James's view, cricket's constitutive role in providing the cultural underpinnings of Victorian nationalism hardly interfered with its appeal in the colonies. On the contrary: 'This signifies, as so often in any deeply national movement, that it contained elements of universality that went beyond the bound of the originating nation' (James: 1993:164).

166 'No more an instrument for socializing black and brown men into the public etiquette of empire, it is now an instrument for mobilizing national sentiment in the service of transnational spectacles and commoditization' (Appadurai, 1996:109). The investment in commodifying national sentiment may, however, be eroded by the emergence of the Indian Premier League, which draws its professional, highly paid players from a pool of top-rated internationals, much like the English Premier League in soccer. I address this development at the end of this chapter.

167 The readmission of South Africa to international cricket without any evidence of racial transformation in the composition of the national team was sharply contested by non-racial national and provincial cricket organisations in the country. For a detailed and impassioned analysis of the politics deferring racial transformation in South African cricket, especially in the period just before and after the democratic transition, see Farred (1997). For a somewhat longer historical treatment, including the infamous D'Oliveira affair, see Murray and Merrett (2004). For Natal, see the comprehensive landmark study by Desai et al. (2002).

168 Symonds had already suffered taunts and monkey gestures from the Indian crowd in matches played only a few months previously in India. Mukul Kesayan (2007) has written an excoriating critique of efforts by the Indian media to pass off such crowd behaviour as expressing little more than working-class barbarism, as opposed to dispositions of the educated middle classes: 'It was Hamish Blair's brilliant photograph of two middle-class Indian men in the Wankhede stands, trying to look like apes and succeeding, that swung Indian public opinion away from denial towards an acknowledgment that there was a problem that needed to be named. And its name is racism. It's silly and deluded to look for anthropological explanations that will turn racist behaviour by Indians into something subtly different. Cricket writing by Indians in English sometimes makes the mistake of thinking of the "average" Indian fan as

non-English speaking and therefore naïve and unsophisticated. This assumption makes it possible for "us" to explain "their" behaviour away as a kind of unschooled brutishness that is unfortunate but not wicked. This is why Blair's photograph is so important: it shows you upwardly mobile men – who probably discuss the virtues of one malt whisky over the other, who possibly holiday abroad, whose children certainly go to private schools that teach in English – using one of the many international codes they've learnt in their cosmopolitan lives, the Esperanto of bigotry. The *mudras* they're making aren't derived from Kathakali: they're straight out of the international style guide to insulting black men.'

169 Menon (1994), for example, shows how communist ideology was appropriated locally in order to provide a political critique of caste inequality in the Malabar region of what is today the Indian state of Kerala. His book draws attention to the socially tenuous and historically contingent ways in which the moral discourse of 'community' becomes yoked to a variety of political projects – ranging from communist-inspired peasant movements against the landed classes to movements for caste unity or caste equality. Bénit-Gbaffou and Lama-Rewal (this volume) show how in India, decentralisation has been most successful in the two states controlled most often by communist governments: Kerala and West Bengal.

170 Hart and Padayachee (2000:703–5) tell a remarkable story of Gandhi's printing legacy that has remained within South Africa – a story that foregrounds the intergenerational transfer and transformation of technology, managerial skill and capital. Virjee Mehta, a Gujarati Hindu who immigrated to Durban in 1908 and was hired by Gandhi as a printer of *Indian Opinion* at the Phoenix settlement, eventually established his own press, Bombay Printers, in 1924. The family business was passed on to his sons, and eventually to his grandsons, who turned it into a modern corporation, Universal Web Printers (now Uniprint). One of the grandsons, Harshish Mehta, became founding chairman of First Asian Investment Corporation, supposedly the first listed empowerment corporation for people of Asian descent.

171 See the extended treatment by Cowen and Shenton (1996) of the concept of trusteeship in the 19th-century British Empire and the way in which it laid the foundation for the 20th-century discourse of development. Interestingly, the concept of trusteeship – used in a slightly different sense to mean the holding of property and wealth in trust for the broader social good – later became an ethical pillar of Gandhian economic philosophy.

172 Oddly, it was after decolonisation that American and European sociology grew increasingly invested in the theory that Indian society was obsessed with sustaining a hierarchy of relative human value organised along an axis defined by purity at one pole and pollution at the other (Dumont, 1981; see Dirks, 2001:43–60). For sociologists

such as Louis Dumont, this obsession with establishing one's proper place on a status scale structured by ideologies of relative purity and value was seen to permeate every facet of cultural action: eating, marriage, sex, occupation, worship, death and physical contact. Of course, such a view required that centuries of Islamic political and cultural permeation be sifted out of Indian social history. Given that this came in the wake of the massive bloodshed attending partition, this constituted a stunning process of political forgetting in the guise of scholarly abstraction and insight.

173 See both Menon (1994) and Rao (2009), who, in different ways and in different regions of India, explore the place of caste ideology and the ideology of caste equality in movements of political modernity. Ebr.-Vally (2001) explores the significance of caste distinctions brought from India and transformed thereafter among Indian South Africans.

174 On the diasporic and unacknowledged transracial mixing of popular musical cultures in Indian-owned taxis in Durban, see Hansen (2006).

175 While there may be strong parallels here with South Asia, it is of some importance that we do not underestimate at least one crucial difference. In southern Africa, social, sexual and kin networks often stretch across the rural–urban divide – a fact that is hardly surprising, given the very long history of labour migration in the region. Here, the ethics of connection have long involved the obligation on the part of the urban to remit wages or make marriage payments to rural affines. For most Africans living in the region south of the Zambezi River, polygynous marriage is not uncommon and 'marriage' itself is understood as a series of exchanges involving rights in labour, sexual access and children unfolding over time. Children are incorporated into the agnatic kin group of the husband, but only if he satisfies a negotiated demand for bridewealth – principally cattle or their monetary equivalent – by the wife's patrikin (Kuper, 1982). Infertility or divorce can eventuate in the return or non-payment of bridewealth, with the wife sometimes returning to her natal family. While generalisation is hazardous, in South Asia the norm, broadly stated, is for the wife to bring marriage payments ('dowry') into the home of her husband's kin. As one moves northward in India, and upward in caste status, the tendency is for wives in Hindu marriages to be seen as permanently 'incorporated' into their husbands' caste, making divorce or widow remarriage unimaginable. As one moves southward in India, and also down in the caste hierarchy – or out of it altogether – the bond to the husband diminishes, as do restrictions on remarriage after his death or divorce (Goody, 1990). For a detailed overview of variations in marriage practices and wedding rituals among 'Indian' South Africans, both Hindu and Muslim, see Ebr.-Vally (2001).

176 The incident and controversy that followed Willem to the finals in Durban is the subject matter of a documentary made by Nishendra Moodley called *Contesting Race* (Ikon South Africa, 2009).

177 The political, cultural and historical intimacy between India and South Africa is subjected to imaginative and sometimes satirical exploration in the special issue of *Chimurenga* (no. 14, April 2009) entitled 'Everyone has their Indian'. The phrase evokes the cozy relationship between now President Jacob Zuma and his financial advisor, Durban businessman Schabir Shaik, who was charged with facilitating the payment of bribes by a French weapons manufacturer in order to secure Zuma's support for arms contracts. Shaik was eventually convicted for corruption and fraud, and jailed. Zuma was relieved of the deputy presidency of South Africa by President Thabo Mbeki in June 2005, a change in political fortunes that was decisively reversed at the ANC convention at Polokwane in December 2007.

178 I have transcribed this quotation directly from the audio segments of the interview. For a discussion of the dilemmas faced by Muslim South Africans as they try to reconcile conflicting ethical demands from overlapping political and religious communities of belonging, see Vally and Worby (2008).

179 One might also reflect on Amla's career in light of the critique made by Farred (1997) of the purely formal gestures made towards racial transformation in South African cricket in the years immediately following apartheid's demise. Amla himself had to face accusations of racial tokenism after his initial selection, although his batting prowess soon put such murmurs to rest.

References

Abraham, I. (2008) From Bandung to NAM: Non-alignment and Indian foreign policy, 1947–65. *Commonwealth and Comparative Politics*, 46(2):195–219.

Abrahams, P. (1970) *Tell Freedom: Memories of Africa*. New York: Collier.

Adams, R. (1997) Epistemology, Afrocentricity, and ideology. In Logan, P. (ed.), *A Howard Reader: An Intellectual and Cultural Quilt of the African-American Experience*, pp. 439–44. Boston: Houghton Mifflin.

Agarwala, R. (2006) From work to welfare. *Critical Asian Studies*, 38(4):419–44.

Ahluwalia, P. (2001) *Politics and Post-colonial Theory: African Inflections*. London: Routledge.

Ajuha, R. (2002) Labour relations in an early colonial context: Madras, c. 1750–1800. *Modern Asian Studies*, 36:793–826.

Alexander, P. (2007) Women and coal mining in India and South Africa, c. 1900–1940. *African Studies*, 66:201–22.

Amin, S. (1990) The future of socialism. In Tabb, W. K. (ed.), *The Future of Socialism: Perspectives from the Left*, pp. 106–23. New York: Monthly Review Press.

Amrith, S. (2005) Asian internationalism: Bandung's echo in a colonial metropolis. *Inter-Asia Cultural Studies*, 6(4):557–69.

ANC (African National Congress) (1994) *Reconstruction and Development Programme*. Johannesburg: Umanyano.

—— . (1997) 'Report by the president of the ANC, Nelson Mandela, to the 50th National Conference of the African National Congress', Mafikeng, 16 December.

Anderson, A. (1925) *Windjammer Yarns: Some Incidents in the Life of a South African Seaman Abroad*. London: Whitby.

Anderson, B. (1991) *Imagined Communities*. London: Verso.

Appadurai, A. (1969) Gandhi's contribution to social theory. *Review of Politics*, 31(3):312–28.

—— . (1996) *Modernity at Large*. Minneapolis: University of Minnesota Press.

Arendt, H. (1951) *The Origins of Totalitarianism, part III, Totalitarianism*. New York: Harcourt Brace.

Atkinson, D. (2007) Taking to the streets: Has developmental local government failed in South Africa? In Buhlungu, S., Daniel, J., Southall, R. & Lutchman, J. (eds), *State of the Nation: South Africa 2007*, pp. 53–77. Cape Town: HSRC Press.

Bagwandeen, D. (1991) *A People on Trial: The Struggle for Land and Housing of the Indian People of Natal, 1940–46*. Durban: Madiba.

Balachandran, G. (2003) Circulation through seafaring: Indian seamen 1890–1945. In Markovits, C., Pouchepadass, J. & Subrahmanyam, S. (eds), *Society and Circulation: Mobile People and Itinerant Cultures in South Asia 1750–1950*, pp. 89–130. New Delhi: Permanent Black.

Ballantine, C. J. (1993) *Marabi Nights: Early South African Jazz Vaudeville*. Johannesburg: Ravan Press.

Ballantyne, T. (2006) *Between Colonialism and Diaspora: Sikh Colonial Formations in an Imperial World*. Durham: Duke University Press.

Ballard, R., Habib, A. & Valodia, I. (eds) (2006) *Voices of Protest: Social Movements in Post-apartheid South Africa*. Pietermaritzburg: University of KwaZulu-Natal Press.

Banaji, J. (1993) Capitalist domination and the small peasantry: The Deccan district in the late nineteenth century. In Prakash, G. (ed.), *The World of the Rural Labourer in Colonial India*, pp. 113–45. New Delhi: Oxford University Press.

Bangabasi (1899) 'Report on native newspapers, no. 1 of 1900, 30 December.' National Archives of India.

——. (1900) 'Report on native newspapers, no. 3 of 1900, 13 January.' National Archives of India.

Banteyerga, H. (1994) An alternative model in teacher education: The classroom in focus. Paper presented at the Pan-African colloquium Educational Innovation in Post-Colonial Africa, University of Cape Town.

Bardhan, P. (1999) The state against society: The great divide in Indian social science discourse. In Bose, S. & Jalal, A. (eds), *Nationalism, Democracy and Development*, pp. 184–95. New Delhi: Oxford University Press.

Barnett, M. R. (1976) *The Politics of Cultural Nationalism in South India*. Princeton: Princeton University Press.

Barthes, R. (1972) The world of wrestling. In *Mythologies*, pp. 15–25. Trans. A. Lavers. New York: Hill & Wang.

Bastos, C. (2005) Race, medicine, and the late Portuguese empire: The role of Goan colonial physicians. *Journal of Romance Studies*, 5(1):23–35.

Baud, I. & Nainan, N. (2008) 'Negotiated spaces' for representation in Mumbai: Ward committees, advanced locality management and the politics of middle class activism. *Environment and Urbanization*, 20(2):483–99.

Bausmati (1899) 'Report on native newspapers, no. 49 of 1899, 20 December.' National Archives of India.

Baviskar, A. (2007) Cows, cars and rickshaws: Bourgeois environmentalism and the battle for Delhi's streets. Paper presented at the workshop on The Middle Classes in India: Identity, Citizenship and the Public Sphere, Institute of Economic Growth, New Delhi, 15–17 March.

Bayly, S. (2004) Imagining 'Greater India': French and Indian visions of colonialism in the Indic mode. *Modern Asian Studies*, 38(3):703–44.

Beall, J., Crankshaw, O. & Parnell, S. (2002) *Uniting a Divided City: Governance and Social Exclusion in Johannesburg*. London: Earthscan.

Beinart, W. (1994) *Twentieth-century South Africa*. Cape Town: Oxford University Press.

Beinart, W. & Bundy, C. (1987) *Hidden Struggles in Rural South Africa: Politics and Popular Movements in the Transkei and Eastern Cape*. London & Berkeley: University of California Press.

Bénit-Gbaffou, C. (2008) Are practices of local participation side-lining participatory channels? Reflections from Johannesburg. *Transformation: Critical Perspectives on Southern Africa,* 66/67:1–33.

——. (2010) Local democracy, clientelism and the (re)politicisation of urban governance: Reflections from Johannesburg stories. In Padayachee, V., Cramer, C., Freund, B., Hart, K. & Pons-Vignon, N. (eds), *The Political Economy of Africa*, pp. 286–300. London: Routledge.

Benjamin, W. (1968) Theses on the philosophy of history. In Benjamin, W. (ed.), *Illuminations*, pp. 253–64. New York: Harcourt, Brace & World.

Bernstein, R. (1999) *Memory against Forgetting*. London: Viking.

Bhabha, H. (1994) *Location of Culture*. New York: Routledge.

Bhana, S. (1997) *Gandhi's Legacy: The Natal Indian Congress*. Pietermaritzburg: University of Natal Press.

Bhana, S. & Brain, J. (1990) *Setting down Roots: Indian Migrants in South Africa 1860–1911*. Johannesburg: Wits University Press.

Bhana, S. & Hunt, J. D. (1989) *Gandhi's Editor: The Letters of M. H. Nazar*. New Delhi: Promilla.

Bhana, S. & Vahed, G. (2005) *The Making of a Political Reformer: Gandhi in South Africa, 1893–1914*. New Delhi: Manohar.

Bhattacharya, D. (1973) *Rabindra-Charya*. Kolkata: General Printers and Publishers.

Bhattacharya, N. (1993) Agricultural labour and production: Central and South-East Punjab, 1870–1940. In Prakash, G. (ed.), *The World of the Rural Labourer in Colonial India*, pp. 146–204. New Delhi: Oxford University Press.

—— . (2006) Introduction. In Behal, R. P. & Van der Linden, M. (eds), *International Review of Social History, Supplement 14*, pp. 7–19. Cambridge: Cambridge University Press.

Bhattacharya, S. N. (1965) *Mahatma Gandhi: The Journalist*. Bombay: Asia Publishing.

Blackburn, R. (1991) *Fin de siècle*: Socialism after the crash. In Blackburn, R. (ed.), *After the Fall: The Failure of Communism and the Future of Socialism*, pp. 173–249. London: Verso.

Blainey, G. (2001) *The Tyranny of Distance: How Distance Shaped Australia's History*. Sydney: Macmillan.

Boggs, C. & Plotke, D. (eds) (1980) *The Politics of Eurocommunism: Socialism in Transition*. Boston: South End.

Bond, P. (2000) *Elite Transition: From Apartheid to Neoliberalism in South Africa*. London: Pluto.

Bonner, P. L. (1990) Desirable or undesirable women? Liquor, prostitution and the migration of Basotho women to the Rand, 1920–1945. In Walker, S. (ed.), *Women and the Organisation of Gender in South African History*, pp. 221–50. Cape Town & London: David Philip/James Currey.

—— . (1993) The shaping of apartheid: Continuity, contradiction and popular struggle, 1943–1962. In Bonner, P., Delius, P. & Posel, D. (eds), *Apartheid's Genesis*, pp. 1–41. Johannesburg: Ravan Press.

—— . (2004a) Migration, urbanization and urban social movements in twentieth century India and South Africa. *Studies in History*, 20(2):215–36.

—— . (2004b) The great migration and the 'Greatest Trek', some reflections. *Journal of Southern African Studies*, 30(1):87–114.

Bonner, P. L. & Ndima, V. (2008) The roots of violence and martial Zuluness on the East Rand. In Carton, B., Laband, J. & Sithole, J. (eds), *Zulu Identities: Being Zulu Past and Present*. Pietermaritzburg: University of KwaZulu-Natal Press.

Bonner, P. L. with Nieftagodien, N. (2008) *Alexandra: A History*. Johannesburg: Wits University Press.

Bonner, P. L. & Segal, L. (1998) *Soweto: A History*. Johannesburg: Maskew Miller Longman.

Bose, A. (1973) *Studies in Indian Urbanization 1901–1970*. Bombay: McGraw-Hill.

Bose, S. (2005) *A Hundred Horizons: The Indian Ocean in an Age of Global Imperialism*. Cambridge, Mass.: Harvard University Press.

——. (2006) *A Hundred Horizons: The Indian Ocean in the Age of Global Empire*. Cambridge, Mass.: Harvard University Press.

Bourdieu, P. (1995) *Outline of a Theory of Practice*. Trans. R. Nice. Cambridge: Cambridge University Press.

Bozzoli, B. (1991) *Women of Phokeng*. Portsmouth & London: Heinemann/James Currey.

Bradford, H. (1987) *A Taste of Freedom: The ICU in Rural South Africa, 1924–1930*. New Haven: Yale University Press.

Brady, W. (1997) Indigenous Australian education and globalization. In Masemann, V. & Welch, A. (eds), *Tradition, Modernity and Post-modernity in Comparative Education*, pp. 413–22. Dordrecht: Kluwer.

Brass, P. R. (1997) *Theft of an Idol: Text and Context in the Representation of Collective Violence*. Princeton: Princeton University Press.

Breman, J. C. (1974) *Patronage and Exploitation: Changing Agrarian Relations in South Gujarat, India*. Berkeley: University of California Press.

——. (1985) *Of Peasants, Migrants and Paupers. Rural Labour Circulation and Capitalist Production in West India*. New Delhi: Oxford University Press.

—— (1996) *Footloose Labour: Working in India's Informal Economy*. Cambridge: Cambridge University Press.

Brett, O. (2008) Cricket's new order. *BBC Sport*, 29 February. <http://news.bbc.co.uk/sport2/hi/cricket/7270944.stm>.

Broeze, F. (ed.) (1997) *Gateways of Asia: Port Cities of Asia in the 13th–20th Centuries*. London: Kegan Paul.

Broeze, F. (1998) *Island Nation: A History of Australians and the Sea*. St Leonard's: Allen & Unwin.

Brown, J. M. (1990) *Gandhi: Prisoner of Hope*. New Delhi: Oxford University Press.

——. (1996) The making of a critical outsider. In Brown, J. M. & Prozesky, M. (eds), *Gandhi and South Africa: Principles and Politics*. Pietermaritzburg: University of Natal Press.

Bulsara, J. F. (1964) *Problems of Rapid Urbanization in India*. Bombay: Popular Prakashan.

——. (1970) *Patterns of Social Life in Metropolitan Areas*. Bombay: Chronicle Press.

Bundy, C. (1991) *The History of the South African Communist Party*. Cape Town: UCT Press.

Burton, A. (2006) Cold War cosmopolitanism: The education of Santha Rama Rau in the age of Bandung, 1945–1954. *Radical History Review*, 95:149–72.

Burton, A., Espiritu, A. & Wilkins, F. C. (2006) Introduction: The fate of nationalisms in the age of Bandung. *Radical History Review*, 95:145–48.

Cachalia, D. N. (1981) The radicalisation of the Transvaal Indian Congress and the moves to joint action, 1946–1952. BA Hons. dissertation, University of the Witwatersrand.

Cahen, M., Couto, D., De Souza, P. R., Marrou, L. & Siqueira, A. (2000) Introduction: Issues of Asian Portuguese-speaking spaces and *lusotopias*. *Lusotopie*, 137–58.

Cameron, R. (ed.) (1999) *Democratisation of South African Local Government: A Tale of Three Cities*. Pretoria: Van Schaik.

Carrim, Y. (2001) From transition to transformation: Challenges of the new local government system. *The African Communist*, 156(1):32–44.

Carrim, Y. & Kondlo, N. (1999) Public–private partnerships: The challenges for local government. *The African Communist*, 151(2):13–19.

Chakrabarty, D. (1989) *Rethinking Working-class History: Bengal 1890–1940*. Princeton: Princeton University Press.

Chandavarkar, R. (1994) *The Origins of Industrial Capitalism in India: Business Strategies and the Working Classes in Bombay, 1900–1940*. Cambridge: Cambridge University Press.

Chandra, K. (2005) The transformation of ethnic politics in India: The decline of Congress and the rise of the Bahujan Samaj Party in Hoshiarpur. *Journal of Asian Studies*, 59(1):26–61.

Chanock, M. (2001) *The Making of South African Legal Culture 1902–1936: Fear, Favour and Prejudice*. Cambridge: Cambridge University Press.

Charlton, S. & Kihato, C. (2008) Reaching the poor? An analysis of the influences on South Africa's housing programme. In Pillay, U., Tomlinson, R. & Du Toit, J. (eds), *Democracy and Delivery: Urban Policy in South Africa*, pp. 252–82. Cape Town: HSRC Press.

Chatterjee, P. (1993) *The Nation and Its Fragments: Colonial and Postcolonial Histories*. Princeton: Princeton University Press.

——. (1997) Our modernity. Lecture published by the South-South Exchange Programme for Research on the History of Development (SEPHIS) and the Council for the Development of Social Science Research in Africa, Rotterdam/Dakar.

——. (2001) Democracy and the violence of the state: A political negotiation of death. *Inter-Asia Cultural Studies*, 2(1):7–21.

——. (2006a) Are Indian cities becoming bourgeois at last? In John, M. E., Jha, P. V. & Jodhka, S. S. (eds), *Contested Transformations: Changing Economies and Identities in Contemporary India*. New Delhi: Tulika.

——. (2006b) Empire and nation: 50 years after Bandung. *Inter-Asia Cultural Studies*, 6(4):487–96.

——. (2007) Democracy and the current economic transformation. Paper presented at the conference on The Great Transformation? India's New Political Economy, Columbia University, 14–16 September.

Chattopadhyaya, H. (1987) *Internal Migration in India: A Case Study of Bengal*, Calcutta & New Delhi: K. P. Bagchi.

Chaudhuri, K. N. (1985) *Trade and Civilisation in the Indian Ocean: An Economic History from the Rise of Islam to 1750*. Cambridge: Cambridge University Press.

Chaudhuri, R. (1993) *Migration and Remittances: Inter-urban and Rural–urban Linkages*. New Delhi: Sage.

Chaudhuri, S. (2006) What difference does a constitutional amendment make? The 1994 Panchayati Raj Act and the attempt to revitalize rural local government in India. In Bardhan, P. & Mookherjee, D. (eds), *Decentralization and Local Governance in Developing Countries*, pp. 153–202. Cambridge: MIT Press.

Chibber, V. (2005) From class compromise to class accommodation: Labor's incorporation into the Indian political economy. In Ray, R. & Katzenstein, M. (eds), *Social Movements in India: Poverty, Power and Politics*, pp. 32–61. New York: Rowman & Littlefield.

Chipkin, I. (2007) *Do South Africans Exist? Nationalism, Democracy and the Identity of 'the People'*. Johannesburg: Wits University Press.

Choudhury, Y. (1995) *Sons of the Empire: Oral History from the Bangladeshi Seamen Who Sailed on British Ships during the 1939–45 War*. Birmingham: Sylheti Social History Group.

Claudin, F. (1975) *The Communist Movement: From Comintern to Cominform*, vols I & II. New York: Monthly Review Press.

Clegg, J. (1984) An examination of the Umzansi dance style. In Tracy, A. (ed.), *Papers Presented at the Third and Fourth Symposia on Ethnic Musicology*, pp. 1–70. Grahamstown: International Library of African Music, Institute of Social and Economic Research, Rhodes University.

Cohen, J. L. & Arato, A. (1992) *Civil Society and Political Theory*. Cambridge, Mass.: MIT Press.

Cohn, B. (1996) *Colonialism and Its Forms of Knowledge*. Princeton: Princeton University Press.

Colaco, A. (1955) *A History of the Seamen's Union of Bombay*. Bombay: Pascal Vaz.

Cole, J. R. I. (2002) Printing and urban Islam in the Mediterranean world, 1890–1920. In Fawaz, L. T. & Bayly, C. A. (eds), *Modernity and Culture: From the Mediterranean to the Indian Ocean*, pp. 344–64. New York: Columbia University Press.

Comaroff, J. & Comaroff, J. (1991) *Of Revelation and Revolution, vol. 1, Christianity, Colonialism, and Consciousness in South Africa*. Chicago: University of Chicago Press.

Connell, R. (2007) *Southern Theory*. Cambridge: Polity Press.

Conrad, J. (2004 [1919]) Confidence. In Stape, J. H. with Burza, A. (eds), *Notes on Life and Letters*, pp. 159–63. Cambridge: Cambridge University Press.

Cooper, F. (1997) The dialectics of decolonization: Nationalism and labor movements in postwar French Africa. In Stoler, A. & Cooper, F. (eds), *Tensions of Empire: Colonial Cultures in a Bourgeois World*, pp. 406–35. Berkeley: University of California Press.

Coplan, D. B. (1985) *In Township Tonight: South Africa's Black City Music and Theatre*. London: Longman.

Corbridge, S. & Harriss, J. (2000) *Reinventing India: Liberalization, Hindu Nationalism and Popular Democracy*. Cambridge: Polity Press.

Corbridge, S., Williams, G., Srivastava, M. & Veron, R. (2005) *Seeing the State: Governance and Governmentality in India*. Cambridge & New York: Cambridge University Press.

Courtios, S., Kramer, M., Panne, J. L., Paczkowski, A., Bartosek, K. & Margolu, J. L. (1999) *The Black Book of Communism: Crimes, Terror, Repression*. Cambridge, Mass.: Harvard University Press.

Cowen, M. & Shenton, R. (1996) *Doctrines of Development*. London: Routledge.

CPI(M) (Communist Party of India [Marxist]) (1990) On certain political-ideological issues related to developments in some socialist countries. Central Committee Resolution 28–31 May. In *Documents of the Communist Movement*. Calcutta: National Book Agency.

—— . (1997 [1967]) The new situation and the new tasks confronting the Party. Central Committee Resolution 1967. In *Documents of the Communist Movement in India, vol. XI (1965–1967)*. Calcutta: National Book Agency.

——. (1998a [1989]) CPI(M) Election manifesto: 1989 Lok Sabha elections. In *Documents of the Communist Movement*, vol. XXIII. Calcutta: National Book Agency.

——. (1998b [1992]) Resolution on certain ideological issues. Congress resolution, Madras, 3–9 January 1992. In *Documents of the Communist Movement,* vol. XXIV. Calcutta: National Book Agency.

Crapanzano, V. (1980) *Tuhami: Portrait of a Moroccan.* Chicago: University of Chicago Press.

Cronin, J. (1994) Bolshevism and socialist transition. *The African Communist,* 136(1):39–41.

——.(1995) The RDP needs class struggle. *The African Communist,* 142(4):1–3.

Crook, N. (1993) *India's Industrial Cities: Essays in Economy and Demography.* New Delhi: Oxford University Press

Crutchley, W. C. (1912) *My Life at Sea: Being a 'Yarn' Loosely Spun for the Purpose of Holding together Certain Reminiscences of the Period from Sail to Steam in the British Merchant Marine (1863–1894).* London: Chapman & Hall.

Dagnino, E. (1998) Culture, citizenship, and democracy: Changing discourses and practices of the Latin American Left. In Alvarez, S. E., Dagnino, E. & Escobar, A. (eds), *Cultures of Politics, Politics of Cultures: Revisioning Latin American Social Movements,* pp. 33–63. Boulder: Westview Press.

Daily Star (Bangladesh) (2008) 'Back to "dark" days?' 14 February.

Dasgupta, K. (2009) The Hawkers' Movement in Kolkata: Negotiating the right to city space. Paper presented at the workshop on The Voice of City Dwellers in Urban Governance. Participation, Mobilisation and Local Democracy – Comparing Indian/ South African Debates, Mumbai University, 12–14 January.

Das Gupta, R. (1976) Factory labour in eastern India: Sources of supply, 1946–1955: Some preliminary findings. *Indian Economic and Social History Review,* 8(3):245–49.

Datta, P. K. (2007) The interlocking worlds of the Anglo-Boer War in South Africa/India. *South African Historical Journal,* 57:35–59.

Davenport, T. R. (1970) The triumph of Colonel Stallard: The transformation of the Natives (Urban Areas) Act between 1923 and 1937. *South African Historical Journal,* 2:77–96.

——. (1971) The beginnings of urban segregation in South Africa: The Natives (Urban Areas) Act of 1923 and its background. Occasional paper no. 15. Grahamstown: Institute of Social and Economic Research, Rhodes University.

Davies, R. (1991) Rethinking socialist economics for South Africa. *The African Communist,* 125(2):37–46.

Deccan Herald (2004) Ship ownership row. 14 March. <http://www.deccanherald.com/archives/mar142004/s17.asp>.

De Haan, A. (1994) *Unsettled Settlers: Migrant Workers and Industrial Capitalism in Calcutta.* Rotterdam & Hilversum: Verloren.

——. (2004) Calcutta's labour migrants' encounters with modernity. In Osella, F. & Gardner, K. (eds), *Migration, Modernity and Social Transformation in South Asia,* pp. 189–215. New Delhi: Sage.

Delius, P. (1996) *A Lion amongst the Cattle.* Johannesburg: Ravan Press.

Dembowski, H. (1999) Courts, civil society and public sphere: Environmental litigation in Calcutta. *Economic and Political Weekly,* 9 January, pp. 49–56.

Department of Economics, University of Bombay (1970) Housing conditions in the slums. In Desai, A. R. & Pillay, S. D. (eds), *Slums and Urbanization*, pp. 153–219. Bombay: Popular Prakashan.

Desai, A., Padayachee, V., Reddy, K. & Vahed, G. (2002) *Blacks in Whites: A Century of Cricket Struggles in KwaZulu-Natal*. Pietermaritzburg: University of Natal Press.

Desai, A. R. & Pillay, S. D. (1972) *A Profile of an Indian Slum*. Bombay: University of Bombay.

Desai, A. & Vahed, G. (2007) *Inside Indenture: A South African Story, 1860–1914*. Durban: Madiba.

Desai, D. (1939) *Maritime Labour in India*. Bombay: Servants of India Society.

De Sousa Santos, B. (2002) Between Prospero and Caliban: Colonialism, postcolonialism, and inter-identity. *Luso-Brazilian Review*, 39(2):9–43.

—— . (2006) *The Rise of the Global Left: The World Social Forum and Beyond*. London: Zed Books.

Dexter, P. (1996) Marxism and the national question in a democratic South Africa. *The African Communist*, 145(3):59–66.

Dhupelia-Mesthrie, U. (2004) *Gandhi's Prisoner? The Life of Gandhi's Son Manilal*. Cape Town: Kwela.

—— . (2007) The place of India in South African history: Academic scholarship, past, present and future. *South African Historical Journal*, 57:12–34.

Dirks, N. B. (2001) *Castes of Mind: Colonialism and the Making of Modern India*. Princeton: Princeton University Press.

Dirlik, A. (n.d.) 'Global South: Predicament and promise.' <http://www.humnet.ucla.edu/mellon/Global%20South.pdf>.

Dixon, C. (1980) Lascars: The forgotten seamen. In Ommer, R. & Ponting, G. (eds), *Working Men Who Got Wet: Proceedings of the Fourth Conference of the Atlantic Canada Shipping Project*, pp. 265–81. St John's: Atlantic Canada Shipping Project.

Dlamini, J. (2010) *Native Nostalgia*. Johannesburg: Jacana Media.

Doke, J. J. (2005) *Gandhi: A Patriot in South Africa*. New Delhi: Ministry of Information and Broadcasting.

Downes, A. G. (1952) *Printer's Saga: Being a History of the South African Typographical Union*. Johannesburg: South African Typographical Union.

Du Bois, W. (1970) The strivings of the negro people. In Weinberg, M. (ed.), *W. E. B. Dubois: A Reader*, pp. 19–25. New York: Harper Torchbooks.

Dumont, L. (1981) *Homo Hierarchicus: The Caste System and Its Implications*. Chicago: University of Chicago Press.

Duverger, M. (1974) *Modern Democracies: Economic Power versus Political Power*. Illinois: Drysden.

Ebr.-Vally, R. (2001) *Kala-Pani: Caste and Colour in South Africa*. Cape Town: Kwela.

Eley, G. (1992) Nations, publics, and political cultures: Placing Habermas in the nineteenth century. In Calhoun, C. (ed.), *Habermas and the Public Sphere*, pp. 289–339. Cambridge: MIT Press.

Erlmann, F. (1996) But hope does not kill: Popular music in Durban, 1913–1939. In Maylam, P. & Edwards, I. (eds), *The People's City: African Life in Twentieth Century Durban*, pp. 67–101. Pietermaritzburg: University of Natal Press.

Erwin, A. (1996) Building the new South Africa's economy. *The African Communist*, 145(3):25–29.

Escobar, A. (1992) Culture, economics, and politics in Latin American social movements theory and practice. In Escobar, A. & Alvarez, S. E. (eds), *The Making of Social Movements in Latin America: Identity, Strategy, and Democracy*, pp. 62–85. Boulder: Westview Press.

Esping-Anderson, G. (1990) *The Three Worlds of Welfare Capitalism*. Princeton: Princeton University Press.

Evans, P. (1995) *Embedded Autonomy: States and Industrial Transformation*. Princeton: Princeton University Press.

—— . (2005) Counter-hegemonic globalization: Transnational social movements in the contemporary global political economy. In Janaski, T., Hicks, A. M. & Schwartz, M. (eds), *The Handbook of Political Sociology*. London: Cambridge University Press.

Ewald, J. J. (2000) Crossers of the sea: Slaves, freedmen and other migrants in the Northwestern Indian Ocean c. 1750–1914. *American Historical Review*, 105(1):69–91.

Eyal, G. (2002) Eastern Europe as laboratory for economic knowledge: The transnational roots of neoliberalism. *American Journal of Sociology*, 108(2):310–52.

Fanon, F. (1967). *The Wretched of the Earth*. Harmondsworth: Penguin.

Farred, G. (1997) The nation in white: Cricket in a post-apartheid South Africa. *Social Text*, 50:9–32.

Fernandes, L. (2006) *India's New Middle Class: Democratic Politics in an Era of Economic Reform*. New Delhi: Oxford University Press.

Fernandes, L. & Heller, P. (2006) Hegemonic aspirations. *Critical Asian Studies*, 38(4):495–522.

Fernandes, N. (2006) Tomb raider: Looking for St Francis Xavier. In Pinto, J. (ed.), *Reflected in Water: Writings on Goa*, pp. 73–84. New Delhi: Penguin Books India.

Fischer, L. (ed.) (1963) *The Essential Gandhi*. London: Allen & Unwin.

Fischer, L. R. & Panting, G. E. (1995) Indian ports and British intercontinental sailing ships. In Mathew, K. S. (ed.), *Mariners, Merchants and Oceans: Studies in Maritime History*, pp. 371–83. New Delhi: Manohar.

Fox, J. (1994) The difficult transition from clientalism to citizenship. *World Politics*, 46(2):151–84.

Fox, S. (2004) *The Ocean Railway: Isambard Kingdom Brunel, Samuel Cunard, and the Revolutionary World of the Great Atlantic Steamships*. London: Harper & Collins.

Frost, D. (ed.) (1995) *Ethnic Labour and British Imperial Trade: A History of Ethnic Seafarers in the UK*. London: Frank Cass.

Frost, M. R. (2002) 'Wider opportunities': Religious revival, nationalist awakening and the global dimension in Colombo, 1870–1920. *Modern Asian Studies*, 36(4):937–67.

—— . (2004) Asia's maritime networks and the colonial public sphere, 1840–1920. *New Zealand Journal of Asian Studies*, 6(2):5–36.

—— . (2010) 'That great ocean of idealism': Calcutta, the Tagore Circle and the idea of Asia, 1900–1920. In Gupta, P., Hofmeyr, I. & Pearson, M. (eds), *Eyes across the Water: Navigating the Indian Ocean*, pp. 75–95. Pretoria: UNISA Press.

Fullard, M. (2004) State repression in the 1960s. In *The Road to Democracy in South Africa vol. I (1960–1970)*, pp. 341–90. Cape Town: Zebra Press.

Gadgil, D. G. (1952) *Poona: A Socio-economic Survey*, vol. 1. Poona: Gokale Institute of Politics and Economics.

Galaty, J. G. (1982) Being 'Maasai'; being 'people-of-cattle': Ethnic shifters in East Africa. *American Ethnologist*, 9(1):1–20.

Gandhi, M. K. (1920) The law of suffering. *Young India*, 16 June. <http://en.wikipedia.org/wiki/Satyagraha#cite_note-9>.

——. (1957) *An Autobiography: The Story of My Experiments with Truth*. Boston: Beacon Press.

——. (1960a) *The Collected Works of Mahatma Gandhi, vol. 1, July 1888–November 1896*. New Delhi: Publications Division, Government of India.

——. (1960b) *The Collected Works of Mahatma Gandhi, vol. 2, 1897–1900*. New Delhi: Publications Division, Government of India.

——. (1960c) *The Collected Works of Mahatma Gandhi, vol. 3, 1901–1903*. New Delhi: Publications Division, Government of India.

——. (1967) Power of satyagraha. In Prabhu, R. K. & Rao, U. R. (eds), *The Mind of Mahatma Gandhi*. Revised edition. Ahmedabad. <http://en.wikipedia.org/wiki/Satyagraha#cite_note-9>.

——. (1968a) *The Collected Works of Mahatma Gandhi, vol. 81, 18 August, 1941–8 February, 1942*. Ahmedabad: Navajivan.

——. (1968b) *The Selected Works of Mahatma Gandhi IV: The Basic Works*. Ahmedabad: Navajivan.

——. (1968c) *The Selected Works of Mahatma Gandhi VI: The Voice of Truth*. Ahmedabad: Navajivan.

Gandhi, P. (1957) *My Childhood with Gandhi*. Ahmedabad: Navajivan.

Ghertner, D. A. (2008) Analysis of new legal discourse behind Delhi's slum demolitions. *Economic and Political Weekly*, 17 May, pp. 57–66.

Ghosh, A. (1992) *In an Antique Land: History in the Guise of a Traveler's Tale*. London: Vintage.

——. (2006) *Popular Publishing and the Politics of Language and Culture in a Colonial Society 1778–1905*. New Delhi: Oxford University Press.

——. (2008) *Sea of Poppies*. London: John Murray.

Ghosh, A. & Tawa Lama-Rewal, S. (2005) *Democratization in Progress: Women and Local Politics in Urban India*. New Delhi: Tulika.

Ghurye, G. S. (1974) Cities of India: Their growth and location. In Rao, M. S. A. (ed.), *Urban Sociology in India*. New Delhi: Orient Longman.

Gilroy, P. (2000) *On Race*. Cambridge, Mass.: Harvard University Press.

Glaser, C. (2000) *Bo-Tsotsi: Youth Gangs of Soweto, 1935–1976*. Portsmouth: Heinemann.

GOI (Government of India) (2002) *State Profiles*. New Delhi.

GOK (Government of Kerala), State Planning Board. (1991) *Draft Eighth Five-year Plan*. Thiruvananthapuram: GOK.

Gomomo, J. (1995) Privatization and the reorganization of state assets. *The African Communist*, 141(2):8–13.

Goodhew, D. (2004) *Respectability and Resistance: A History of Sophiatown*. Westport: Praeger.

Goody, J. (1990) *The Oriental, the Ancient and the Primitive: Systems of Marriage and the Family in the Pre-industrial Societies of Eurasia.* Cambridge: Cambridge University Press.

Goonam, K. (1992) *Coolie Doctor.* Durban: Madiba.

Gore, M. S. (1970) *Immigration and Neighbourhoods: Two Aspects of Life in a Metropolitan City.* Bombay: Tata Institute of Social Sciences.

Gostner, K. & Joffe, A. (2000) Negotiating the future: Labour's role in NEDLAC. In Adler, G. (ed.), *Engaging the State and Business: The Labour Movement and Co-determination in Contemporary South Africa*, pp. 75–100. Johannesburg: Wits University Press.

Govender, S. (2007) Judges flee after Xhosa girl wins Miss Teen India. *Sunday Times* (South Africa), 29 July.

Greenstein, R. (2003) State, civil society and the reconfiguration of power in post-apartheid South Africa. Paper presented at a WISER seminar, University of the Witwatersrand, Johannesburg, 28 August.

Grossberg, L. (1994) Introduction: Bringin' it all back home: Pedagogy and cultural studies. In Giroux, H. & McLaren, P. (eds), *Between Borders: Pedagogy and the Politics of Cultural Studies*, pp. 23–42. New York: Routledge.

Guha, S. (1985) *The Agrarian Economy of the Bombay Deccan, 1818–1941.* New Delhi: Oxford University Press.

Gupta, A. D. (2004) *India and the Indian Ocean World: Trade and Politics.* New Delhi: Oxford University Press.

Gupta, D. (1982) *Nativism in a Metropolis.* New Delhi: Manohar.

Gupta, P. (1997) What about Goa? The role of the press in the politics of Goan independence, 1947–1961. Unpublished paper.

——. (2007) Mapping Portuguese decolonization in the Indian Ocean: A research agenda. *South African Historical Journal*, 57:93–112.

Gupta, P., Hofmeyr, I. & Pearson, M. (eds) (2010) *Eyes across the Water: Navigating the Indian Ocean.* Pretoria: UNISA Press.

Gupta, V. (ed.) (2003) *Dhanyavaad India: A Tribute to the Heroes and Heroines of India who Supported the Liberation Struggle of South Africa.* New Delhi: High Commission of the Republic of South Africa.

Gurnah, A. (1994) *Paradise.* New York: New Press.

——. (2005) *By the Sea.* London: Bloomsbury.

Habermas, J. (1989) *The Structural Transformation of the Public Sphere: An Inquiry into a Category of Bourgeois Society.* Cambridge, Mass.: MIT Press.

——. (1991) What does socialism mean today? The revolutions or recuperation and the need for new thinking. In Blackburn, R. (ed.), *After the Fall: The Failure of Communism and the Future of Socialism*, pp. 25–46. London: Verso.

——. (1996) *Between Facts and Norms: Contributions to a Discourse Theory of Law and Democracy.* Cambridge, Mass.: MIT Press.

Habermas, J. & Pensky, M. (2001) *The Postnational Constellation: Political Essays.* Cambridge, Mass.: MIT Press.

Habib, A. & Valodia, I. (2006) Reconstructing a social movement in an era of globalisation: A caste study of COSATU. In Ballard, R., Habib, A. & Valodia, I. (eds), *Voices of Protest: Social Movements in Post-apartheid South Africa*, pp. 225–54. Durban: University of KwaZulu-Natal Press.

Hansen, T. B. (2001a) *Urban Violence in India: Identity Politics, 'Mumbai' and the Postcolonial City*. New Delhi: Permanent Black.

—— . (2001b) *Wages of Violence: Naming and Identity in Postcolonial Bombay*. Princeton: Princeton University Press.

—— . (2005) Sovereigns beyond the state: On legality and authority in urban India. In Hansen, T. B. & Stepputat, F. (eds), *Sovereign Bodies: Citizens, Migrants and States in the Postcolonial World*, pp. 169–91. Princeton: Princeton University Press.

—— . (2006) Sounds of freedom: Music, taxis, and racial imagination in urban South Africa. *Public Culture*, 18(1):185–208.

Hantrais, L. (2009) *International Comparative Research: Theory, Methods and Practice*. New York: Palgrave Macmillan.

Hardiman, D. (2003) *Gandhi in His Time and Ours: The Global Legacy of His Ideas*. Pietermaritzburg: University of Natal Press.

Harper, T. N. (2002) Empire, diaspora and the languages of globalism, 1850–1914. In Hopkins, A. G. (ed.), *Globalization in World History*, pp. 141–66. London: Pimlico.

Harries, P. (1994) *Work Culture and Society*. Portsmouth: Heinemann.

Harrison, N. (1905) *A Manual of Lascari-Hindustani with Technical Phrases and Terms*. London: Imray, Laurie, Norrie & Wilson.

Harriss, J. (2007) Antinomies of empowerment: Observations on civil society, politics and urban governance in India. *Economic and Political Weekly*, 42(26):2716–24.

Hart, K. & Padayachee, V. (2000) Indian business in South Africa after apartheid: New and old trajectories. *Comparative Studies in Society and History*, 4:683–712.

Hart, M. & Negri, A. (2001) *Empire*. Cambridge, Mass.: Harvard University Press.

Heller, P. (1999) *The Labor of Development: Workers and the Transformation of Capitalism in Kerala, India*. Ithaca: Cornell University Press.

—— . (2000) Degrees of democracy: Some comparative lessons from India. *World Politics*, 52(4):484–519.

—— . (2003) Reclaiming democratic spaces: Civics and politics in post-transition Johannesburg. In Tomlinson, R., Beauregard, R., Bremner, L. & Mangcu, X. (eds), *Emerging Johannesburg: Perspectives on the Postapartheid State*, pp. 155–84. New York: Routledge.

—— . (2008) Local democracy and development in comparative perspective. In Van Donk, M., Swilling, M., Pieterse, E. & Parnell, S. (eds), *Consolidating Developmental Local Government: Lessons from the South African Experience*, pp. 153–74. Cape Town: UCT Press.

Heller, P. & Ntlokonkulu, L. (2001) *A Civic Movement or a Movement of Civics? The South African National Civic Organisation (SANCO) in the Post-apartheid Period*. Johannesburg: Centre for Policy Studies.

Hemson, D. (1977) Dock workers, labour circulation and class struggles in Durban, 1940–59. *Journal of Southern African Studies*, 4(1):88–124.

Hemson, D. & O'Donnovan, M. (2007) Putting numbers on the scorecard: Presidential targets and the state of delivery. In Buhlungu, S., Daniel, J., Southall, R. & Lutchman, J. (eds), *State of the Nation: South Africa 2007*, pp. 11–45. Cape Town: HSRC Press.

Hipsher, P. (1998) Democratic transitions as protest cycles: Social movement dynamics in democratizing Latin America. In Tarrow, S. & Meyer, D. (eds), *The Social Movement Society*, pp. 152–72. New York: Rowman & Littlefield.

Hirson, B. & Vivian, L. (1992) *The Seamen's Strike of 1925 in Britain, South Africa and Australia*. London: Clio.

Hitavadi (1899a) 'Report on native newspapers, no. 47 of 1899, 17 November.' National Archives of India.

—— . (1899b) 'Report on native newspapers, no. 48 of 1899, 1 December.' National Archives of India.

Ho, E. (2004) Empires through diasporic eyes: A view from the other boat. *Comparative Study of Society and History*, 46(1):210–46.

—— . (2006) *The Graves of Tarim: Genealogy and Mobility across the Indian Ocean*. Berkeley: University of California Press.

Hobsbawm, E. (1991) Out of the ashes. In Blackburn, R. (ed.), *After the Fall: The Failure of Communism and the Future of Socialism*, pp. 115–25. London: Verso.

Hofmeyr, I. (2007) The idea of 'Africa' in Indian nationalism: Reporting the diaspora in the *Modern Review* 1907–1929. *South African Historical Journal*, 57:60–81.

—— . (2008) Indian Ocean lives and letters. *English in Africa*, 33(1):11–28.

—— . (forthcoming) Universalizing the Indian Ocean. *PMLA*.

Hogan, P. C. (2000) *Colonialism and Cultural Identity: Crises of Tradition in the Anglophone Literatures of India, Africa, and the Caribbean*. Albany: State University of New York Press.

Holloway, J. (2002) *Change the World without Taking Power: The Meaning of Revolution Today*. London: Pluto.

Hood, W. H. (1903) *The Blight of Insubordination: The Lascar Question and the Rights and Wrongs of the British Shipmaster, including the Mercantile Marine Committee Report*. London: Spottiswoode.

Huntington, S. (1968) *Political Order in Changing Societies*. New Haven: Yale University Press.

—— . (1992) *The Third Wave: Democratization in the Late Twentieth Century*. Norman: University of Oklahoma Press.

Hyslop, J. (1995) The white working class, women, and the invention of apartheid: 'Purified' Afrikaner nationalist agitation for legislation against 'mixed marriages' 1934–9. *Journal of African History*, 36:57–81.

Isaac, T. M. T. (1994) The Left movement in Kerala: Lessons of the past and challenges of the present. In *International Congress on Kerala Studies Documents, vol. I, 27–29 April*. Thiruvananthapuram: AKG Centre for Research and Studies.

Isaac, T. M. T. & Franke, R. (2001 [2000]) *Local Democracy and Development: People's Campaign for Decentralized Planning in Kerala*. New Delhi: Leftword.

Isaac, T. M. T. & Heller, P. (2003) Democracy and development: Decentralized planning in Kerala. In Fung, A. & Wright, E. O. (eds), *Deepening Democracy: Institutional Innovations in Empowered Participatory Governance*, pp. 77–110. London & New York: Verso.

James, C. L. R. (1993 [1963]) *Beyond a Boundary.* Durham: Duke University Press.

Jayal, N. G. (2006) Democratic dogmas and disquiets. *Seminar,* 557, January:12–14.

——. (2007) The transformation of citizenship in the 1990s. Paper presented at the conference on The Great Transformation? India's New Political Economy, Columbia University, 14–16 September.

Jayasuriya, S. de S. & Pankhurst, R. (2003) On the African diaspora in the Indian Ocean. In Jayasuriya, S. de S. & Pankhurst, R. (eds), *The African Diaspora in the Indian Ocean,* pp. 1–17. Trenton: Africa World Press.

Jenkins, R. (2010) NGOs and Indian politics. In Jayal, N. G. & Mehta, P. B. (eds), *The Oxford Companion to Indian Politics.* New Delhi: Oxford University Press.

Jenkinson, J. (1987) The 1919 race riots in Britain: Their background and consequences. PhD thesis, University of Edinburgh.

Jeppie, S. (2007) *Language, Identity and Modernity: The Arabic Study Circle of Durban.* Pretoria: HSRC Press.

Jochelson, K. (2001) *The Colour of Disease: Syphilis and Racism in South Africa 1880–1950.* Basingstoke: Palgrave.

Johnstone, F. A. (1976) *Class, Race and Gold.* London: Routledge/Kegan Paul.

Jones, N. (2006) *The Plimsoll Sensation: The Great Campaign to Save Lives at Sea.* London: Little, Brown.

Joshi, C. (1985) Bonds of community, ties of religion: Kanpur textile workers in the early twentieth century. *Indian Economic and Social History Review,* 22(3):251–80.

——. (2003) *Lost Worlds: Indian Labour and Forgotten Histories.* New Delhi: Permanent Black.

Joshi, H. & Joshi, V. (1976) *Surplus Labour and the City: A Study of Bombay.* Bombay: Oxford University Press.

Jowitt, K. (1992) *New World Disorder: The Leninist Extinction.* Berkeley: University of California Press.

Kaarsholm, P. (1988) The South African War and the response of the international socialist community to imperialism between 1896 and 1908. In Van Halthoon, F. & Van der Linden, M. (eds), *Internationalism in the Labour Movement, 1830–1940.* Leiden: Brill.

——. (1989) Pro Boers. In Samuel, R. (ed.), *Patriotism: The Making and Unmaking of British National Identity,* vol. 1. London & New York: Routledge.

Kapuscinksi, R. (1987) *Another Day of Life.* London: Penguin.

Karnik, S. (1998) Goans in Mozambique. *Africa Quarterly,* 38(3):96–118.

Katzenstein, M. & Ray, R. (2005) Introduction: In the beginning there was the Nehruvian state. In Ray, R. & Katzenstein, M. (eds), *Social Movements in India: Poverty, Power and Politics,* pp. 1–32. New York: Rowman & Littlefield.

Kaviraj, S. (2000) Democracy and social inequality. In Frankel, F., Hasan, Z., Bhargava, R. & Arora, B. (eds), *Transforming India,* pp. 89–119. New Delhi: Oxford University Press.

Kaviraj, S. & Katzenstein, M. F. (1981) *Equality and Ethnicity: Shiv Sena Party and Preferential Policies in Bombay.* Ithaca: Cornell University Press.

Keane, J. (ed.) (1995) *South Africa in World War Two: A Pictorial History.* Cape Town: Human & Rousseau.

Kelly, J. (1991) *A Politics of Virtue: Hinduism, Sexuality and Countercolonial Discourse in Fiji*. Chicago: University of Chicago Press.

Kerr, I. A. (2006) On the move: Circulating labour in pre-colonial, colonial and post-colonial India. In Behal, R. P. & Van der Linden, M. (eds), *International Review of Social History, Supplement 14*, pp. 85–109. Cambridge: Cambridge University Press.

Kesayan, M. (2007) No room for bigotry. *Cricinfo Magazine*, 20 August. <http://www.cricinfo.com/magazine/content/story/316219.html>.

Kies, B. (1953) The contribution of non-European peoples to world civilisation. A. J. Abrahamse Memorial Lecture. Cape Town: Teachers' League of South Africa.

Klein, N. (2004) Reclaiming the commons. In Mertes, T. (ed.), *A Movement of Movements: Is Another World Really Possible?*, pp. 219–29. London: Verso.

Koch, E. (1983) Doornfontein and its African working class. MA dissertation, University of the Witwatersrand.

Kohli, A. (1990) *Democracy and Discontent: India's Growing Crisis of Governability*. Cambridge & New York: Cambridge University Press.

—— . (2007) State and redistributive development in India. Paper prepared for the project on Poverty Reduction and Policy Regimes sponsored by the UN Research Institute for Social Development.

Kothari, R. (1989) Decentralization: The real issue. *Seminar*, 360, August:14–19.

Krishnamurty, J. (1993) The growth of agricultural labour in India: A note. In Prakash, G. (ed.), *The World of the Rural Labourer in Coloured India*, pp. 12–14. New Delhi: Oxford University Press.

Kumar, D. (1989) *Land and Caste in South India*. Cambridge: Cambridge University Press.

Kumar Bawa, V. (1980) *Indian Metropolis, Urbanization Planning and Management*. New Delhi: Inter Indian.

Kumar, G. (2006) *Local Democracy in India: Interpreting Decentralization*. New Delhi: Sage.

Kumar, N. & Rai, M. (2006) *Dalit Leadership in Panchayats: A Comparative Study of Four States*. New Delhi: IIDS & Rawat.

Kumble, M. D. (1982) *Migrants in an Indian Metropolis: A Study of Madras Metropolis*. New Delhi: Uphal.

Kuper, A. (1982) *Cattle for Wives*. London: Routledge/Kegan Paul.

Kuper, J. (1975) The Goan community in Kampala. In Twaddle, M. (ed.), *Expulsion of a Minority: Essays on Ugandan Asians*, pp. 53–69. London: Athlone.

—— . (1979) 'Goan' and 'Asian' in Uganda: An analysis of racial identity and cultural categories. In Shack, W. & Skinner, E. (eds), *Strangers in African Societies*, pp. 243–59. Berkeley: University of California Press.

Larkin, B. (1997) Indian films and Nigerian lovers: Media and the creation of parallel modernities. *Africa*, 67(3):406–40.

Legassick, M. (1977) Gold, agriculture and secondary industry in South Africa, 1885–1970: From periphery to sub-metropole, as a forced labour system. In Palmer, R. & Parsons, N. (eds), *The Roots of Rural Poverty in Central and Southern Africa*, pp. 75–200. London: Heinemann.

Lewandowski, S. (1980) *Migration and Ethnicity in Urban India*. New Delhi: Manohar.

Lieberman, E. S. (2003) *Race and Regionalism in the Politics of Taxation in Brazil and South Africa*. Cambridge & New York: Cambridge University Press.

Linton, M. (2001) *The Politics of Virtue in Enlightenment France*. New York: Palgrave.

Linz, J. J. & Stepan, A. C. (1996) *Problems of Democratic Transition and Consolidation: Southern Europe, South America, and Post-Communist Europe*. Baltimore: Johns Hopkins University Press.

Linz, J., Stepan, A. & Yadav, Y. (2006) 'Nation state' or 'state nation'? India in comparative perspective. In Bajpai, S. (ed.), *Democracies and Diversity: India and the American Experience*, pp. 50–106. New Delhi & Oxford: Oxford University Press.

Lloyd, L. (1991) A family quarrel: The development of the dispute over Indians in South Africa. *Historical Journal*, 34(3):203–38.

Ludden, D. (1996) Caste society and units of production in early-modern south India. In Stein, B. & Subrahmanyan, S. (eds), *Institutions and Economic Changes in South Asia*, pp. 105–33. New Delhi: Oxford University Press.

Maciel, C. (2007) Bantu oral narratives in the training of EFL teachers in Mozambique. PhD thesis, Department of Linguistics, Illinois State University.

Maciel, D. (2003) *Fragmentos da Minha Vida*. Maputo: Imprensa Universitária, Universidade Eduardo Mondlane.

MacKenzie, J. M. (2004) Locks, rivers and oceans: Technology, ethnicity and the shipping of empire in the late nineteenth century. In Killingray, D. & Lincoln, M. (eds), *Maritime Empires: British Imperial Maritime Trade in the Nineteenth Century*, pp. 111–27. Woodbridge: Boydell/National Maritime Museum.

Mager, A. K. (1999) *Gender and the Making of a South African Bantustan: A Social History of the Ciskei*. Oxford: James Currey.

Mahajan, G. (1999) Civil society and its avatars: What happened to freedom and democracy? *Economic and Political Weekly*, 34, pp. 1188–96.

Mail & Guardian Online (2010). State decides against prosecuting Gupta. 27 September. <http://www.mg.co.za/article/2010-09-27-state-decides-against-prosecuting-gupta>.

Majumdar, P. S. & Majumdar, I. (1978) *Rural Migrants in an Urban Setting: A Study of Two Shanty Colonies in the Capital City of India*. New Delhi: Hindustani.

Makgetla, N. S. (2007) Local government budgets and development: A tale of two towns. In Buhlungu, S., Daniel, J., Southall, R. & Lutchman, J. (eds), *State of the Nation: South Africa 2007*, pp. 146–70. Cape Town: HSRC Press.

Makgoba, M. (ed.) (1999) *African Renaissance: The New Struggle*. Sandton: Mafube.

Maksoud, C. (1993) Redefining non-alignment: The Global South in the new global equation. In Bennis, P. & Moushabeck, M. (eds), *Altered State: A Reader in the New World Order*, pp. 28–37. New York: Olive Branch.

Makura, D. (1999) The MDM, civil society and social transformation. *Umrabulo*, 7(3):17.

'Malem Sahib' (1892) *Lascari-Bat: A Collection of Sentences Used in the Daily Routine of a Modern Passenger Ship*. London: Miller.

Malinga, P. (1990) Nationalization or free enterprise? *The African Communist*, 123(4):20–33.

Mamdani, M. (1996) *Citizen and Subject: Contemporary Africa and the Legacy of Late Colonialism*. Princeton: Princeton University Press.

——. (1999) There can be no African renaissance without an African-focused intelligentsia. In Makgoba, M. W. (ed.), *African Renaissance: The New Struggle*, pp. 125–36. Sandton: Mafube.

Mandela, N. (1994) *Long Walk to Freedom*. London: Abacus.

Mangan, J. A. (1986) *The Games Ethic and Imperialism*. Middlesex: Viking.

——. (ed.) (1992) *The Cultural Bond: Sport, Empire, Society*. London: Frank Cass.

Mangcu, X. (2008) *To the Brink: The State of Democracy in South Africa*. Durban: University of KwaZulu-Natal Press.

Manning, F. E. (1981) Celebrating cricket: The symbolic construction of Caribbean politics. *American Ethnologist*, 8(3):616–32.

Manor, J. (2004) User committees: A potentially damaging second wave of decentralisation? *European Journal of Development Research*, 16(1):192–213.

Marais, H. (1994) Radical as reality. *The African Communist*, 138(3):15–20.

——. (1996) All GEARed up. *The African Communist*, 145(3):30–42.

Markovits, C. (2003) *The Un-Gandhian Gandhi: The Life and Afterlife of the Mahatma*. New Delhi: Permanent Black.

Mathur, O. P. (2006) Urban finance. In *India Infrastructure Report 2006*. New Delhi: Oxford University Press.

Mawdsley, E. (2004) India's middle classes and the environment. *Development and Change*, 35:79–103.

Mayer, P. & Mayer, I. (1971) *Townsmen or Tribesmen? Conservatism and the Process of Urbanization in a South African City*. Cape Town: Oxford University Press.

Mazrui, A. (1991) Africa between Gandhi and Nehru: An Afro-Asian intersection. Background paper for the Wits Spring Festival 'Cultural Identity in a New South Africa', University of the Witwatersrand, 5 September.

Mbeki, T. (2001) Address at the Third African Renaissance Festival. Durban, 31 March.

Mbembe, A. (2001) *On the Postcolony*. Berkeley: University of California Press.

McDonald, D. & Pape, J. (2002) *Cost Recovery and the Crisis of Service Delivery in South Africa*. Pretoria: HSRC Press.

McGill, M. (2003) *American Literature and the Culture of Reprinting 1834–1853*. Philadelphia: University of Pennsylvania Press.

McIntyre, S. (1998) *The Reds*. St Leonard's: Allen & Unwin.

McLane, J. (1977) *Indian Nationalism and the Early Congress*. Princeton: Princeton University Press.

McPherson, K. (1993) *The Indian Ocean: A History of the People and the Sea*. New Delhi & New York: Oxford University Press.

McRae, D. (2008) After terrorist jibe, Amla is ready for bat to do talking. *Guardian Online*, 8 July. <http://www.guardian.co.uk/sport/2008/jul/08/englandvsouthafrica2008. sportinterviews>.

Meer, F. (1969) *Portrait of Indian South Africans*. Durban: Avon House.

Meer, I. C. (2002) *Ismail Meer: A Fortunate Man*. Cape Town: Zebra Press.

Mehta, P. B. (2007) The rise of judicial sovereignty. *Journal of Democracy*, 18(2):70–83.

Mehta, V. (1976) *Mahatma Gandhi and His Apostles*. Harmondsworth: Penguin.

Melville, H. (1986 [1849]) *Redburn: His First Voyage*. London: Penguin.

Menon, D. (1994) *Caste, Nationalism and Communism in South India: Malabar, 1900–1948*. Cambridge: Cambridge University Press.

Mertes, T. (2004) Grassroots globalism. In Mertes T. (ed.), *A Movement of Movements: Is Another World Really Possible?*, pp. 237–46. London: Verso.

Mesthrie, U. S. (1987) From advocacy to mobilization: *Indian Opinion*, 1903–1914. In Switzer, L. (ed.), *South Africa's Alternative Press: Voices of Protest and Resistance, 1880s–1990s*. Cambridge: Cambridge University Press.

Metcalf, T. (2007) *Imperial Connections: India in the Indian Ocean Arena, 1860–1920*. Berkeley: University of California Press.

Miller, S. M. (2005) In support of the 'Imperial Mission'? Volunteering for the South African War, 1899–1902. *Journal of Military History*, 69(3):691–711.

Milliband, R. (1991) Reflections on the crisis of communist regimes. In Blackburn, R. (ed.), *After the Fall: The Failure of Communism and the Future of Socialism*, pp. 6–17. London: Verso.

Miraftab, F. (2006) Feminist praxis, citizenship and informal politics: Reflections on South Africa's Anti-Eviction Campaign. *International Feminist Journal of Politics*, 8(2):194–218.

Mitra, S. (2002) Planned urbanisation through public participation: Case of the new town, Kolkata. *Economic and Political Weekly*, 16 March, pp. 1048–54.

Mokone, S. (1982) Majority rule: Some notes. Reprinted from the *Educational Journal of the Teachers' League of South Africa*. Cape Town: Teachers' League of South Africa.

Moleketi, J. (1993) Is a retreat from national democratic revolution to national bourgeois revolution imminent? *The African Communist*, 133(2):11–19.

Moodie, D. (1994) *Going for Gold: Men, Mines and Migration*. Berkeley: University of California Press.

Morrell, R. (2001) *From Boys to Gentlemen: Settler Masculinity in Colonial Natal 1880–1920*. Pretoria: UNISA Press.

Muckherjee, R. (1961) Ways of dwelling in the communities of India. In Theodorsan, G. T. (ed.), *Studies in Human Ecology*. Evanston: Row, Peterson.

Muckerjee, R. & Singh, B. (1961) *Social Profiles of a Metropolis: Social Economic Structure of Lucknow, 1954–56*. Bombay: Asia Publishing House.

Mukherji, P. N. (2008) Mahatma Gandhi and the legacy of democratic decentralisation in India. *ISAS Insights*, 25:29–38.

Murray, B. & Merrett, C. (2004) *Caught Behind: Race and Politics in Springbok Cricket*. Johannesburg: Wits University Press & University of KwaZulu-Natal Press.

Mzamane, N. (1999) Eurocentric and Afrocentric perspectives on ancient African history. In Makgoba, M. W. (ed.), *African Renaissance: The New Struggle*, pp. 173–83. Sandton: Mafube.

Naicker, M. P. (1969) From Gandhi to Mandela: In commemoration of the 75th anniversary of the formation of the NIC by Mahatma Gandhi, Sechaba, 3, 5, May.' In Naidoo, L. (ed.), *Don't Mourn, Mobilise! A Biography of the Late M. P. Naicker*. Unpublished manuscript.

Naipaul, V. S. (1980) *A Bend in the River*. Harmondsworth: Penguin.

—— . (1998) *India: A Million Mutinies Now*. London: Vintage House.

Nair, J. (2006) 'Social municipalism' and the new metropolis. In John, M. E., Jha, P. K. & Jodhka, S. S. (eds), *Contested Transformations: Changing Economies and Identities in Contemporary India*, pp. 125–46. New Delhi: Tulika.

Nair, K. S. (1978) *Ethnicity and Organization: A Case Study of Ethnic Identity of South Indian Migrants in Poona*. New Delhi: Ajanta.

Namboodiripad, E. M. S. (1994) Presidential address. In *Kerala Studies Congress Documents, vol. I, 27–29 August*. Thiruvananthapuram: AKG Centre for Research and Studies.

Namibiar, P. K. (1970) Slums in a Madras city. In Desai, A. R. & Devandas Pillay, S. (eds), *Slums and Urbanisation*. Bombay: Popular Prakash.

Nandy, A. (1998) The politics of secularism and the recovery of religious toleration. In Bhargava, R. (ed.), *Secularism and Its Critics*, pp. 321–44. New Delhi: Oxford University Press.

—— . (2002) *Time Warps: The Insistent Politics of Silent and Evasive Pasts*. New Delhi: Permanent Black.

—— . (2005) *Exiled at Home*. New Delhi: Oxford University Press.

Narain, I. (1965) The concept of panchayati raj and its institutional implications in India. *Asian Survey*, 5(9):456–66.

Narayan, J. P. (2001 [1959]) A plea for the reconstruction of the Indian polity. *Seminar*, 506.

Nekhwevha, F. (1999) No matter how long the night, the day is sure to come: Culture and educational transformation in post-colonial Namibia and post-apartheid South Africa. In Soudien, C. & Kallaway, P. (eds), *Education, Equity and Transformation*, pp. 491–503. Dordrecht: Kluwer.

Netshitenzhe, J. (2000) The national democratic revolution and class struggle. *The African Communist*, 154(2):12–20.

Newitt, M. (1995) *A History of Mozambique*. London: Hurst.

Newman, R. (1981) *Workers and Unions in Bombay, 1918–1929: A Study of Organisation in the Cotton Mills*. Canberra: Australian National University.

Ngwane, Z. (2003) Apartheid under education: Schooling, initiation and domestic reproduction in post-apartheid South Africa. In Kallaway, P. (ed.), *The History of Education under Apartheid, 1948–1994*, pp. 270–87. Cape Town: Pearson.

Niranjana, T. (1999) Left to the imagination: Indian nationalism and female sexuality in Trinidad. *Public Culture*, 11(1):223–43.

Nondwangu, S. (1996) An alternative macro-economic strategy? *The African Communist*, 145(3):43–48.

Nqakula, C. (1994) Forward with a people-driven RDP. *The African Communist*, 138(3):7–14.

Ntsebeza, L. (2005) *Democracy Compromised: Chiefs and the Politics of Land in South Africa*. Cape Town: HSRC Press.

Nugent, S. (2002) 'Gente Boa, elites in and of Amazonia. In Shore, C. & Nugent, S. (eds), *Elite Cultures: Anthropological Perspectives*, pp. 61–73. London: Routledge.

Nzimande, B. (1996) The role of the working class in consolidating and deepening the National Democratic Revolution. *The African Communist*, 145(3):12–24.

O'Donnell, G. (1993) On the state, democratization and some conceptual problems: A Latin American view with glances at some postcommunist countries. *World Development*, 21(8):1355–59.

Oldenburg, P. (1976) *Big City Government in India: Councilor, Administrator and Citizen in Delhi*. New Delhi: Manohar.

Oldfield, S. (2008) Participatory mechanisms and community politics: Building consensus and conflict. In Van Donk, M., Swilling, M., Pieterse, E. & Parnell, S. (eds), *Consolidating Developmental Local Government: Lessons from the South African Experience*, pp. 487–500. Cape Town: UCT Press.

Oliphant, J. (2009) Teacher educators' professional identities in Lesotho. PhD thesis, University of Cape Town.

Omvedt, G. (1998) The struggle for social justice and the expansion of the public sphere. In Mahajan, G. (ed.), *Democracy, Difference and Social Justice*, pp. 130–45. New Delhi: Oxford University Press.

——. (2002) Ambedkar and after: The Dalit Movement in India. In Shah, G. (ed.), *Social Movements and the State*, pp. 292–309. New Delhi: Sage.

Osella, F. & Gardner, K. (2004) *Migration, Modernity and Social Transformation in South Asia*. New Delhi: Sage.

Pandian, A. & Ali, D. (eds) (2010) *Ethical Life in South Asia*. Bloomington: Indiana University Press.

Panitch, L. (2001) *Renewing Socialism: Democracy, Strategy, and Imagination*. Boulder: Westview Press.

Pape, J. (2001) The myth of 'South Fundamentals': South Africa and global economic crises. *The African Communist*, 156(1):45–59.

Parel, A. J. (ed.) (2009) *Hind Swaraj and Other Writings*. New Delhi: Cambridge University Press.

Parnell, S. (1993) Johannesburg slums and racial segregation in South African cities. PhD thesis, University of the Witwatersrand.

Parnell, S., Pieterse, E., Swilling, M. & Wooldridge, D. (2002) *Democratising Local Government: The South African Experiment*. Cape Town: UCT Press.

Parry, J. P. (2004) Nehru's dream and the village waiting room: Long distance labour migrants to a central Indian steel town. In Osella, F. & Gardner, K. (eds), *Migration, Modernity and Social Transformation in South Asia*, pp. 217–49. New Delhi: Sage.

Patel, K. (1963) *Rural Labour in Industrial Bombay*. Bombay: Popular Prakash.

Patel, S. J. (1952) *Agricultural Labourers in Modern India and Pakistan*. Bombay: Current Book House.

Paul, S. (2006) Public spending, outcomes and accountability: Citizen report card as a catalyst for public action. *Economic and Political Weekly*, 28 January, pp. 333–40.

Pearson, M. N. (1998) *Port Cities and Intruders: The Swahili Coast, India, and Portugal in the Early Modern Era*. Baltimore: Johns Hopkins University Press.

——. (2003) *The Indian Ocean*. London: Routledge.

——. (2006) Littoral society: The concept and the problems. *Journal of World History*, 17(4):353–73.

——. (2007) Studying the Indian Ocean world: Problems and opportunities. In Ray, H. P. & Alpers, E. (eds), *Cross Currents and Community Networks: The History of the Indian Ocean World*, pp. 15–33. Oxford: Oxford University Press.

Pethe, A. & Ghodke, M. (2002) Funding urban infrastructure: From government to markets. *Economic and Political Weekly*, 22 June, pp. 2467–70.

Pierson, C. (1995) *Socialism after Communism: The New Market Socialism.* Cambridge: Polity Press.

Pillay, U., Tomlinson, R. & Du Toit, J. (2008) *Democracy and Delivery: Urban Policy in South Africa.* Cape Town: HSRC Press.

Pinto, R. (2007) *Between Empires: Print and Politics in Goa.* New Delhi: Oxford University Press.

Piper, L. & Deacon, R. (2008) Party politics, elite accountability and public participation: Ward committee politics in the Msunduzi municipality. *Transformation* 66/67:61–82.

Polak, M. (1931) *Mr. Gandhi: The Man.* London: George Allen & Unwin.

Posel, D. (1991) *The Making of Apartheid, 1948–1961: Conflict and Compromise.* Oxford: Clarendon Press.

Prah, K. (1999) African renaissance or warlordism? In Makgoba, M. W. (ed.), *African Renaissance: The New Struggle*, pp. 37–61. Sandton: Mafube.

Prakash, G. (ed.) (1993) *The World of the Rural Labourer in Colonial India.* New Delhi: Oxford University Press.

—— . (1999) *Another Reason.* Princeton: Princeton University Press.

Prakash, O. (2004) *Bullion for Goods: European and Indian Merchants in the Indian Ocean Trade, 1500–1800.* New Delhi: Manohar.

Prakash Rao, U. C. S. (1983) *Urbanization in India: Spatial Dimensions.* New Delhi: Concept.

Prinz, M. (1997) Intercultural links between Goa and Mozambique in their colonial and contemporary history. In Borges, C. & Feldmann, H. (eds), *Goa and Portugal: Their Cultural Links*, pp. 111–27. New Delhi: Concept.

Purcell, M. (2006) Urban democracy and the local trap. *Urban Studies*, 43(11):1921–41.

Puri, E. (2004) Understanding participation: Theoretical foundations and practical implications. *Economic and Political Weekly*, 12 June, pp. 2511–17.

Pyarelal (1980) *The Discovery of Satyagraha: On the Threshold*, vol. 2. Bombay: Sevak Prakasha.

—— . (1986) *The Birth of Satyagraha: From Petitioning to Passive Resistance*, vol. 3. Ahmedabad: Navajivan.

Rabinowitch, A. (1978 [1976]) *The Bolsheviks Come to Power: The Revolution of 1917 in Petrograd.* New York: Norton.

Raman, P. (2004) Yusuf Dadoo: Transnational politics, South African belonging. *South African Historical Journal*, 50:27–48.

—— . (2006) Being Indian the South African way: The development of Indian identity in 1940s Durban. In Coombes, A. E. (ed.), *Rethinking Settler Colonialism: History and Memory in Australia, Canada, Aotearoa New Zealand and South Africa*, pp. 193–208. Manchester: Manchester University Press.

Ramanathan, R. (2007) Federalism, urban decentralization and citizen participation. *Economic and Political Weekly*, 24 February, pp. 674–81.

Ramaphosa, C. (1993) The role of trade unions in transition. *The African Communist*, 133(2):32–38.

Rao, A. (2009) *The Caste Question: Dalits and the Politics of Modern India.* Berkeley: University of California Press.

Rao, R. N. (1990) *Social Organisation in an Indian Slum.* New Delhi: Mittal.

Rastogi, S. R. (1996) *Socio-economic Dimensions of Rural Migration in Uttar Pradesh.* Survey report no. 27. Lucknow.

Ray, R. K. (1979) *Social Conflict and Political Unrest in Bengal, 1875–1927.* New Delhi: Oxford University Press.

Reddy, E. (1991) Are Gandhiji's ideas relevant in a new South Africa? Lecture at the Spring Festival of the University of the Witwatersrand, 15 September.

Ricoeur, P. (2007) *Reflections on the Just.* Trans. D. Pellauer. Chicago: University of Chicago Press.

Rihani, A. (1930) *Around the Coasts of Arabia.* Boston & New York: Houghton Mifflin.

Risso, P. (1995) *Merchants and Faith: Muslim Commerce and Culture in the Indian Ocean.* Boulder: Westview Press.

Roff, W. J. (2000) Early steamships in eastern waters. In Gardiner, R. & Greenhill, B. (eds), *The Advent of Steam: The Merchant Steamship before 1900*, pp. 28–43. Edison: Chartwell Books.

Rolls, E. (1992) *Sojourners: Flowers and the Wide Sea: The Epic Story of China's Centuries-old Relationship with Australia.* St Lucia: University of Queensland Press.

Rosenthal, D. B. (ed.) (1976) *The City in Indian Politics.* Faridabad: Thomson.

Roux, E. (1966) *Time Longer than Rope: A History of the Black Man's Struggle for Freedom in South Africa.* Madison: University of Wisconsin Press.

Rowe, W. L. (1973) Caste, kinship and association in urban India. In Southall, A. (ed.), *Urban Anthropology*, pp. 211–39. New York: Oxford University Press.

Roychowdhury, S. (2008) Slums and civil society: The limits of urban activism. In Mahadevia, D. (ed.), *Inside the Transforming Urban Asia: Processes, Policies and Public Actions*, pp. 601–18. New Delhi: Concept.

Rudolph, L. I. & Rudolph, S. H. (2006) *Postmodern Gandhi and Other Essays: Gandhi in the World and at Home.* Chicago: University of Chicago Press.

Ruet, J. & Tawa Lama-Rewal, S. (eds) (2009) *Governing India's Metropolises.* New Delhi: Routledge.

Rule, P. (1993) *Nokukhanya: Mother of Light.* South Africa: The Grail.

Rummonds, R. G. (2004) *Nineteenth-century Printing Practices and the Iron Handpress*, vols 1 & 2. Delaware & London: Oak Knoll Press & British Library.

Runkle, G. (1976) Is violence always wrong? *Journal of Politics*, 38(2):367–89.

Russell, B. (1991) *Autobiography.* London: Routledge.

SACP (South African Communist Party) (1963) Road to South African Freedom. Programme adopted in 1962. *The African Communist*, 1:24–70.

—— . (1989) The Path to Power. SACP programme adopted at 7th Congress, Cuba.

—— . (1990) Editorial. *The African Communist*, 122(3):5–17.

—— . (1995) Socialism is the future: Build it now: Strategic perspectives. Strategy and tactics adopted at SACP 9th National Congress, 6–8 April.

—— . (1997) Economic policy in the alliance. *The African Communist*, 147(3):15–25.

—— . (1998) Build People's Power – Build Socialism Now! SACP programme adopted at 10th National Congress, July.

—— . (1999) Discussion documents. SACP Strategy Conference, 3–5 September.

Samiran (1899) 'Report on native newspapers, 8 November.' National Archives of India.

Sarkar, S. (2007) Labour history in India and South Africa: Some affinities and contrasts. *African Studies*, 66(2):181–200.

Satgar, V. (1997) Workplace forums and autonomous self-management. *The African Communist*, 147(3):68–73.

—— . (2001) Critical literature review and discussion paper: Worker owned co-operatives, development, and neo-liberal economic adjustment. *The African Communist*, 156(1):60–77.

Satgar, V. & Mantashe, G. (1996) The labour market and job creation. *The African Communist*, 144(2):11–19.

Satyagraha: In Pursuit of Truth (n.d.) <http://images.google.com/imgres?imgurl=http:// www.gandhiserve.org/arts/exhibitions/satyagraha/satyagraha_06_800. jpg&imgrefurl=http://www.gandhiserve.org/arts/exhibitions/satyagraha/ satyagraha.html&h=800&w=577&sz=57&hl=en&start=10&tbnid=E4EeQ244I05Bt M:&tbnh=143&tbnw=103&prev=/images%3Fq%3Dgandhi%2Bprinting%2Bpress% 26gbv%3D2%26svnum%3D10%26hl%3Den>.

Schmidt, E. (1992) *Peasants, Traders and Wives: Shona Women in the History of Zimbabwe 1870–1939*. London: Heinemann.

Scott, D. (1995) Colonial governmentality. *Social Text*, Fall:191–220.

Scott, J. (1998) *Seeing Like a State*. New Haven: Yale University Press.

Seidman, G. W. (2000) Blurred lines: Nonviolence in South Africa. *Political Science and Politics*, 33(2):161–67.

Sekhar, S. & Bidarkar, S. (1999) Municipal budgets in India. *Economic and Political Weekly*, 15 May.

Selby, J. (1973) *A Short History of South Africa*. London: George Allen & Unwin.

Selznick, P. (1952) *Organizational Weapon*. Santa Monica: Rand Corporation.

Sen, A. (2000) Culture and development. Unpublished talk at World Bank meeting, 13 December, mimeo.

Sen, A. K. (1999) *Development as Freedom*. New York: Knopf.

Sen, S. (1999) *Women and Labour in Late Colonial India*. Cambridge: Cambridge University Press.

Sen, S. N. (1960) *The City of Calcutta: A Socio-economic Survey 1954–5 to 1957–8*. Calcutta: Bookland Private.

Shah, G. (ed.) (2002) *Social Movements and the State*. New Delhi: Sage.

Shapiro, I. (2003) *The State of Democratic Theory*. Princeton: Princeton University Press.

Shaw, G. W. (1977a) Printing at Mangalore and Tellicherry by the Basel Mission. *Libri*, 27(2):154–64.

—— . (1977b) The Cuttack Mission Press and early Oriya printing. *British Library Journal*, 3(1):29–43.

Sheth, D. L. (2004) Globalisation and new politics of micro-movements. *Economic and Political Weekly*, 3 January, p. 4558.

Shore, C. (2002) Introduction. In Shore, C. & Nugent, S. (eds), *Elite Cultures: Anthropological Perspectives*, pp. 1–21. London: Routledge.

Shukla, C. (ed.) (1951) *Reminiscences of Gandhiji.* Bombay: Vora. <http://www.gandhimuseum.org/sarvodaya/articles/owe.htm>.

Sinha, D. (1972) Life in a Calcutta slum. In Sinha, S. (ed.), *Cultural Profile of Calcutta*, pp. 87–107. Calcutta: Indian Anthropological Society.

Sivaramakrishnan, K. C. (2000) *Power to the People? The Politics and Progress of Decentralisation.* New Delhi: Konark.

Slovo, J. (1976) South Africa: No middle road. In Davidson, B., Slovo, J. & Wilkinson, A. R. (eds), *Southern Africa: The New Politics of Revolution*, pp. 106–210. New York & Harmondsworth: Pelican.

—— . (1989) *The South African Working Class and the National Democratic Revolution.* Johannesburg: SACP.

—— . (1990) Has socialism failed? In Tabb, W. K. (ed.), *The Future of Socialism: Perspectives from the Left*, pp. 48–63. New York: Monthly Review Press.

Smith, S. A. (1983) *Red Petrograd: Revolution in the Factories, 1917–1918.* Cambridge: Cambridge University Press.

Somers, M. R. (1993) Citizenship and the place of the public sphere: Law, community, and political culture in the transition to democracy. *American Sociological Review*, 58:587–620.

Soudien, C. (2004) Inside but below: The puzzle of education in the global order. In Zajda, J. & Zajda, R. (eds), *Globalisation, Education and Policy Research: Changing Paradigms: International Handbook on Globalisation, Education and Policy Research*, pp. 239–48. Dordrecht: Kluwer.

—— . (2007) Caste, class and race: Continuities and discontinuities across Indian and South African schools. *South African Historical Journal*, 57:113–33.

Southern News (n.d.) Tamil Nadu. <http://www.newindpress.com> (accessed 28 September 2007).

Spencer, J. (2002) The vanishing elite, the political and cultural work of the nationalist revolution in Sri Lanka. In Shore, C. & Nugent, S. (eds), *Elite Cultures: Anthropological Perspectives*, pp. 91–109. London: Routledge.

Staniland, L. (2008) They know me, I won't get any job: Participation, patronage and the sedation of civil society in a Capetonian township. *Transformation*, 66/67:34–60.

Stark, U. (2004) Hindi publishing in the heart of an Indo-Persian cultural metropolis: Lucknow's Newal Kishore Press (1858–1895). In Blackburn, S. & Dalmia, V. (eds), *India's Literary History: Essays on the Nineteenth Century*, pp. 251–79. New Delhi: Permanent Black.

—— . (2007) *Empire of Books: The Naval Kishore Press and the Diffusion of the Printed Word in Colonial India.* New Delhi: Oxford University Press.

Stauffer, C. (2010) Patterns of social reciprocity in the 'new' South Africa. PhD thesis, University of the Witwatersrand.

Stichter, S. (1985) *Migrant Labourers.* Cambridge: Cambridge University Press.

Stiles, D. (2004) The dragon of imperialism: Martin Butler, Butler's *Journal*, the Canadian democrat and anti-imperialism. *Canadian Historical Review*, 85(3):481–505.

Stoler, A. (1989) Making empire respectable: The politics of race and sexual morality in 20th century colonial cultures. *American Ethnologist*, 16(3):634–60.

Stoler, A. & Cooper, F. (1997) Between metropole and colony: Rethinking a research agenda. In Stoler, A. & Cooper, F. (eds), *Tensions of Empire: Colonial Cultures in a Bourgeois World*, pp. 1–56. Berkeley: University of California Press.

Subrahmanyam, S. (1995) Introduction: The Portuguese and early modern Asia. In Subrahmanyam, S. (ed.), *Sinners and Saints: The Successors of Vasco da Gama*, pp. 5–12. New Delhi: Oxford University Press.

—— . (1997a) Connected histories: Notes towards a reconfiguration of early modern Eurasia. *Modern Asian Studies*, 31(3):735–62.

—— . (1997b) *The Career and Legend of Vasco da Gama*. Cambridge: Cambridge University Press.

—— . (2005) *Explorations in Connected History: Mughals and Franks*. New Delhi: Oxford University Press.

Swan, M. (1985) *Gandhi: The South African Experience*. Johannesburg: Ravan Press.

Swanson, M. W. (1983) 'The Asiatic menace': Creating segregation in Durban, 1870–1900. *International Journal of African Historical Studies*, 16(3):401–21.

Tabili, L. (1994) *'We Ask for British Justice': Workers and Racial Difference in Late Imperial Britain*. Ithaca: Cornell University Press.

Talmon, J. L. (1952) *The Origins of Totalitarian Democracy*. London: Secker & Warburg.

Tarrow, S. (1967) *Peasant Communism in Southern Italy*. New Haven: Yale University Press.

Tawa Lama-Rewal, S. (ed.) (2005) *Electoral Reservations, Political Representation and Social Change in India: A Comparative Perspective*. New Delhi: Manohar.

—— . (2007) Neighborhood associations and local democracy: Delhi municipal elections 2007. *Economic and Political Weekly*, 52(47):51–60.

Thakkar, U. (2004) Mohalla committees of Mumbai: Candles in ominous darkness. *Economic and Political Weekly*, 7 February, pp. 580–86.

Thorner, D. & Thorner, A. (1962) *Land and Labour in India*. Bombay: Asia Publishing House.

Times of India (2006) Choppy waters ahead for Gandhi's ship. 5 October. <http://timesofindia.indiatimes.com/articleshow/2099998.coms>.

Tomlinson, R. & Singh, A. (2008) India's Twenty20 cricket imports cheerleaders, grabs U.K. stars. Bloomberg, 25 September. <http://www.bloomberg.com/apps/news?pid=newsarchive&sid=agXm3oIJqEUA>.

Tonkin, E. (2002) Settlers and the elites in Kenya and Liberia. In Shore, C. & Nugent, S. (eds), *Elite Cultures: Anthropological Perspectives*, pp. 129–44. London: Routledge.

Tripartite Alliance (1993) Strategic objectives of the national liberation struggle. Alliance discussion paper. *The African Communist*, 133(2):3–10.

—— . (1994) Broad strategic tasks facing the ANC after April 28. Discussion paper, ANC National Conference on Reconstruction and Strategy, Johannesburg, 21–23 January. *The African Communist*, 136(1):56–57.

—— . (1995). The need for an effective ANC-led political centre. *The African Communist*, 142(3):7–16.

—— . (1997) The role of the state. *The African Communist*, 148(4):13–18.

Troup, F. (1950) *In Face of Fear: Michael Scott's Challenge to South Africa*. London: Faber & Faber.

Tupper, E. (1938) *Seaman's Torch*. London: Hutchinson.

UN (United Nations) (2004) *Human Development Report*. New York: UN.

—— . (2009) *Human Development Report*. <http://hdrstats.undp.org/en/countries/country_fact_sheets/cty_fs_ZAF.html>.

Uppal, J. N. (1995) *Gandhi: Ordained in South Africa*. New Delhi: Ministry of Information and Broadcasting, Government of India.

Vahed, G. (2000) 'African Gandhi': The South African War and the limits of imperial identity. *Historia*, 45(1):201–19.

Vahed, G., Padayachee, V. & Desai, A. (2006) Beyond apartheid: Race, transformation and governance in KwaZulu-Natal cricket. *Transformation*, 61:63–88.

—— . (2010) Between black and white: A case study of the KwaZulu-Natal Cricket Union. In Desai, A. (ed.), *The Race to Transform: Sport in Post-apartheid South Africa*, pp. 222–58. Cape Town: HSRC Press.

Vail, L. (ed.) (1989) *The Creation of Tribalism in Southern Africa*. Berkeley: University of California Press.

Valenti, A. L. (1896) *Lascari-Bat: A Collection of Sentences Used in the Daily Routine of Modern Steamers where Lascars Are Carried as the Deck Crew*. London: Miller.

Vally, R. & Worby, E. (2008) Introduction: Public religiosity and Muslim dilemmas of citizenship. *South Africa Historical Journal*, 60(4):579–82.

Van der Veer, P. (ed.) (1995) *Nation and Migration: The Politics of Space in the South Asian Diaspora*. Philadelphia: University of Pennsylvania Press.

Van Donk, M., Swilling, M., Parnell, S. & Pieterse, E. (eds) (2008) *Consolidating Developmental Local Government: Lessons from the South Africa Experiment*. Cape Town: UCT Press.

Varshney, A. (2000) Is India becoming more democratic? *Journal of Asian Studies*, 59(1): 3–25.

Vergès, F. (2003) Writing on water: Peripheries, flows, capital, and struggles in the Indian Ocean. *Positions: East Asia Cultures Critique*, 11(1):241–57.

Véron, R. (2006) Remaking urban environments: The political ecology of air pollution in Delhi. *Environment and Planning A*, 38:2093–109.

Villiers, A. (1969) *Sons of Sinbad: The Great Tradition of Arab Seamanship in the Indian Ocean*. New York: Scribner.

Vink, M. P. M. (2007) Indian Ocean Studies and the 'New Thalassology'. *Journal of Global History*, 2:41–62.

Visram, R. (1986) *Ayahs, Lascars and Princes: Indians in Britain 1700–1947*. London: Pluto.

Wallerstein, I. (1990) Anti-systemic movements: History and dilemmas. In Amin, S., Arrighi, G., Gunder Frank, A. & Wallerstein, I. (eds), *Transforming the Revolution: Social Movements and the World System*. New York: Monthly Review Press.

Warwick, P. (1983) *Black People and the South African War, 1899–1902*. Cambridge: Cambridge University Press.

Washbrook, D. (1993) Land and labour in late eighteenth-century South India: The golden age of the pariah? In Robb, P. (ed.), *Dalit Movements and the Meanings of Labour in India*, pp. 68–86. New Delhi: Oxford University Press.

Webster, E. & Buhlungu, S. (2004) Between marginalisation and revitalisation? The state of the trade union movement in South Africa. *Review of African Political Economy*, 31(100):229–45.

Weiner, M. & Osgoofield, J. (1976) India's urban constituencies. *Comparative Politics*, 8(2):183–222.

White, L. (1997) Cars out of place: Vampires, technology, and labor in East and Central Africa. In Stoler, A. & Cooper, F. (eds), *Tensions of Empire: Colonial Cultures in a Bourgeois World*, pp. 436–60. Berkeley: University of California Press.

Williams, J. (2001) *Cricket and Race*. Oxford & New York: Berg.

Williams, M. (2008) *The Roots of Participatory Democracy: Democratic Communists in South Africa and Kerala, India*. New York & London: Palgrave Macmillan.

Williams, R. (1977) Structures of feeling. In *Marxism and Literature*, pp. 128–35. Oxford: Oxford University Press.

Wilson, F. (1972) *Labour in the South African Gold Mines 1911–1969*. Cambridge: Cambridge University Press.

Wilson, J. H. (1925) *My Stormy Voyage through Life*. London: Co-operative Printing Society.

Windschuttle, K. (2004) *The White Australia Policy*. Sydney: Macleay.

Wink, A. (2002) From the Mediterranean to the Indian Ocean: Medieval history in geographic perspective. *Comparative Study of Society and History*, 44(3):416–45.

Wolpe, H. (1972) Capitalism and cheap labour-power in South Africa: From segregation to apartheid. *Economy and Society*, 1:425–56.

Worby, E. (1994) Maps, names and ethnic games: The epistemology and iconography of colonial power in northwestern Zimbabwe. *Journal of Southern African Studies*, 24(3):371–92.

—— . (1995) Not to plough my master's field: Discourses of ethnicity and the production of inequality in Botswana. *Journal of Social Studies*, 67:71–108.

World Bank (2006a) 'Country profile: India at a glance.' <http://devdata.worldbank.org/AAG/ind_aag.pdf>.

—— . (2006b) 'Country profile: South Africa at a glance.' <http://devdata.worldbank.org/AAG/ind_aag.pdf>.

—— . (2009a) 'Country profile: India at a glance.' <http://devdata.worldbank.org/AAG/ind_aag.pdf>.

—— . (2009b) 'Country profile: South Africa at a glance.' <http://devdata.worldbank.org/AAG/zaf_aag.pdf>.

Wright, E. O. (2006) The socialist compass. In *Sociological Marxism*, chap. 4. Unpublished ms.

—— . (2010) *Envisioning Real Utopias*. London: Verso.

Wright, E. O. & Burawoy, M. (2004) Taking seriously the social in socialism. In *Sociological Marxism*, draft chap. 2. Unpublished ms.

Yadav, Y. (1999) Understanding the second democratic upsurge. In Frankel, F., Bhargava, R. & Arora, B. (eds), *Transforming India*. New Delhi: Oxford University Press.

Zachariah, K. C. (1964) *A Historical Study of Internal Migration in the Indian Subcontinent*. London: Asia Publishing House.

—— . (1968) *Migrants in Greater Bombay*. Bombay: Asia Publishing House.

Zakaria, F. (2008) *The Post-American World*. London: Allen Lane.

Zérah, M.-H. (2007a) Middle class neighbourhood associations as political players in Mumbai. *Economic and Political Weekly*, 52(47):61–68.

—— . (2007b) Urban governance in Mumbai. Paper presented at the seminar on Urban Actors, Policies and Governance in Four Indian Metropolitan Cities, New Delhi, 23–24 January.

Zita, L. (1993) Moving beyond the social contract. *The African Communist*, 133(2):20–31.

Zizek, S. (1996) *The Indivisible Remainder: On Schelling and Related Matters*. London: Verso.

Zunes, S. (1999) The role of non-violent action in the downfall of apartheid. *Journal of Modern African Studies*, 37(1):137–69.

About the Authors

Claire Bénit-Gbaffou has a PhD in Urban Geography and is a fellow of the Ecole Normale Superieure (Ulm, Paris). She is currently a senior lecturer in the School of Architecture and Planning at the University of the Witwatersrand, and a research associate to CUBES (Centre for Urbanism and the Built Environment Studies at Wits) and Gecko (Comparative Perspectives on Cities from the North and the South, University of Paris Ouest-Nanterre-La Defense). Her research interests focus on urban governance, community participation, party politics and spatial justice. She is currently coordinating a research network entitled *The Voice of the Poor in Urban Governance: Participation, Mobilization and Politics in South African Cities*, as well as comparative research on governance in Indian and South African cities.

Phil Bonner is professor of History and the director of the research programme Local Histories and Present Realities. He heads a team of 14 researchers who are conducting research on small towns and their rural hinterlands in the Mpumalanga, Limpopo, North-West, Gauteng and the Free State provinces of South Africa. He is personally researching Limpopo Province, particularly Polokwane and its surroundings and the Mokopane/Waterberg area.

Pradip Kumar Datta has taught, conducted research and published on literature, modern Indian history and politics. His main areas of interest are the history of communalism especially of the Hindu Right, literary subject formations and contemporary politics. His books include *Carving Blocs: Communal Ideology in Twentieth Century Bengal* (1999), *Khaki Shorts Saffron Flags: A Study of the Hindu Right* (co-author, 1993), and *Rabindranath Tagore's The Home and the World: A Critical Companion* (edited, 2002). His collection of essays entitled *Heterogeneities: Identity Formations in Modern India* is due to be published shortly. He is currently professor in a multidisciplinary position in the Department of Political Science, University of Delhi.

Pamila Gupta is a senior researcher at WISER (Wits Institute for Social and Economic Research) at the University of the Witwatersrand in Johannesburg, South Africa. She holds a PhD in Socio-cultural Anthropology from Columbia University, New York. Her recent publications include 'Introduction: Islandness in the Indian Ocean' in P. Gupta, I. Hofmeyr and M. Pearson (eds), *Eyes Across the Water: Navigating the Indian Ocean* (UNISA Press and Penguin India, 2010); 'A voyage of convalescence: Richard Burton and the imperial ills of Portuguese India', *South African Historical Journal*, 61(4):802–16 (2009); 'Le Futur de la nostalgie, ou rumination sur les ruines', *Écologie & Politique*, 37:87–90 (2008); '"Signs of wonder": The postmortem travels of Francis Xavier in the Indian Ocean world' in A. Jamal and S. Moorthy (eds), *Indian Ocean Studies: Cultural, Social and Political Perspectives* (Routledge Press, Indian Ocean Series, 2010); and 'Introduction: The life of the corpse: Framing reflections and questions', co-author and editor with Deborah Posel, special issue, *African Studies*, 68(3):299–309 (December 2009). Her areas of interest include the history and anthropology of South Asia, Mozambique and South Africa; Portuguese colonial and missionary history; Indian Ocean studies (migration, islands); post-colonial studies and visual cultures; heritage and tourism studies; corporeality, cults and state pageantry; and historical anthropology.

Patrick Heller is a professor of Sociology and International Studies at Brown University in the United States. His primary area of research is the comparative study of democratic deepening. He is the author of *The Labor of Development: Workers and the Transformation of Capitalism in Kerala, India* (Cornell University Press, 1999) and a co-author of *Social Democracy in the Periphery* (Cambridge University Press, 2007). He has written on a range of topics, including democratic consolidation, the politics of decentralisation, local democracy, urban transformation and social movements. He is currently finishing a four-year research project on the post-apartheid city (<http://www.s4.brown.edu/southafrica/homepage.htm>). The project uses both GIS data and qualitative fieldwork to examine the impact of planned transformation on the racial and economic reconfiguration of South Africa's three largest cities. He is also finishing a book on urban governance in Brazil with Gianpaolo Baiocchi and Marcelo Kunrath Silva (Stanford University Press) and working on a book that explores the relationship among development, democracy and civil society through a comparative analysis of India, Brazil and South Africa. He is the director of the Watson Institute's Graduate Program in Development.

Isabel Hofmeyr is a professor of African Literature at the University of the Witwatersrand in Johannesburg, South Africa. Her first monograph, *We Spend Our Years as a Tale that Is Told: Oral Historical Narrative in a South African Chiefdom* (1994) was shortlisted for the Herskovits Prize. *The Portable Bunyan: A Transnational History of The Pilgrim's Progress* won the 2007 Richard L. Greaves Award from the International John Bunyan Society. Until 2009, she was acting director for the Centre of Indian Studies in Africa (<http://www.cisa wits.org>). She is currently working on textual circulation in the Indian Ocean.

Jonathan Hyslop is Professor in the Department of Sociology, University of Pretoria. He has published widely on the social history of 19th and 20th Century South Africa. In 2010-11 he is A Lindsay O'Connor Visiting Professor at Colgate University, Hamilton, New York. He is author of *The Notorious Syndicalist* (Johannesburg, Jacana, 2004).

Crain Soudien is a professor and former director of the School of Education at the University of Cape Town and currently Deputy Vice Chancellor. He has written over 120 articles, reviews, reports and book chapters in the areas of social difference, culture, educational policy, comparative education, educational change, public history and popular culture. He is also the co-editor of three books on District Six, Cape Town, and another on comparative education, and the author of *The Making of Youth Identity in Contemporary South Africa: Race, Culture and Schooling* and the co-author of *Inclusion and Exclusion in South African and Indian Schools*. He was educated at the universities of Cape Town and South Africa, and holds a PhD from the State University of New York at Buffalo. He is involved in a number of local, national, and international social and cultural organisations and is the chairperson of the District Six Museum Foundation, board member of the Cape Town Festival, immediate past-president of the World Council of Comparative Education Societies and was the chair of a Ministerial Committee on Transformation in Higher Education.

Stéphanie Tawa Lama-Rewal is a senior research fellow at the Centre for Indian and South Asian Studies (CEIAS, CNRS-EHESS), Paris. Her research focusses on urban democracy in India, with a focus on micro-local mobilisations. Her published works include *Femmes et politique en Inde et au Népal: image et présence* (2004); *Electoral Reservations, Political Representation, and Social Change in India: A Comparative Perspective* (edited, 2005); *Democratization in Progress: Women and Local Politics in Urban India* (co-authored with Archana Ghosh, 2005); and *Governing India's Metropolises* (co-edited with Joël Ruet, 2009).

Goolam Vahed is an associate professor of History at the University of KwaZulu-Natal. He has published widely on Indian South Africans. He is co-author of *Inside Indenture: A South African Story 1860–1914* and *Monty Naicker: Between Reason and Treason*.

Michelle Williams is a senior lecturer in the Department of Sociology at the University of the Witwatersrand. Her publications include *The Roots of Participatory Democracy: Democratic Communists in South Africa and Kerala, India* (Palgrave, 2008). She is the chair person of the Global Labour University MA Programme at the University of the Witwatersrand, Johannesburg.

Eric Worby is currently a fellow at the Center for Advanced Study in the Behavioral Sciences at Stanford University, on leave from the University of the Witwatersrand, where he served as head of the School of Social Sciences from 2006 to 2010. He will return to Wits in mid-2011 to become director of the Graduate Centre for the Humanities. An anthropologist, he has conducted field research in Zimbabwe, Botswana, Tanzania, South Africa and Bangladesh. His recent publications include *Go Home or Die Here: Violence, Xenophobia and the Reinvention of Difference in South Africa* (Wits University Press), co-edited with Shireen Hassim and Tawana Kupe, and two special issues of the *South African Historical Journal*, co-edited with Rehana Vally, on the theme of 'Islam, Democracy and Public Life'.

Index

G

H

I

J

post-colonialism 83–84, 86, 90, 98, 100–103, 126, 171, 225, 244–248, 250, 252, 261, 265, 268
poverty/the poor 3, 12, 14, 17, 78, 99, 163, 166–167, 169, 173, 190, 192–194, 196, 202, 217, 220, 224–225, 232–234
Prakash, G 137, 226
pre-colonial society 45, 142–144, 223
Pretoria 70, 108–109
privatisation/outsourcing 162–163, 188
public health 3, 156, 168, 188, 203, 213–214, 216–217
Pune 220, 230, 234, 236

R

race 16, 85, 101, 103, 144, 147–148, 153, 159, 247–248, 253, 263
racial segregation 16, 29, 91, 106–108, 180, 229, 249, 253, 256–257, 262
racial stereotyping 267
'coolie' vs 'free' Indian 67–69
racialisation/racial exclusion 11, 43, 48, 53–54, 67, 74–75, 91, 246–247, 249, 252, 256, 263–265
racism/racial discrimination 39, 48, 60, 63, 67–68, 74, 76, 78, 80, 97, 126, 132, 166, 171, 247, 250, 260
Raj 7, 55, 60, 71, 106, 247
reconstruction 183–184
Reconstruction and Development Programme (RDP) 162, 165, 188, 205, 209
Reddy, E 135
redistribution/redistributive reform 165, 173, 181, 200–201, 205, 213, 216, 250, 253
representation see political participation, access to
resistance/struggle 4, 42, 96–97, 99, 106, 115–117, 119, 124, 153, 174, 201, 252, 258
1976 Soweto uprising 180
rights, social/political 148, 150, 152–154, 156, 158–160, 163, 167, 170, 172, 194, 196, 203, 206, 219, 235–236
Rihani, Ameen 43
rule of law 157, 171
Runkle, G 124
rural-urban differences/divide 15–16. 142. 162. 167, 172, 178–179, 182–183, 195, 233, 252, 262
Russell, Bertrand 57

Russia/Soviet Union 17, 73, 77–78, 197–198, 208, 213–214, 251

S

Sen, Amita 237–238
Sastri, Srinivasa 106, 114
Seamen's Union of Bombay 54
secularism 155, 167–168
Seidman, Gay W 119, 124
self-rule/*Hind Swaraj* 63, 96, 154, 255–256
service delivery 162–163, 181–182, 190
    commodification of 166
    urban protests over 182
Shapiro, I 151
Shembe, Isaiah 40
Shiv Sena 183, 192
Shore, Chris 86
Shukla, C 105, 113
Siddis 6
Sisulu, Walter 116–117, 119
slavery 3–4, 44
Slovo, Joe 204
Smuts, Jan 109, 114
social movements 161, 163–166, 169, 173–175, 191–192, 205, 251
    civic/urban 12, 160, 165, 169–170, 180–181, 183–184, 191–193, 195
    neighbourhood activism 194
social/family stability 16, 71, 154, 235–236, 240, 242
    crime 12, 147, 236–239
    issue of generation 16, 239, 242
    juvenile delinquency 16, 235, 238–239
    violence 12, 236, 239
socialism 15, 24, 56–57, 197–198
    coexistence with capitalism 15, 197, 201, 210
socio-political comparative work, benefits of 2–4, 11–14
software engineering 3
South African Communist Party (SACP) 3, 12, 15, 115, 120, 157, 181, 191, 197–206, 208–218, 251
South African Congress of Trade Unions (SACTU) 117–118, 120
South African Indian Congress (SAIC) 11, 34, 117, 121–123
South African National Civic Organisation (SANCO) 165, 170, 181
South African War 231
South Asia 3